NO, BUT I SAW THE MOVIE

A librarian, archivist, collector of books and recordings, and avid film buff, David Wheeler is currently the co-director of the Archive of Contemporary Music, which he founded with Bob George in 1985. He has also contributed to a number of books on writers and writing as a free-lance editor and writer. He lives in New York City.

No, But I Saw the Movie

The Best Short Stories Ever Made into Film

EDITED BY DAVID WHEELER
With a Foreword
by Bruce Jay Friedman

PENGUIN BOOKS

PENGUIN BOOKS
Published by the Penguin Group
Viking Penguin, a division of Penguin Books USA Inc.,
40 West 23rd Street, New York, New York 10010, U.S.A.
Penguin Books Ltd, 27 Wrights Lane,
London W8 5TZ, England
Penguin Books Australia Ltd, Ringwood,
Victoria, Australia
Penguin Books Canada Ltd, 2801 John Street,
Markham, Ontario, Canada L3R 1B4
Penguin Books (N.Z.) Ltd, 182–190 Wairau Road,
Auckland 10, New Zealand

Penguin Books Ltd, Registered Offices:
Harmondsworth, Middlesex, England

First published in Penguin Books 1989
Published simultaneously in Canada

10 9 8 7 6 5 4 3 2 1

LIBRARY OF CONGRESS CATALOGING-IN-PUBLICATION DATA
No, but I saw the movie : the best short stories ever made into film /
edited by David Wheeler ; introduction by David Wheeler.
p.   cm.
ISBN 0 14 01.1090 9 (pbk.)
1. Film adaptations—Catalogs. 2. Short stories—Film and video
adaptations—Catalogs.   I. Wheeler, David, 1957–   .
PN1997.85.N6 1989
016.79143'75—dc19   88-39795

Printed in the United States of America
Set in Garamond Light
Designed by Ann Gold

FOREWORD

It may come as a surprise to the casual moviegoer, as it did to me, that classic Hollywood films such as *All About Eve, Rear Window, Bad Day at Black Rock and It's A Wonderful Life* were based on short stories with sturdy credentials of their own. I doubt that there has been a deliberate plan to sweep this information under the rug. Nor do I recall an effort to make it known. It has always been Hitchcock's *Psycho,* and Capra's *It's A Wonderful Life* and Carl Foreman's *High Noon,* just as it became Coppola's and not Puzo's *Godfather* and it is sure to be someone other than Tom Wolfe's *Bonfire of the Vanities.* People who work in the fanciful world of moviemaking—from auteurs to accountants— quickly develop rich imaginations of their own. It represents only a minor leap for the man who distributed *Snows of Kilimanjaro* to begin to feel that he wrote it.

This is not to minimize the Hitchcock touch or the brilliance and complexity of a Joseph Mankiewicz screenplay. Anyone who has spent a day on a movie set will come away with the feeling that directors are underpaid. Screenplay writing, which lies somewhere between prose and calculus, is the most rigorous and maddening of enterprises. But the movies cited in David Wheeler's entertaining volume did not appear to their creators as visions in the night. They had considerable assistance, as will quickly become clear to the reader of this book. With their sweep and panache, the stories collected here would have made a formidable anthology had there been no movies attached to them. But then the phone from the Coast would have been ringing off the hook with offers to seize them up as properties.

The traditional short story requires economy, ruthless attention to plot and narrative, particularization of character and tone and offers little opportunity for its author to stop and admire the scenery. It would seem to provide the perfect road map for the moviemaker. Yet Mr. Wheeler informs me that short stories are far less frequently looked upon by the film colony as fertile ground for source material.

Assuming that this is an unattractive state of affairs, how did it come about? The first impulse is to blame villainous Hollywood. It is not difficult to imagine the M.B.A. in charge of creative affairs at a studio saying: "Why should we buy this? It's only six pages. For a few dollars more, we can get a big fat novel." As I write this scenario, I begin to like it, but I doubt that it reflects a pattern. More than likely, the culprit is the short story itself which for the moment has taken a minimalist turn. From a filmmaker's point of view, this is unfortunate. Warhol is gone and the man running a vacuum cleaner in a high rise, speculating on the cosmos does not lead us to *Double Indemnity*. Nor does the tale of a housewife who flees the K-Mart to sit in a marsh and watch the geese fly over produce *It Happened One Night*. The magazines and pulps that published many of the stories in this volume have themselves been put to rest. The ones that have replaced them have not put the short story of any kind, much less the traditional one, at their core.

On a personal note—I have run into fiction writers who sit in bars with clenched fists and bemoan the rude treatment their works have received in Hollywood. I can recriminate as bitterly as the next one, but my experience with "Change of Plan" (a.k.a. *The Heartbreak Kid)* could not have been more pleasing. The screenplay was written by the estimable Neil Simon. The director was the gifted Elaine May. The movie stretched out before me as if I had written not just the story but the screenplay as well. (In time, and following in a grand Hollywood tradition, I began to feel that I *had* written it). To cap it off, an envelope soon arrived from Proctor and Gamble. Thinking it was a toothpaste sample, I threw it away. Fortunately, after considering my shaky situation, I retrieved it. It contained that rarest of specimens, a profit-participation check, Proctor and Gamble having been a sponsor of the film. In all, a satisfying experience and one I recommend to any writer who is thinking of having a short story snapped up by the films.

Not long ago, in a Manhattan restaurant, a man at a nearby table was pointed out to me as being Joseph Mankiewicz.

"Now there," I said, "is a sophisticated man."

It's an uneasy label and one I hope I haven't thrown around too often. But how else to describe the man responsible for that most sophisticated of all comedy dramas, *All About Eve*. This episode took place before I became aware of Mary Orr's short story "The Wisdom of Eve," whose opening sentences instantly establish the astringent tone which is the movie's most enduring quality. The Orr story did not turn itself into a movie. The Mankiewicz contribution was monumental. But in the future, while continuing to be in awe of Mr. Mankiewicz, I plan to reserve a share of my admiration for Mary Orr's jewel of a story as well.

—Bruce Jay Friedman
Water Mill, N.Y.

ACKNOWLEDGMENTS

Putting a work like this together is never wholly the effort of a single individual, and this book would not have existed without the contributions of many diverse hands. A part of this work belongs to all of them.

Bob Atwan not only suggested the idea for this collection, but also gave generously of his advice and expertise at every stage of its development;

For their assistance in everything from bibliographical research, location of source materials, preparation of manuscript, and general support, I am indebted to the following individuals and organizations: Alan Bisbort, Robert Fass, Bob George and The Archive of Contemporary Music, Mark Matucci, Margaux Ravis, Daniel Von Behren, Grace Wherry, Toby Wherry, Pamela Wilkins, and The Writer's Guild. Very special thanks are owed to Errol Somay of the New York Public Library;

Bruce Jay Friedman kindly lent his enthusiasm and talents as a writer;

Without the belief and dedication of my agent, Sandy Choron (who still hasn't stopped!) and Trish Todd, none of this would have happened, and the professional attention of my editor, Pam Dorman, and Ellen McFarland made the whole job easier and a lot more pleasant;

Finally, JoAnn Jacobsen provided that rare combination of emotional support, common sense, friendship and honesty that is seldom encountered outside of fiction.

This volume is dedicated to the memory of Michael Weinman, filmmaker, storyteller, and friend, whose works are sadly absent from these pages.

CONTENTS

INTRODUCTION

Conventional wisdom loves to tell us how opposites attract. If we accept Ingmar Bergman's assumption that "film has nothing to do with literature" and that "the character and substance of the two art forms are usually in conflict" then surely fiction and cinema must be two of the strangest and most fertile bedfellows in the world of modern artistic expression. They share a mutual love of narrative, of well-drawn character, and of the examination of human joy and suffering in both the grandest and simplest terms. They can also quarrel bitterly over the ways their respective visions are rendered. The world of the written word is static; that of the motion picture, kinetic. Yet, since its earliest days as an artistic and entertainment medium, film has regularly depended upon works of literature for the vast wealth of rich and compelling source material it has to offer.

The French film pioneer George Melies (sometimes called "The Father of the Motion Picture") drew heavily on the work of fellow countryman Jules Verne as well as on H.G. Wells for his brilliant turn-of-the-century fantasies, and American director D.W. Griffith used a wide variety of literary forms from theatrical melodramas to poetry in creating his own landmark productions. Over the last eighty years, scarcely any writer of note has gotten by without seeing at least one of his efforts translated into film. In many cases these same writers were recruited to write directly for the screen: William Faulkner, F. Scott Fitzgerald, Graham Greene, Clifford Odets, and John Steinbeck—to name a very few—all spent brief stints as screenwriters.

To this day the relationship between film and fiction remains a closely-knit, if often curious one. Novels in particular have benefited the most from motion-picture tie-ins. Older, established works are continually brought back into print, glossily repackaged and marketed to coincide with their appearance on the big screen, and fans of contemporary popular works eagerly await the film version of current favorites. In a bizarre kind of reverse adaptation, "novelizations" are often manufactured from the original films themselves to satisfy the public's insatiable appetite for more of the same good story—no matter how it's presented. As is sometimes the case, a motion picture has served as the substitute (like Cliff Notes for the college student) for reading great classics and popular novels alike. All of us have at some point invoked the now standard cliché/excuse, "No, but I saw the movie." Despite the slight embarrassment we show at not having read a particular masterpiece or potboiler, this confession basically says, "Yes, I do know the story." We may not have read *Moby Dick,* but we at least know who Captain Ahab is, and why he limps. For better or worse, motion pictures have provided vast numbers of viewers with an introduction to the work of our world's many great novelists and playwrights.

But what about the short story? Just as many directors and producers have turned to short fiction for their inspiration as they have to the novel. Yet because of their transitory nature and lack of visibility, these sibling gems have been kept out of the public eye and have rarely been associated with their counterparts on film. When was the last time you had a friend scoop you on a preview for a film based on that great story that ran in *Esquire* two years ago? Rarely have short stories had the luxury of basking in the limelight that pours from a glittering marquee. They don't tend to leap into our hands off of airport book racks or advertise themselves on subway placards and the sides of city buses. Nor can they aspire to the "blockbuster" status of their considerably fleshier—and flashier!—big brothers. There are exceptions of course, but for the most part these pieces have enjoyed only the occasional reprint in an annual reader while the bulk of their brethren sleep fitfully on reels of microfilm in the world's libraries. Ironically, it could be convincingly argued that short fiction, (perhaps more than any other literary form) is most appropriately suited to the direct interests of filmmaking. Alfred Hitchcock, one of the most purely visual artists in the history of cinema, once remarked that "the nearest art form to the motion picture is, I think, the short story. It's the only form when you ask the audience to sit down and read it in one sitting."

The fact is the short story was a much sought after and much used commodity in Hollywood (and in the film world in general) for the better part of this century, precisely because it contained the basic elements that the motion picture industry was looking for in a neat, uncomplicated package: plot, character, and theme. There were also other factors that made them immensely attractive.

First of all, short stories were available in abundance. All of the major magazines or "glossies" including *The Saturday Evening Post, Collier's, Cosmopolitan, Argosy,* and *Munsey's* offered a regular outlet for writers of fiction whether they were established names or promising literary prospects. Additionally, there were literally hundreds of "pulps" like *Black Mask, Adventure, Astounding Stories, Ace High Western,* and others that catered to the tastes of readers of detective thrillers, science-fiction, westerns, and romances. Anyone from a high-ranking production executive to a lowly studio slush reader with an eye for potentially salable material could choose from a wide assortment of storylines that just *might* launch the next big film. When a likely property for adaptation was discovered, the rights would usually be obtained at a modest expense (sometimes with the author himself in the same deal), and so, from a financial standpoint, the studios could afford to retain a writer "on spec" with relatively little risk. Moreover, the simple skeleton of a short story gave the final scriptwriter considerable elbowroom with which to play.

On the other side of the coin, the movie business opened up an extremely attractive new market for writers of fiction. No longer restricted to books and magazines, a clever author with an enterprising agent could conceivably translate a modest publication fee into significant earnings with a movie option. Philip Van Doren Stern made numerous unsuccessful attempts to sell his short fable, "The Greatest Gift," to magazines and ended up sending it out to friends as a Christmas card. Frank Capra's film company happened upon it, bought the rights for $50,000, and turned it in to *It's A Wonderful Life* (1946). Hollywood beckoned like a goldrush to legions of fiction writers who saw the opportunity to transform their historically non-lucrative craft into a satisfying, full-time profession. In those days, the word "story" was loosely used, indeed. It wasn't uncommon for a feature film to proceed on the basis of anything from a standard published work to an eight-page treatment or even a single-page scenario. The career of screenwriter Norman Krasna (he created the original story and screenplay for classics like Fritz Lang's *Fury* (1936) and Alfred Hitchcock's only romantic comedy, *Mr. & Mrs. Smith* (1941)) is a perfect example. According to his widow, Krasna never once set pen to paper for his basic ideas—he simply sat down in a producer's office and told the story like a raconteur, take it or leave it.

By no means, however, should this suggest that the writer's place in the movie business was—or presently is—an exalted or easy one. In his autobiography, director Frank Capra described the hard realities of the job with no pretensions to glamour. "There are writers who work for groceries, writers who work for big money, and writers who work for the love of writing. . . . You name the reason for writing, Hollywood will furnish the writer—and his frustrations. Because writing—for whatever reason—is a personal expression. You write *alone*. Except in Hollywood, where writing is *not* a personal expression. You write for, and sometimes with, producers, directors, stars. . . . It can be a galling, ego-bruising, unspotlighted experience." Once bought and paid for, the film industry has proved time and again that it will do what it likes with a writer's work, authorial integrity be damned. The inclusion of a romantic interest or a happy ending, was typical of concessions made in the name of "what the people want."

Even so, it is undeniable that for many years the cinema effectively interpreted, gave new life to, and sometimes championed some of the finest works of short literature by writers from around the world. (Even Vladimir Nabokov, while still a rather obscure young writer living in Russian-emigre Berlin, was approached to write for Hollywood in the 1930s on the basis of his short fiction.) The two forms complemented and enhanced one another in surprising and delightful ways, and for years it seemed as if they were destined for a long and fruitful marriage.

Unfortunately, the 1950s irrevocably changed all of that and by 1960 it became clear that the honeymoon was over. The emergence and immediate appeal of television claimed a large percentage of Hollywood's film-going audience and its writers with it. The successful "pulps" that had provided a seemingly unquenchable market for short fiction dwindled to a handful; the national magazines that had actively solicited short fiction significantly curtailed their pursuit of stories in favor of more topical non-fiction; and the movie moguls in California also had their reasons for cutting back on the capricious expenditure for movie rights. The Consent Decree of 1948 (handed down by the Supreme Court) finally put an end to the film industry's control of what movie played when, where and for how long in any given theater (until then, they had monopolized every aspect of production, distribution *and* exhibition).

Producers were, now much less inclined to buy the rights to any story that might be a hit down the line. They simply could no longer afford to speculate on every literary property that showed future potential. And considering the several million dollars it costs to launch a major motion picture today, the movie business banks almost exclusively on original screenplays and the guaranteed appeal of popular best-selling novels. Of the more than 1,500 short stories included in the list that was compiled for research on this book, only a small fraction are represented by films from the last twenty years.

Still, despite its relative decline as the narrative springboard for modern films, there are still clear indications that the short story is far from extinct in the movie business. In the past year alone, John Huston's final directorial effort, *The Dead* (from James Joyce's short masterpiece) was released and greeted with great acclaim, as was the adaptation of Isak Dinesen's *Babette's Feast,* which won the Academy Award for Best Foreign Film. In his acceptance speech for the Irving G. Thalberg Award at the Oscar ceremonies in 1986, Steven Spielberg (whose first film *Duel* was taken from a taut, short thriller by Richard Matheson) said, "We are first and foremost storytellers . . . and I think it's time to renew our romance with the written word."

The purpose of this collection is to bring together some of the best short stories that have served as the bases for a wide variety of classic, noteworthy, and cult films. The selections have been chosen to cover a wide span of both time (from the first talkie to the present) and genre (drama, comedy, adventure, suspense, horror, science-fiction, the western, and even the musical). Many of these tales have been only sporadically reprinted—in some cases not since their very first appearance!—and despite their quality and the fame of the pictures they inspired many are real "sleepers." They contain elements that should provide readers with a pleasurable combination of both recognition and surprise. Film buffs will discover, I think, a fascinating new angle on their film favorites, and lovers of literature can relish an equally delectable introduction to some of the greatest achievements in the history of cinema—you've got a real treat in store for you. The criterion that governed the choice of material was a simple one: good stories that became good movies. A quick word of warning to purists in both camps, particularly film: what you saw is *NOT* necessarily what you get. Do not be overly distressed if a particular story doesn't match with your memory of one director's ultimate realization of his personal view. In the final analysis, a story, a film, or any work of art for that matter, is good or bad on its own terms. What the following stories have in common is neither plot, character, setting, nor gimmick. Rather, they share the ability to create a powerful and pervasive image in the mind's eye. It just so happens that the images created from these pieces have become some of the most enduring works of art of our time. We *read* stories, we *see* films. Here is an opportunity to *see* a story and to *read* a film. If nothing else, one of the richest joys in experiencing any creative effort is that in doing so, we make it our own. So settle into your seat, and let the filmmaker inside your own head get to work.

—David Wheeler
New York City, 1988

NO,
BUT I SAW
THE MOVIE

ALL ABOUT EVE

(1950)

THE WISDOM OF EVE
MARY ORR

In the early 1940s, a young woman named Mary Orr visited with Elizabeth Bergner, a renowned Austrian actress vacationing in Woodstock, Vermont. Over dinner, Bergner told the story of a young girl, an adoring fan whom the older actress had taken under her wing until it became clear that the intentions of this admirer were far from benign. Thinking that the story illustrated a novel approach to "making it" on the stage, Orr went back to her room at the Woodstock Inn and emerged four days later with "The Wisdom of Eve," her first effort at fiction-writing. Unlike the heroine of her tale, says Orr, "success couldn't have been further from my mind."

All About Eve, which charts the conniving rise of Eve Harrington from stage-door waif to Hollywood star, won Academy Awards in 1950 for Best Picture, Best Director (Joseph Mankiewicz), and Best Supporting Actor (George Sanders, as a reptilian theater critic). Cynical, melodramatic, and hilarious, the film is a rich evocation of backstage Broadway with all of its gossip, glamour, and ruthless ambition. The performances are first-rate (even Marilyn Monroe's ditzy blonde shines) and the movie itself is one of the entertainment industry's best attempts at self-scrutiny.

MARY ORR was born in Brooklyn in 1918 and is the author of five novels and numerous plays and television scripts. She has been a professional actress on Broadway since the mid-1930s and is still performing regularly on the stage.

ALL ABOUT EVE

Released: 1950
Production: Darryl F. Zanuck for Twentieth Century-Fox (Academy Award)
Direction: Joseph L. Mankiewicz (Academy Award)
Screenplay: Joseph L. Mankiewicz (Academy Award)
Cinematography: Milton Krasner
Editing: Barbara McLean
Costume design: Edith Head and Charles LeMaire (Academy Award)
Running time: 138 minutes

PRINCIPAL CHARACTERS:

Margo Channing	Bette Davis
Eve Harrington	Anne Baxter
Addison De Witt (Narrator)	George Sanders (Academy Award)
Karen Richards	Celeste Holm
Bill Sampson	Gary Merrill
Lloyd Richards	Hugh Marlowe
Miss Caswell (Girl at Party)	Marilyn Monroe

A young girl is on her way to Hollywood with a contract for one thousand dollars a week from a major film company in her pocketbook. I shall call her Eve Harrington because that is not her name, though the Eve part of the alias is not unapt, considering the original's snaky activities in a once-peaceful garden. In a year or two, I am sure Miss Harrington will be as much a household word to you as Ingrid Bergman or Joan Fontaine. When she is a star, I am equally positive that the slick publicity agents of Hollywood who surround these celestial beings with glamour will give you their version of her success. But no matter what they concoct, it will not be as interesting or ironic as her real story. It would never occur to them to tell you the truth. Stars must be presented to their public in a warm, sympathetic light, and one could scratch a long time before kindling any such spark from the personality of Eve Harrington.

I first saw her on a cold, snowy night in January. I was sitting snugly under a fur rug in the back seat of Margola Cranston's town car. We were parked at the stage entrance of Margola's theater, waiting for her to come out. By we, I mean her chauffeur Henry and I. Henry sat patiently in front of me, displaying the proper fortitude of one whose chief occupation in life was to wait. But marking time is not my long suit, and my gloved fingers played an irritated tattoo on Margola's polychrome upholstery. I am an actress myself and am able to get in and out of my makeup with the same speed that I duck in and out of a cold shower. Not so Margola. Rarely did she leave the theater before a quarter to twelve. What went on in her dressing room for three quarters of an hour was a mystery known only to her maid, Alice, and herself. Consequently, if one wanted to see Margola after the theater one waited. However, it was not a lone vigil.

There was a crowd at the stage door. They were the usual autograph fans, all with little books open and fountain pens dripping ink. Some appeared to be intelligent theatergoers; they carried programs for Margola to sign and had obviously seen the play that evening. I could hear their enthusiastic comments through the tiny opening where I had lowered the car window to let my cigarette smoke escape. A few were boys in uniform with dreams of dating Margola—dreams that would not come true. There was only one person standing there I could not catalogue. She stood nearest the car, and I could see her face clearly in the light of the streetlamp.

It was a young, unusual face, but not in the least pretty. Because she was rather plain, the amount of makeup she was wearing seemed to me very odd. What I mean is, false eyelashes can look very much at home on Lana Turner, but the same pair could be incongruous on a schoolteacher. This girl had a serious, prim expression. She was dressed in a warm, practical red coat. On her head she wore a small dark tam-o'-shanter which didn't seem to agree with the coat. She also wore high-heeled, open-toed shoes, and standing there in the slush her feet must have been cold. Her hands were thrust into her coat pockets and a shabby purse dangled from her left arm. Her manner was shy and reticent. Under their long lashes, her eyes stared at the ground. She stood first on one foot and then on the other to keep warm, but displayed no fatigue at the long wait.

I continued to wonder who she was and why she was there until Margola finally appeared at the stage entrance. I had seen her come out many times. It was a superb act. I knew perfectly well she was not in the least surprised to see the crowd gathered there, but her expression was one of delighted amazement. So many people gathered there to see her! It could not be! She smiled and signed the autograph books and spoke first to one and then to another. She radiated graciousness. Everyone would go away exclaiming, "What charm!" "So modest!" "How kind!"

Margola would then climb into the car and apologize for keeping me waiting by saying, "Those tiresome people! Such bores! What fools!"

I was one of Margola's few women friends. My husband, Lloyd Richards, had written the play in which she was then appearing with great success. Lloyd had also written another one of her most popular vehicles. No one knew better than he that a large part of their success was due to Margola's performance. Without her, they might have run five, six, or seven weeks. With her, the first play had lasted two years, and the current smash hit showed stubborn signs of outdoing it. For there was no doubt that Margola was a truly great actress.

Watching her sign the autographs, I wondered for the thousandth time what made her so great. Nobody would guess it to see her out of the theater. She was tiny, with the childish figure of a Botticelli angel. On stage, her clothes were done by Carnegie, Valentia, and Mainbocher. Offstage, they were done by Cranston. They consisted generally of old sweaters and tweed skirts. I had once peeked into her closet and discovered a dozen gowns utterly unworn. I have known her six years and seen her twice in a decent dress. Once was at a funeral of a big producer for whom she had no respect and once when she had to receive a Critics Award she didn't want.

Her hair was another cross her friends had to bear. When she was not on stage, it was generally piled on the top of her head as if she had just fallen out of the bath. Even on stage it could sometimes be said to resemble a theater cleaner's mop. That night it was tucked beneath a hand-painted handkerchief which she had tied under her chin, peasant fashion. She wore a mink coat, true enough, but on her it might have been an old muskrat. It was down to her ankles and six years out of style. Nobody but a genius could dress as she did and get away with it.

Lloyd has always said that for him she is utterly devoid of sex appeal. To me she is tremendously attractive. He gives her one asset in the way of beauty—a very obvious one—a pair of enormous eyes, which behind the footlights can betray every thought in a character's mind with crystal clarity. Also, she seems to have the secret of eternal youth. I have seen her in the bright sunshine with no makeup on and she doesn't look a day over twenty-nine or thirty. If Margola ever sees forty-five again, I'll have my eyes lifted.

We got along together from the first day we met. I often disagreed with her, argued with her, and wisecracked at her expense. Sometimes Lloyd would look worried and tell me not to go too far, to remember that I owed my penthouse and sables largely to her. However, in spite of my acid tongue, to this day she has preferred my company to most other women's.

Being Margola's best friend is in many ways a bit of a bore. I'm the type of female who only feels at home dressed in a Daché hat at the Stork Club or El Morocco. As Margola always looks like a tourist, it is well nigh impossible to persuade her to have supper at any café-society haunt. She favors a bar behind some delicatessen shop, Sardi's, or her own home.

On the night in question it was home—and home to Margola is a nest of forty rooms at Great Neck, Long Island, called Capulet's Cottage. That meant I had to stay all night, for first there would be a huge supper, and then conversation until three or four in the morning, as Margola loves to talk by the light of the moon. Consequently, my overnight bag rested uncomfortably on my feet. Lloyd had kissed me good-bye when I'd left for the theater and gone off with a gleam in his eye to a stag poker session.

"Have a nice cat party" had been his parting words, and I knew that he was privately relieved we were not having a foursome with Margola's husband, Clement Howell. Clement is a clever enough director and producer but very English and pompous. Lloyd can take only a certain number of broad A's.

Margola was close to the car when the shabby little girl with the red coat suddenly stepped into her line of vision. I saw Margola's eyes cloud up and her expression change to one of annoyance. The girl spoke a few words and looked at her in the most supplicating way, her large eyes filled with tears. But she didn't succeed in melting the star's icy attitude. I couldn't hear what Margola said to her exactly, but I knew it wasn't nice, and I did catch the last phrase, which was, "I don't want you pestering me every night." With that, she climbed into the car and slammed the door. "Get going, Henry," she commanded the chauffeur and sank back into the corner of the seat like a sulky child.

"Well," I said in my most sarcastic tone, "I thought you were always so charming to your public. What's the matter with little Miss Redcoat? Is she selling something?"

Margola glared at me. "You don't know what I've been through with that girl. You can't imagine what she's said and done to me. How she lied to me and made a fool of me."

"Now, Margola," I said, "don't act. Don't be so dramatic. What could a poor girl like that do to you?"

"It's too long a story," she said. "Besides, I get in a rage every time I think about it."

I lighted a cigarette and handed it to her. "Come on," I said. "You'll have to tell me now. We've got a long drive ahead and nothing to do but talk."

She inhaled deeply. "Her name's Eve Harrington," she said. "Translated, it spells—well, she is the most awful girl I've ever met. There are no lengths to which she won't go."

"Start at the beginning," I urged. "Not with the third act. How did you happen to meet this paragon of all the virtues?"

"It was Clement's fault," Margola sighed after a moment's pause. "He first drew my attention to her. He asked me if I'd ever noticed the girl who stood at the stage entrance and simply watched me come out. She didn't ask for an autograph or a picture or try to speak to me—just stood there and looked.

"I said that I hadn't.

"He said she always wore a red coat and to be sure to give a look next time."

"She was wearing a red coat tonight," I interrupted.

"I know." She flicked my remark aside impatiently. "Well, the next time I went into the theater—for a matinee it was—I saw her. She was there when the afternoon performance was over. I saw her again when

I came back after dinner, and when the evening performance was over she was still there.

"This time, when I got rid of the crowd, I spoke to her. I asked her if there was anything I could do for her, and she said no. I said I had noticed her at the matinee and that my husband had seen her before. She said she stood there every night. I couldn't believe my ears. I said, 'Well, what do you want?' She said, 'Nothing.' I said, 'There must be something,' and finally she said that she knew if she stood there long enough eventually I would speak to her. I asked if that was all she wanted and she said yes, that she had first seen me in San Francisco when I toured in *Have a Heart*." That was my husband's first play in which Margola had appeared. "She said she had followed me to Los Angeles and eventually come on to New York."

"Just to stand at your stage door?" I asked, amazed.

"She went to the play," Margola added, "as often as she could afford to."

"What devotion," I said.

"That," said Margola sadly, "is what I assumed. I was most impressed. I thought: This is my most ardent fan. She follows me clear across the Great Divide. She sees my plays constantly when she obviously has very little money. She stands night after night at my stage door just to see me come out and finally have me speak to her. I was moved."

"So what went on?" I urged.

"Well," Margola answered, "I felt that I had to do something to repay this child for her admiration. She was only twenty-two. I thought: I'll give her an evening she'll always remember. So I invited her to come home with me. She acted as if she were in a seventh heaven. She had a slight accent which she told me was Norwegian.

"She said that her people had come over here six or seven years before and had finally left her with an aunt and gone back to Norway on a trip. Of course, because of the war they hadn't been able to return, and she hadn't heard from them in months. In the meantime, she had married a young American flier and had been living in San Francisco because he had gone to the Pacific from there. I asked her how she got along and she said that at first she had had her husband's allotment, but then he had been killed over Bougainville and since then she had lived very meagerly on his insurance."

"How sad."

"Exactly what I thought," Margola said. "She told me that seeing me act and watching my plays had been her only happiness since she had had the wire about her husband. It seemed to me that I must do something for her. I found out that she could type and do shorthand. She'd worked as a secretary in San Francisco. It suddenly came to me that this girl might make just the secretary for me. You know I'm hard to please, but here was someone who adored me, who would be loyal, who was quiet and at the same time well bred. She spoke English beautifully and seemed intelligent.

"So I asked her if she'd like to work for me. You've never seen such a response. She burst into tears and kissed my hand. I generally hate that sort of thing because I know it's insincere, but this time I was sure it was genuine. She was so naive, so unsubtle."

"The way you read that line suggests she wasn't."

"Don't jump cues," Margola snapped. And for my impatience, I had to wait until she had drawn three or four puffs on her cigarette.

"Well, I gave the wretched girl clothes to wear. I gave her twenty-five dollars a week. All she had to do was tend to my correspondence, send out pictures, and so forth. Some letters she was to answer without bothering me, but anything that she felt needed my particular attention she was to show to me. At first she was ideal. Then after a month or so she began to annoy me."

"How?" I couldn't help asking.

"By staring at me. She stared at me all the time. I would turn around suddenly and catch her eyes on me. It gave me the creeps. Finally, I couldn't stand it any longer. I suddenly realized that she was studying me, imitating my gestures, my ways of speech, almost doing the same things. It was like having a living shadow. At last I told Clement that he should use the girl at the office, that she could attend to my mail there instead of at home. I wanted to get her out of the house, and at the same time I didn't want to fire her. I still felt sorry for her. Besides, her work was very satisfactory.

"Clement was delighted with her," Margola continued, a little thin-lipped. "His own secretary had just left to be married and this girl fitted right into her place. She began to read plays for us and made some quite intelligent observations. Then one day we had a rehearsal—it was when we were putting Miss Caswell into the sister part—and I had a toothache and didn't go.

"My understudy hadn't been called. She was out, and the stage manager wasn't able to get in touch with her. Eve had gone to the rehearsal with Clement to take his notes, and when there wasn't anybody to do my part, she volunteered. Clement told the stage manager to give her the script so that she could read it, and to his amazement she said, 'Oh, I don't need that.' Well, my dear"—Margola leaned closer to me as the car spun around a corner—"would you believe it, she knew every line of my part? Not only every line but every *inflection,* every *gesture.* Clement was there to watch Miss Caswell and he said he forgot all about her, he was so fascinated by Eve's unexpected performance."

"Was she really good?"

"Good?" Margola raised a penciled eyebrow. "Good? She was marvelous! Clement even hinted she was slightly better than I am. He didn't dare say so, of course, but he teased me that she was. He said if he'd closed his eyes he wouldn't have known the difference."

"What about the Norwegian accent?"

"Apparently"—Margola shrugged—"that just went. I understand why now."

"I don't," I said.

"You will," Margola stated bluntly. "Anyway, Clement was so amazed at the girl's exhibition that he took her out to tea afterward. She confessed to him that she had always wanted to be an actress and asked him to help her. Asked *him*—not me! Don't you think that was hatefully deceitful?"

I admitted that it was, but I thought privately that the girl had been rather smart. Great actresses are not noted for encouraging brilliant ingenues.

"She told him that she'd only stood around my stage door because she wanted to meet *him,* that she considered him the most brilliant director and producer in New York. He didn't tell me that. I found it out later. But Clem was very flattered. After all, he's only a man, and I get more than my share of attention. He's always introduced as Miss Cranston's husband—it probably irritates him more than he admits. But here was somebody looking up at him with saucer eyes, telling him he was wonderful, and he fell for it. He told me she was the most talented young girl he had seen in years, that we must help her. I said nothing. I knew I had to handle this very carefully. I asked Eve why she hadn't told *me* she wanted to be an actress and asked *me* to help her. She had the nerve"—Margola paused for effect—"to tell me she knew I wouldn't like the competition."

I laughed out loud. It was ridiculous. Even the best actors in her supporting casts have a tendency to melt into the scenery when Margola gets into her stride. "She doesn't lack ego," I chuckled.

"Ego!" Margola stubbed out her cigarette in the ashtray. "Wait till I tell you about the letter! It arrived several days after this rehearsal. Eve came to my dressing room before the performance with four or five letters. This particular one was among them. She told me that she thought I ought to give them my personal attention. I put them into my purse, took them home, and forgot about them.

"Several days later, Eve asked me if I had read them, and I said that I hadn't. She particularly urged me to do so. I promised to, but I still put it off. I hate reading mail. In a few days, she was nagging me again to know if I had read the letters. I still hadn't. That night Alice told me that Miss Harrington had come to my dressing room while I was on stage and had gone through my pockets and my purse looking for something.

"I didn't like that, and after the show I called Eve down for it. She said she was looking for those letters, that there was one that, on second thought, she felt I ought not to see. I said that as she had given me the letter in the first place it was a little absurd to decide now that I shouldn't see it. But whether I read the letters or not, she was never again to go through my things.

"She burst into tears and cried that she only wanted to spare me pain. I had been so kind to her, she didn't want my feelings hurt. She had only given me the letter because when she had first read it she had been so thrilled that she wanted me to see it; thinking it over, she realized that it might hurt me.

"I remarked that after the things critics had written about me, nothing in any letter could possibly faze me.

"I realize now that this entire performance was to get me to read that letter without any more delay, and I'm sorry to say it worked. That night when I got home it was the first thing I did. It was very easy to pick out the one she was referring to. It went something like this—

"Dear Miss Cranston,

"Today I was buying a ticket to see a performance of your play. The door to the theater was open, and as I could hear voices and no one was watching the door I wandered inside to see what was going on. It seemed to be a rehearsal. A young girl was playing the part that I recognized, when I saw the actual performance, as your role—I presume she was your understudy. I know that stars of your caliber are always jealous of the ability of young people, but my dear Miss Cranston, I put you above such petty feelings. I am sure that loving the theater as you do, you will wish to enrich it. In your company, hidden backstage, is the most brilliant young performer I have ever seen. I was spellbound. She brought all your ability plus youth to the part. I waited outside for this young girl and asked her name. It was Harrington. Do help her to get the break she so richly deserves.

"It was signed 'One of your devoted followers.'"

"Of course she wrote it herself," I gasped.

"I think so," Margola said. "I was positive, but it was typewritten, so I couldn't prove it. The next day I merely said to Eve that it was quite a coincidence that the theater door was ajar when she happened to be rehearsing my part. We never mentioned it again."

I resisted comment. I could sense Margola was working up to a big scene.

"Not long after this, the John Bishop auditions came up."

I nodded. John Bishop is one of Broadway's better producers. Every season he holds auditions where talented unknowns can come and do a scene of their own choosing on the stage of his theater. The judges are other producers, talent scouts from film companies, and agents. Mr. Bishop's official reason for this competition is his altruistic desire to give embryonic thespians a chance to be seen—the winner often steps right into a Broadway show.

"Well, darling," Margola went on, "Eve was crazy to participate in Johnny's auditions. She went to Clem and pleaded with him to give her an introduction to Johnny. He said it wasn't necessary, that she merely had to fill in the application blank in Johnny's office and when her turn came she would be called. She found that to be true, and from then on she was no use as a secretary at all. She was in a complete dither about what scene to do and wanted Clement to advise her and coach her. I told her to do a scene from *A Kiss for Cinderella* as I felt she was rather the pathetic, wistful type, but Clem picked out a bit of Ibsen—Hilda in *The Master Builder*—because it would suit her Scandinavian accent.

"She naturally took Clement's advice—not mine. She studied the scene, and when she had memorized it Clement heard her go through it. He came home enthralled. Again, he thought she was marvelous. He insisted that I come down to the theater and give her some suggestions. By this time I was so curious to see the future Jeanne Eagels that I consented. One day before the matinee, I went to the theater early and she did the scene for me."

"Was she really terrific?" I asked.

"I was impressed," Margola admitted reluctantly. "She was talented, there was no question about that. She had a marvelous voice and she read the lines with great sincerity, though this didn't disguise the fact that she was utterly inexperienced and awkward. I suppose that didn't show up when she was copying me in my part because she had me for a model. I did what I could to help her to hide these defects and showed her a few other little tricks, and she picked them up quickly enough. I wasn't as excited as Clement, but I could see that there was something to his statements.

"The auditions took place in a few days. She got down to the finals, and then, on the big day, won them. Everybody was terribly excited about her. Movie scouts knocked themselves out to make tests of her, agents wanted to put her on their files. She thought she was made. She was a star overnight, so now the story could come out."

"What story?"

"Her story. Her true story. Pathetic, wistful, naive Eve Harrington gave out an interview to the newspapers on how she had fooled the finest actress in the theater for several months!"

"Fooled you? How?"

"In every way. Her entire story was a piece of fiction. She'd never been any closer to San Francisco than Milwaukee, where she was born. She was Norwegian by descent, but had picked up her accent from a waitress in her father's restaurant. Her parents were safely in Wisconsin."

"Why did she want an accent?"

"Glamour, my dear. So many foreign actresses are successful here. She thought an accent would make her."

"But the parents being trapped by the war in Norway. What was the point of that?" I asked.

"Sympathy. The husband was a plea in the same direction."

"You mean she wasn't a widow?"

"She'd never been married."

"My God!" I said.

"The entire plot was a masterpiece of detail," Margola went on, enjoying my amazement. "In Milwaukee she had been a secretary with stage ambitions. She saved enough money to come to New York and live for six months. Once here, she laid a careful campaign to get ahead in the theater. She made up her mind to become acquainted with Clem and me. I think her ideas went even further. I believe she planned to break up our marriage.

"Being married to a big producer-director would just suit Eve. She once made a remark to me that every important actress in the theater had a successful man behind her. That part hadn't jelled, but the rest had worked pretty well. As Clem's secretary she had met most of the big agents, playwrights, and important actors. Now, in addition to these contacts, she'd received a chance to show her ability and had come off the winner.

"It looked very amusing in print that director Clement Howell had had a genius right in his own office and that it had remained for another producer to discover her. Poor Clem took a lot of kidding on that score. That interview was the loudest crowing I ever read. The funniest part was how I had fallen for that stuff about her being my great fan. It made her out an even greater actress—that she had played a role in real life so convincingly that we had both been taken completely for a ride. I could have strangled her. Naturally, she didn't wait to be fired. She resigned as Clem's secretary—told him she couldn't be tied down to an office any longer.

"She began to dress in clothes and costumes that would be noticed. And she began to wear makeup in quantity because the report on most of her screen tests was 'no sex appeal.' "

"Why is she still standing at your stage door?" I asked. "I don't understand."

"That's where we had the last laugh," said Margola brightly. "The only thing happened that she hadn't bargained for. You know what Broadway is like. One day you're the toast of the town and the next you're forgotten. She was too inexperienced to have learned that real and lasting success is built only on a long-term foundation. She thought she was all set, and it went to her head. She took a few more screen tests but didn't photograph well enough to be sensational, and Hollywood doesn't bother to experiment with lights and makeup unless you have a real hit behind you. She was an odd type—certainly not the conventional ingenue—and no part turned up for her. Pretty soon the agents and producers just forgot about her. She couldn't even get in to see John Bishop himself, and she was his official protegee.

"That's when she came crying back to Clem and me. She says she'll stand at the stage door every night until I forgive her, that she was a silly fool when she gave out that interview. That she really did adore me and at first her only thought had been to get to know me. That she'll be everlastingly grateful if we will only help her to get a part. But I don't fall into the same trap twice," said Margola determinedly. "So far as I'm concerned she can stand at that entrance until she turns into a statue. I shan't lift a finger to help her."

"It's rather a pity," I said, "since you say she really is talented."

"So what?" Margola said. "Lots of girls are talented and never get a chance to show it. She had a chance, and she muffed it by her own conceit. She'll never get another opportunity."

"Probably not." I sighed and stared through the car window at the reflected stars twinkling like footlights in Little Neck Bay. No, I thought to myself, the little girl with the red coat will probably spend the rest of her life in obscurity.

But I was wrong. So was Margola. Eve Harrington had that rare second chance. I curse the day that she got it. For Margola was right. Eve was a bitch. I know, for it was through me that opportunity knocked twice on her door.

Several weeks after Margola told me this story, Lloyd finished his new play and a prominent manager made immediate plans to produce it. It was a strange play, different from anything Lloyd had written before and very hard to cast. There was one part which presented a real dilemma. It required a young emotional actress of great strength and power. At the same time, it wasn't large enough for a star, having only three scenes.

Lloyd and the manager tried actress after actress, and no one was right. He wanted a certain timid quality that was apparently unobtainable from the synthetic blondes of Broadway. I knew where he could find it. I knew the perfect girl was standing at Margola's stage door. I had never forgotten the shy expression in Eve Harrington's wide eyes. Finally, when in desperation the manager was about to call the production off, I suggested her to Lloyd.

"Go around there," I suggested. "She always wears a red coat. You can't miss her. If you wash the makeup off her face, you'll have exactly the right type. Furthermore, I hear she really can act."

Lloyd thought I was kidding, but finally he did as I told him. Eve read the part the next day, and they gave it to her. The search was over.

All through rehearsals, Lloyd and the director carefully coached Eve to hide her awkwardness. Lloyd began taking her out to lunch to talk about the part. On the opening night, she walked off with the show. It was a hit, and I had to admit it was partly her performance.

Her notices were amazing. The movies got excited about her all over again. This time, with her success behind her, her tests were a different story. What had once struck Hollywood as a lack of sex appeal now was called "a rare quality." So Eve is on the train with her contract in her pocket.

I'm going on a trip, also. I'm heading for Reno to get a divorce. For in spite of her success, Eve had found the time to get engaged to a famous playwright. She's going to marry my husband, Lloyd Richards.

BAD DAY
AT BLACK ROCK

(1954)

BAD TIME AT HONDA
HOWARD BRESLIN

The sun- and sand-beaten outpost of Black Rock is the ideal backdrop for this gripping depiction of a town with a guilty conscience and the one-armed veteran (Spencer Tracy) who arrives to uncover its shameful secret. *Bad Day at Black Rock* has been viewed as an indictment of U.S. persecution of Japanese-Americans during World War II, as a cautionary message to post-Korean War society, and as a thinly-veiled attack on McCarthy's Hollywood blacklisting. Whatever its intended social commentary, *Bad Day at Black Rock* is a pitiless examination of small-town bigotry and civic injustice, and offers up a superb example of the suspense thriller in its most pared-down form. The same story was loosely adapted for the somewhat inferior 1960 film, *Platinum High School*. In addition to the fine performances and the scrupulous direction by John Sturges [*The Magnificent Seven* (1960), *The Great Escape* (1963), *Ice Station Zebra* (1968)], the film also features the early Hollywood work of composer André Previn, who went on to score a number of Academy Award-winning soundtracks.

HOWARD BRESLIN (1912–1964) was the author of six full-length works of fiction, including a post-film novelization of the following story under the pseudonym Michael Niall.

BAD DAY AT BLACK ROCK

Released: 1954
Production: Dore Schary for MGM
Direction: John Sturges
Screenplay: Millard Kaufman
Cinematography: William C. Mellor
Editing: Newell P. Kimlin
Running time: 81 minutes

PRINCIPAL CHARACTERS:

John J. MacReedy	Spencer Tracy
Reno Smith	Robert Ryan
Liz Wirth	Anne Francis
Tim Horn	Dean Jagger
Doc Velie	Walter Brennan
Pete Wirth	John Erickson
Coley Trimble	Ernest Borgnine
Hector David	Lee Marvin

Honda sprawls between the bluff and the railroad tracks. The tracks, four strips of steel, bright in the sunlight, fence the endless Southwestern plain from the false fronts of the town. The plain is Honda's only view; from behind the buildings the bluff, a huge, red-brown mound, roughly shaped like the crown of an enormous sombrero, rises to the sky. Against the bluff's ancient mass the houses of Honda's single street are garish and new, in spite of peeling paint and battered tin signs. The glaring sunshine has baked everything, thoroughly, into one color—sepia. Even the dust that swirls up as the Streamliner passes is the same thinned-out, tired brown.

The long red and silver fatly curved Streamliner streaks past Honda,

heading west, three mornings a week. Eastbound, it rattles by in the
night, a sound, sudden and fleeting. But on the mornings when it is ·
seen, its length alive with glints from the ever-present sunlight, the
Streamliner is an event to Honda, a glimpse of the sleekness and wealth,
the silver-chromium speed, that belong to other places.

That is why the morning the Streamliner stopped it was more than
an event; it was a shock. It was wrong, not normal. The whole town
felt it; the range, when it heard, felt it. And even then, that morning,
the feeling was that this happening would mean a bad time for Honda.

There was no warning. The shimmering heat above the railroad tracks
seemed to become audible with a low humming.

Doc Velie, lounging on the porch of Sullivan's Bar, let his chair
down and looked at his watch. "That'll be her," Doc told the other
loungers. "On time today."

Honda prepared for the expected passage in its usual way. Papa
Delvecchio came out of his grocery store: Liz Brooks climbed up from
the grease pit of her garage and stood waiting, wiping her hands vig-
orously on a piece of waste.

The humming increased in volume. The station door banged, and
Hastings, the station agent, peered down the tracks. Hastings was wearing black dust cuffs, and he raised an arm to shield his bald head from
the sun.

"Here she comes," said Doc Velie, leaning forward. Then his mouth
popped open. The Streamliner wasn't racing into Honda; she had cut
her speed, and was slowing.

The loungers stared. Liz Brooks dropped her waste. Papa Delvecchio
began beckoning wildly to somebody inside the store. Hastings stood
as if frozen until the train slid smoothly to a stop. The moment the
train ceased motion, Hastings jerked into life, running along the track.
But the passenger was on the ground, and the porter was swinging
back up the steps, before the station agent reached the open car door.

The Streamliner slid away, picking up speed with each yard out of
Honda. Every glance in town watched it go. Then all the heads turned
back in unison, to view the man the train had left behind.

He was a big man, bulky. His clothes looked rumpled and well
worn. Towering over the excited Hastings, the man hefted his large,
black Gladstone bag with an ease that matched his size.

Hastings's voice was shrill; it carried across the quiet morning: "You for Honda?"

"That's right," said the big man. He didn't look at Hastings. He was gazing at the town with a pair of calm, untroubled, brown eyes. There was nothing shrewd nor speculative about his gaze, but it seemed to record every feature of Honda with the emotionless efficiency of a camera.

"But there must be some mistake!" Hastings spluttered, disbelief in his tone. "I'm the agent here! Nobody told me about this! Nobody wired me the liner was stopping!"

The big man looked at Hastings, then, and smiled. He said again, softly and amused, "That's right."

Hastings sucked in his breath noisily and swallowed. "You being met?" he asked. "You visiting folks here?"

"No."

The monosyllable was so casually dropped that Hastings wasn't sure he'd heard it. "No?" he repeated.

The stranger nodded toward a two-story frame building that had a sign hanging vertically down one corner, with the single word, HOTEL. "That's for me," he said, and started for it.

Hastings followed him across the dust of the street, up the steps, and into the hotel. The slap of the screen door closing seemed to stir Honda into action. Liz Brooks turned and walked briskly around the corner of her garage. Papa Delvecchio herded his daughter back into the grocery store.

In front of Sullivan's, the loungers could hear the jangle of a telephone bell as Sullivan cranked for a connection. The bar's big Saturday trade came from the ranches, and its owner would make sure that they were informed. The loungers stirred uneasily and looked at one another.

Doc Velie brought out his knife and cut a chew off his tobacco plug. He said, munching, "Walks light for a big man."

They knew that much themselves. A voice asked, low and quick, "What do you think, Doc?"

"How should I know?" Doc Velie answered. "He ain't no salesman, that's sure. Not off the Streamliner." He laughed, a harsh, dry sound without mirth, and jabbed the point of his knife into a pillar of the porch. "Why ask me? It's no hair off my chest, whoever he is!"

A slender, wiry man in a faded blue shirt and jeans came out of the shoemaker's. He stood a moment in the street, smoking, and looked at the loungers. The face under a dust-colored hat was thin and tanned, and his hands were the same. He stood motionless, except for the wisp of smoke from the cigarette between his lips, and the loungers were silent. Not even Doc Velie spoke.

Snapping his cigarette away, the slender man climbed into a light truck and kicked its motor awake. He swung the truck in a smooth, competent U-turn and drove out of town.

Doc Velie spat tobacco at the settling dust. "Ask him," he said. "Ask Lancey Horn. See what it gets you." Again the sharp laughter rattled.

The sun climbed higher, and the shadows of Honda shortened as they always did. It was hot, the dry, breathless furnace heat that Honda expected at midday. But this day was different. Doc Velie shuffled into Sullivan's before his usual time, and the others followed. They stood along the bar, talking quietly, drinking. Sullivan, a small, dark Irishman with a tight mouth, served his customers swiftly and said nothing. The whole room was waiting. But when Hastings came they learned only how the big man had registered:

Peter Macreedy, Chicago.

The name passed from lip to lip. No man recognized it. Sullivan slipped under his bar, went into his back room where the phone was, and shut the door. They all watched when he came back. Sullivan shook his head. The name meant nothing on the range, either.

Doc Velie tossed down a drink and slammed his glass on the bar. "He ain't no cattle buyer, then! Not if Circle T don't know his name!" He stopped, staring at Sullivan.

Hands on the bar propping him higher, Sullivan was on tiptoe, looking over their heads into the street. Through the window, Macreedy's bulk was plain.

The big man was sauntering along easily, hands in his pockets, his feet stirring the dust. As he passed Sullivan's, he glanced at the row of faces behind the window, and smiled. Macreedy went on down the street, not hurrying, and turned into the garage.

There was no one there. The gas pump in the doorway seemed to droop beneath the sun. Macreedy leaned into the car that was over the grease pit, and put his thumb on its horn. The sound was sudden and raucous.

It brought Liz Brooks from her house behind the garage. She came out to the front, walking with a long, man's stride, saw Macreedy, and checked herself. She was a tall girl, and she carried herself well. Even the stained coverall she wore only accented the curves of her figure.

Macreedy said, "Lady at the hotel—Mrs. Jiminez. She says you rent cars."

Liz brushed a strand of black hair off her forehead, as if to see him more clearly. "Sometimes," she said.

"This one of the times?"

"Maybe."

They were facing, standing apart like duelists, trying to find the range with each quiet sentence.

Macreedy moved closer. Both his manner and his voice were bland. "I need this car," he said, "for a trip. To a place called Adobe Wells."

The girl's face didn't change, but she couldn't keep a crisp note from her tone. "Why are you going there?" she asked.

"I have to," said Macreedy simply.

Frowning, Liz said, "There's nothing at the Wells." She waited for Macreedy to speak, but he just looked at her. Her next words had an edge: "Nothing and nobody!" Again she stopped, and again the big man outwaited her, his silence forcing her into speech: "What are you after, anyway?"

"A car," Macreedy said.

LIZ BROOKS took a deep breath, and tightened her lips over it. She turned toward a battered station wagon. Over her shoulder she said, "I'll drive you myself." It sounded like a challenge.

Macreedy nodded, followed her, and got into the car. He watched while the girl backed the station wagon out into the street, and glanced once through the rear window. If he noticed the crowd staring from Sullivan's, he said nothing. They were away from the town, dragging a curtain of dust behind them, when Macreedy unfolded a map on his lap.

"I won't get lost!" said Liz Brooks savagely. She drove faster, looking straight ahead, her knuckles white on the steering wheel.

Rocking on the seat beside her, Macreedy watched the landscape. He tilted his hat forward to shield his eyes from the glare.

The road paralleled the railroad tracks, and then swung away in a wide curve around the shoulder of the bluff behind Honda. After that they were on the plain for miles, the vast flatland slipping away beneath them. Nothing grew higher than a fence post, and only a few cattle moved.

Liz turned off the main road and bounced toward what looked like a low cloud on the horizon. They sped on. The floorboards under Macreedy's feet became uncomfortably hot. Suddenly, the cloud ahead was a jumble of low hills. Macreedy counted them. There were four, tumbled together like carelessly piled grain sacks. In the white glare, each stood clearly etched, as if cut from cardboard, baked into the sepia of the country.

Adobe Wells was a pocket between two of the hills. A barbed-wire fence still stretched across the pocket, but its open gate hung listlessly by one hinge. Liz Brooks steered the station wagon through the gateway and braked abruptly beneath two shadeless, twisted trees.

"Here!" She practically barked the word.

Macreedy grunted, and got out of the car. Turning his body in a complete circle, he looked the place over. He gazed up at the hills, along the line of the fence. Only when his circuit was completed did the big man turn his attention to what had been buildings.

Two adobe walls maintained a right angle, but their fellows had crumbled. Inside the angle lay a mass of charred and blackened timbers. Behind this ruin, scattered dark patches on the rank brown grass showed that fire had taken to the outbuildings, too.

Beside Macreedy, Liz Brooks glared up at him. "I told you," she said. "There's nothing here! Nothing!"

"Since?"

"Not for years!"

The loud twang of metal on metal startled them. There was the high whine of a ricochet, and then, from the hills, the flat slap of a rifle.

Macreedy moved fast. He took one step, hooked a leg behind Liz's knees, deftly shouldered her over, and fell on top of her. They were on the ground before the station wagon's bullet-scarred fender stopped quivering.

"Stay down," said Macreedy. The girl twisted beneath him, and he pushed her flat, holding her there with a hand on her shoulder, his arm rigid. He took a quick look at the fender, and relaxed. "It's all right. He's on the other side of the car." He rolled away from Liz, and rose to a crouch, balancing on one fist like a football player. Macreedy's other hand held a gun, a square black automatic, compact and heavy.

Liz Brooks, prone, watched, her face white and tense. But it was the paleness of anger, not fear. With sudden violence, she pounded her fist against the ground. "Fool!" she muttered. "Fool!"

"Who is?" asked Macreedy. Then, as she whirled herself to a sitting position, he said sharply, "Watch it! Down!"

"He wasn't shooting at me! And it was only a warning, anyway!" The girl's eyes were scornful. "You're too big a target to miss, if a man was trying."

"Maybe," agreed Macreedy, smiling. But he watched the hills for a long time through the car's windows, before he nodded. He helped Liz Brooks to her feet, noticed her glance at his automatic, and slid it back under his arm. "Habit, I guess. At his range I might just as well have thrown it at him."

"Now will you go away?" asked Liz. "There's nothing here!"

"Nothing?" Macreedy's finger stroked the furrow in the fender. "Somebody doesn't agree with you." His head turned in a slow, deliberate survey. Shrugging, he climbed back into the car. "Let's go."

They drove back in silence. Once, on the flatlands, Macreedy spoke. "That gun of mine," he said. "It's a Beretta. Italian make. You might mention it around Honda. I'm not fond of people shooting at me." Getting no reply, he sighed, settled himself more comfortably, and dozed.

Alongside the railroad tracks a car honked and swept past them. Liz Brooks said, "Circle T. The range is coming in."

"That's nice," said Macreedy tonelessly.

The sun was lower in the sky when they came back into Honda, but it was still the same pale, yellow disk. Along the street there were more cars parked, and even a saddled horse drooped in front of Sullivan's. Four men watching Papa Delvecchio water his vegetables stopped talking and stared at the station wagon. When Liz Brooks skidded to a stop before the hotel, a puncher in a parked sedan touched his horn twice.

Macreedy got out of the station wagon, looked at the puncher calmly, smiled. The girl shook her head impatiently, then said, gazing at Honda, "Look. Whatever you're starting, drop it. You can't ride these folks too long."

"I'm not," Macreedy said. "They're riding themselves." He paid Liz and mopped his face. After the wind of motion the heat was stifling. He went into the hotel.

Three men were waiting in Mrs. Jiminez's dining room. They rose from behind an oil-cloth-covered table when Macreedy entered. The biggest of the three wore a seersucker suit and a bow tie. Except for his low-crowned Stetson he might have been a Midwestern banker.

"You're Macreedy," he said, without preamble. "I'm Coogan Trimble."

"Circle T." Macreedy nodded.

Trimble introduced the others: "Mort Lane, of the 31 spread. Randy Cameron. He manages Rancho Mesa."

Lane was a square, stocky man with short bowed legs. Cameron, lanky, had a lean, shrewd face. They were both coatless, wearing clean white shirts.

Macreedy said, "Pleasure." He drew a chair out and sat down. He waited, smiling, attentive. Trimble took a place across the table. The two ranchers stood behind the Circle T owner's chair.

Trimble spoke with the easy assurance of a man to whom people listened. He grinned, teeth very white against sunburned skin, and said, "I'm a frank man, Macreedy. Your arrival was kind of a surprise to Honda. We welcome you." The grin flashed again. "But we're curious. What brought you here?"

"Business."

"Fine. Just what kind?"

"Mine."

The word hung in the quiet room. Color slowly rose behind the bronze of Trimble's face. His grin stiffened, and disappeared. "We're not sitting in on your game," he said evenly. "But we all have a stake in what happens around here."

"Sure." Macreedy glanced at each of the three in turn. "I know. Big outfits. It'd be pretty hard to burn those out."

Lane sucked his breath, audibly. Cameron's voice was flat, uninterested; the tone of a dealer calling the cards. He said, distinctly, "Adobe Wells."

"Your trail's cold," Trimble said. "Why not let it lie? What happened, happened. You can't prove anything, anyway."

"What is there to prove?" asked Macreedy.

"An old Jap squatter!" Lane spat the sentence out as if it tasted bitter.

"Born in the United States," Macreedy said.

"Was he?" Trimble shrugged. "I never knew that. God knows what brought him to this part of the country."

Macreedy said, "I know that, too. He didn't like the talk on the Coast. Too much Emperor routine. He drifted this way. To be let alone."

Trimble's face was blank. "You're well informed."

"Except about the finish."

"About that." The rancher rubbed his chin. "I'm not saying it should have happened, Macreedy. But you know how folks felt after Pearl Harbor. And it was Sunday, and the boys were liquored up."

"So."

Trimble laid his palms flat on the table and leaned forward. "Maybe some of those boys rode for me. Maybe not. Nobody knows for sure. If they did, I'll stand behind them."

Lane and Cameron nodded in unison.

"Other places," said Trimble, not pausing, "settled it other ways. Camps. Things like that. We only had the one. We ran him out. Burned him out. That's all."

"You don't know that's all," said Macreedy.

"Oh, yes, I do," Trimble said. "That's the story I'm taking. And it's all anybody's going to know. The old man lived alone. There'd been some kids, but they went away years ago. Maybe a little arson spurred the old man into leaving, but that's all anybody can say."

Macreedy smiled. "Or wants to."

"Or wants to." Trimble rose, pushing back his chair. "We've played fair, Macreedy. You've got your story. Take it, and run along. There are others around here who might not just talk."

"Lancey Horn, for one," said Cameron, in his quiet, unaccented voice. "Liz Brooks threw him over on account of this thing."

Macreedy looked at him, not speaking. Cameron met the gaze steadily.

"You're sticking?" asked Trimble.

"I'm sticking."

"Why? What's your stake in this? What'll it get you?"

"There are reasons," said Macreedy.

With a snort, Trimble turned and pushed his way through the other two to the door. There he swung around. "One thing. Are you from the government?"

"No." Macreedy shook his head. He watched them go, not moving until he heard the screen door shut behind them. He took out a cigarette, and lit it. The tiny match flame was doubled in eyes that were cold and hard.

Not many customers came in for supper. Those who did, ate hurriedly, talking low, ignoring the big man alone at his table. Macreedy gave all his attention to his meal.

When he had finished he sat on the hotel's porch for a while. In the clear brightness of the moonlight, Honda's street was less shabby than by day. Overhead were countless stars; the street itself was splashed with streams of light from doors and windows. Voices, and the loud music of a jukebox, made Sullivan's neon sign unnecessary. Beneath it, in the shadows, several red dots showed where men smoked. Two punchers, coming out of the hotel, swerved away from Macreedy's bulk and hurried toward Sullivan's. A voice carried back through the quiet: "Yeah. That's the guy." Macreedy smiled into the night, stretched, and went to bed.

Most of Honda stayed up late. Even the light in the back of Papa Delvecchio's store didn't go out until after midnight. Sullivan's was packed and busy. But the jukebox music couldn't drown the uneasy note in men's laughter, and the arguments at the poker table were sudden and frequent. Doc Velie, drunk, started the only fight, a quick flurry of punches that ended with Doc's being carried out to sleep it off. When Sullivan's finally closed, men hung about the street, reluctant to go home. And in the back room a select few waited with Coogan Trimble for a phone call he had put through to Chicago.

By the time Macreedy came down for breakfast, everyone in Honda knew the result of that phone call. Mrs. Jiminez, knowing, served him nervously. The big man had been a cop. Very much a cop. A boss one, they said. Mrs. Jiminez spilled the coffee. This Macreedy had been laid off since the war's start, but who could be certain of anything with cops, except they were always bad luck?

Macreedy didn't seem to do anything. He took one look at the sun blazing over Honda, winced, and borrowed a pack of cards from Mrs. Jiminez. He spent the morning playing solitaire in the hotel dining room.

It wasn't quite noon when three riders from Cameron's Rancho Mesa drifted into Sullivan's. The bartender served them, surprised. "No work today?" he asked.

The three shuffled their feet. They didn't look at Sullivan. One said,

"We got our time. We're drifting." Sullivan stared: Doc Velie, nursing his head in a corner, snickered. Another of the riders said angrily, "Better pay, south a-ways!" The third gulped his drink and glanced through the window toward the hotel. "Yeah," he said. "Let's get along."

In spite of the heat they spurred their horses to a trot through the town. Macreedy heard them pass the hotel, but never looked up from his card game.

He left it only once all that day. He walked through Honda to Liz Brooks's garage. Macreedy noticed that there were more men in town; all along the street they fell silent as he passed. He noticed another thing, too. Nearly every man had a gun belt buckled on.

Liz Brooks saw him coming, waited for him.

Macreedy raised his hat and asked one question: "Who fired that shot yesterday?"

The girl looked at him with tired, red-rimmed eyes. She shook her head.

"It might go easier if you'd tell me," Macreedy said.

Liz Brooks shook her head again.

Macreedy turned and walked back to the hotel. He could feel the tension along the street. It was like the heat, steady, oppressive, mounting. It even followed him into the hotel.

He stayed there through the rest of the day, playing game after game, stopping only to eat. Outside, Honda baked and speculated.

Night brought relief only from the sun. Macreedy finished his supper, pushed the dishes aside, dealt the cards. Doc Velie, glaring, stamped out of the room. Coogan Trimble, drawn irresistibly, came all the way from Sullivan's to stand over Macreedy's table.

"Won't the game come out?" Trimble asked.

"Eventually," Macreedy said.

That night, after Macreedy had gone to bed, the tension broke in Honda. A puncher in Sullivan's denied, heatedly, that he'd ever been to Adobe Wells. The word "lie" snapped out; a name was shouted. The saloon rocked with the roaring of gunfire. Before it was over, two men were dead, another was badly wounded, and the state police were on their way.

The shots woke Macreedy. He lay listening until the shouting had stopped, then got up and went to the open window. In the white floodlight beam of a full moon, Honda seemed crowded with men.

One group was under Macreedy's window, and from it a voice cursed Macreedy savagely, blaming him for the shooting.

A colder voice, Trimble's, cut across the swearing: "Shut up, you fool! That's what he wants!"

With a sudden silence, every face in the group was a white patch lifted toward Macreedy's window. The big man stiffened. He was a clear target in the moonlight, and he knew it, and he was careful not to move. Any sudden motion might bring a gunshot from the street, instead of hatred. Macreedy gazed down on the group, until it quietly broke up and drifted off in fragments. Then he let his breath out slowly.

He stayed at the window, watching, until the state police cars had come and gone. Then he went back to bed. He was asleep when the tap came on his door.

Macreedy was out of bed with a leap, and his gun was in his hand. The room was darker. The moon was gone; the window showed blue instead of silver. Macreedy put his back against the wall by the door, and spoke very quietly: "What is it?"

Through the thin panel a voice said, "Liz Brooks sent me."

Macreedy didn't turn on the light. He unlocked the door, then raised his gun. "Open it," he said. "And come slow."

A man walked into the room, a slender shadow in the half-light.

"The bulb's over your head," said Macreedy. "Pull it on."

The man reached up, fumbled, found the light, and turned it on. Then he walked across to the window and pulled the shade down. He turned, as Macreedy shut the door.

"Your name would be Horn," said Macreedy.

"You're good."

"That was easy. That's the one thing they gave me."

"Like that." Horn didn't sound surprised. "That would be Cameron. He's always wanted my place. So I'm elected." He lit a cigarette, not hurrying, and blew smoke toward the ceiling. "I walked in alone, Macreedy. I'll walk out alone. Italian gun or not."

"Out at the Wells. That shot. The girl knew it was you."

Horn smiled. "Testing. You didn't scare."

Macreedy wasn't smiling. He asked, "Was it you the night they burned the old man out?"

"I was there. But I'm not going to be the goat."

"Tell me what happened."

"Showdown, eh?" Horn took the cigarette out of his mouth and looked at Macreedy for a long time. "All right," he said finally. He sat down on the edge of the rumpled bed. "Liz didn't want me to go out there with the crowd. I went. You don't have to believe I went to herd them off, to slow them down. On the other hand, I don't have to tell you anything."

Macreedy nodded. "Go on."

"I went. They were drunk. They had a rope. You've seen those trees out there; they're not big enough for that. I thought it might save the old man. But they started burning the buildings. He broke away. Ran for it."

Macreedy nodded again.

"He ran up the hill. You could see him plain, in all that fire. They started to chase him. But I called for the shot. I cursed them out, and called for it. Like I was one of them. I meant to miss."

"Yes," Macreedy said.

"He couldn't run very fast. I gave him all the time I could. He was almost to the top when I shot. I put it beside him, into a shadow so they wouldn't see it hit. I couldn't believe it when he dropped."

"You hit him?"

"No. There wasn't a mark on him. But nobody knows that but me. The rest of them beat it. I buried him over at my own place. He was dead, all right. Fright, I guess. Or running up that hill. He wasn't young. But there was no bullet in him."

"The town doesn't know that."

"No. I got the credit. Even with Liz." Horn bared his teeth. "But that's the truth. I liked the old bird. Used to get vegetables from him."

Horn stood up, suddenly tense. "Liz talked me into coming here, ending this thing. You've got it. You don't have to believe it. There's no proof. I could show you an unmarked skeleton, but you wouldn't know it was the Jap's. There was never any proof about what really happened. That's why I never told my story. . . . Take it or leave it."

Macreedy sighed, and tossed his gun on the bed. He said, "You couldn't stop them?"

"You can't stop a stampede, Macreedy."

"I guess that's all," said Macreedy. "And thanks." He went to the window and raised the shade. "Almost dawn."

Horn heard the dismissal in the words, and started for the door. He had his hand on the knob when he paused. "Why, Macreedy?" he asked. "Why, after four years? What brought you to Honda?" But Macreedy just stood, looking out the window, and Horn left.

Macreedy slept late, and he spoke to Hastings as soon as he breakfasted. The station agent raced to Sullivan's with the news: "He's leaving! He wants me to flag the eastbound Streamliner tonight!"

It spread through Honda like a cool wind. Sullivan passed it on to the ranches. Doc Velie took off his gun. Even Papa Delvecchio beamed when he heard, and pressed a free apple on the man who told him. And all through another scorching day Honda scoffed at Macreedy's solitaire as the gesture of a beaten man.

Sullivan's was crowded and happy that night. The jukebox was the only noise in the room, and Macreedy was standing in the doorway. The crowd drew back from him. Somebody pulled the plug of the jukebox out, and the silence was like a shot.

"Now, listen," said Macreedy. "All of you. I came here to find Old Man Kamotka. You know what happened to him. So do I—now." He could hear the breathing in the room, and he went on: "This is why I came. There was a kid named Jimmy Kamotka. He left here years ago. He never wrote his father. The old man couldn't read. I met Jimmy in the Army. In Italy. He asked me to look in here."

Macreedy's smile was not a pleasant one. "Jimmy Kamotka was killed in Italy. I think maybe this town should know that. And remember it. I'm not a cop any more, and you're all safe enough. But just remember what I told you."

Along the railroad tracks came the humming of an approaching train.

Macreedy looked the crowd over with his calm gaze. Then he spoke, and the word crackled like an insult: "Honda!"

The big man turned and went out. He reached the station just as the Streamliner slid to a stop. Macreedy climbed aboard without looking back.

BLOW-UP

(1966)

BLOW-UP
JULIO CORTAZAR

By the very nature of the medium, cinema has from its earliest days manipulated and questioned the manner in which we perceive reality by pitting fantasy against fact, subjectivity against objectivity. For his first English-language film, Italian director Michelangelo Antonioni chose the story of a photographer who snaps a shot of what appears to be an innocent lovers' tryst in a park. On closer analysis, the picture discloses elements that are malevolent, dangerous, and possibly murderous. Rejecting the traditional approach to plot and character development, Antonioni used a fabric of abstract imagery better suited to the film's exploration of perceived truth. The director's timing couldn't have been better—in 1966, European "art films" were being received enthusiastically worldwide. The movie also capitalized on the audience's latent voyeurism by supplying glimpses of nudity and a vicarious entree into the trendy world of London culture (the seminal British rock band, the Yardbirds, makes a cameo appearance performing "Train Kept A-Rollin'," replete with instrument-smashing finale). The film became an international box-office hit. In 1975, Antonioni once again explored the themes suggested in *Blow-Up* with *The Passenger,* this time as they related to personal identity.

Born in 1914 and raised outside Buenos Aires, Argentina, JULIO CORTÁZAR is recognized as one of the most influential writers of contemporary Latin and South American literature. Because he is a practitioner of fantasy and fabulism, he is often compared to his fellow countryman, Jorge Luis Borges. In 1951, he settled in Paris, where he continued to write and to work as a freelance translator for UNESCO until his death in 1984. Of his many novels and short stories, his best-known work is *Hopscotch*.

BLOW-UP

Released: 1966
Production: Carlo Ponti for MGM
Direction: Michelangelo Antonioni
Screenplay: Michelangelo Antonioni and Tonino Guerra, English dialogue in
    collaboration with Edward Bond
Cinematography: Carlo di Palma
Editing: Frank Clarke
Music: Herbert Hancock, with the song "Train Kept A-Rollin' " written and
    performed by the Yardbirds
Running time: 110 minutes

PRINCIPAL CHARACTERS:

Thomas	David Hemmings
The Girl	Vanessa Redgrave
Patricia	Sarah Miles
Bill	John Castle
Ron	Peter Bowles
The Blonde	Jane Birkin
The Brunette	Gillian Hills

It'll never be known how this has to be told, in the first person or in the second, using the third person plural or continually inventing modes that will serve for nothing. If one might say: I will see the moon rose, or: we hurt me at the back of my eyes, and especially: you the

blonde woman was the clouds that race before my your his our yours
their faces. What the hell.

Seated ready to tell it, if one might go to drink a bock over there,
and the typewriter continue by itself (because I use the machine), that
would be perfection. And that's not just a manner of speaking. Perfection, yes, because here is the aperture which must be counted also as
a machine (of another sort, a Contax 1.1.2) and it is possible that one
machine may know more about another machine than I, you, she—
the blonde—and the clouds. But I have the dumb luck to know that
if I go this Remington will sit turned to stone on top of the table with
the air of being twice as quiet that mobile things have when they are
not moving. So, I have to write. One of us all has to write, if this is
going to get told. Better that it be me who am dead, for I'm less
compromised than the rest; I who see only the clouds and can think
without being distracted, write without being distracted (there goes
another, with a grey edge) and remember without being distracted, I
who am dead (and I'm alive, I'm not trying to fool anybody, you'll see
when we get to the moment, because I have to begin some way and
I've begun with this period, the last one back, the one at the beginning,
which in the end is the best of the periods when you want to tell
something).

All of a sudden I wonder why I have to tell this, but if one begins
to wonder why he does all he does do, if one wonders why he accepts
an invitation to lunch (now a pigeon's flying by and it seems to me a
sparrow), or why when someone has told us a good joke immediately
there starts up something like a tickling in the stomach and we are not
at peace until we've gone into the office across the hall and told the
joke over again; then it feels good immediately, one is fine, happy, and
can get back to work. For I imagine that no one has explained this,
that really the best thing is to put aside all decorum and tell it, because,
after all's done, nobody is ashamed of breathing or of putting on his
shoes; they're things that you do, and when something weird happens,
when you find a spider in your shoe or if you take a breath and feel
like a broken window, then you have to tell what's happening, tell it
to the guys at the office or to the doctor. Oh, doctor, every time I take
a breath.... Always tell it, always get rid of that tickle in the stomach
that bothers you.

And now that we're finally going to tell it, let's put things a little bit
in order, we'd be walking down the staircase in this house as far as

Sunday, November 7, just a month back. One goes down five floors and stands then in the Sunday in the sun one would not have suspected of Paris in November, with a large appetite to walk around, to see things, to take photos (because we were photographers, I'm a photographer). I know that the most difficult thing is going to be finding a way to tell it, and I'm not afraid of repeating myself. It's going to be difficult because nobody really knows who it is telling it, if I am I or what actually occurred or what I'm seeing (clouds, and once in a while a pigeon) or if, simply, I'm telling a truth which is only my truth, and then is the truth only for my stomach, for this impulse to go running out and to finish up in some manner with, this, whatever it is.

We're going to tell it slowly, what happens in the middle of what I'm writing is coming already. If they replace me, if, so soon, I don't know what to say, if the clouds stop coming and something else starts (because it's impossible that this keep coming, clouds passing continually and occasionally a pigeon), if something out of all this. . . . And after the "if" what am I going to put if I'm going to close the sentence structure correctly? But if I begin to ask questions, I'll never tell anything, maybe to tell would be like an answer, at least for someone who's reading it.

Roberto Michel, French-Chilean, translator and in his spare time an amateur photographer, left number 11, rue Monsieur-le-Prince Sunday November 7 of the current year (now there're two small ones passing, with silver linings). He had spent three weeks working on the French version of a treatise on challenges and appeals by José Norberto Allende, professor at the University of Santiago. It's rare that there's wind in Paris, and even less seldom a wind like this that swirled around corners and rose up to whip at old wooden venetian blinds behind which astonished ladies commented variously on how unreliable the weather had been these last few years. But the sun was out also, riding the wind and friend of the cats, so there was nothing that would keep me from taking photos of the Conservatoire and Sainte-Chapelle. It was hardly ten o'clock, and I figured that by eleven the light would be good, the best you can get in the fall; to kill some time I detoured around by the Isle Saint-Louis and started to walk along the quai D'Anjou, I stared for a bit at the hôtel de Lauzun, I recited bits from Apollinaire which always get into my head whenever I pass in front of the hôtel de Lauzun (and at that I ought to be remembering the other poet, but Michel is an obstinate beggar), and when the wind stopped all at once and the sun came out at least twice as hard (I mean warmer, but really it's the same thing), I sat down on the parapet and felt terribly happy in the Sunday morning.

One of the many ways of contesting level-zero, and one of the best, is to take photographs, an activity in which one should start becoming an adept very early in life, teach it to children since it requires discipline, aesthetic education, a good eye, and steady fingers. I'm not talking about waylaying the lie like any old reporter, snapping the stupid silhouette of the VIP leaving Number 10 Downing Street, but in all ways when one is walking about with a camera, one has almost a duty to be attentive, to not lose that abrupt and happy rebound of sun's rays off an old stone, or the pigtails-flying run of a small girl going home with a loaf of bread or a bottle of milk. Michel knew that the photographer always worked as a permutation of his personal way of seeing the world as other than the camera insidiously imposed upon it (now a large cloud is going by, almost black), but he lacked no confidence in himself, knowing that he had only to go out without the Contax to recover the keynote of distraction, the sight without a frame around it, light without the diaphragm aperture or 1/250 sec. Right now (what a word, *now,* what a dumb lie) I was able to sit quietly on the railing overlooking the river watching the red and black motorboats passing below without it occurring to me to think photographically of the scenes, nothing more than letting myself go in the letting go of objects, running immobile in the stream of time. And then the wind was not blowing.

After, I wandered down the quai de Bourbon until getting to the end of the isle where the intimate square was (intimate because it was small, not that it was hidden, it offered its whole breast to the river and the sky), I enjoyed it, a lot. Nothing there but a couple and, of course, pigeons; maybe even some of those which are flying past now so that I'm seeing them. A leap up and I settled on the wall, and let myself turn about and be caught and fixed by the sun, giving it my face and ears and hands (I kept my gloves in my pocket). I had no desire to shoot pictures, and lit a cigarette to be doing something; I think it was that moment when the match was about to touch the tobacco that I saw the young boy for the first time.

What I'd thought was a couple seemed much more now a boy with his mother, although at the same time I realized that it was not a kid and his mother, and that it was a couple in the sense that we always allegate to couples when we see them leaning up against the parapets or embracing on the benches in the squares. As I had nothing else to do, I had more than enough time to wonder why the boy was so nervous, like a young colt or a hare, sticking his hands into his pockets, taking them out immediately, one after the other, running his fingers through his hair, changing his stance, and especially why was he afraid, well, you could guess that from every gesture, a fear suffocated by his shyness, an impulse to step backwards which he telegraphed, his body standing as if it were on the edge of flight, holding itself back in a final, pitiful decorum.

All this was so clear, ten feet away—and we were alone against the parapet at the tip of the island—that at the beginning the boy's fright didn't let me see the blonde very well. Now, thinking back on it, I see her much better at that first second when I read her face (she'd turned around suddenly, swinging like a metal weathercock, and the eyes, the eyes were there), when I vaguely understood what might have been occurring to the boy and figured it would be worth the trouble to stay and watch (the wind was blowing their words away and they were speaking in a low murmur). I think that I know how to look, if it's something I know, and also that every looking oozes with mendacity, because it's that which expels us furthest outside ourselves, without the least guarantee, whereas to smell, or (but Michel rambles on to himself easily enough, there's no need to let him harangue on this way). In any case, if the likely inaccuracy can be seen beforehand, it becomes possible again to look; perhaps it suffices to choose between looking and the reality looked at, to strip things of all their unnecessary clothing. And surely all that is difficult besides.

As for the boy I remember the image before his actual body (that will clear itself up later), while now I am sure that I remember the woman's body much better than the image. She was thin and willowy, two unfair words to describe what she was, and was wearing an almost-black fur coat, almost long, almost handsome. All the morning's wind (now it was hardly a breeze and it wasn't cold) had blown through her blonde hair which pared away her white, bleak face—two unfair words—and put the world at her feet and horribly alone in front of her dark eyes, her eyes fell on things like two eagles, two leaps into nothingness, two puffs of green slime. I'm not describing it. And I said two puffs of green slime.

Let's be fair, the boy was well enough dressed and was sporting yellow gloves which I would have sworn belonged to his older brother, a student of law or sociology; it was pleasant to see the fingers of the gloves sticking out of his jacket pocket. For a long time I didn't see his face, barely a profile, not stupid—a terrified bird, a Fra Filippo angel, rice pudding with milk—and the back of an adolescent who wants to take up judo and has had a scuffle or two in defense of an idea or his sister. Turning fourteen, perhaps fifteen, one would guess that he was dressed and fed by his parents but without a nickel in his pocket, having to debate with his buddies before making up his mind to buy a coffee, a cognac, a pack of cigarettes. He'd walk through the streets thinking of the girls in his class, about how good it would be to go to the movies and see the latest film, or to buy novels or neckties or bottles of liquor with green and white labels on them. At home (it would be a respectable home, lunch at noon and romantic landscapes on the walls, with a dark entryway and a mahogany umbrella stand inside the door) there'd be the slow rain of time, for studying, for being mama's hope, for looking like dad, for writing to his aunt in Avignon. So that there was a lot of walking the streets, the whole of the river for him (but without a nickel) and the mysterious city of fifteen-year-olds with its signs in doorways, its terrifying cats, a paper of fried potatoes for thirty francs, the pornographic magazine folded four ways, a solitude like the emptiness of his pockets, the eagerness for so much that was incomprehensible but illumined by a total love, by the availability analogous to the wind and the streets.

This biography was of the boy and of any boy whatsoever, but this particular one now, you could see he was insular, surrounded solely by the blonde's presence as she continued talking with him. (I'm tired of insisting, but two long ragged ones just went by. That morning I don't think I looked at the sky once, because what was happening with the boy and the woman appeared so soon I could do nothing but look at them and wait, look at them and . . .) To cut it short, the boy was agitated and one could guess without too much trouble what had just occurred a few minutes before, at most half-an-hour. The boy had come onto the tip of the island, seen the woman and thought her marvelous. The woman was waiting for that because she was there waiting for that, or maybe the boy arrived before her and she saw him from one of the balconies or from a car and got out to meet him, starting the conversation with whatever, from the beginning she was sure that he was going to be afraid and want to run off, and that, naturally, he'd stay, stiff and sullen, pretending experience and the pleasure of the adventure. The rest was easy because it was happening ten feet away from me, and anyone could have gauged the stages of the game, the derisive, competitive fencing; its major attraction was not that it was happening but in foreseeing its denouement. The boy would try to end it by pretending a date, an obligation, whatever, and would go stumbling off disconcerted, wishing he were walking with some assurance, but naked under the mocking glance which would follow him until he was out of sight. Or rather, he would stay there, fascinated or simply incapable of taking the initiative, and the woman would begin to touch his face gently, muss his hair, still talking to him voicelessly, and soon would take him by the arm to lead him off, unless he, with an uneasiness beginning to tinge the edge of desire, even his stake in the adventure, would rouse himself to put his arm around her waist and to kiss her. Any of this could have happened, though it did not, and perversely Michel waited, sitting on the railing, making the settings almost without looking at the camera, ready to take a picturesque shot of a corner of the island with an uncommon couple talking and another looking at one another.

Strange how the scene (almost nothing: two figures there mismatched in their youth) was taking on a disquieting aura. I thought it was I imposing it, and that my photo, if I shot it, would reconstitute things in their true stupidity. I would have liked to know what he was thinking, a man in a grey hat sitting at the wheel of a car parked on the dock which led up to the footbridge, and whether he was reading the paper or asleep. I had just discovered him because people inside a parked car have a tendency to disappear, they get lost in that wretched, private cage stripped of the beauty that motion and danger give it. And nevertheless, the car had been there the whole time, forming part (or deforming that part) of the isle. A car: like saying a lighted streetlamp, a park bench. Never like saying wind, sunlight, those elements always new to the skin and the eyes, and also the boy and the woman, unique, put there to change the island, to show it to me in another way. Finally, it may have been that the man with the newspaper also became aware of what was happening and would, like me, feel that malicious sensation of waiting for everything to happen. Now the woman had swung around smoothly, putting the young boy between herself and the wall, I saw them almost in profile, and he was taller, though not much taller, and yet she dominated him, it seemed like she was hovering over him (her laugh, all at once, a whip of feathers), crushing him just by being there, smiling, one hand taking a stroll through the air. Why wait any longer? Aperture at sixteen, a sighting which would not include the horrible black car, but yes, that tree, necessary to break up too much grey space . . . .

I raised the camera, pretended to study a focus which did not include them, and waited and watched closely, sure that I would finally catch the revealing expression, one that would sum it all up, life that is rhythmed by movement but which a stiff image destroys, taking time in cross section, if we do not choose the essential imperceptible fraction of it. I did not have to wait long. The woman was getting on with the job of handcuffing the boy smoothly, stripping from him what was left of his freedom a hair at a time, in an incredibly slow and delicious torture. I imagined the possible endings (now a small fluffy cloud appears, almost alone in the sky), I saw their arrival at the house (a basement apartment probably, which she would have filled with large cushions and cats) and conjectured the boy's terror and his desperate decision to play it cool and to be led off pretending there was nothing new in it for him. Closing my eyes, if I did in fact close my eyes, I set the scene: the teasing kisses, the woman mildly repelling the hands which were trying to undress her, like in novels, on a bed that would have a lilac-colored comforter, on the other hand she taking off his clothes, plainly mother and son under a milky yellow light, and everything would end up as usual, perhaps, but maybe everything would go otherwise, and the initiation of the adolescent would not happen, she would not let it happen, after a long prologue wherein the awkwardnesses, the exasperating caresses, the running of hands over bodies would be resolved in who knows what, in a separate and solitary pleasure, in a petulant denial mixed with the art of tiring and disconcerting so much poor innocence. It might go like that, it might very well go like that; that woman was not looking for the boy as a lover, and at the same time she was dominating him toward some end impossible to understand if you do not imagine it as a cruel game, the desire to desire without satisfaction, to excite herself for someone else, someone who in no way could be that kid.

Michel is guilty of making literature, of indulging in fabricated unrealities. Nothing pleases him more than to imagine exceptions to the rule, individuals outside the species, not-always-repugnant monsters. But that woman invited speculation, perhaps giving clues enough for the fantasy to hit the bull's-eye. Before she left, and now that she would fill my imaginings for several days, for I'm given to ruminating, I decided not to lose a moment more. I got it all into the view-finder (with the tree, the railing, the eleven-o'clock sun) and took the shot. In time to realize that they both had noticed and stood there looking at me, the boy surprised and as though questioning, but she was irritated, her face and body flat-footedly hostile, feeling robbed, ignominiously recorded on a small chemical image.

I might be able to tell it in much greater detail but it's not worth the trouble. The woman said that no one had the right to take a picture without permission, and demanded that I hand over the film. All this in a dry, clear voice with a good Parisian accent, which rose in color and tone with every phrase. For my part, it hardly mattered whether she got the roll of film or not, but anyone who knows me will tell you, if you want anything from me, ask nicely. With the result that I restricted myself to formulating the opinion that not only was photography in public places not prohibited, but it was looked upon with decided favor, both private and official. And while that was getting said, I noticed on the sly how the boy was falling back, sort of actively backing up though without moving, and all at once (it seemed almost incredible) he turned and broke into a run, the poor kid, thinking that he was walking off and in fact in full flight, running past the side of the car, disappearing like a gossamer filament of angel-spit in the morning air.

But filaments of angel-spittle are also called devil-spit, and Michel had to endure rather particular curses, to hear himself called meddler and imbecile, taking great pains meanwhile to smile and to abate with simple movements of his head such a hard sell. As I was beginning to get tired, I heard the car door slam. The man in the grey hat was there, looking at us. It was only at that point that I realized he was playing a part in the comedy.

He began to walk toward us, carrying in his hand the paper he had been pretending to read. What I remember best is the grimace that twisted his mouth askew, it covered his face with wrinkles, changed somewhat both in location and shape because his lips trembled and the grimace went from one side of his mouth to the other as though it were on wheels, independent and involuntary. But the rest stayed fixed, a flour-powdered clown or bloodless man, dull dry skin, eyes deepset, the nostrils black and prominently visible, blacker than the eyebrows or hair or the black necktie. Walking cautiously as though the pavement hurt his feet; I saw patent-leather shoes with such thin soles that he must have felt every roughness in the pavement. I don't know why I got down off the railing, nor very well why I decided to not give them the photo, to refuse that demand in which I guessed at their fear and cowardice. The clown and the woman consulted one another in silence: we made a perfect and unbearable triangle, something I felt compelled to break with a crack of a whip. I laughed in their faces and began to walk off, a little more slowly, I imagine, than the boy. At the level of the first houses, beside the iron footbridge, I turned around to look at them. They were not moving, but the man had dropped his newspaper; it seemed to me that the woman, her back to the parapet, ran her hands over the stone with the classical and absurd gesture of someone pursued looking for a way out.

What happened after that happened here, almost just now, in a room on the fifth floor. Several days went by before Michel developed the photos he'd taken on Sunday; his shots of the Conservatoire and of Sainte-Chapelle were all they should be. Then he found two or three proof-shots he'd forgotten, a poor attempt to catch a cat perched astonishingly on the roof of a rambling public urinal, and also the shot of the blonde and the kid. The negative was so good that he made an enlargement; the enlargement was so good that he made one very much larger, almost the size of a poster. It did not occur to him (now one wonders and wonders) that only the shots of the Conservatoire were worth so much work. Of the whole series, the snapshot of the tip of the island was the only one which interested him; he tacked up the enlargement on one wall of the room, and the first day he spent some time looking at it and remembering, that gloomy operation of comparing the memory with the gone reality; a frozen memory, like any photo, where nothing is missing, not even, and especially, nothingness, the true solidifier of the scene. There was the woman, there was the boy, the tree rigid above their heads, the sky as sharp as the stone of the parapet, clouds and stones melded into a single substance and inseparable (now one with sharp edges is going by, like a thunderhead). The first two days I accepted what I had done, from the photo itself to the enlargement on the wall, and didn't even question that every once in a while I would interrupt my translation of José Norberto Allende's treatise to encounter once more the woman's face, the dark splotches on the railing. I'm such a jerk; it had never occurred to me that when we look at a photo from the front, the eyes reproduce exactly the position and the vision of the lens; it's these things that are taken for granted and it never occurs to anyone to think about them. From my chair, with the typewriter directly in front of me, I looked at the photo ten feet away, and then it occurred to me that I had hung it exactly at the point of view of the lens. It looked very good that way; no doubt, it was the best way to appreciate a photo, though the angle from the diagonal doubtless has its pleasures and might even divulge different aspects. Every few minutes, for example when I was unable to find the way to say in good French what José Norberto Allende was saying in very good Spanish, I raised my eyes and looked at the photo; sometimes the woman would catch my eye, sometimes the boy, sometimes the pavement where a dry leaf had fallen admirably situated to heighten a lateral section. Then I rested a bit from my labors, and I enclosed myself again happily in that morning in which the photo was drenched, I recalled ironically the angry picture of the woman demanding I give her the photograph, the boy's pathetic and ridiculous flight, the entrance on the scene of the man with the white face. Basically, I was satisfied with myself; my part had not been too brilliant, and since the French have been given the gift of the sharp response, I did not see very well why I'd chosen to leave without a complete demonstration of the rights, privileges and prerogatives of citizens. The important thing, the really important thing was having helped the kid to escape in time (this in case my theorizing was correct, which was not sufficiently proven, but the running away itself seemed to show it so). Out of plain meddling, I had given him the opportunity finally to take advantage of his fright to do something useful; now he would be regretting it, feeling his honor impaired, his manhood diminished. That was better than the attentions of a woman capable of looking as she had looked at him on that island. Michel is something of a puritan at times, he believes that one should not seduce someone from a position of strength. In the last analysis, taking that photo had been a good act.

Well, it wasn't because of the good act that I looked at it between paragraphs while I was working. At that moment I didn't know the reason, the reason I had tacked the enlargement onto the wall; maybe all fatal acts happen that way, and that is the condition of their fulfillment. I don't think the almost-furtive trembling of the leaves on the tree alarmed me, I was working on a sentence and rounded it out successfully. Habits are like immense herbariums, in the end an en-

largement of 32 × 28 looks like a movie screen, where, on the tip of
the island, a woman is speaking with a boy and a tree is shaking its
dry leaves over their heads.

But her hands were just too much. I had just translated: "In that
case, the second key resides in the intrinsic nature of difficulties which
societies . . ."—when I saw the woman's hand beginning to stir slowly,
finger by finger. There was nothing left of me, a phrase in French which
I would never have to finish, a typewriter on the floor, a chair that
squeaked and shook, fog. The kid had ducked his head like boxers do
when they've done all they can and are waiting for the final blow to
fall; he had turned up the collar of his overcoat and seemed more a
prisoner than ever, the perfect victim helping promote the catastrophe.
Now the woman was talking into his ear, and her hand opened again
to lay itself against his cheekbone, to caress and caress it, burning it,
taking her time. The kid was less startled than he was suspicious, once
or twice he poked his head over the woman's shoulder and she continued talking, saying something that made him look back every few
minutes toward that area where Michel knew the car was parked and
the man in the grey hat, carefully eliminated from the photo but present
in the boy's eyes (how doubt that now) in the words of the woman,
in the woman's hands, in the vicarious presence of the woman. When
I saw the man come up, stop near them and look at them, his hands
in his pockets and a stance somewhere between disgusted and demanding, the master who is about to whistle in his dog after a frolic
in the square, I understood, if that was to understand, what had to
happen now, what had to have happened then, what would have to
happen at that moment, among these people, just where I had poked
my nose in to upset an established order, interfering innocently in that
which had not happened, but which was now going to happen, now
was going to be fulfilled. And what I had imagined earlier was much
less horrible than the reality, that woman, who was not there by herself,
she was not caressing or propositioning or encouraging for her own
pleasure, to lead the angel away with his tousled hair and play the
tease with his terror and his eager grace. The real boss was waiting
there, smiling petulantly, already certain of the business; he was not
the first to send a woman in the vanguard, to bring him the prisoners
manacled with flowers. The rest of it would be so simple, the car, some
house or another, drinks, stimulating engravings, tardy tears, the awakening in hell. And there was nothing I could do, this time I could do

absolutely nothing. My strength had been a photograph, that, there, where they were taking their revenge on me, demonstrating clearly what was going to happen. The photo had been taken, the time had run out, gone; we were so far from one another, the abusive act had certainly already taken place, the tears already shed, and the rest conjecture and sorrow. All at once the order was inverted, they were alive, moving, they were deciding and had decided, they were going to their future; and I on this side, prisoner of another time, in a room on the fifth floor, to not know who they were, that woman, that man, and that boy, to be only the lens of my camera, something fixed, rigid, incapable of intervention. It was horrible, their mocking me, deciding it before my impotent eye, mocking me, for the boy again was looking at the flour-faced clown and I had to accept the fact that he was going to say yes, that the proposition carried money with it or a gimmick, and I couldn't yell for him to run, or even open the road to him again with a new photo, a small and almost meek intervention which would ruin the framework of drool and perfume. Everything was going to resolve itself right there, at that moment; there was like an immense silence which had nothing to do with physical silence. It was stretching it out, setting itself up. I think I screamed, I screamed terribly, and that at that exact second I realized that I was beginning to move toward them, four inches, a step, another step, the tree swung its branches rhythmically in the foreground, a place where the railing was tarnished emerged from the frame, the woman's face turned toward me as though surprised, was enlarging, and then I turned a bit, I mean that the camera turned a little, and without losing sight of the woman, I began to close in on the man who was looking at me with the black holes he had in place of eyes, surprised and angered both, he looked, wanting to nail me onto the air, and at that instant I happened to see something like a large bird outside the focus that was flying in a single swoop in front of the picture, and I leaned up against the wall of my room and was happy because the boy had just managed to escape, I saw him running off, in focus again, sprinting with his hair flying in the wind, learning finally to fly across the island, to arrive at the footbridge, return to the city. For the second time he'd escaped them, for the second time I was helping him to escape, returning him to his precarious paradise. Out of breath, I stood in front of them; no need to step closer, the game was played out. Of the woman you could see just maybe a shoulder and a bit of hair, brutally cut off by the frame of the picture; but the man was directly center, his mouth half open, you could see a shaking black tongue, and he lifted his hands slowly, bringing them into the foreground, an instant still in perfect focus, and then all of him a lump that blotted out the island, the tree, and I shut my eyes, I didn't want to see any more, and I covered my face and broke into tears like an idiot.

Now there's a big white cloud, as on all these days, all this untellable time. What remains to be said is always a cloud, two clouds, or long hours of a sky perfectly clear, a very clean, clear rectangle tacked up with pins on the wall of my room. That was what I saw when I opened my eyes and dried them with my fingers: the clear sky, and then a cloud that drifted in from the left, passed gracefully and slowly across and disappeared on the right. And then another, and for a change sometimes, everything gets grey, all one enormous cloud, and suddenly the splotches of rain cracking down, for a long spell you can see it raining over the picture, like a spell of weeping reversed, and little by little, the frame becomes clear, perhaps the sun comes out, and again the clouds begin to come, two at a time, three at a time. And the pigeons once in a while, and a sparrow or two.

THE BODY SNATCHER

(1945)

THE BODY SNATCHER
ROBERT LOUIS STEVENSON

The horror film has perhaps enjoyed greater longevity and staying-power than any other cinematic style, even greater than the western, the science-fiction film, or film noir. From the silent Lon Chaney masterpieces, through the Universal "monster" pictures of the 1930s and '40s, to the current efforts of directors like Roger Corman and George Romero, the horror picture has always been viewed as a worthwhile box-office risk, based on its appeal to one of the most basic of human drives: the confrontation of fear. Granted, it has produced endless reels of the most execrable footage in the form of hackneyed sequels and the current assembly line of slasher films; yet, in its long history, some astonishing works of cinematic art have surfaced. *The Body Snatcher* is one such film. Set in early nineteenth-century Edinburgh, the film concerns the trafficking of disinterred corpses to medical schools for anatomical research and features performances by two grand screen ghouls, Boris Karloff and Bela Lugosi. This was one of the last (and generally considered the best) of producer Val Lewton's high-quality, low-budget mood thrillers made for RKO during the 1940s. It also showcases the early work of director Robert Wise (*The Day the Earth Stood Still* (1951), *West Side Story* (1961), *The Sound of Music* (1965)).

With the exception of Edgar Allan Poe's, the writings of ROBERT LOUIS STEVENSON (1850–1894) have been used more frequently as the source for horror films than those of any other writer. In addition to many versions of *Dr. Jekyll & Mr. Hyde,* the Stevenson oeuvre has produced such films as *The Suicide Club* (1936) and *The Strange Door* (1951).

THE BODY SNATCHER

Released: 1945
Production: Val Lewton for RKO/Radio
Direction: Robert Wise
Screenplay: Philip MacDonald and Carlos Keith (Val Lewton)
Cinematography: Robert de Grasse
Editing: J. R. Whittredge
Running time: 77 minutes

PRINCIPAL CHARACTERS:

Gray	Boris Karloff
Dr. Macfarlane	Henry Daniell
Fettes	Russell Wade
Mrs. Marsh	Rita Corday
Georgina Marsh	Sharyn Moffett
Joseph	Bela Lugosi

Every night in the year, four of us sat in the small parlour of the *George* at Debenham—the undertaker, and the landlord, and Fettes, and myself. Sometimes there would be more; but blow high, blow low, come rain or snow or frost, we four would be each planted in his own particular armchair. Fettes was an old drunken Scotsman, a man of education obviously, and a man of some property, since he lived in idleness. He had come to Debenham years ago, while still young, and by a mere continuance of living had grown to be an adopted townsman.

His blue camlet cloak was a local antiquity, like the church-spire. His place in the parlour at the *George,* his absence from church, his old, crapulous, disreputable vices, were all things of course in Debenham. He had some vague Radical opinions and some fleeting infidelities, which he would now and again set forth and emphasize with tottering slaps upon the table. He drank rum—five glasses regularly every evening; and for the greater portion of his nightly visit to the *George* sat, with his glass in his right hand, in a state of melancholy alcoholic saturation. We called him the Doctor, for he was supposed to have some special knowledge of medicine and had been known, upon a pinch, to set a fracture or reduce a dislocation; but beyond these slight particulars, we had no knowledge of his character and antecedents.

One dark winter night—it had struck nine some time before the landlord joined us—there was a sick man in the *George,* a great neighbouring proprietor suddenly struck down with apoplexy on his way to Parliament; and the great man's still greater London doctor had been telegraphed to his bedside. It was the first time that such a thing had happened in Debenham, for the railway was but newly open, and we were all proportionately moved by the occurrence.

"He's come," said the landlord, after he had filled and lighted his pipe.

"He?" said I. "Who?—not the doctor?"

"Himself," replied our host.

"What is his name?"

"Dr. Macfarlane," said the landlord.

Fettes was far through his third tumbler, stupidly fuddled, now nodding over, now staring mazily around him; but at the last word he seemed to awaken and repeated the name "Macfarlane" twice, quietly enough the first time, but with sudden emotion at the second.

"Yes," said the landlord, "that's his name, Dr. Wolfe Macfarlane."

Fettes became instantly sober; his eyes awoke, his voice became clear, loud and steady, his language forcible and earnest. We were all startled by the transformation, as if a man had risen from the dead.

"I beg your pardon," he said, "I am afraid I have not been paying much attention to your talk. Who is this Wolfe Macfarlane?" And then, when he had heard the landlord out, "It cannot be, it cannot be," he added; "and yet I would like well to see him face to face."

"Do you know him, Doctor?" asked the undertaker, with a gasp.

"God forbid!" was the reply. "And yet the name is a strange one; it were too much to fancy two. Tell me, landlord, is he old?"

"Well," said the host, "he's not a young man, to be sure, and his hair is white; but he looks younger than you."

"He is older, though; years older. But," with a slap upon the table, "it's the rum you see in my face—rum and sin. This man, perhaps, may have an easy conscience and a good digestion. Conscience! Hear me speak. You would think I was some good, old, decent Christian, would you not? But no, not I; I never canted. Voltaire might have canted if he'd stood in my shoes; but the brains"—with a rattling fillip on his bald head—"the brains were clear and active and I saw and made no deductions."

"If you know this doctor," I ventured to remark, after a somewhat awful pause, "I should gather that you do not share the landlord's good opinion."

Fettes paid no regard to me.

"Yes," he said, with sudden decision, "I must see him face to face."

There was another pause and then a door was closed rather sharply on the first floor and a step was heard upon the stair.

"That's the doctor," cried the landlord. "Look sharp and you can catch him."

It was but two steps from the parlour to the door of the old *George* inn; the wide oak staircase landed almost in the street; there was room for a Turkey rug and nothing more between the threshold and the last round of the descent; but this little space was every evening brilliantly lit up, not only by the light upon the stair and the great signal-lamp below the sign, but by the warm radiance of the barroom window. The *George* thus brightly advertised itself to passers-by in the cold street. Fettes walked steadily to the spot and we, who were hanging behind, beheld the two men meet, as one of them had phrased it, face to face. Dr. Macfarlane was alert and vigorous. His white hair set off his pale and placid, although energetic, countenance. He was richly dressed in the finest of broadcloth and the whitest of linen, with a great gold watchchain, and studs and spectacles of the same precious material. He wore a broad-folded tie, white and speckled with lilac, and he carried on his arm a comfortable driving-coat of fur. There was no doubt but he became his years, breathing, as he did, of wealth and consideration; and it was a surprising contrast to see our parlour sot—

bald, dirty, pimpled and robed in his old camlet cloak—confront him at the bottom of the stairs.

"Macfarlane!" he said somewhat loudly, more like a herald than a friend.

The great doctor pulled up short on the fourth step, as though the familiarity of the address surprised and somewhat shocked his dignity.

"Toddy Macfarlane!" repeated Fettes.

The London man almost staggered. He stared for the swiftest of seconds at the man before him, glanced behind him with a sort of scare, and then in a startled whisper, "Fettes!" he said, "you!"

"Ay," said the other, "me! Did you think I was dead too? We are not so easy shut of our acquaintance."

"Hush, hush!" exclaimed the doctor. "Hush, hush! this meeting is so unexpected—I can see you are unmanned. I hardly knew you, I confess, at first, but I am overjoyed—overjoyed to have this opportunity. For the present it must be how-d'ye-do and goodbye in one, for my fly is waiting and I must not fail the train; but you shall—let me see—yes—you shall give me your address and you can count on early news of me. We must do something for you, Fettes. I fear you are out at elbows; but we must see to that for auld lang syne, as once we sang at suppers."

"Money!" cried Fettes; "money from you! The money that I had from you is lying where I cast it in the rain."

Dr. Macfarlane had talked himself into some measure of superiority and confidence, but the uncommon energy of this refusal cast him back into his first confusion.

A horrible, ugly look came and went across his almost venerable countenance. "My dear fellow," he said, "be it as you please; my last thought is to offend you. I would intrude on none. I will leave you my address, however—"

"I do not wish it—I do not wish to know the roof that shelters you," interrupted the other. "I heard your name; I feared it might be you; I wished to know if, after all, there were a God; I know now that there is none. Begone!"

He still stood in the middle of the rug, between the stair and the doorway; and the great London physician, in order to escape, would be forced to step to one side. It was plain that he hesitated before the thought of this humiliation. White as he was, there was a dangerous glitter in his spectacles; but while he still paused uncertain, he became aware that the driver of his fly was peering in from the street at this unusual scene and caught a glimpse at the same time of our little body from the parlour, huddled by the corner of the bar. The presence of so many witnesses decided him at once to flee. He crouched together, brushing on the wainscot, and made a dart like a serpent, striking for the door. But his tribulation was not yet entirely at an end, for even as he was passing Fettes clutched him by the arm and these words came in a whisper, and yet painfully distinct, "Have you seen it again?"

The great rich London doctor cried out aloud with a sharp, throttling cry; he dashed his questioner across the open space, and, with his hands over his head, fled out of the door like a detected thief. Before it had occurred to one of us to make a movement, the fly was already rattling towards the station. The scene was over like a dream, but the dream had left proofs and traces of its passage. Next day the servant found the fine gold spectacles broken on the threshold, and that very night we were all standing breathless by the barroom window, and Fettes at our side, sober, pale, and resolute in look.

"God protect us, Mr. Fettes!" said the landlord, coming first into possession of his customary senses. "What in the universe is all this? These are strange things you have been saying."

Fettes turned towards us; he looked us each in succession in the face. "See if you can hold your tongues," said he. "That man Macfarlane is not safe to cross; those that have done so already have repented it too late."

And then, without so much as finishing his third glass, far less waiting for the other two, he bade us goodbye and went forth, under the lamp of the hotel, into the black night.

We three turned to our places in the parlour, with the big red fire and four clear candles; and as we recapitulated what had passed the first chill of our surprise soon changed into a glow of curiosity. We sat late; it was the latest session I have known in the old *George*. Each man, before we parted, had his theory that he was bound to prove; and none of us had any nearer business in this world than to track out the past of our condemned companion, and surprise the secret that he shared with the great London doctor. It was no great boast, but I believe I was a better hand at worming out a story than either of my fellows at the *George;* and perhaps there is now no other man alive who would narrate to you the following foul and unnatural events.

In his young days Fettes studied medicine in the schools of Edinburgh. He had talent of a kind, the talent that picks up swiftly what it hears and readily retails it for its own. He worked little at home; but he was civil, attentive, and intelligent in the presence of his masters. They soon picked him out as a lad who listened closely and remembered well; nay, strange as it seemed to me when I first heard it, he was in those days well favoured, and pleased by his exterior. There was, at that period, a certain extramural teacher of anatomy, whom I shall here designate by the letter K. His name was subsequently too well known. The man who bore it skulked through the streets of Edinburgh in disguise, while the mob that applauded at the execution of Burke called loudly for the blood of his employer. But Mr. K—— was then at the top of his vogue; he enjoyed a popularity due partly to his own talent and address, partly to the incapacity of his rival, the university professor. The students, at least, swore by his name, and Fettes believed himself, and was believed by others, to have laid the foundations of success when he had acquired the favour of this meteorically famous man. Mr. K—— was a *bon vivant* as well as an accomplished teacher; he liked a sly allusion no less than a careful preparation. In both capacities Fettes enjoyed and deserved his notice, and by the second year of his attendance he held the half-regular position of second demonstrator or sub-assistant in his class.

In this capacity, the charge of the theatre and lecture-room developed in particular upon his shoulders. He had to answer for the cleanliness of the premises and the conduct of the other students, and it was a part of his duty to supply, receive, and divide the various subjects. It was with a view to this last—at that time very delicate—affair that he was lodged by Mr. K—— in the same wynd, and at last in the same building, with the dissecting-rooms. Here, after a night of turbulent pleasures, his hand still tottering, his sight still misty and confused, he would be called out of bed in the black hours before the winter dawn by the unclean and desperate interlopers who supplied the table. He would open the door to these men, since infamous throughout the land. He would help them with their tragic burthen, pay them their sordid price, and remain alone, when they were gone, with the unfriendly relics of humanity. From such a scene he would return to snatch another hour or two of slumber, to repair the abuses of the night, and refresh himself for the labours of the day.

Few lads could have been more insensible to the impressions of a life thus passed among the ensigns of mortality. His mind was closed against all general considerations. He was incapable of interest in the fate and fortunes of another, the slave of his own desires and low ambitions. Cold, light, and selfish in the last resort, he had that modicum of prudence, miscalled morality, which keeps a man from inconvenient drunkenness or punishable theft. He coveted, besides, a measure of consideration from his masters and his fellow-pupils, and he had no desire to fail conspicuously in the external parts of life. Thus he made it his pleasure to gain some distinction in his studies, and day after day rendered unimpeachable eye-service to his employer, Mr. K——. For his day of work he indemnified himself by nights of roaring, blackguardly enjoyment; and when that balance had been struck, the organ that he called his conscience declared itself content.

The supply of subjects was a continual trouble to him as well as to his master. In that large and busy class, the raw material of the anatomists kept perpetually running out; and the business thus rendered necessary was not only unpleasant in itself, but threatened dangerous consequences to all who were concerned. It was the policy of Mr. K—— to ask no questions in his dealings with the trade. "They bring the body, and we pay the price," he used to say, dwelling on the alliteration—"*quid pro quo.*" And again, and somewhat profanely, "Ask no questions," he would tell his assistants, "for conscience' sake." There was no understanding that the subjects were provided by the crime of murder. Had that idea been broached to him in words, he would have recoiled in horror; but the lightness of his speech upon so grave a matter was, in itself, an offence against good manners, and a temptation to the men with whom he dealt. Fettes, for instance, had often remarked to himself upon the singular freshness of the bodies. He had been struck again and again by the hang-dog, abominable looks of the ruffians who came to him before the dawn; and, putting things together clearly in his private thoughts, he perhaps attributed a meaning too immoral and too categorical to the unguarded counsels of his master. He understood his duty, in short, to have three branches: to take what was brought, to pay the price, and to avert the eye from any evidence of crime.

One November morning this policy of silence was put sharply to the test. He had been awake all night with a racking toothache—pacing his room like a caged beast or throwing himself in fury on his bed—and had fallen at last into that profound, uneasy slumber that so often follows on a night of pain, when he was awakened by the third or fourth angry repetition of the concerted signal. There was a thin, bright moonshine: it was bitter cold, windy, and frosty; the town had not yet awakened, but an indefinable stir already preluded the noise and business of the day. The ghouls had come later than usual, and they seemed more than usually eager to be gone. Fettes, sick with sleep, lighted them upstairs. He heard their grumbling Irish voices through a dream; and as they stripped the sack from their sad merchandise he leaned dozing with his shoulder propped against the wall; he had to shake himself to find the men their money. As he did so his eyes lighted on the dead face. He started; he took two steps nearer, with the candle raised.

"God Almighty!" he cried. "That is Jane Galbraith!"

The men answered nothing, but they shuffled nearer the door.

"I know her, I tell you," he continued. "She was alive and hearty yesterday. It's impossible she can be dead; it's impossible you should have got this body fairly."

"Sure, sir, you're mistaken entirely," asserted one of the men.

But the other looked Fettes darkly in the eyes, and demanded the money on the spot.

It was impossible to misconceive the threat or to exaggerate the danger. The lad's heart failed him. He stammered some excuses, counted out the sum, and saw his hateful visitors depart. No sooner were they gone than he hastened to confirm his doubts. By a dozen unquestionable marks he identified the girl he had jested with the day before. He saw, with horror, marks upon her body that might well betoken violence. A panic seized him, and he took refuge in his room. There he reflected at length over the discovery that he had made; considered soberly the bearing of Mr. K——'s instructions and the danger to himself of interference in so serious a business, and at last, in sore perplexity, determined to wait for the advice of his immediate superior, the class assistant.

This was a young doctor, Wolfe Macfarlane, a high favourite among all the restless students, clever, dissipated, and unscrupulous to the last degree. He had travelled and studied abroad. His manners were agreeable and a little forward. He was an authority on the stage, skilful on the ice or the links with skate or golf-club; he dressed with nice audacity, and, to put the finishing touch upon his glory, he kept a gig and a strong trotting-horse. With Fettes he was on terms of intimacy; indeed their relative positions called for some community of life; and when subjects were scarce the pair would drive far into the country in Macfarlane's gig, visit and desecrate some lonely graveyard, and return before dawn with their booty to the door of the dissecting room.

On that particular morning Macfarlane arrived somewhat earlier than his wont. Fettes heard him, and met him on the stairs, told him his story, and showed him the cause of his alarm. Macfarlane examined the marks on her body.

"Yes," he said with a nod, "it looks fishy."

"Well, what should I do?" asked Fettes.

"Do?" repeated the other. "Do you want to do anything? Least said soonest mended, I should say."

"Someone else might recognize her," objected Fettes. "She was as well known as the Castle Rock."

"We'll hope not," said Macfarlane, "and if anybody does—well you didn't, don't you see, and there's an end. The fact is, this has been going on too long. Stir up the mud, and you'll get K—— into the most unholy trouble; you'll be in a shocking box yourself. So will I, if you come to that. I should like to know how any one of us would look, or what the devil we should have to say for ourselves, in any Christian witness-box. For me, you know there's one thing certain—that, practically speaking, all our subjects have been murdered."

"Macfarlane!" cried Fettes.

"Come now!" sneered the other. "As if you hadn't suspected it yourself!"

"Suspecting is one thing—"

"And proof another. Yes, I know; and I'm as sorry as you are this should have come here," tapping the body with his cane. "The next best thing for me is not to recognize it; and," he added coolly, "I don't. You may, if you please. I don't dictate, but I think a man of the world would do as I do; and I may add, I fancy that is what K—— would look for at our hands. The question is, why did he choose us two for his assistants? And I answer, because he didn't want old wives."

This was the tone of all others to affect the mind of a lad like Fettes. He agreed to imitate Macfarlane. The body of the unfortunate girl was duly dissected, and no one remarked or appeared to recognize her.

One afternoon, when his day's work was over, Fettes dropped into a popular tavern and found Macfarlane sitting with a stranger. This was a small man, very pale and dark, with coal-black eyes. The cut of his features gave a promise of intellect and refinement which was but

feebly realized in his manners, for he proved, upon a nearer acquaintance, coarse, vulgar, and stupid. He exercised, however, a very remarkable control over Macfarlane; issued orders like the Great Bashaw;
became inflamed at the least discussion or delay, and commented
rudely on the servility with which he was obeyed. This most offensive
person took a fancy to Fettes on the spot, plied him with drinks, and
honoured him with unusual confidences on his past career. If a tenth
part of what he confessed were true, he was a very loathsome rogue;
and the lad's vanity was tickled by the attention of so experienced a
man.

"I'm a pretty bad fellow myself," the stranger remarked, "but Macfarlane is the boy—Toddy Macfarlane I call him. Toddy, order your
friend another glass." Or it might be, "Toddy, you jump up and shut
the door." "Toddy hates me," he said again. "Oh, yes, Toddy, you do!"

"Don't call me that confounded name," growled Macfarlane.

"Hear him! Did you ever see the lads play knife? He would like to
do that all over my body," remarked the stranger.

"We medicals have a better way than that," said Fettes. "When we
dislike a dead friend of ours, we dissect him."

Macfarlane looked up sharply, as though this jest was scarcely to his
mind.

The afternoon passed. Gray, for that was the stranger's name, invited
Fettes to join them at dinner, ordered a feast so sumptuous that the
tavern was thrown in commotion, and when all was done commanded
Macfarlane to settle the bill. It was late before they separated; the man
Gray was incapably drunk. Macfarlane, sobered by his fury, chewed
the cud of the money he had been forced to squander and the slights
he had been obliged to swallow. Fettes, with various liquors singing
in his head, returned home with devious footsteps and a mind entirely
in abeyance. Next day Macfarlane was absent from the class, and Fettes
smiled to himself as he imagined him still squiring the intolerable Gray
from tavern to tavern. As soon as the hour of liberty had struck he
posted from place to place in quest of his last night's companions. He
could find them, however, nowhere; so returned early to his rooms,
went early to bed, and slept the sleep of the just.

At four in the morning he was awakened by the well-known signal.
Descending to the door, he was filled with astonishment to find Macfarlane with his gig, and in the gig one of those long and ghastly
packages with which he was so well acquainted.

"What?" he cried. "Have you been out alone? How did you manage?"

But Macfarlane silenced him roughly, bidding him turn to business. When they had got the body upstairs and laid it on the table, Macfarlane made at first as if he were going away. Then he paused and seemed to hesitate; and then, "You had better look at the face," said he, in tones of some constraint. "You had better," he repeated, as Fettes only stared at him in wonder.

"But where, and how, and when did you come by it?" cried the other.

"Look at the face," was the only answer.

Fettes was staggered; strange doubts assailed him. He looked from the young doctor to the body, and then back again. At last, with a start, he did as he was bidden. He had almost expected the sight that met his eyes, and yet the shock was cruel. To see, fixed in the rigidity of death and naked on that coarse layer of sack-cloth, the man whom he had left well-clad and full of meat and sin upon the threshold of a tavern, awoke, even in the thoughtless Fettes, some of the terrors of the conscience. It was a *cras tibi* which re-echoed in his soul, that two whom he had known should have come to lie upon these icy tables. Yet these were only secondary thoughts. His first concern regarded Wolfe. Unprepared for a challenge so momentous, he knew not how to look his comrade in the face. He durst not meet his eye, and he had neither words nor voice at his command.

It was Macfarlane himself who made the first advance. He came up quietly behind and laid his hand gently but firmly on the other's shoulder.

"Richardson," said he, "may have the head."

Now Richardson was a student who had long been anxious for that portion of the human subject to dissect. There was no answer, and the murderer resumed: "Talking of business, you must pay me; your accounts, you see, must tally."

Fettes found a voice, the ghost of his own: "Pay you!" he cried. "Pay you for that?"

"Why, yes, of course you must. By all means and on every possible account, you must," returned the other. "I dare not give it for nothing, you dare not take it for nothing; it would compromise us both. This is another case like Jane Galbraith's. The more things are wrong the more we must act as if all were right. Where does old K—— keep his money—"

"There," answered Fettes hoarsely, pointing to a cupboard in the corner.

"Give me the key, then," said the other, calmly, holding out his hand.

There was an instant's hesitation, and the die was cast. Macfarlane could not suppress a nervous twitch, the infinitesimal mark of an immense relief, as he felt the key turn between his fingers. He opened the cupboard, brought out pen and ink and a paper-book that stood in one compartment, and separated from the funds in a drawer a sum suitable to the occasion.

"Now, look here," he said, "there is the payment made—first proof of your good faith: first step to your security. You have now to clinch it by a second. Enter the payment in your book, and then you for your part may defy the devil."

The next few seconds were for Fettes an agony of thought; but in balancing his terrors it was the most immediate that triumphed. Any future difficulty seemed almost welcome if he could avoid a present quarrel with Macfarlane. He set down the candle which he had been carrying all the time, and with a steady hand entered the date, the nature, and the amount of the transaction.

"And now," said Macfarlane, "it's only fair that you should pocket the lucre. I've had my share already. By-the-by, when a man of the world falls into a bit of luck, has a few shillings extra in his pocket—I'm ashamed to speak of it, but there's a rule of conduct in the case. No treating, no purchase of expensive classbooks, no squaring of old debts; borrow, don't lend."

"Macfarlane," began Fettes, still somewhat hoarsely. "I have put my neck in a halter to oblige you."

"To oblige me?" cried Wolfe. "Oh, come! You did, as near as I can see the matter, what you downright had to do in self defence. Suppose I got into trouble, where would you be? This second little matter flows clearly from the first. Mr. Gray is the continuation of Miss Galbraith. You can't begin and then stop. If you begin, you must keep on beginning; that's the truth. No rest for the wicked."

A horrible sense of blackness and the treachery of fate seized hold upon the soul of the unhappy student.

"My God!" he cried, "but what have I done? and when did I begin? To be made a class assistant—in the name of reason, where's the harm in that? Service wanted the position; Service might have got it. Would *he* have been where *I* am now?"

"My dear fellow," said Macfarlane, "what a boy you are! What harm *has* come to you? What harm *can* come to you if you hold your tongue? Why, man, do you know what this life is? There are two squads of us— the lions and the lambs. If you're a lamb, you'll come to lie upon these tables like Gray or Jane Galbraith; if you're a lion, you'll live and drive a horse like me, like K——, like all the world with any wit or courage. You're staggered at the first. But look at K——! My dear fellow, you're clever, you have pluck. I like you, and K—— likes you. You were born to lead the hunt; and I tell you, on my honour and my experience of life, three days from now you'll laugh at all these scarecrows like a high-school boy at a farce."

And with that Macfarlane took his departure and drove off up the wynd in his gig to get under cover before daylight. Fettes was thus left alone with his regrets. He saw the miserable peril in which he stood involved. He saw, with inexpressible dismay, that there was no limit to his weakness, and that, from concession to concession, he had fallen from the arbiter of Macfarlane's destiny to his paid and helpless accomplice. He would have given the world to have been a little braver at the time, but it did not occur to him that he might still be brave. The secret of Jane Galbraith and the cursed entry in the daybook closed his mouth.

Hours passed; the class began to arrive; the members of the unhappy Gray were dealt out to one and to another, and received without remark. Richardson was made happy with the head; and before the hour of freedom rang Fettes trembled with exultation to perceive how far they had already gone towards safety.

For two days he continued to watch, with increasing joy, the dreadful process of disguise.

On the third day Macfarlane made his appearance. He had been ill, he said; but he made up for lost time by the energy with which he directed the students. To Richardson in particular he extended the most valuable assistance and advice, and that student, encouraged by the praise of the demonstrator, burned high with ambitious hopes, and saw the medal already in his grasp.

Before the week was out Macfarlane's prophecy had been fulfilled. Fettes had outlived his terrors and had forgotten his baseness. He began to plume himself upon his courage, and had so arranged the story in his mind that he could look back on these events with an unhealthy pride. Of his accomplice he saw but little. They met, of course, in the business of the class; they received their orders together from Mr. K——. At times they had a word or two in private, and Macfarlane was from first to last particularly kind and jovial. But it was plain that he avoided any reference to their common secret; and even when Fettes whispered to him that he had cast in his lot with the lions and forsworn the lambs, he only signed to him smilingly to hold his peace.

At length an occasion arose which threw the pair once more into a closer union. Mr. K—— was again short of subjects; pupils were eager, and it was a part of this teacher's pretensions to be always well supplied. At the same time there came the news of a burial in the rustic graveyard of Glencorse. Time has little changed the place in question. It stood then, as now, upon the crossroad, out of call of human habitations, and buried fathom deep in the foliage of six cedar trees. The cries of the sheep upon the neighbouring hills, the streamlets upon either hand, one loudly singing among pebbles, the other dripping furtively from pond to pond, the stir of the wind in mountainous old flowering chestnuts, and once in seven days the voice of the bell and the old tunes of the precentor, were the only sounds that disturbed the silence around the rural church. The Resurrection Man—to use a by-name of the period—was not to be deterred by any of the sanctities of customary piety. It was part of his trade to despise and desecrate the scrolls and trumpets of old tombs, the paths worn by the feet of worshipers and mourners, and the offerings and the inscriptions of bereaved affection. To rustic neighborhoods, where love is more than commonly tenacious, and where some bonds of blood or fellowship unite the entire society of a parish, the body-snatcher, far from being repelled by natural respect, was attracted by the ease and safety of the task. To bodies that had been laid in earth, in joyful expectation of a far different awakening, there came that hasty, lamp-lit, terror-haunted resurrection of the spade and mattock. The coffin was forced, the cerements torn, and the melancholy relics, clad in sack-cloth, after being rattled for hours on moonless by-ways, were at length exposed to uttermost indignities before a class of gaping boys.

Somewhat as two vultures may swoop upon a dying lamb, Fettes and Macfarlane were to be let loose upon a grave in that green and quiet resting-place. The wife of a farmer, a woman who had lived for sixty years, and been known for nothing but good butter and a godly conversation, was to be rooted from her grave at midnight and carried, dead and naked, to that faraway city that she had always honoured with her Sunday best; the place beside her family was to be empty till the crack of doom; her innocent and almost venerable members to be exposed to that last curiosity of the anatomist.

Late one afternoon the pair set forth, well wrapped in cloaks and furnished with a formidable bottle. It rained without remission—a cold, dense, lashing rain. Now and again there blew a puff of wind, but these sheets of falling water kept it down. Bottle and all, it was a sad and silent drive as far as Penicuik, where they were to spend the evening. They stopped once, to hide their implements in a thick bush not far from the churchyard, and once again at the Fisher's Tryst, to have a toast before the kitchen fire and vary their nips of whisky with a glass of ale. When they reached their journey's end the gig was housed, the horse was fed and comforted, and the two young doctors in a private room sat down to the best dinner and the best wine the house afforded. The lights, the fire, the beating rain upon the window, the cold, incongruous work that lay before them, added zest to their enjoyment of the meal. With every glass their cordiality increased. Soon Macfarlane handed a little pile of gold to his companion.

"A compliment," he said. "Between friends these little damned accommodations ought to fly like pipe-lights."

Fettes pocketed the money, and applauded the sentiment to the echo. "You are a philosopher," he cried. "I was an ass till I knew you. You and K—— between you, by the Lord Harry! but you'll make a man of me."

"Of course we shall," applauded Macfarlane. "A man? I tell you, it required a man to back me up the other morning. There are some big, brawling, forty-year-old cowards who would have turned sick at the look of the damned thing; but not you—you kept your head. I watched you."

"Well, and why not?" Fettes thus vaunted himself. "It was no affair of mine. There was nothing to gain on the one side but disturbance, and on the other I could count on your gratitude, don't you see?" And he slapped his pocket till the gold pieces rang.

Macfarlane somehow felt a certain touch of alarm at these unpleasant words. He may have regretted that he had taught his young companion so successfully, but he had no time to interfere, for the other noisily continued in this boastful strain:

"The great thing is not to be afraid. Now, between you and me, I don't want to hang—that's practical; but for all cant, Macfarlane, I was born with a contempt. Hell, God, Devil, right, wrong, sin, crime, and all the old gallery of curiosities—they may frighten boys, but men of the world, like you and me, despise them. Here's to the memory of Gray!"

It was by this time growing somewhat late. The gig, according to order, was brought round to the door with both lamps brightly shining, and the young men had to pay their bill and take the road. They announced that they were bound for Pebbles, and drove in that direction till they were clear of the last houses of the town; then, extinguishing the lamps, returned upon their course, and followed a by-road towards Glencorse. There was no sound but that of their own passage, and the incessant, strident pouring of the rain. It was pitch dark; here and there a white gate or a white stone in the wall guided them for a short space across the night; but for the most part it was at a foot pace, and almost groping, that they picked their way through that resonant blackness to their solemn and isolated destination. In the sunken woods that traverse the neighbourhood of the burying-ground the last glimmer failed them, and it became necessary to kindle a match and re-illumine one of the lanterns of the gig. Thus, under the dripping trees, and environed by huge and moving shadows, they reached the scene of their unhallowed labours.

They were both experienced in such affairs, and powerful with the spade; and they had scarce been twenty minutes at their task before they were rewarded by a dull rattle on the coffin lid. At the same moment Macfarlane, having hurt his hand upon a stone, flung it carelessly above his head. The grave, in which they now stood almost to the shoulders, was close to the edge of the plateau of the graveyard; and the gig lamp had been propped, the better to illuminate their labours, against a tree, and on the immediate verge of the steep bank descending to the stream. Chance had taken a sure aim with the stone. Then came a clang of broken glass; night fell upon them; sounds alternately dull and ringing announced the bounding of the lantern down the bank, and its occasional collision with the trees. A stone or two, which it had dislodged in its descent rattled behind it into the profundities of the glen; and then silence, like night, resumed its sway; and they might bend their hearing to its utmost pitch, but naught was to be heard except the rain, now marching to the wind, now steadily falling over miles of open country.

They were so nearly at an end of their abhorred task that they judged it wisest to complete it in the dark. The coffin was exhumed and broken open; the body inserted in the dripping sack and carried between them to the gig; one mounted to keep it in its place, and the other, taking the horse by the mouth, groped along by the wall and bush until they reached the wider road by the Fisher's Tryst. Here was a faint disused radiancy, which they hailed like daylight; by that they pushed the horse to a good pace and began to rattle along merrily in the direction of the town.

They had both been wetted to the skin during their operations, and now, as the gig jumped among the deep ruts, the thing that stood propped between them fell now upon one and now upon the other. At every repetition of the horrid contact each instinctively repelled it with greater haste; and the process, natural although it was, began to tell upon the nerves of the companions. Macfarlane made some ill-favoured jest about the farmer's wife, but it came hollowly from his lips, and was allowed to drop in silence. Still their unnatural burthen bumped from side to side; and now the head would be laid, as if in confidence, upon their shoulders, and now the drenching sackcloth would flap icily about their faces. A creeping chill began to possess the soul of Fettes. He peered at the bundle, and it seemed somehow larger than at first. All over the countryside, and from every degree of distance, the farm dogs accompanied their passage with tragic ululations; and it grew and grew upon his mind that some unnatural miracle had been achieved, that some nameless change had befallen the dead body, and that it was in fear of their unholy burthen that the dogs were howling.

"For God's sake," said he, making a great effort to arrive at speech, "for God's sake, let's have a light!"

Seemingly Macfarlane was affected in the same directon; for though he made no reply, he stopped the horse, passed the reins to his companion, got down, and proceeded to kindle the remaining lamp. They had by that time got no farther than the crossroad down to Auchendinny. The rain still poured as though the deluge were returning, and it was no easy matter to make a light in such a world of wet and darkness. When at last the flickering blue flame had been transferred to the wick and began to expand and clarify, and shed a wide circle of misty brightness round the gig, it became possible for the two young men to see each other and the thing they had along with them. The rain had moulded the rough sacking to the outlines of the body underneath; the head was distinct from the trunk, the shoulders plainly modelled; something at once spectral and human riveted their eyes upon the ghastly comrade of their drive.

For some time Macfarlane stood motionless, holding up the lamp. A nameless dread was swathed, like a wet sheet, about the body, and tightened the white skin upon the face of Fettes; a fear that was meaningless, a horror of what could not be, kept mounting to his brain. Another beat of the watch, and he had spoken. But his comrade forestalled him.

"That is not a woman," said Macfarlane, in a hushed voice.

"It was a woman when we put her in," whispered Fettes.

"Hold that lamp," said the other. "I must see her face."

And as Fettes took the lamp his companion untied the fastenings of the sack and drew down the cover from the head. The light fell very clear upon the dark, well-moulded features and smooth-shaven cheeks of a too familiar countenance, often beheld in dreams of both of these young men. A wild yell rang up into the night; each leaped from his own side into the roadway; the lamp fell, broke, and was extinguished; and the horse, terrified by this unusual commotion, bounded and went off toward Edinburgh at a gallop, bearing along with it, sole occupant of the gig, the body of the dead and long-dissected Gray.

DON'T LOOK NOW

(1973)

DON'T LOOK NOW
DAPHNE DU MAURIER

Set in the rainy bleakness of Venice in winter, *Don't Look Now* is part contemporary Gothic thriller, part psychological mystery. Church restoration expert John Baxter and his wife Laura, grief-stricken at the recent drowning death of their young daughter, cross paths with an English spinster and her blind, clairvoyant sister who warns the bereaved couple of further, undefined dangers. The film, executed with exquisite visual richness, offers an eerie study of the deceptive nature of human sight and psychic vision. (There were even reports of paranormal activities in Venice at the time the film was being shot.)

For many years an immensely successful cinematographer [*Petulia* (1967) and *Far from the Madding Crowd* (1968)], Nicholas Roeg has been described as a director who can make *anything* look scary. Indeed, with his effective manipulation of the brooding Venetian locations, Roeg creates a cinematic landscape in which every face, every gesture, and every object is potentially sinister and threatening.

_____

An immensely popular British writer, DAPHNE DU MAURIER was born in London in 1907, but has lived for many years in rural Cornwall, which provides the setting for most of her stories and novels. She is no stranger to the cinema; a number of her works have been adapted to the screen, most notably by Alfred Hitchcock who scored back-to-back hits with *Jamaica Inn* (1939) and *Rebecca* (1940), and chose her story "The Birds" as the basis for his 1963 apocalyptic nightmare of the same name.

DON'T LOOK NOW

Released: 1973
Production: Peter Katz for Paramount
Direction: Nicholas Roeg
Screenplay: Allan Scott and Chris Bryant
Cinematography: Anthony Richmond
Editing: Graeme Clifford
Running time: 110 minutes

PRINCIPAL CHARACTERS:

John Baxter	Donald Sutherland
Laura Baxter	Julie Christie
Mystic	Hilary Mason
Wendy	Clelia Mantana
Bishop Barbarrigo	Massimo Serato
Christine	Sharon Williams

_____

"Don't look now," John said to his wife, "but there are a couple of old girls two tables away who are trying to hypnotise me."

Laura, quick on cue, made an elaborate pretence of yawning, then tilted her head as though searching the skies for a non-existent aeroplane.

"Right behind you," he added. "That's why you can't turn round at once—it would be much too obvious."

Laura played the oldest trick in the world and dropped her napkin, then bent to scrabble for it under her feet, sending a shooting glance over her left shoulder as she straightened once again. She sucked in her cheeks, the first tell-tale sign of suppressed hysteria, and lowered her head.

"They're not old girls at all," she said. "They're male twins in drag."

Her voice broke ominously, the prelude to uncontrolled laughter, and John quickly poured some more chianti into her glass.

"Pretend to choke," he said, "then they won't notice. You know what it is—they're criminals doing the sights of Europe, changing sex at each stop. Twin sisters here on Torcello. Twin brothers tomorrow in Venice, or even tonight, parading arm-in-arm across the Piazza San Marco. Just a matter of switching clothes and wigs."

"Jewel thieves or murderers?" asked Laura.

"Oh, murderers, definitely. But why, I ask myself, have they picked on me?"

The waiter made a diversion by bringing coffee and bearing away the fruit, which gave Laura time to banish hysteria and regain control.

"I can't think," she said, "why we didn't notice them when we arrived. They stand out to high heaven. One couldn't fail."

"That gang of Americans masked them," said John, "and the bearded man with a monocle who looked like a spy. It wasn't until they all went just now that I saw the twins. Oh God, the one with the shock of white hair has got her eye on me again."

Laura took the powder compact from her bag and held it in front of her face, the mirror acting as a reflector.

"I think it's me they're looking at, not you," she said. "Thank heaven I left my pearls with the manager at the hotel." She paused, dabbing the sides of her nose with powder. "The thing is," she said after a moment, "we've got them wrong. They're neither murderers nor thieves. They're a couple of pathetic old retired schoolmistresses on holiday, who've saved up all their lives to visit Venice. They come from some place with a name like Walabanga in Australia. And they're called Tilly and Tiny."

Her voice, for the first time since they had come away, took on the old bubbling quality he loved, and the worried frown between her brows had vanished. At last, he thought, at last she's beginning to get over it. If I can keep this going, if we can pick up the familiar routine of jokes shared on holiday and at home, the ridiculous fantasies about people at other tables, or staying in the hotel, or wandering in art galleries and churches, then everything will fall into place, life will become as it was before, the wound will heal, she will forget.

"You know," said Laura, "that really was a very good lunch. I did enjoy it."

Thank God, he thought, thank God. . . . Then he leant forward, speaking low in a conspirator's whisper. "One of them is going to the loo," he said. "Do you suppose he, or she, is going to change her wig?"

"Don't say anything," Laura murmured. "I'll follow her and find out. She may have a suitcase tucked away there, and she's going to switch clothes."

She began to hum under her breath, the signal, to her husband, of content. The ghost was temporarily laid, and all because of the familiar holiday game, abandoned too long, and now, through mere chance, blissfully recaptured.

"Is she on her way?" asked Laura.

"About to pass our table now," he told her.

Seen on her own, the woman was not so remarkable. Tall, angular, aquiline features, with the close-cropped hair which was fashionably called an Eton crop, he seemed to remember, in his mother's day, and about her person the stamp of that particular generation. She would be in her middle sixties, he supposed, the masculine shirt with collar and tie, sports jacket, grey tweed skirt coming to mid-calf. Grey stockings and laced black shoes. He had seen the type on golf courses and at dog shows—invariably showing not sporting breeds but pugs—and if you came across them at a party in somebody's house they were quicker on the draw with a cigarette lighter than he was himself, a mere male, with pocket matches. The general belief that they kept house with a more feminine, fluffy companion was not always true. Frequently they boasted, and adored, a golfing husband. No, the striking point about this particular individual was that there were two of them. Identical twins cast in the same mould. The only difference was that the other one had whiter hair.

"Supposing," murmured Laura, "when I find myself in the *toilette* beside her she starts to strip?"

"Depends on what is revealed," John answered. "If she's hermaphrodite, make a bolt for it. She might have a hypodermic syringe concealed and want to knock you out before you reached the door."

Laura sucked in her cheeks once more and began to shake. Then, squaring her shoulders, she rose to her feet. "I simply must not laugh," she said, "and whatever you do, don't look at me when I come back, especially if we come out together." She picked up her bag and strolled self-consciously away from the table in pursuit of her prey.

John poured the dregs of the chianti into his glass and lit a cigarette. The sun blazed down upon the little garden of the restaurant. The Americans had left, and the monocled man, and the family party at the far end. All was peace. The identical twin was sitting back in her chair with her eyes closed. Thank heaven, he thought, for this moment at any rate, when relaxation was possible, and Laura had been launched upon her foolish, harmless game. The holiday could yet turn into the cure she needed, blotting out, if only temporarily, the numb despair that had seized her since the child died.

"She'll get over it," the doctor said. "They all get over it, in time. And you have the boy."

"I know," John had said, "but the girl meant everything. She always did, right from the start, I don't know why. I suppose it was the difference in age. A boy of school age, and a tough one at that, is someone in his own right. Not a baby of five. Laura literally adored her. Johnnie and I were nowhere."

"Give her time," repeated the doctor, "give her time. And anyway, you're both young still. There'll be others. Another daughter."

So easy to talk. . . . How replace the life of a loved lost child with a dream? He knew too well. Another child, another girl, would have her own qualities, a separate identity, she might even induce hostility because of this very fact. A usurper in the cradle, in the cot, that had been Christine's. A chubby, flaxen replica of Johnnie, not the little waxen dark-haired sprite that had gone.

He looked up, over his glass of wine, and the woman was staring at him again. It was not the casual, idle glance of someone at the nearby table, waiting for her companion to return, but something deeper, more intent, the prominent, light blue eyes oddly penetrating, giving him a sudden feeling of discomfort. Damn the woman! All right, bloody stare, if you must. Two can play at that game. He blew a cloud of cigarette smoke into the air and smiled at her, he hoped offensively. She did not register. The blue eyes continued to hold his, so that he was obliged to look away himself, extinguish his cigarette, glance over his shoulder for the waiter and call for the bill. Settling for this, and fumbling with the meal, brought composure, but a prickly feeling on his scalp remained, and an odd sensation of unease. Then it went, as abruptly as it had started, and stealing a furtive glance at the other table he saw that her eyes were closed again, and she was sleeping, or dozing, as she had done before. The waiter disappeared. All was still.

Laura, he thought, glancing at his watch, is being a hell of a time. Ten minutes at least. Something to tease her about, anyway. He began to plan the form the joke would take. How the old dolly had stripped to her smalls, suggesting that Laura should do likewise. And then the manager had burst in upon them both, exclaiming in horror, the reputation of the restaurant damaged, the hint that unpleasant consequences might follow unless . . . The whole exercise turning out to be a plant, an exercise in blackmail. He and Laura and the twins taken in a police launch back to Venice for questioning. Quarter of an hour . . . . Oh, come on, come on . . . .

There was a crunch of feet on the gravel, Laura's twin walked slowly past, alone. She crossed over to her table and stood there a moment, her tall, angular figure interposing itself between John and her sister. She was saying something, but he couldn't catch the words. What was the accent, though—Scottish? Then she bent, offering an arm to the seated twin, and they moved away together across the garden to the break in the little hedge beyond, the twin who had stared at John leaning on her sister's arm. Here was the difference again. She was not quite so tall, and she stooped more—perhaps she was arthritic. They disappeared out of sight, and John, becoming impatient, got up and was about to walk back into the hotel when Laura emerged.

"Well, I must say, you took your time," he began, and then stopped, because of the expression on her face.

"What's the matter, what's happened?" he asked.

He could tell at once there was something wrong. Almost as if she were in a state of shock. She blundered towards the table he had just vacated and sat down. He drew up a chair beside her, taking her hand.

"Darling, what it is? Tell me—are you ill?"

She shook her head, and then turned and looked at him. The dazed expression he had noticed at first had given way to one of dawning confidence, almost of exaltation.

"It's quite wonderful," she said slowly, "the most wonderful thing that could possibly be. You see, she isn't dead, she's still with us. That's why they kept staring at us, those two sisters. They could see Christine."

Oh God, he thought. It's what I've been dreading. She's going off her head. What do I do? How do I cope?

"Laura, sweet," he began, forcing a smile, "look, shall we go? I've paid the bill, we can go and look at the cathedral and stroll around, and then it will be time to take off in that launch again for Venice."

She wasn't listening, or at any rate the words didn't penetrate.

"John, love," she said, "I've got to tell you what happened. I followed her, as we planned, into the *toilette* place. She was combing her hair and I went into the loo, and then came out and washed my hands in the basin. She was washing hers in the next basin. Suddenly she turned and said to me, in a strong Scots accent, 'Don't be unhappy any more. My sister has seen your little girl. She was sitting between you and your husband, laughing.' Darling, I thought I was going to faint. I nearly did. Luckily, there was a chair, and I sat down, and the woman bent over me and patted my head. I'm not sure of her exact words, but she said something about the moment of truth and joy being as sharp as a sword, but not to be afraid, all was well, but the sister's vision had been so strong they knew I had to be told, and that Christine wanted it. Oh John, don't look like that. I swear I'm not making it up, this is what she told me, it's all true."

The desperate urgency in her voice made his heart sicken. He had to play along with her, agree, soothe, do anything to bring back some sense of calm.

"Laura, darling, of course I believe you," he said, "only it's a sort of shock, and I'm upset because you're upset . . . ."

"But I'm not upset," she interrupted. "I'm happy, so happy that I can't put the feeling into words. You know what it's been like all these weeks, at home and everywhere we've been on holiday, though I tried to hide it from you. Now it's lifted, because I know, I just know, that the woman was right. Oh Lord, how awful of me, but I've forgotten their name—she did tell me. You see, the thing is that she's a retired doctor, they come from Edinburgh, and the one who saw Christine went blind a few years ago. Although she's studied the occult all her life and been very psychic, it's only since going blind that she has really seen things, like a medium. They've had the most wonderful experiences. But to describe Christine as the blind one did to her sister, even down to the little blue-and-white dress with the puff sleeves that she wore at her birthday party, and to say she was smiling happily . . . . Oh, darling, it's made me so happy I think I'm going to cry."

No hysteria. Nothing wild. She took a tissue from her bag and blew her nose, smiling at him. "I'm all right, you see, you don't have to worry. Neither of us need worry about anything any more. Give me a cigarette."

He took one from his packet and lighted it for her. She sounded normal, herself again. She wasn't trembling. And if this sudden belief was going to keep her happy he couldn't possibly begrudge it. But ... but ... he wished, all the same, it hadn't happened. There was something uncanny about thought-reading, about telepathy. Scientists couldn't account for it, nobody could, and this is what must have happened just now between Laura and the sisters. So the one who had been staring at him was blind. That accounted for the fixed gaze. Which somehow was unpleasant in itself, creepy. Oh hell, he thought, I wish we hadn't come here for lunch. Just chance, a flick of a coin between this, Torcello, and driving to Padua, and we had to choose Torcello.

"You didn't arrange to meet them again or anything, did you?" he asked, trying to sound casual.

"No darling, why should I?" Laura answered. "I mean, there was nothing more they could tell me. The sister had had her wonderful vision, and that was that. Anyway, they're moving on. Funnily enough, it's rather like our original game. They *are* going round the world before returning to Scotland. Only I said Australia, didn't I? The old dears.... Anything less like murderers and jewel thieves."

She had quite recovered. She stood up and looked about her. "Come on," she said. "Having come to Torcello we must see the cathedral."

They made their way from the restaurant across the open piazza, where the stalls had been set up with scarves and trinkets and postcards, and so along the path to the cathedral. One of the ferryboats had just decanted a crowd of sightseers, many of whom had already found their way into Santa Maria Assunta. Laura, undaunted, asked her husband for the guidebook, and, as had always been her custom in happier days, started to walk slowly through the cathedral, studying mosaics, columns, panels from left to right, while John, less interested, because of his concern at what had just happened, followed close behind, keeping a weather eye alert for the twin sisters. There was no sign of them. Perhaps they had gone into the church of Santa Fosca close by. A sudden encounter would be embarrassing, quite apart from the effect it might have upon Laura. But the anonymous, shuffling tourists, intent upon culture, could not harm her, although from his own point of view they made artistic appreciation impossible. He could not concentrate, the cold clear beauty of what he saw left him untouched, and when Laura touched his sleeve, pointing to the mosaic of the Virgin and Child standing above the frieze of the Apostles, he nodded in sympathy yet saw nothing, the long, sad face of the Virgin infinitely remote, and turning on sudden impulse stared back over the heads of the tourists towards the door, where frescoes of the blessed and the damned gave themselves to judgment.

The twins were standing there, the blind one still holding on to her sister's arm, her sightless eyes fixed firmly upon him. He felt himself held, unable to move, and an impending sense of doom, of tragedy, came upon him. His whole being sagged, as it were, in apathy, and he thought, "This is the end, there is no escape, no future." Then both sisters turned and went out of the cathedral and the sensation vanished, leaving indignation in its wake, and rising anger. How dare those two old fools practise their mediumistic tricks on him? It was fraudulent, unhealthy; this was probably the way they lived, touring the world making everyone they met uncomfortable. Give them half a chance and they would have got money out of Laura—anything.

He felt her tugging at his sleeve again. "Isn't she beautiful? So happy, so serene."

"Who? What?" he asked.

"The Madonna," she answered. "She has a magic quality. It goes right through to one. Don't you feel it too?"

"I suppose so. I don't know. There are too many people around."

She looked up at him, astonished. "What's that got to do with it? How funny you are. Well, all right, let's get away from them. I want to buy some postcards anyway."

Disappointed, she sensed his lack of interest, and began to thread her way through the crowd of tourists to the door.

"Come on," he said abruptly, once they were outside, "there's plenty of time for postcards, let's explore a bit," and he struck off from the path, which would have taken them back to the centre where the little houses were, and the stalls, and the drifting crowd of people, to a narrow way amongst uncultivated ground, beyond which he could see a sort of cutting, or canal. The sight of water, limpid, pale, was a soothing contrast to the fierce sun above their heads.

"I don't think this leads anywhere much," said Laura. "It's a bit muddy, too, one can't sit. Besides, there are more things the guidebook says we ought to see."

"Oh, forget the book," he said impatiently, and, pulling her down beside him on the bank above the cutting, put his arms round her.

"It's the wrong time of day for sightseeing. Look, there's a rat swim-ming there on the other side."

He picked up a stone and threw it in the water, and the animal sank, or somehow disappeared, and nothing was left but bubbles.

"Don't," said Laura. "It's cruel, poor thing," and then suddenly, putting her hand on his knee, "Do you think Christine is sitting here beside us?"

He did not answer at once. What was there to say? Would it be like this forever?

"I expect so," he said slowly, "if you feel she is."

The point was, remembering Christine before the onset of the fatal meningitis, she would have been running along the bank excitedly, throwing off her shoes, wanting to paddle, giving Laura a fit of appre-hension. "Sweetheart, take care, come back . . . ."

"The woman said she was looking so happy, sitting beside us, smil-ing," said Laura. She got up, brushing her dress, her mood changed to restlessness. "Come on, let's go back," she said.

He followed her with a sinking heart. He knew she did not really want to buy postcards or see what remained to be seen; she wanted to go in search of the women again, not necessarily to talk, just to be near them. When they came to the open place by the stalls he noticed that the crowd of tourists had thinned, there were only a few stragglers left, and the sisters were not amongst them. They must have joined the main body who had come to Torcello by the ferry service. A wave of relief seized him.

"Look, there's a mass of postcards at the second stall," he said quickly, "and some eye-catching head scarves. Let me buy you a head scarf."

"Darling, I've so many!" she protested. "Don't waste your lire."

"It isn't a waste. I'm in a buying mood. What about a basket? You know we never have enough baskets. Or some lace. How about lace?"

She allowed herself, laughing, to be dragged to the stall. While he rumpled through the goods spread out before them, and chatted up the smiling woman who was selling her wares, his ferociously bad Italian making her smile the more, he knew it would give the body of tourists more time to walk to the landing stage and catch the ferry service, and the twin sisters would be out of sight and out of their life.

"Never," said Laura, some twenty minutes later, "has so much junk been piled into so small a basket," her bubbling laugh reassuring him that all was well, he needn't worry any more, the evil hour had passed. The launch from the *Cipriani* that had brought them from Venice was waiting by the landing stage. The passengers who had arrived with them, the Americans, the man with the monocle, were already assembled. Earlier, before setting out, he had thought the price for lunch and transport, there and back, decidedly steep. Now he grudged none of it, except that the outing to Torcello itself had been one of the major errors of this particular holiday in Venice. They stepped down into the launch, finding a place in the open, and the boat chugged away down the canal and into the lagoon. The ordinary ferry had gone before, steaming towards Murano, while their own craft headed past San Francesco del Deserto and so back direct to Venice.

He put his arm around her once more, holding her close, and this time she responded, smiling up at him, her head on his shoulder.

"It's been a lovely day," she said. "I shall never forget it, never. You know, darling, now at last I can begin to enjoy our holiday."

He wanted to shout with relief. It's going to be all right, he decided, let her believe what she likes, it doesn't matter, it makes her happy. The beauty of Venice rose before them, sharply outlined against the glowing sky, and there was still so much to see, wandering there together, that might now be perfect because of her change of mood, the shadow having lifted, and aloud he began to discuss the evening to come, where they would dine—not the restaurant they usually went to, near the Fenice theatre, but somewhere different, somewhere new.

"Yes, but it must be cheap," she said, falling in with his mood, "because we've already spent so much today."

Their hotel by the Grand Canal had a welcoming, comforting air. The clerk smiled as he handed over their key. The bedroom was familiar, like home, with Laura's things arranged neatly on the dressing table but with it the little festive atmosphere of strangeness, of excitement, that only a holiday bedroom brings. This is ours for the moment, but no more. While we are in it we bring it life. When we have gone it no longer exists, it fades into anonymity. He turned on both taps in the bathroom, the water gushing into the bath, the steam rising. "Now," he thought afterwards, "now at last is the moment to make love," and he went back into the bedroom, and she understood, and opened her arms and smiled. Such blessed relief after all those weeks of restraint.

"The thing is," she said later, fixing her earrings before the looking glass, "I'm not really terribly hungry. Shall we just be dull and eat in the dining room here?"

"God, no!" he exclaimed. "With all those rather dreary couples at the other tables? I'm ravenous. I'm also gay. I want to get rather sloshed."

"Not bright lights and music, surely?"

"No, no ... some small, dark, intimate cave, rather sinister, full of lovers with other people's wives."

"H'm," sniffed Laura, "we all know what *that* means. You'll spot some Italian lovely of sixteen and smirk at her through dinner, while I'm stuck high and dry with a beastly man's broad back."

They went out laughing into the warm soft night, and the magic was about them everywhere. "Let's walk," he said, "let's walk and work up an appetite for our gigantic meal," and inevitably they found themselves by the Molo and the lapping gondolas dancing upon the water, the lights everywhere blending with the darkness. There were other couples strolling for the same sake of aimless enjoyment, backwards, forwards, purposeless, and the inevitable sailors in groups, noisy, gesticulating, and dark-eyed girls whispering, clicking on high heels.

"The trouble is," said Laura, "walking in Venice becomes compulsive once you start. Just over the next bridge, you say, and then the next one beckons. I'm sure there are no restaurants down here, we're almost at those public gardens where they hold the Biennale. Let's turn back. I know there's a restaurant somewhere near the church of San Zaccaria, there's a little alleyway leading to it."

"Tell you what," said John, "if we go down here by the Arsenal, and cross that bridge at the end and head left, we'll come upon San Zaccaria from the other side. We did it the other morning."

"Yes, but it was daylight then. We may lose our way, it's not very well lit."

"Don't fuss. I have an instinct for these things."

They turned down the Fondamenta dell'Arsenale and crossed the little bridge short of the Arsenal itself, and so on past the church of San Martino. There were two canals ahead, one bearing right, the other left, with narrow streets beside them. John hesitated. Which one was it they had walked beside the day before?

"You see," protested Laura, "we shall be lost, just as I said."

"Nonsense," replied John firmly. "It's the left-hand one, I remember the little bridge."

The canal was narrow, the houses on either side seemed to close in upon it, and in the daytime, with the sun's reflection on the water and the windows of the houses open, bedding upon the balconies, a canary singing in a cage, there had been an impression of warmth, of secluded shelter. Now, ill-lit, almost in darkness, the windows of the houses shuttered, the water dank, the scene appeared altogether different, neglected, poor, and the long narrow boats moored to the slippery steps of cellar entrances looked like coffins.

"I swear I don't remember this bridge," said Laura, pausing, and holding on to the rail, "and I don't like the look of that alleyway beyond."

"There's a lamp halfway up," John told her. "I know exactly where we are, not far from the Greek quarter."

They crossed the bridge, and were about to plunge into the alleyway when they heard the cry. It came, surely, from one of the houses on the opposite side, but which one it was impossible to say. With the shutters closed each one of them seemed dead. They turned, and stared in the direction from which the sound had come.

"What was it?" whispered Laura.

"Some drunk or other," said John briefly. "Come on."

Less like a drunk than someone being strangled, and the choking cry suppressed as the grip held firm.

"We ought to call the police," said Laura.

"Oh, for heaven's sake," said John. Where did she think she was— Piccadilly?

"Well, I'm off, it's sinister," she replied, and began to hurry away up the twisting alleyway. John hesitated, his eye caught by a small figure which suddenly crept from a cellar entrance below one of the opposite houses, and then jumped into a narrow boat below. It was a child, a little girl—she couldn't have been more than five or six—wearing a short coat over her minute skirt, a pixie hood covering her head. There were four boats moored, line upon line, and she proceeded to jump from one to the other with surprising agility, intent, it would seem, upon escape. Once her foot slipped and he caught his breath, for she was within a few feet of the water, losing balance; then she recovered, and hopped onto the furthest boat. Bending, she tugged at the rope, which had the effect of swinging the boat's after-end across the canal, almost touching the opposite side and another cellar entrance, about thirty feet from the spot where John stood watching her. Then the child jumped again, landing upon the cellar steps, and vanished into the house, the boat swinging back into mid-canal behind her. The whole episode could not have taken more than four minutes. Then he heard the quick patter of feet. Laura had returned. She had seen none of it, for which he felt unspeakably thankful. The sight of a child, a little girl, in what must have been near danger, her fear that the scene he had just witnessed was in some way a sequel to the alarming cry, might have had a disastrous effect on her overwrought nerves.

"What are you doing?" she called. "I daren't go on without you. The wretched alley branches in two directions."

"Sorry," he told her. "I'm coming."

He took her arm and they walked briskly along the alley, John with an apparent confidence he did not possess.

"There were no more cries, were there?" she asked.

"No," he said, "no, nothing. I tell you, it was some drunk."

The alley led to a deserted *campo* behind a church, not a church he knew, and he led the way across, along another street and over a further bridge.

"Wait a minute," he said. "I think we take this right-hand turning. It will lead us into the Greek quarter—the church of San Giorgio is somewhere over there."

She did not answer. She was beginning to lose faith. The place was like a maze. They might circle round and round forever, and then find themselves back again, near the bridge where they had heard the cry. Doggedly he led her on, and then surprisingly, with relief, he saw people walking in the lighted street ahead, there was a spire of a church, the surroundings became familiar.

"There, I told you," he said. "That's San Zaccaria, we've found it all right. Your restaurant can't be far away."

And anyway, there would be other restaurants, somewhere to eat, at least here was the cheering glitter of lights, of movement, canals beside which people walked, the atmosphere of tourism. The letters "Ristorante," in blue lights, shone like a beacon down a left-hand alley.

"Is this your place?" he asked.

"God knows," she said. "Who cares? Let's feed there anyway."

And so into the sudden blast of heated air and hum of voices, the smell of pasta, wine, waiters, jostling customers, laughter. "For two? This way, please." Why, he thought, was one's British nationality always so obvious? A cramped little table and an enormous menu scribbled in an indecipherable mauve biro, with the waiter hovering, expecting the order forthwith.

"Two very large Camparis, with soda," John said. "*Then* we'll study the menu."

He was not going to be rushed. He handed the bill of fare to Laura and looked about him. Mostly Italians—that meant the food would be good. Then he saw them. At the opposite side of the room. The twin sisters. They must have come into the restaurant hard upon Laura's and his own arrival, for they were only now sitting down, shedding their coats, the waiter hovering beside the table. John was seized with the irrational thought that this was no coincidence. The sisters had noticed them both, in the street outside, and had followed them in. Why, in the name of hell, should they have picked on this particular spot, in the whole of Venice, unless . . . unless Laura herself, at Torcello, had suggested a further encounter, or the sister had suggested it to her? A small restaurant near the church of San Zaccaria, we go there sometimes for dinner. It was Laura, before the walk, who had mentioned San Zaccaria . . . .

She was still intent upon the menu, she had not seen the sisters, but any moment now she would have chosen what she wanted to eat, and then she would raise her head and look across the room. If only the drinks would come. If only the waiter would bring the drinks, it would give Laura something to do.

"You know, I was thinking," he said quickly, "we really ought to go to the garage tomorrow and get the car, and do that drive to Padua. We could lunch in Padua, see the cathedral and touch St. Anthony's tomb and look at the Giotto frescoes, and come back by the way of those various villas along the Brenta that the guidebook cracks up."

It was no use, though. She was looking up, across the restaurant, and she gave a little gasp of surprise. It was genuine. He could swear it was genuine.

"Look," she said, "how extraordinary! How really amazing!"

"What?" he said sharply.

"Why, there they are. My wonderful old twins. They've seen us, what's more. They're staring this way." She waved her hand, radiant, delighted. The sister she had spoken to at Torcello bowed and smiled. False old bitch, he thought. I know they followed us.

"Oh, darling, I must go and speak to them," she said impulsively, "just to tell them how happy I've been all day, thanks to them."

"Oh, for heaven's sake!" he said. "Look, here are the drinks. And we haven't ordered yet. Surely you can wait until later, until we've eaten?"

"I won't be a moment," she said, "and anyway I want scampi, nothing first. I told you I wasn't hungry."

She got up, and, brushing past the waiter with the drinks, crossed the room. She might have been greeting the loved friends of years. He watched her bend over the table and shake them both by the hand, and because there was a vacant chair at their table she drew it up and sat down, talking, smiling. Nor did the sisters seem surprised, at least not the one she knew, who nodded and talked back, while the blind sister remained impassive.

"All right," thought John savagely, "then I *will* get sloshed," and he proceeded to down his Campari and soda and order another, while he pointed out something quite unintelligible on the menu as his own choice, but remembered scampi for Laura. "And a bottle of Soave," he added, "with ice."

The evening was ruined anyway. What was to have been an intimate, happy celebration would now be heavy-laden with spiritualistic visions, poor little dead Christine sharing the table with them, which was so damned stupid when in earthly life she would have been tucked up hours ago in bed. The bitter taste of the Campari suited his mood of sudden self-pity, and all the while he watched the group at the table in the opposite corner, Laura apparently listening while the more active sister held forth and the blind one sat silent, her formidable sightless eyes turned in his direction.

"She's phoney," he thought, "she's not blind at all. They're both of them frauds, and they could be males in drag after all, just as we pretended at Torcello, and they're after Laura."

He began on his second Campari and soda. The two drinks, taken on an empty stomach, had an instant effect. Vision became blurred. And still Laura went on sitting at the other table, putting in a question now and again, while the active sister talked. The waiter appeared with the scampi, and a companion beside him to serve John's own order, which was totally unrecognisable, heaped with a livid sauce.

"The signora does not come?" enquired the first waiter, and John shook his head grimly, pointing an unsteady finger across the room.

"Tell the signora," he said carefully, "her scampi will get cold."

He stared down at the offering placed before him, and prodded it delicately with a fork. The pallid sauce dissolved, revealing two enormous slices, rounds, of what appeared to be boiled pork, bedecked with garlic. He forked a portion to his mouth and chewed, and yes, it was pork, steamy, rich, the spicy sauce having turned it curiously sweet. He laid down his fork, pushing the plate away, and became aware of Laura, returning across the room and sitting beside him. She did not say anything, which was just as well, he thought, because he was too near nausea to answer. It wasn't just the drink, but reaction from the whole nightmare day. She began to eat her scampi, still not uttering. She did not seem to notice he was not eating. The waiter, hovering at his elbow, anxious, seemed aware that John's choice was somehow an error, and discreetly removed the plate. "Bring me a green salad," murmured John, and even then Laura did not register surprise, or, as she might have done in more normal circumstance, accuse him of having had too much to drink. Finally, when she had finished her scampi and was sipping her wine, which John had waved away, to nibble at his salad in small mouthfuls like a sick rabbit, she began to speak.

"Darling," she said, "I know you won't believe it, and it's rather frightening in a way, but after they left the restaurant in Torcello the sisters went to the cathedral, as we did, although we didn't see them in the crowd, and the blind one had another vision. She said Christine was trying to tell her something about us, that we should be in danger if we stayed in Venice. Christine wanted us to go away as soon as possible."

So that's it, he thought. They think they can run our lives for us. This is to be our problem from henceforth. Do we eat? Do we get up? Do we go to bed? We must get in touch with the twin sisters. They will direct us.

"Well?" she said. "Why don't you say something?"

"Because," he answered, "you are perfectly right, I don't believe it. Quite frankly, I judge your old sisters as being a couple of freaks, if nothing else. They're obviously unbalanced, and I'm sorry if this hurts you, but the fact is they've found a sucker in you."

"You're being unfair," said Laura. "They are genuine, I know it. I just know it. They were completely sincere in what they said."

"All right. Granted. They're sincere. But that doesn't make them well-balanced. Honestly, darling, you meet that old girl for ten minutes in a loo, she tells you she sees Christine sitting beside us—well, anyone with a gift for telepathy could read your unconscious mind in an instant—and then, pleased with her success, as any old psychic expert would be, she flings a further mood of ecstasy and wants to boot us out of Venice. Well, I'm sorry, but to hell with it."

The room was no longer reeling. Anger had sobered him. If it would not put Laura to shame he would get up and cross to their table, and tell the old fools where they got off.

"I knew you would take it like this," said Laura unhappily. "I told them you would. They said not to worry. As long as we left Venice tomorrow everything would come all right."

"Oh, for God's sake," said John. He changed his mind, and poured himself a glass of wine.

"After all," Laura went on, "we have really seen the cream of Venice. I don't mind going on somewhere else. And if we stayed—I know it sounds silly, but I should have a nasty nagging sort of feeling inside me, and I should keep thinking of darling Christine being unhappy and trying to tell us to go."

"Right," said John with ominous calm, "that settles it. Go we will. I suggest we clear off to the hotel straight away and warn the reception we're leaving in the morning. Have you had enough to eat?"

"Oh, dear," sighed Laura, "don't take it like that. Look, why not come over and meet them, and then they can explain about the vision to you? Perhaps you would take it seriously then. Especially as you are the one it most concerns. Christine is more worried over you than me. And the extraordinary thing is that the blind sister says you're psychic and don't know it. You are somehow *en rapport* with the unknown, and I'm not."

"Well, that's final," said John. "I'm psychic, am I? Fine. My psychic intuition tells me to get out of this restaurant now, at once, and we can decide what we do about leaving Venice when we are back at the hotel."

He signalled to the waiter for the bill and they waited for it, not speaking to each other, Laura unhappy, fiddling with her bag, while John, glancing furtively at the twins' table, noticed that they were tucking into plates piled high with spaghetti, in very unpsychic fashion. The bill disposed of, John pushed back his chair.

"Right. Are you ready?" he asked.

"I'm going to say good-bye to them first," said Laura, her mouth set sulkily, reminding him instantly, with a pang, of their poor lost child.

"Just as you like," he replied, and walked ahead of her out of the restaurant, without a backward glance.

The soft humidity of the evening, so pleasant to walk about in earlier, had turned to rain. The strolling tourists had melted away. One or two people hurried by under umbrellas. This is what the inhabitants who live here see, he thought. This is the true life. Empty streets by night, and the dank stillness of a stagnant canal beneath shuttered houses. The rest is a bright façade put on for show, glittering by sunlight.

Laura joined him and they walked away together in silence, and emerging presently behind the ducal palace came out into the Piazza San Marco. The rain was heavy now, and they sought shelter with the few remaining stragglers under the colonnades. The orchestras had packed up for the evening. The tables were bare. Chairs had been turned upside down.

The experts are right, he thought. Venice is sinking. The whole city is slowly dying. One day the tourists will travel here by boat to peer down into the waters, and they will see pillars and columns and marble far, far beneath them, slime and mud uncovering for brief moments a lost underworld of stone. Their heels made a ringing sound on the pavement and the rain splashed from the gutterings above. A fine ending to an evening that had started with brave hope, with innocence.

When they came to their hotel Laura made straight for the lift, and John turned to the desk to ask the night porter for the key. The man handed him a telegram at the same time. John stared at it a moment. Laura was already in the lift. Then he opened the envelope and read the message. It was from the headmaster of Johnnie's preparatory school.

"Johnnie under observation suspected appendicitis in city hospital here. No cause for alarm but surgeon thought wise advise you.
Charles Hill"

He read the message twice, then walked slowly towards the lift where Laura was waiting for him. He gave her the telegram. "This came when we were out," he said. "Not awfully good news." He pressed the lift button as she read the telegram. The lift stopped at the second floor, and they got out.

"Well, this decides it, doesn't it?" she said. "Here is the proof. We have to leave Venice because we're going home. It's Johnnie who's in danger, not us. This is what Christine was trying to tell the twins."

The first thing John did the following morning was to put a call through to the headmaster at the preparatory school. Then he gave notice of their departure to the reception manager, and they packed while they waited for the call. Neither of them referred to the events of the preceding day, it was not necessary. John knew the arrival of the telegram and the foreboding of danger from the sister was coincidence, nothing more, but it was pointless to start an argument about it. Laura was convinced otherwise, but intuitively she knew it was best to keep her feelings to herself. During breakfast they discussed ways and means of getting home. It should be possible to get themselves, and the car, to the special car train that ran from Milan through to Calais, since it was early in the season. In any event, the headmaster had said there was no urgency.

The call from England came while John was in the bathroom. Laura answered it. He came into the bedroom a few minutes later. She was still speaking, but he could tell from the expression in her eyes that she was anxious.

"It's Mrs. Hill," she said. "Mr. Hill is in class. She says they reported from the hospital that Johnnie had a restless night and the surgeon may have to operate, but he doesn't want to unless it's absolutely necessary. They've taken X-rays and the appendix is in a tricky position, it's not awfully straightforward."

"Here, give it to me," he said.

The soothing but slightly guarded voice of the headmaster's wife came down the receiver. "I'm so sorry this may spoil your plans," she said, "but both Charles and I felt you ought to be told, and that you might feel rather easier if you were on the spot. Johnnie is very plucky, but of course he has some fever. That isn't unusual, the surgeon says, in the circumstances. Sometimes an appendix can get displaced, it appears, and this makes it more complicated. He's going to decide about operating this evening."

"Yes, of course, we quite understand," said John.

"Please do tell your wife not to worry too much," she went on. "The hospital is excellent, a very nice staff, and we have every confidence in the surgeon."

"Yes," said John, "yes," and then broke off because Laura was making gestures beside him.

"If we can't get the car on the train, I can fly," she said. "They're sure to be able to find me a seat on a plane. Then at least one of us would be there this evening."

He nodded agreement. "Thank you so much, Mrs. Hill," he said, "we'll manage to get back all right. Yes, I'm sure Johnnie is in good hands. Thank your husband for us. Goodbye."

He replaced the receiver and looked round him at the tumbled beds, suitcases on the floor, tissue paper strewn. Basket, maps, books, coats, everything they had brought with them in the car. "Oh God," he said, "what a bloody mess. All this junk." The telephone rang again. It was the hall porter to say he had succeeded in booking a sleeper for them both, and a place for the car, on the following night.

"Look," said Laura, who had seized the telephone, "could you book one seat on the midday plane from Venice to London today, for me? It's imperative one of us gets home this evening. My husband could follow with the car tomorrow."

"Here, hang on," interrupted John. "No need for panic stations. Surely twenty-four hours wouldn't make all that difference?"

Anxiety had drained the colour from her face. She turned to him, distraught.

"It mightn't to you, but it does to me," she said. "I've lost one child, I'm not going to lose another."

"All right, darling, all right . . . ." He put his hand out to her but she brushed it off, impatiently, and continued giving directions to the porter. He turned back to his packing. No use saying anything. Better for it to be as she wished. They could, of course, both go by air, and then when all was well, and Johnnie better, he could come back and fetch the car, driving home through France as they had come. Rather a sweat, though, and the hell of an expense. Bad enough Laura going by air and himself with the car on the train from Milan.

"We could, if you like, both fly," he began tentatively, explaining the sudden idea, but she would have none of it. "That really *would* be absurd," she said impatiently. "As long as I'm there this evening, and you follow by train, it's all that matters. Besides, we shall need the car, going backwards and forwards to the hospital. And our luggage. We couldn't go off and just leave all this here."

No, he saw her point. A silly idea. It was only—well, he was as worried about Johnnie as she was, though he wasn't going to say so.

"I'm going downstairs to stand over the porter," said Laura. "They always make more effort if one is actually on the spot. Everything I want tonight is packed. I shall only need my overnight case. You can bring everything else in the car." She hadn't been out of the bedroom five minutes before the telephone rang. It was Laura. "Darling," she said, "it couldn't have worked out better. The porter has got me on a charter flight that leaves Venice in less than an hour. A special motor launch takes the party direct from San Marco in about ten minutes. Some passenger on the charter flight cancelled. I shall be at Gatwick in less than four hours."

"I'll be down right away," he told her.

He joined her by the reception desk. She no longer looked anxious and drawn, but full of purpose. She was on her way. He kept wishing they were going together. He couldn't bear to stay on in Venice after she had gone, but the thought of driving to Milan, spending a dreary night in a hotel there alone, the endless dragging day which would follow, and the long hours in the train the next night, filled him with intolerable depression, quite apart from the anxiety about Johnnie. They walked along to the San Marco landing stage, the Molo bright and glittering after the rain, a little breeze blowing, the postcards and scarves and tourist souvenirs fluttering on the stalls, the tourists themselves out in force, strolling, contented, the happy day before them.

"I'll ring you tonight from Milan," he told her. "The Hills will give you a bed, I suppose. And if you're at the hospital they'll let me have the latest news. That must be your charter party. You're welcome to them!"

The passengers descending from the landing stage down into the waiting launch were carrying hand luggage with Union Jack tags upon them. They were mostly middle-aged, with what appeared to be two Methodist ministers in charge. One of them advanced towards Laura, holding out his hand, showing a gleaming row of dentures when he smiled. "You must be the lady joining us for the homeward flight," he said. "Welcome aboard, and to the Union of Fellowship. We are all delighted to make your acquaintance. Sorry we hadn't a seat for hubby, too."

Laura turned swiftly and kissed John, a tremor at the corner of her mouth betraying inward laughter. "Do you think they'll break into hymns?" she whispered. "Take care of yourself, hubby. Call me tonight."

The pilot sounded a curious little toot upon his horn, and in a moment Laura had climbed down the steps into the launch and was standing amongst the crowd of passengers, waving her hand, her scarlet coat a gay patch of colour amongst the more sober suiting of her companions. The launch tooted again and moved away from the landing stage, and he stood there watching it, a sense of immense loss filling his heart. Then he turned and walked away, back to the hotel, the bright day all about him desolate, unseen.

There was nothing, he thought, as he looked about him presently in the hotel bedroom, so melancholy as a vacated room, especially when the recent signs of occupation were still visible about him. Laura's suitcases on the bed, a second coat she had left behind. Traces of powder on the dressing table. A tissue, with a lipstick smear, thrown in the wastepaper basket. Even an old toothpaste tube squeezed dry, lying on the glass shelf above the washbasin. Sounds of the heedless traffic on the Grand Canal came as always from the open window, but Laura wasn't there any more to listen to it, or to watch from the small balcony. The pleasure had gone. Feeling had gone.

John finished packing, and leaving all the baggage ready to be collected he went downstairs to pay the bill. The reception clerk was welcoming new arrivals. People were sitting on the terrace overlooking the Grand Canal reading newspapers, the pleasant day waiting to be planned.

John decided to have an early lunch, here on the hotel terrace, on familiar ground, and then have the porter carry the baggage to one of the ferries that steamed direct between San Marco and the Porta Roma, where the car was garaged. The fiasco meal of the night before had left him empty, and he was ready for the trolley of hors d'oeuvres when they brought it to him, around midday. Even here, though, there was change. The headwaiter, their especial friend, was off duty, and the table where they usually sat was occupied by new arrivals, a honeymoon couple, he told himself sourly, observing the gaiety, the smiles, while he had been shown to a small single table behind a tub of flowers.

"She's airborne now," John thought, "she's on her way," and he tried to picture Laura seated between the Methodist ministers, telling them, no doubt, about Johnnie ill in hospital, and heaven knows what else besides. Well, the twin sisters anyway could rest in psychic peace. Their wishes would have been fulfilled.

Lunch over, there was no point in lingering with a cup of coffee on the terrace. His desire was to get away as soon as possible, fetch the car, and be en route for Milan. He made his farewells at the reception desk, and, escorted by a porter who had piled his baggage onto a wheeled trolley, made his way once more to the landing stage of San Marco. As he stepped onto the steam ferry, his luggage heaped beside him, a crowd of jostling people all about him, he had one momentary pang to be leaving Venice. When, if ever, he wondered, would they come again? Next year . . . in three years . . . . glimpsed first on honey-moon, nearly ten years ago, and then a second visit *en passant,* before a cruise, and now this last abortive ten days that had ended so abruptly.

The water glittered in the sunshine, buildings shone, tourists in dark glasses paraded up and down the rapidly receding Molo, already the terrace of their hotel was out of sight as the ferry churned its way up the Grand Canal. So many impressions to seize and hold, familiar loved façades, balconies, windows, water lapping the cellar steps of decaying palaces, the little red house where d'Annunzio lived, with its garden— our house, Laura called it, pretending it was theirs—and too soon the ferry would be turning left on the direct route to the Piazzale Roma, so missing the best of the Canal, the Rialto, the further palaces.

Another ferry was heading downstream to pass them, filled with passengers, and for a brief foolish moment he wished he could change places, be amongst the happy tourists bound for Venice and all he had left behind him. Then he saw her. Laura, in her scarlet coat, the twin sisters by her side, the active sister with her hand on Laura's arm, talking earnestly, and Laura herself, her hair blowing in the wind, gesticulating, on her face a look of distress. He stared, astounded, too astonished to shout, to wave, and anyway they would never have heard or seen him, for his own ferry had already passed and was heading in the opposite direction.

What the hell had happened? There must have been a holdup with the charter flight and it had never taken off, but in that case why had Laura not telephoned him at the hotel? And what were those damned sisters doing? Had she run into them at the airport? Was it coincidence? And why did she look so anxious? He could think of no explanation. Perhaps the flight had been cancelled. Laura, of course, would go straight to the hotel, expecting to find him there, intending, doubtless, to drive with him after all to Milan and take the train the following night. What a blasted mix-up. The only thing to do was to telephone the hotel immediately his ferry reached the Piazzale Roma and tell her to wait—he would return and fetch her. As for the damned interfering sisters, they could get stuffed.

The usual stampede ensued when the ferry arrived at the landing stage. He had to find a porter to collect his baggage, and then wait while he discovered a telephone. The fiddling with change, the hunt for the number, delayed him still more. He succeeded at last in getting through, and luckily the reception clerk he knew was still at the desk.

"Look, there's been some frightful muddle," he began, and explained how Laura was even now on her way back to the hotel—he had seen her with two friends on one of the ferry services. Would the reception clerk explain and tell her to wait? He would be back by the next available service to collect her. "In any event, detain her," he said. "I'll be as quick as I can." The reception clerk understood perfectly, and John rang off.

Thank heaven Laura hadn't turned up before he had put through his call, or they would have told her he was on his way to Milan. The porter was still waiting with the baggage, and it seemed simplest to walk with him to the garage, hand everything over to the chap in charge of the office there and ask him to keep it for an hour, when he would be returning with his wife to pick up the car. Then he went back to the landing station to await the next ferry to Venice. The minutes dragged, and he kept wondering all the time what had gone wrong at the airport and why in heaven's name Laura hadn't telephoned. No use conjecturing. She would tell him the whole story at the hotel. One thing was certain: he would not allow Laura and himself to be saddled with the sisters and become involved with their affairs. He could imagine Laura saying that they also had missed a flight, and could they have a lift to Milan?

Finally the ferry chugged alongside the landing stage and he stepped aboard. What an anticlimax, thrashing back past the familiar sights to which he had bidden a nostalgic farewell such a short while ago! He didn't even look about him this time, he was so intent on reaching his destination. In San Marco there were more people than ever, the afternoon crowds walking shoulder to shoulder, every one of them on pleasure bent.

He came to the hotel and pushed his way through the swing door, expecting to see Laura, and possibly the sisters, waiting in the lounge to the left of the entrance. She was not there. He went to the desk. The reception clerk he had spoken to on the telephone was standing there, talking to the manager.

"Has my wife arrived?" John asked.

"No, sir, not yet."

"What an extraordinary thing. Are you sure?"

"Absolutely certain, sir. I have been here ever since you telephoned me at a quarter of two. I have not left the desk."

"I just don't understand it. She was on one of the vaporettos passing by the Accademia. She would have landed at San Marco about five minutes later and come on here."

The clerk seemed nonplussed. "I don't know what to say. The signora was with friends, did you say?"

"Yes. Well, acquaintances. Two ladies we had met at Torcello yesterday. I was astonished to see her with them on the vaporetto, and of course I assumed that the flight had been cancelled, and she had somehow met up with them at the airport and decided to return here with them, to catch me before I left."

Oh hell, what was Laura doing? It was after three. A matter of moments from San Marco landing stage to the hotel.

"Perhaps the signora went with her friends to their hotel instead. Do you know where they are staying?"

"No," said John, "I haven't the slightest idea. What's more, I don't even know the names of the two ladies. They were sisters, twins, in fact—looked exactly alike. But anyway, why go to their hotel and not here?"

The swing door opened but it wasn't Laura. Two people staying in the hotel.

The manager broke into the conversation. "I tell you what I will do," he said. "I will telephone the airport and check with the flight. Then at least we will get somewhere." He smiled apologetically. It was not usual for arrangements to go wrong.

"Yes, do that," said John. "We may as well know what happened there."

He lit a cigarette and began to pace up and down the entrance hall. What a bloody mix-up. And how unlike Laura, who knew he would be setting off for Milan directly after lunch—indeed, for all she knew he might have gone before. But surely, in that case, she would have telephoned at once, on arrival at the airport, had the flight been cancelled.

The manager was ages telephoning, he had to be put through on some other line, and his Italian was too rapid for John to follow the conversation. Finally he replaced the receiver.

"It is more mysterious than ever, sir," he said. "The charter flight was not delayed, it took off on schedule with a full complement of passengers. As far as they could tell me, there was no hitch. The signora must simply have changed her mind." His smile was more apologetic than ever.

"Changed her mind," John repeated. "But why on earth should she do that? She was so anxious to be home tonight."

The manager shrugged. "You know how ladies can be, sir," he said. "Your wife may have thought that after all she would prefer to take the train to Milan with you. I do assure you, though, that the charter party was most respectable, and it was a Caravelle aircraft, perfectly safe."

"Yes, yes," said John impatiently, "I don't blame your arrangements in the slightest. I just can't understand what induced her to change her mind, unless it was meeting with these two ladies."

The manager was silent. He could not think of anything to say. The reception clerk was equally concerned. "Is it possible," he ventured, "that you made a mistake, and it was not the signora that you saw on the vaporetto?"

"Oh no," replied John, "it was my wife, I assure you. She was wearing her red coat, she was hatless, just as she left here. I saw her as plainly as I can see you. I would swear to it in a court of law."

"It is unfortunate," said the manager, "that we do not know the name of the two ladies, or the hotel where they were staying. You say you met these ladies at Torcello yesterday?"

"Yes . . . but only briefly. They weren't staying there. At least, I am certain they were not. We saw them at dinner in Venice later, as it happens."

"Excuse me . . . ." Guests were arriving with luggage to check in, the clerk was obliged to attend to them. John turned in desperation to the manager. "Do you think it would be any good telephoning the hotel in Torcello in case the people there knew the name of the ladies, or where they were staying in Venice?"

"We can try," replied the manager. "It is a small hope, but we can try."

John resumed his anxious pacing, all the while watching the swing

door, hoping, praying, that he would catch sight of the red coat and
Laura would enter. Once again there followed what seemed an interminable telephone conversation between the manager and someone
at the hotel in Torcello.

"Tell them two sisters," said John, "two elderly ladies dressed in
grey, both exactly alike. One lady was blind," he added. The manager
nodded. He was obviously giving a detailed description. Yet when he
hung up he shook his head. "The manager at Torcello says he remembers the two ladies well," he told John, "but they were only there for
lunch. He never learnt their names."

"Well, that's that. There's nothing to do now but wait."

John lit his third cigarette and went out onto the terrace, to resume
his pacing there. He stared out across the canal, searching the heads
of the people on passing steamers, motorboats, even drifting gondolas.
The minutes ticked by on his watch, and there was no sign of Laura.
A terrible foreboding nagged at him that somehow this was prear-
ranged, that Laura had never intended to catch the aircraft, that last
night in the restaurant she had made an assignation with the sisters.
Oh God, he thought, that's impossible, I'm going paranoiac.... Yet
why, why? No, more likely the encounter at the airport was fortuitous,
and for some incredible reason they had persuaded Laura not to board
the aircraft, even prevented her from doing so, trotting out one of their
psychic visions, that the aircraft would crash, that she must return with
them to Venice. And Laura, in her sensitive state, felt they must be right,
swallowed it all without question.

But granted all these possibilities, why had she not come to the
hotel? What was she doing? Four o'clock, half-past four, the sun no
longer dappling the water. He went back to the reception desk.

"I just can't hang around," he said. "Even if she does turn up, we
shall never make Milan this evening. I might see her walking with these
ladies, in the Piazza San Marco, anywhere. If she arrives while I'm out,
will you explain?"

The clerk was full of concern, "Indeed, yes," he said. "It is very
worrying for you, sir. Would it perhaps be prudent if we booked you
in here tonight?"

John gestured, helplessly. "Perhaps, yes, I don't know. Maybe...."

He went out of the swing door and began to walk towards the Piazza
San Marco. He looked into every shop up and down the colonnades,

crossed the piazza a dozen times, threaded his way between the tables in front of Florian's, in front of Quadri's, knowing that Laura's red coat and the distinctive appearance of the twin sisters could easily be spotted, even amongst this milling crowd, but there was no sign of them. He joined the crowd of shoppers in the Merceria, shoulder to shoulder with idlers, thrusters, window-gazers, knowing instinctively that it was useless, they wouldn't be here. Why should Laura have deliberately missed her flight to return to Venice for such a purpose? And even if she had done so, for some reason beyond his imagining, she would surely have come first to the hotel to find him.

The only thing left to him was to try to track down the sisters. Their hotel could be anywhere amongst the hundreds of hotels and pensions scattered through Venice, or even across the other side at the Zattere, or farther again on the Guidecca. These last possibilities seemed remote. More likely they were staying in a small hotel or pension somewhere near San Zaccaria handy to the restaurant where they had dined last night. The blind one would surely not go far afield in the evening. He had been a fool not to have thought of this before, and he turned back and walked quickly away from the brightly lighted shopping district towards the narrower, more cramped quarter where they had dined last evening. He found the restaurant without difficulty, but they were not yet open for dinner, and the waiter preparing tables was not the one who had served them. John asked to see the *padrone,* and the waiter disappeared to the back regions, returning after a moment or two with the somewhat dishevelled-looking proprietor in shirt sleeves, caught in a slack moment, not in full tenue.

"I had dinner here last night, " John explained. "There were two ladies sitting at that table there in the corner." He pointed to it.

"You wish to book that table for this evening?" asked the proprietor.

"No," said John. "No, there were two ladies there last night, two sisters, *due sorelle,* twins, *gemelle"*—what was the right word for twins?—"Do you remember? Two ladies, *sorelle vecchie . . ."*

"Ah," said the man, *"si, si, signore, la povera signorina."* He put his hands to his eyes to feign blindness. "Yes, I remember."

"Do you know their names?" asked John. "Where they were staying? I am very anxious to trace them."

The proprietor spread out his hands in a gesture of regret. "I am ver' sorry, signore, I do not know the names of the signorine, they have been here once, twice, perhaps for dinner, they do not say where they were staying. Perhaps if you come again tonight they might be here? Would you like to book a table?"

He pointed around him, suggesting a whole choice of tables that might appeal to a prospective diner, but John shook his head.

"Thank you, no. I may be dining elsewhere. I am sorry to have troubled you. If the signorine should come . . ." he paused, "possibly I may return later," he added. "I am not sure."

The proprietor bowed, and walked with him to the entrance. "In Venice the whole world meets," he said smiling. "It is possible the signore will find his friends tonight. Arrivederci, signore."

Friends? John walked out into the street. More likely kidnappers . . . . Anxiety had turned to fear, to panic. Something had gone terribly wrong. Those women had got hold of Laura, played upon her suggestibility, induced her to go with them, either to their hotel or elsewhere. Should he find the Consulate? Where was it? What would he say when he got there? He began walking without purpose, finding himself as they had done the night before, in streets he did not know, and suddenly came upon a tall building with the word "Questura" above it. This is it, he thought. I don't care, something has happened, I'm going inside. There were a number of police in uniform coming and going, the place at any rate was active, and, addressing himself to one of them behind a glass partition, he asked if there was anyone who spoke English. The man pointed to a flight of stairs and John went up, entering a door on the right where he saw that another couple were sitting, waiting, and with relief he recognised them as fellow countrymen, tourists, obviously a man and his wife, in some sort of predicament.

"Come and sit down," said the man. "We've waited half an hour but they can't be much longer. What a country! They wouldn't leave us like this at home."

John took the proffered cigarette and found a chair beside him.

"What's your trouble?" he asked.

"My wife had her handbag pinched in one of those shops in the Merceria," said the man. "She simply put it down one moment to look at something, and you'd hardly credit it, the next moment it had gone. I say it was a sneak thief, she insists it was the girl behind the counter. But who's to say? These Ities are all alike. Anyway, I'm certain we shan't get it back. What have you lost?"

"Suitcase stolen," John lied rapidly. "Had some important papers in it."

How could he say he had lost his wife? He couldn't even begin . . . .

The man nodded in sympathy. "As I said, these Ities are all alike. Old Musso knew how to deal with them. Too many Communists around these days. The trouble is, they're not going to bother with our troubles much, not with this murderer at large. They're all out looking for him."

"Murderer? What murderer?" asked John.

"Don't tell me you've not heard about it?" The man stared at him in surprise. "Venice has talked of nothing else. It's been in all the papers, on the radio, and even in the English papers. A grizzly business. One woman found with her throat slit last week—a tourist too—and some old chap discovered with the same sort of knife wound this morning. They seem to think it must be a maniac, because there doesn't seem to be any motive. Nasty thing to happen in Venice in the tourist season."

"My wife and I never bother with the newspapers when we're on holiday," said John. "And we're neither of us much given to gossip in the hotel."

"Very wise of you," laughed the man. "It might have spoilt your holiday, especially if your wife is nervous. Oh well, we're off tomorrow anyway. Can't say we mind, do we, dear?" He turned to his wife. "Venice has gone downhill since we were here last. And now this loss of the handbag really is the limit."

The door of the inner room opened, and a senior police officer asked John's companion and his wife to pass through.

"I bet we don't get any satisfaction," murmured the tourist, winking at John, and he and his wife went into the inner room. The door closed behind them. John stubbed out his cigarette and lighted another. A strange feeling of unreality possessed him. He asked himself what he was doing here, what was the use of it? Laura was no longer in Venice but had disappeared, perhaps forever, with those diabolical sisters. She would never be traced. And just as the two of them had made up a fantastic story about the twins, when they first spotted them in Torcello, so, with nightmare logic, the fiction would have basis in fact; the women were in reality disguised crooks, men with criminal intent who lured unsuspecting persons to some appalling fate. They might even be the murderers for whom the police sought. Who would ever suspect two elderly women of respectable appearance, living quietly in some second-rate pension or hotel? He stubbed out his cigarette, unfinished.

"This," he thought, "is really the start of paranoia. This is the way people go off their heads." He glanced at his watch. It was half-past six. Better pack this in, this futile quest here in police headquarters, and keep to the single link of sanity remaining. Return to the hotel, put a call through to the prep school in England, and ask about the latest news of Johnnie. He had not thought about poor Johnnie since sighting Laura on the vaporetto.

Too late, though. The inner door opened, the couple were ushered out.

"Usual claptrap," said the husband sotto voce to John. "They'll do what they can. Not much hope. So many foreigners in Venice, all of 'em thieves! The locals all above reproach. Wouldn't pay 'em to steal from customers. Well, I wish you better luck."

He nodded, his wife smiled and bowed, and they had gone. John followed the police officer into the inner room.

Formalities began. Name, address, passport. Length of stay in Venice, etc., etc. Then the questions, and John, the sweat beginning to appear on his forehead, launched into his interminable story. The first encounter with the sisters, the meeting at the restaurant, Laura's state of suggestibility because of the death of their child, the telegram about Johnnie, the decision to take the chartered flight, her departure, and her sudden inexplicable return. When he had finished he felt as exhausted as if he had driven three hundred miles nonstop after a severe bout of flu. His interrogator spoke excellent English with a strong Italian accent.

"You say," he began, "that your wife was suffering the aftereffects of shock. This had been noticeable during your stay here in Venice."

"Well, yes," John replied, "she had really been quite ill. The holiday didn't seem to be doing her much good. It was only when she met these two women at Torcello yesterday that her mood changed. The strain seemed to have gone. She was ready, I suppose, to snatch at every straw, and this belief that our little girl was watching over her had somehow restored her to what appeared normality."

"It would be natural," said the police officer, "in the circumstances. But no doubt the telegram last night was a further shock to you both."

"Indeed, yes. That was the reason we decided to return home."

"No argument between you? No difference of opinion?"

"None. We were in complete agreement. My one regret was that I could not go with my wife on this charter flight."

The police officer nodded. "It could well be that your wife had a sudden attack of amnesia, and meeting the two ladies served as a link, she clung to them for support. You have described them with great accuracy, and I think they should not be too difficult to trace. Meanwhile, I suggest you should return to your hotel, and we will get in touch with you as soon as we have news."

At least, John thought, they believed his story. They did not consider him a crank who had made the whole thing up and was merely wasting their time.

"You appreciate," he said, "I am extremely anxious. These women may have some criminal design upon my wife. One has heard of such things . . . ."

The police officer smiled for the first time. "Please don't concern yourself," he said. "I am sure there will be some satisfactory explanation."

All very well, thought John, but in heaven's name, what?

"I'm sorry," he said, "to have taken up so much of your time. Especially as I gather the police have their hands full hunting down a murderer who is still at large."

He spoke deliberately. No harm in letting the fellow know that for all any of them could tell there might be some connection between Laura's disappearance and this other hideous affair.

"Ah, that," said the police officer, rising to his feet. "We hope to have the murderer under lock and key very soon."

His tone of confidence was reassuring. Murderers, missing wives, lost handbags were all under control. They shook hands, and John was ushered out of the door and so downstairs. Perhaps, he thought, as he walked slowly back to the hotel, the fellow was right. Laura had suffered a sudden attack of amnesia, and the sisters happened to be at the airport and had brought her back to Venice, to their own hotel, because Laura couldn't remember where she and John had been staying. Perhaps they were even now trying to track down his hotel. Anyway, he could do nothing more. The police had everything in hand, and, please God, would come up with the solution. All he wanted to do right now was to collapse upon a bed with a stiff whisky, and then put through a call to Johnnie's school.

The page took him up in the lift to a modest room on the fourth floor at the rear of the hotel. Bare, impersonal, the shutters closed, with a smell of cooking wafting up from a courtyard down below.

"Ask them to send me up a double whisky, will you?" he said to the boy. "And a ginger ale," and when he was alone he plunged his face under the cold tap in the washbasin, relieved to find that the minute portion of visitor's soap afforded some measure of comfort. He flung off his shoes, hung his coat over the back of a chair and threw himself down on the bed. Somebody's radio was blasting forth an old popular song, now several seasons out-of-date, that had been one of Laura's favorites a couple of years ago. "I love you, Baby...." He reached for the telephone, and asked the exchange to put through the call to England. Then he closed his eyes, and all the while the insistent voice persisted, "I love you, Baby... I can't get you out of my mind."

Presently there was a tap at the door. It was the waiter with his drink. Too little ice, such meagre comfort, but what desperate need. He gulped it down without a ginger ale, and in a few moments the ever-nagging pain was eased, numbed, bringing, if only momentarily, a sense of calm. The telephone rang, and now, he thought, bracing himself for ultimate disaster, the final shock, Johnnie probably dying, or already dead. In which case nothing remained. Let Venice be engulfed....

The exchange told him that the connection had been made, and in a moment he heard the voice of Mrs. Hill at the other end of the line. They must have warned her that the call came from Venice, for she knew instantly who was speaking.

"Hullo?" she said. "Oh, I am so glad you rang. All is well. Johnnie has had his operation, the surgeon decided to do it at midday rather than wait, and it was completely successful. Johnnie is going to be all right. So you don't have to worry any more, and will have a peaceful night."

"Thank God," he answered.

"I know," she said, "we are all so relieved. Now I'll get off the line and you can speak to your wife."

John sat up on the bed, stunned. What the hell did she mean? Then he heard Laura's voice, cool and clear.

"Darling? Darling, are you there?"

He could not answer. He felt the hand holding the receiver go clammy cold with sweat. "I'm here," he whispered.

"It's not a very good line," she said, "but never mind. As Mrs. Hill told you, all is well. Such a nice surgeon, and a very sweet Sister on Johnnie's floor, and I really am happy about the way it's turned out. I came straight down here after landing at Gatwick —the flight was OK, by the way, but such a funny crowd, it'll make you hysterical when I tell you about them—and I went to the hospital, and Johnnie was coming round. Very dopey, of course, but so pleased to see me. And the Hills are being wonderful, I've got their spare room, and it's only a short taxi drive into the town and the hospital. I shall go to bed as soon as we've had dinner, because I'm a bit fagged, what with the flight and the anxiety. How was the drive to Milan? And where are you staying?"

John did not recognize the voice that answered as his own. It was the automatic response of some computer.

"I'm not in Milan," he said. "I'm still in Venice."

"Still in Venice? What on earth for? Wouldn't the car start?"

"I can't explain," he said. "There was a stupid sort of mix-up . . . ."

He felt suddenly so exhausted that he nearly dropped the receiver, and, shame upon shame, he could feel tears pricking behind his eyes.

"What sort of mix-up?" Her voice was suspicious, almost hostile. "You weren't in a crash?"

"No . . . no . . . nothing like that."

A moment's silence, and then she said, "Your voice sounds very slurred. Don't tell me you went and got pissed."

Oh Christ . . . If she only knew! He was probably going to pass out any moment, but not from the whisky.

"I thought," he said slowly. "I thought I saw you, in a vaporetto, with those two sisters."

What was the point of going on? It was hopeless trying to explain.

"How could you have seen me with the sisters?" she said. "You knew I'd gone to the airport. Really, darling, you are an idiot. You seem to have got those two poor old dears on the brain. I hope you didn't say anything to Mrs. Hill just now."

"No."

"Well, what are you going to do? You'll catch the train at Milan tomorrow, won't you?"

"Yes, of course," he told her.

"I still don't understand what kept you in Venice," she said. "It all sounds a bit odd to me. However . . . thank God Johnnie is going to be all right and I'm here."

"Yes," he said, "yes."

He could hear the distant boom-boom sound of a gong from the headmaster's hall.

"You had better go," he said. "My regards to the Hills, and my love to Johnnie."

"Well, take care of yourself, darling, and for goodness' sake don't miss the train tomorrow, and drive carefully."

The telephone clicked and she had gone. He poured the remaining drop of whisky into his empty glass, and sousing it with ginger ale drank it down at a gulp. He got up, and crossing the room threw open the shutters and leant out of the window. He felt lightheaded. His sense of relief, enormous, overwhelming, was somehow tempered with a curious feeling of unreality, almost as though the voice speaking from England had not been Laura's after all but a fake, and she was still in Venice, hidden in some furtive pension with the two sisters.

The point was, he *had* seen all three of them on the vaporetto. It was not another woman in a red coat. The women *had* been there, with Laura. So what was the explanation? That he was going off his head? Or something more sinister? The sisters, possessing psychic powers of formidable strength, had seen him as their two ferries had passed, and in some inexplicable fashion had made him believe Laura was with them. But why, and to what end? No, it didn't make sense. The only explanation was that he had been mistaken, the whole episode an hallucination. In which case he needed psychoanalysis, just as Johnnie had needed a surgeon.

And what did he do now? Go downstairs and tell the management he had been at fault and had just spoken to his wife, who had arrived in England safe and sound from her charter flight? He put on his shoes and ran his fingers through his hair. He glanced at his watch. It was ten minutes to eight. If he nipped into the bar and had a quick drink it would be easier to face the manager and admit what had happened. Then, perhaps, they would get in touch with the police. Profuse apologies all round for putting everyone to enormous trouble.

He made his way to the ground floor and went straight to the bar, feeling self-conscious, a marked man, half-imagining everyone would look at him, thinking, "There's the fellow with the missing wife." Luckily the bar was full and there wasn't a face he knew. Even the chap behind the bar was an underling who hadn't served him before. He downed his whisky and glanced over his shoulder to the reception hall. The desk was momentarily empty. He could see the manager's back framed in the doorway of an inner room, talking to someone within. On impulse, coward-like, he crossed the hall and passed through the swing door to the street outside.

"I'll have some dinner," he decided, "and then go back and face them. I'll feel more like it once I've some food inside me."

He went to the restaurant nearby where he and Laura had dined once or twice. Nothing mattered any more, because she was safe. The nightmare lay behind him. He could enjoy his dinner, despite her absence, and think of her sitting down with the Hills to a dull, quiet evening, early to bed, and on the following morning going to the hospital to sit with Johnnie. Johnnie was safe, too. No more worries, only the awkward explanations and apologies to the manager at the hotel.

There was a pleasant anonymity sitting down at a corner table alone in the little restaurant, ordering vitello alla Marsala and half a bottle of Merlot. He took his time, enjoying his food but eating in a kind of haze, a sense of unreality still with him, while the conversation of his nearest neighbours had the same soothing effect as background music.

When they rose and left, he saw by the clock on the wall that it was nearly half-past nine. No use delaying matters any further. He drank his coffee, lighted a cigarette and paid his bill. After all, he thought, as he walked back to the hotel, the manager would be greatly relieved to know that all was well.

When he pushed through the swing door, the first thing he noticed was a man in police uniform, standing talking to the manager at the desk. The reception clerk was there too. They turned as John approached, the manager's face lighted up with relief.

"Eccolo!" he exclaimed. "I was certain the signore would not be far away. Things are moving, signore. The two ladies have been traced, and they very kindly agreed to accompany the police to the Questura. If you will go there at once, this *agente di polizia* will escort you."

John flushed. "I have given everyone a lot of trouble," he said. "I meant to tell you before going out to dinner, but you were not at the desk. The fact is that I have contacted my wife. She did make the flight to London after all, and I spoke to her on the telephone. It was all a great mistake."

The manager looked bewildered. "The signora is in London?" he repeated. He broke off, and exchanged a rapid conversation in Italian with the policeman. "It seems that the ladies maintain they did not go out for the day, except for a little shopping in the morning," he said, turning back to John. "Then who was it the signore saw on the vaporetto?"

John shook his head. "A very extraordinary mistake on my part which I still don't understand," he said. "Obviously, I did not see either my wife or the two ladies. I really am extremely sorry."

More rapid conversation in Italian. John noticed the clerk watching him with a curious expression in his eyes. The manager was obviously apologising on John's behalf to the policeman, who looked annoyed and gave tongue to the effect, his voice increasing in volume, to the manager's concern. The whole business had undoubtedly given enormous trouble to a great many people, not least the two unfortunate sisters.

"Look," said John, interrupting the flow, "will you tell the *agente* I will go with him to headquarters and apologise in person both to the police officer and to the ladies?"

The manager looked relieved. "If the signore would take the trouble," he said. "Naturally, the ladies were much distressed when a policeman interrogated them at their hotel, and they offered to accompany him to the Questura only because they were so distressed about the signora."

John felt more and more uncomfortable. Laura must never learn any of this. She would be outraged. He wondered if there were some penalty for giving the police misleading information involving a third party. His error began, in retrospect, to take on criminal proportions.

He crossed the Piazza San Marco, now thronged with after-dinner strollers and spectators at the cafés, all three orchestras going full blast in harmonious rivalry, while his companion kept a discreet two paces to his left and never uttered a word.

They arrived at the police station and mounted the stairs to the same inner room where he had been before. He saw immediately that it was not the officer he knew but another who sat behind the desk, a sallow-faced individual with a sour expression, while the two sisters, obviously upset—the active one in particular—were seated on chairs nearby, some underling in uniform standing behind them. John's escort went at once to the police officer, speaking in rapid Italian, while John himself, after a moment's hesitation, advanced towards the sisters.

"There has been a terrible mistake," he said. "I don't know how to apologise to you both. It's all my fault, mine entirely, the police are not to blame."

The active sister made as though to rise, her mouth twitching nervously, but he restrained her.

"We don't understand," she said, the Scots inflection strong. "We said good night to your wife last night at dinner, and we have not seen her since. The police came to our pension more than an hour ago and told us your wife was missing and you had filed a complaint against us. My sister is not very strong. She was considerably disturbed."

"A mistake. A frightful mistake," he repeated.

He turned towards the desk. The police officer was addressing him, his English very inferior to that of the previous interrogator. He had John's earlier statement on the desk in front of him, and tapped it with a pencil.

"So?" he queried. "This document all lies? You not speaka the truth?"

"I believed it to be true at the time," said John. "I could have sworn in a court of law that I saw my wife with these two ladies on a vaporetto in the Grand Canal this afternoon. Now I realise I was mistaken."

"We have not been near the Grand Canal all day," protested the sister, "not even on foot. We made a few purchases in the Merceria this morning, and remained indoors all afternoon. My sister was a little unwell. I have told the police officer this a dozen times, and the people at the pension would corroborate our story. He refused to listen."

"And the signora?" rapped the police officer angrily. "What happen to the signora?"

"The signora, my wife, is safe in England," explained John patiently. "I talked to her on the telephone just after seven. She did join the charter flight from the airport, and is now staying with friends."

"Then who you see on the vaporetto in the red coat?" asked the furious police officer. "And if not these signorine here, then what signorine?"

"My eyes deceived me," said John, aware that his English was likewise becoming strained. "I think I see my wife and these ladies but no, it was not so. My wife in aircraft, these ladies in pension all the time."

It was like talking stage Chinese. In a moment he would be bowing and putting his hands in his sleeves.

The police officer raised his eyes to heaven and thumped the table. "So all this work for nothing," he said. "Hotels and pensiones searched for the signorine and a missing signora inglese, when here we have plenty, plenty other things to do. You maka a mistake. You have perhaps too much vino at mezzo giorno and you see hundred signore in red coats in hundred vaporetti." He stood up, rumpling the papers on his desk. "And you, signorine," he said, "you wish to make complaint against this person?" He was addressing the active sister.

"Oh no," she said, "no, indeed. I quite see it was all a mistake. Our only wish is to return at once to our pension."

The police officer grunted. Then he pointed at John. "You very lucky man," he said. "These signorine could file complaint against you— very serious matter."

"I'm sure," began John, "I'll do anything in my power...."

"Please don't think of it," exclaimed the sister, horrified. "We would not hear of such a thing." It was her turn to apologise to the police officer. "I hope we need not take up any more of your valuable time," she said.

He waved a hand of dismissal and spoke in Italian to the underling. "This man walk with you to the pension," he said. "*Buona sera,* signorine," and, ignoring John, he sat down again at his desk.

"I'll come with you," said John, "I want to explain exactly what happened."

They trooped down the stairs and out of the building, the blind sister leaning on her twin's arm, and once outside she turned her sightless eyes to John.

"You saw us," she said, "and your wife too. But not today. You saw us in the future."

Her voice was softer than her sister's, slower, she seemed to have some slight impediment in her speech.

"I don't follow," replied John, bewildered.

He turned to the active sister and she shook her head at him, frowning, and put her finger on her lips.

"Come along, dear," she said to her twin. "You know you're very tired, and I want to get you home." Then sotto voce to John, "She's psychic. Your wife told you, I believe, but I don't want her to go into trance here in the street."

God forbid, thought John, and the little procession began to move slowly along the street, away from police headquarters, a canal to the left of them. Progress was slow, because of the blind sister, and there were two bridges. John was completely lost after the first turning, but it couldn't have mattered less. Their police escort was with them, and anyway, the sisters knew where they were going.

"I must explain," said John softly. "My wife would never forgive me if I didn't," and as they walked he went over the whole inexplicable story once again, beginning with the telegram received the night before and the conversation with Mrs. Hill, the decision to return to England the following day, Laura by air, and John himself by car and train. It no longer sounded as dramatic as it had done when he had made his statement to the police officer, when, possibly because of his conviction of something uncanny, the description of the two vaporettos passing one another in the middle of the Grand Canal had held a sinister quality, suggesting abduction on the part of the sisters, the pair of them holding a bewildered Laura captive. Now that neither of the women had any further menace for him he spoke more naturally, yet with great sincerity, feeling for the first time that they were somehow both in sympathy with him and would understand.

"You see," he explained, in a final endeavour to make amends for having gone to the police in the first place, "I truly believed I had seen you with Laura, and I thought . . . ." he hesitated, because this had been the police officer's suggestion and not his, "I thought that perhaps Laura had some sudden loss of memory, had met you at the airport, and you had brought her back to Venice to wherever you were staying."

They had crossed a large square and were approaching a house at one end of it, with a sign, "Pensione," above the door. Their escort paused at the entrance.

"Is this it?" asked John.

"Yes," said the sister. "I know it is nothing much from the outside, but it is clean and comfortable, and was recommended by friends." She turned to the escort. *"Grazie,"* she said to him, *"grazie* tanto."

The man nodded briefly, wished them "Buona notte," and disappeared across the campo.

"Will you come in?" asked the sister. "I am sure we can find you some coffee, or perhaps you prefer tea?"

"No, really," John thanked her, "I must get back to the hotel. I'm making an early start in the morning. I just want to make quite sure you do understand what happened, and that you forgive me."

"There is nothing to forgive," she replied. "It is one of the many examples of second sight that my sister and I have experienced time and time again, and I should very much like to record it for our files, if you will permit it."

"Well as to that, of course," he told her, "but I myself find it hard to understand. It has never happened to me before."

"Not consciously, perhaps," she said, "but so many things happen to us of which we are not aware. My sister felt you had psychic understanding. She told your wife. She also told your wife, last night in the restaurant, that you were to experience trouble, danger, that you should leave Venice. Well, don't you believe now that the telegram was proof of this? Your son was ill, possibly dangerously ill, and so it was necessary for you to return home immediately. Heaven be praised your wife flew home to be by his side."

"Yes, indeed," said John, "but why should I see her on the vaporetto with you and your sister when she was actually on her way to England?"

"Thought transference, perhaps," she answered. "Your wife may have been thinking about us. We gave her our address, should you wish to get in touch with us. We shall be here another ten days. And she knows that we would pass on any message that my sister might have from your little one in the spirit world."

"Yes," said John awkwardly, "yes, I see. It's very good of you." He had a sudden rather unkind picture of the two sisters putting on headphones in their bedroom, listening for a coded message from poor Christine. "Look, this is our address in London," he said. "I know Laura will be pleased to hear from you."

He scribbled their address on a sheet torn from his pocket diary, even, as a bonus thrown in, the telephone number, and handed it to her. He could imagine the outcome. Laura springing it on him one evening that the "old dears" were passing through London on their way to Scotland, and the least they could do was to offer them hospitality, even the spare room for the night. Then a séance in the living room, tambourines appearing out of thin air.

"Well, I must be off," he said. "Good night, and apologies, once again, for all that has happened this evening." He shook hands with the first sister, then turned to her blind twin. "I hope," he said, "that you are not too tired."

The sightless eyes were disconcerting. She held his hand fast and would not let it go. "The child," she said, speaking in an odd staccato voice, "the child . . . I can see the child . . ." and then, to his dismay, a bead of froth appeared at the corner of her mouth, her head jerked back, and she half-collapsed in her sister's arms.

"We must get her inside," said the sister hurriedly. "It's all right, she's not ill, it's the beginning of a trance state."

Between them they helped the twin, who had gone rigid, into the house, and sat her down on the nearest chair, the sister supporting her. A woman came running from some inner room. There was a strong smell of spaghetti from the back regions. "Don't worry," said the sister, "the signorina and I can manage. I think you had better go. Sometimes she is sick after these turns."

"I'm most frightfully sorry . . ." John began, but the sister had already turned her back and, with the signorina, was bending over her twin, from whom peculiar choking sounds were proceeding. He was obviously in the way, and after a final gesture of courtesy, "Is there anything I can do?" which received no reply, he turned on his heel and began walking across the square. He looked back once, and saw they had closed the door.

What a finale to the evening! And all his fault. Poor old girls, first dragged to police headquarters and put through an interrogation, and then a psychic fit on top of it all. More likely epilepsy. Not much of a life for the other sister, but she seemed to take it in her stride. An additional hazard, though, if it happened in a restaurant or in the street. And not particularly welcome under his and Laura's roof should the sisters ever find themselves beneath it, which he prayed would never happen.

Meanwhile, where the devil was he? The square, with the inevitable church at one end, was quite deserted. He could not remember which way they had come from police headquarters, there had seemed to be so many turnings.

Wait a minute, the church itself had a familiar appearance. He drew nearer to it, looking for the name which was sometimes on notices at the entrance. San Giovanni in Bragora, that rang a bell. He and Laura had gone inside one morning to look at a painting by Cima da Co-

negliano. Surely it was only a stone's throw from the Riva degli Schiavoni and the open wide waters of the San Marco lagoon, with all the
bright lights of civilisation and the strolling tourists? He remembered
taking a small turning from the Schiavoni and they had arrived at the
church. Wasn't that the alleyway ahead? He plunged along it, but halfway
down he hesitated. It didn't seem right, although it was familiar for
some unknown reason.

Then he realised that it was not the alley they had taken the morning
they visited the church, but the one they had walked along the previous
evening, only he was approaching it from the opposite direction. Yes,
that was it, in which case it would be quicker to go on and cross the
little bridge over the narrow canal, and he would find the Arsenal on
his left and the street leading down to the Riva degli Schiavoni to his
right. Simpler than retracing his steps and getting lost once more in
the maze of back streets.

He had almost reached the end of the alley, and the bridge was in
sight, when he saw the child. It was the same little girl with the pixie
hood who had leapt between the tethered boats the preceding night
and vanished up the cellar steps of one of the houses. This time she
was running from the direction of the church the other side, making
for the bridge. She was running as if her life depended on it, and in
a moment he saw why. A man was in pursuit, who, when she glanced
backwards for a moment, still running, flattened himself against a wall,
believing himself unobserved. The child came on, scampering across
the bridge, and John, fearful of alarming her further, backed into an
open doorway that led into a small court.

He remembered the drunken yell of the night before which had
come from one of the houses near where the man was hiding now.
This is it, he thought, the fellow's after her again, and with a flash of
intuition he connected the two events, the child's terror then and now,
and the murders reported in the newspapers, supposedly the work of
some madman. It could be coincidence, a child running from a drunken
relative, and yet, and yet . . . . His heart began thumping in his chest,
instinct warning him to run himself, now, at once, back along the alley
the way he had come—but what about the child? What was going to
happen to the child?

Then he heard her running steps. She hurtled through the open
doorway into the court in which he stood, not seeing him, making for

the rear of the house that flanked it, where steps led presumably to a back entrance. She was sobbing as she ran, not the ordinary cry of a frightened child, but the panic-stricken intake of breath of a helpless being in despair. Were there parents in the house who would protect her, whom he could warn? He hesitated a moment, then followed her down the steps and through the door at the bottom, which had burst open at the touch of her hands as she hurled herself against it.

"It's all right," he called. "I won't let him hurt you, it's all right," cursing his lack of Italian, but possibly an English voice might reassure her. But it was no use—she ran sobbing up another flight of stairs, which were spiral, twisting, leading to the floor above, and already it was too late for him to retreat. He could hear sounds of the pursuer in the courtyard behind, someone shouting in Italian, a dog barking. This is it, he thought, we're in it together, the child and I. Unless we can bolt some inner door above he'll get us both

He ran up the stairs after the child, who had darted into a room leading off a small landing, and followed her inside and slammed the door, and, merciful heaven, there was a bolt which he rammed into its socket. The child was crouching by the open window. If he shouted for help someone would surely hear, someone would surely come before the man in pursuit threw himself against the door and it gave, because there was no one but themselves, no parents, the room was bare except for a mattress on an old bed, and a heap of rags in one corner.

"It's all right," he panted, "it's all right," and held out his hand, trying to smile.

The child struggled to her feet and stood before him, the pixie hood falling from her head onto the floor. He stared at her, incredulity turning to horror, to fear. It was not a child at all but a little thick-set woman dwarf, about three feet high, with a great square adult head too big for her body, grey locks hanging shoulder-length, and she wasn't sobbing any more, she was grinning at him, nodding her head up and down.

Then he heard the footsteps on the landing outside and the hammering on the door, and a barking dog, and not one voice but several voices, shouting, "Open up! Police!" The creature fumbled in her sleeve, drawing a knife, and as she threw it at him with hideous strength, piercing his throat, he stumbled and fell, the sticky mess covering his protecting hands.

And he saw the vaporetto with Laura and the two sisters steaming down the Grand Canal, not today, not tomorrow, but the day after that, and he knew why they were together and for what purpose they had come. The creature was gibbering in its corner. The hammering and the voices and the barking dog grew fainter, and, "Oh, God," he thought, "what a bloody silly way to die . . . ."

THE FLY

(1958)

THE FLY
GEORGE LANGELAAN

"Once it was human . . . even as you and I . . . this monster created by atoms gone wild." So read the original advertisement for *The Fly,* one of the most successful films ever in the sci-fi genre. (In the first 3 years of play it made its producers over $3,000,000.) Drawing on the Frankenstein fable of the dangers of science tampering with nature, the story involves a scientist who, through an experimental accident in his matter-transfer device, is rendered a human monster with the head and claw of a housefly. Many critics found the film "ludicrous and revolting" while other more generous reviewers saw it as a technologized version of Franz Kafka's "The Metamorphosis." Regardless of the critical response it received, *The Fly* had immediate mass appeal and contains moments of unforgettable shock value. As with many blockbusters, it was followed by two dreadful sequels and was remade in 1986 (with even greater emphasis on gruesome detail) by Canadian director David Cronenberg. Of note in the film's production credits is the early scriptwork of James Clavell, who later wrote the screenplays for *The Great Escape* (1963) and *To Sir, With Love* (1966) before becoming a best-selling novelist with *Shogun* and *Noble House.*

Born in France in 1910, British writer and journalist GEORGE LANGELAAN was active for many years in the U.S. before returning to Europe. He is the author of several works in French and his one English-language collection, *Out of Time,* was published in 1964.

THE FLY

Released: 1958
Production: Kurt Neumann for Twentieth Century-Fox
Direction: Kurt Neumann
Screenplay: James Clavell
Cinematography: Karl Struss
Special Effects: Lyle B. Abbott
Music: Paul Sawtell
Running Time: 94 minutes

PRINCIPAL CHARACTERS:

André	Al "David" Hedison
Hélène	Patricia Owens
Francois	Vincent Price
Phillipe	Charles Herbert
Inspector Charas	Herbert Marshall
Emma	Kathleen Freeman
Dr. Ejoute	Eugene Borden

Telephones and telephone bells have always made me uneasy. Years ago, when they were mostly wall fixtures, I disliked them, but nowadays, when they are planted in every nook and corner, they are a downright intrusion. We have a saying in France that a coalman is master in his own house; with the telephone that is no longer true, and I suspect that even the Englishman is no longer king in his own castle.

At the office, the sudden ringing of the telephone annoys me. It means that, no matter what I am doing, in spite of the switchboard operator, in spite of my secretary, in spite of doors and walls, some unknown person is coming into the room and on to my desk to talk right into my very ear, confidentially—whether I like it or not. At home,

the feeling is still more disagreeable, but the worst is when the telephone rings in the dead of night. If anyone could see me turn on the
light and get up blinking to answer it, I suppose I would look like any
other sleepy man annoyed at being disturbed. The truth in such a case,
however, is that I am struggling against panic, fighting down a feeling
that a stranger has broken into the house and is in my bedroom. By
the time I manage to grab the receiver and say: *"Ici Monsieur Delambre.
Je vous écoute,"* I am outwardly calm, but I only get back to a more
normal state when I recognize the voice at the other end and when I
know what is wanted of me.

The effort at dominating a purely animal reaction and fear had
become so effective that when my sister-in-law called me at two in the
morning, asking me to come over, but first to warn the police that she
had just killed my brother, I quietly asked her how and why she had
killed André.

"But, François! . . . I can't explain all that over the telephone. Please
call the police and come quickly."

"Maybe I had better see you first, Hélène."

"No, you'd better call the police first; otherwise they will start asking
you all sorts of awkward questions. They'll have enough trouble as it
is to believe that I did it alone. . . . And, by the way, I suppose you ought
to tell them that André . . . André's body is down at the factory. They
may want to go there first."

"Did you say that André is at the factory?"

"Yes . . . under the steam hammer."

"Under the what?"

"The steam hammer! But don't ask so many questions. Please come
quickly, François! Please understand that I'm afraid . . . that my nerves
won't stand it much longer!"

Have you ever tried to explain to a sleepy police officer that your
sister-in-law has just phoned to say that she has killed your brother
with a steam hammer? I tried to repeat my explanation, but he would
not let me.

"Oui, monsieur, oui, I hear . . . but who are you? What is your name?
Where do you live? I said, where do you live!"

It was then that Commissaire Charas took over the line and the
whole business. He at least seemed to understand everything. Would
I wait for him? Yes, he would pick me up and take me over to my
brother's house. When? In five or ten minutes.

I had just managed to pull on my trousers, wriggle into a sweater and grab a hat and coat, when a black Citroen, headlights blazing, pulled up at the door.

"I assume you have a night watchman at your factory, Monsieur Delambre. Has he called you?" asked Commissaire Charas, letting in the clutch as I sat down beside him and slammed the door of the car.

"No, he hasn't. Though of course my brother could have entered the factory through his laboratory where he often works late at night ... all night sometimes."

"Is Professor Delambre's work connected with your business?"

"No, my brother is, or was, doing research work for the Ministère de l'Air. As he wanted to be away from Paris and yet within reach of where skilled workmen could fix up or make gadgets big and small for his experiments, I offered him one of the old workshops of the factory and he came to live in the first house built by our grandfather on the top of the hill at the back of the factory."

"Yes, I see. Did he talk about his work? What sort of research work?"

"He rarely talked about it, you know; I suppose the Air Ministry could tell you. I only know that he was about to carry out a number of experiments he had been preparing for some months, something to do with the disintegration of matter, he told me."

Barely slowing down, the commissaire swung the car off the road, slid it through the open factory gate and pulled up sharp by a policeman apparently expecting him.

I did not need to hear the policeman's confirmation. I knew now that my brother was dead; it seemed that I had been told years ago. Shaking like a leaf, I scrambled out after the commissaire.

Another policeman stepped out of a doorway and led us towards one of the shops where all the lights had been turned on. More policemen were standing by the hammer, watching two men setting up a camera. It was tilted downwards, and I made an effort to look.

It was far less horrid than I had expected. Though I had never seen my brother drunk, he looked just as if he were sleeping off a terrific binge, flat on his stomach across the narrow line on which the white-hot slabs of metal were rolled up to the hammer. I saw at a glance that his head and arm could only be a flattened mess, but that seemed quite impossible; it looked as if he had somehow pushed his head and arm right into the metallic mass of the hammer.

Having talked to his colleagues, the commissaire turned towards me:

"How can we raise the hammer, Monsieur Delambre?"

"I'll raise it for you."

"Would you like us to get one of your men over?"

"No, I'll be all right. Look, here is the switchboard. It was originally a steam hammer, but everything is worked electrically here now. Look, commissaire, the hammer has been set at fifty tons and its impact at zero."

"At zero . . . ?"

"Yes, level with the ground if you prefer. It is also set for single strokes, which means that it has to be raised after each blow. I know what Hélène, my sister-in-law, will have to say about all this, but one thing I am sure of: she certainly did not know how to set and operate the hammer."

"Perhaps it was set that way last night when work stopped?"

"Certainly not. The drop is never set at zero, monsieur le commissaire."

"I see. Can it be raised gently?"

"No. The speed of the upstroke cannot be regulated. But in any case it is not very fast when the hammer is set for single strokes."

"Right. Will you show me what to do? It won't be very nice to watch, you know."

"No, no, monsieur le commissaire. I'll be all right."

"All set?" asked the commissaire of the others. "All right then, Monsieur Delambre. Whenever you like."

Watching my brother's back, I slowly but firmly pushed the upstroke button.

The unusual silence of the factory was broken by the sigh of compressed air rushing into the cylinders, a sigh that always makes me think of a giant taking a deep breath before solemnly socking another giant, and the steel mass of the hammer shuddered and then rose swiftly. I also heard the sucking sound as it left the metal base and thought I was going to panic when I saw André's body heave forward as a sickly gush of blood poured all over the ghastly mess bared by the hammer.

"No danger of it coming down again, Monsieur Delambre?"

"No, none whatever," I mumbled as I threw the safety switch and, turning around, I was violently sick in front of a young green-faced policeman.

For weeks after, Commissaire Charas worked on the case, listening, questioning, running all over the place, making out reports, telegraphing and telephoning right and left. Later, we became quite friendly and he owned up that he had for a long time considered me as suspect number one, but had finally given up that idea because, not only was there no clue of any sort, there was not even a motive.

Hélène, my sister-in-law, was so calm throughout the whole business that the doctors finally confirmed what I had long considered the only possible solution: that she was mad. That being the case, there was of course no trial.

My brother's wife never tried to defend herself in any way and even got quite annoyed when she realized that people thought her mad, and this of course was considered proof that she was indeed mad. She owned up to the murder of her husband and proved easily that she knew how to handle the hammer; but she would never say why, exactly how, or under what circumstances she had killed my brother. The great mystery was how and why had my brother so obligingly stuck his head under the hammer, the only possible explanation for his part in the drama.

The night watchman had heard the hammer all right; he had even heard it twice, he claimed. This was strange, and the stroke counter, which was always set back to nought after a job, seemed to prove him right, since it marked the figure two. Also, the foreman in charge of the hammer confirmed that after cleaning up the day before the murder, he had as usual turned the stroke counter back to nought. In spite of this, Hélène maintained that she had only used the hammer once, and this seemed just another proof of her insanity.

Commissaire Charas, who had been put in charge of the case, at first wondered if the victim were really my brother. But of that there was no possible doubt, if only because of the great scar running from his knee to his thigh, the result of a shell that had landed within a few feet of him during the retreat in 1940; and there were also the fingerprints of his left hand which corresponded to those found all over his laboratory and his personal belongings up at the house.

A guard had been put on his laboratory and the next day half a dozen officials came down from the Air Ministry. They went through all his papers and took away some of his instruments, but before leaving, they told the commissaire that the most interesting documents and instruments had been destroyed.

The Lyons police laboratory, one of the most famous in the world, reported that André's head had been wrapped in a piece of velvet when it was crushed by the hammer, and one day Commissaire Charas showed me a tattered drapery which I immediately recognized as the brown velvet cloth I had seen on a table in my brother's laboratory, the one on which his meals were served when he could not leave his work.

After only a very few days in prison, Hélène had been transferred to a nearby asylum, one of the three in France where insane criminals are taken care of. My nephew Henri, a boy of six, the very image of his father, was entrusted to me, and eventually all legal arrangements were made for me to become his guardian and tutor.

Hélène, one of the quietest patients of the asylum, was allowed visitors and I went to see her on Sundays. Once or twice the commissaire had accompanied me and, later, I learned that he had also visited Hélène alone. But we were never able to obtain any information from my sister-in-law, who seemed to have become utterly indifferent. She rarely answered my questions and hardly ever those of the commissaire. She spent a lot of her time sewing, but her favourite pastime seemed to be catching flies which she invariably released unharmed after having examined them carefully.

Hélène only had one fit of raving— more like a nervous breakdown than a fit, said the doctor who had administered morphia to quieten her—the day she saw a nurse swatting flies.

The day after Hélène's one and only fit, Commissaire Charas came to see me.

"I have a strange feeling that there lies the key to the whole business, Monsieur Delambre," he said.

I did not ask him how it was that he already knew all about Hélène's fit.

"I do not follow you, commissaire. Poor Madame Delambre could have shown an exceptional interest for anything else, really. Don't you think that flies just happen to be the border-subject of her tendency to raving?"

"Do you believe she is really mad?" he asked.

"My dear commissaire, I don't see how there can be any doubt. Do you doubt it?"

"I don't know. In spite of all the doctors say, I have the impression that Madame Delambre has a very clear brain . . . even when catching flies."

"Supposing you were right, how would you explain her attitude with regard to her little boy? She never seems to consider him as her own child."

"You know, Monsieur Delambre, I have thought about that also. She may be trying to protect him. Perhaps she fears the boy or, for all we know, hates him?"

"I'm afraid I don't understand, my dear commissaire."

"Have you noticed, for instance, that she never catches flies when the boy is there?"

"No. But come to think of it, you are quite right. Yes, that is strange . . . . Still, I fail to understand."

"So do I, Monsieur Delambre. And I'm very much afraid that we shall never understand, unless perhaps your sister-in-law should *get better*."

"The doctors seem to think that there is no hope of any sort, you know."

"Yes. Do you know if your brother ever experimented with flies?"

"I really don't know, but I should think so. Have you asked the Air Ministry people? They knew all about the work."

"Yes, and they laughed at me."

"I can understand that."

"You are very fortunate to understand anything, Monsieur Delambre. I do not . . . but I hope to someday."

"Tell me, Uncle, do flies live a long time?"

We were just finishing our lunch and, following an established tradition between us, I was just pouring some wine into Henri's glass for him to dip a biscuit in.

Had Henri not been staring at his glass gradually being filled to the brim, something in my look might have frightened him.

This was the first time that he had ever mentioned flies, and I shuddered at the thought that Commissaire Charas might quite easily have been present. I could imagine the glint in his eye as he would have answered my nephew's question with another question. I could almost hear him saying:

"I don't know, Henri. Why do you ask?"

"Because I have again seen the fly that Maman was looking for."

And it was only after drinking off Henri's own glass of wine that I realized that he had answered my spoken thought.

"I did not know that your mother was looking for a fly."

"Yes, she was. It has grown quite a lot, but I recognized it all right."

"Where did you see this fly, Henri, and . . . how did you recognize it?"

"This morning on your desk, Uncle François. Its head is white instead of black, and it has a funny sort of leg."

Feeling more and more like Commissaire Charas, but trying to look unconcerned, I went on:

"And when did you see this fly for the first time?"

"The day that Papa went away. I had caught it, but Maman made me let it go. And then after, she wanted me to find it again. She'd changed her mind," and shrugging his shoulders just as my brother used to, he added, "you know how women are."

"I think that fly must have died long ago, and you must be mistaken, Henri," I said, getting up and walking to the door.

But as soon as I was out of the dining room, I ran up the stairs to my study. There was no fly anywhere to be seen.

I was bothered, far more than I cared to even think about. Henri had just proved that Charas was really closer to a clue than it had seemed when he told me about his thoughts concerning Hélène's pastime.

For the first time I wondered if Charas did not really know much more than he let on. For the first time also, I wondered about Hélène. Was she really insane? A strange horrid feeling was growing on me, and the more I thought about it, the more I felt that, somehow, Charas was right: Hélène was *getting away with it!*

What could possibly have been the reason for such a monstrous crime? What had led up to it? Just what had happened?

I thought of all the hundreds of questions that Charas had put to Hélène, sometimes gently like a nurse trying to soothe, sometimes stern and cold, sometimes barking them furiously. Hélène had answered very few, always in a calm quiet voice and never seeming to pay any attention to the way in which the question had been put. Though dazed, she had seemed perfectly sane then.

Refined, well-bred, and well-read, Charas was more than just an intelligent police official. He was a keen psychologist and had an amazing

way of smelling out a fib or an erroneous statement even before it was
uttered. I knew that he had accepted as true the few answers she had
given him. But then there had been all those questions which she had
never answered: the most direct and important ones. From the very
beginning, Hélène had adopted a very simple system. "I cannot answer
that question," she would say in her low, quiet voice. And that was
that! The repetition of the same question never seemed to annoy her.
In all the hours of questioning that she underwent, Hélène did not
once point out to the commissaire that he had already asked her this
or that. She would simply say, "I cannot answer that question," as
though it was the very first time that that particular question had been
asked and the very first time she had made that answer.

This cliché had become the formidable barrier beyond which Commissaire Charas could not even get a glimpse, an idea of what Hélène
might be thinking. She had very willingly answered all questions about
her life with my brother—which seemed a happy and uneventful one—
up to the time of his end. About his death, however, all that she would
say was that she had killed him with the steam hammer, but she refused
to say why, what had led up to the drama and how she got my brother
to put his head under it. She never actually refused outright; she would
just go blank and, with no apparent emotion, would switch over to, "I
cannot answer that question."

Hélène, as I have said, had shown the commissaire that she knew
how to set and operate the steam hammer.

Charas could only find one single fact which did not coincide with
Hélène's declarations, the fact that the hammer had been used twice.
Charas was no longer willing to attribute this to insanity. That evident
flaw in Hélène's stonewall defence seemed a crack which the commissaire might possibly enlarge. But my sister-in-law finally cemented
it by acknowledging:

"All right, I lied to you. I did use the hammer twice. But do not ask
me why, because I cannot tell you."

"Is that your only . . . misstatement, Madame Delambre?" the commissaire had asked. Trying to follow up what looked at last like an
advantage.

"It is . . . and you know it, monsieur le commissaire."

And, annoyed, Charas had seen that Hélène could read him like an
open book.

I had thought of calling on the commissaire, but the knowledge that he would inevitably start questioning Henri made me hesitate. Another reason also made me hesitate, a vague sort of fear that he would look for and find the fly Henri had talked of. And that annoyed me a good deal because I could find no satisfactory explanation for that particular fear.

André was definitely not the absent-minded sort of professor who walks about in pouring rain with a rolled umbrella under his arm. He was human, had a keen sense of humour, loved children and animals, and could not bear to see anyone suffer. I had often seen him drop his work to watch a parade of the local fire brigade, or see the Tour de France cyclists go by, or even follow a circus parade all around the village. He liked games of logic and precision, such as billiards and tennis, bridge and chess.

How was it then possible to explain his death? What could have made him put his head under that hammer? It could hardly have been the result of some stupid bet or a test of his courage. He hated betting and had no patience with those who indulged in it. Whenever he heard a bet proposed, he would invariably remind all present that, after all, a bet was but a contract between a fool and a swindler, even if it turned out to be a toss-up as to which was which.

It seemed there were only two possible explanations for André's death. Either he had gone mad, or else he had a reason for letting his wife kill him in such a strange and terrible way. And just what could have been his wife's role in all this? They surely could not have been both insane?

Having finally decided not to tell Charas about my nephew's innocent revelations, I thought I myself would try to question Hélène.

She seemed to have been expecting my visit, for she came into the parlour almost as soon as I had made myself known to the matron and been allowed inside.

"I wanted to show you my garden," explained Hélène as I looked at the coat slung over her shoulders.

As one of the "reasonable" inmates, she was allowed to go into the garden during certain hours of the day. She had asked for and obtained the right to a little patch of ground where she could grow flowers, and I had sent her seeds and some rosebushes out of my garden.

She took me straight to a rustic wooden bench which had been made in the men's workshop and only just set up under a tree close to her little patch of ground.

Searching for the right way to broach the subject of André's death, I sat for a while tracing vague designs on the ground with the end of my umbrella.

"François, I want to ask you something," said Hélène after a while.

"Anything I can do for you, Hélène?"

"No, just something I want to know. Do flies live very long?"

Staring at her, I was about to say that her boy had asked the very same question a few hours earlier when I suddenly realized that here was the opening I had been searching for and perhaps even the possibility of striking a great blow, a blow perhaps powerful enough to shatter her stonewall defence, be it sane or insane.

Watching her carefully, I replied:

"I don't really know, Hélène; but the fly you were looking for was in my study this morning."

No doubt about it, I had struck a shattering blow. She swung her head round with such force that I heard the bones crack in her neck. She opened her mouth, but said not a word; only her eyes seemed to be screaming with fear.

Yes, it was evident that I had crashed through something, but what? Undoubtedly, the commissaire would have known what to do with such an advantage; I did not. All I knew was that he would never have given her time to think, to recuperate, but all I could do, and even that was a strain, was to maintain my best poker face, hoping against hope that Hélène's defences would go on crumbling.

She must have gone quite a while without breathing, because she suddenly gasped and put both her hands over her still open mouth.

"François. . . . Did you kill it?" she whispered, her eyes no longer fixed, but searching every inch of my face.

"No."

"You have it then . . . . You have it on you! Give it to me!" she almost shouted, touching me with both her hands, and I knew that had she felt strong enough, she would have tried to search me.

"No, Hélène, I haven't got it."

"But you know now . . . . You have guessed, haven't you?"

"No, Hélène. I only know one thing, and that is that you are not insane. But I mean to know all, Hélène, and somehow I am going to find out. You can choose: either you tell me everything and I'll see what is to be done, or . . ."

"Or what? Say! Say it!"

"I was going to say it, Hélène ... or I assure you that your friend the commissaire will have that fly first thing tomorrow morning."

She remained quite still, looking down at the palms of her hands on her lap and although it was getting chilly, her forehead and hands were moist.

Without even brushing aside a wisp of long brown hair blown across her mouth by the breeze, she murmured:

"If I tell you ... will you promise to destroy that fly before doing anything else?"

"No, Hélène. I can make no such promise before knowing."

"But François, you must understand. I promised André that fly would be destroyed. That promise must be kept and I can say nothing until it is."

I could sense the deadlock ahead. I was not yet losing ground, but I was losing the initiative. I tried a shot in the dark:

"Hélène, of course you understand that as soon as the police examine that fly, they will know that you are not insane, and then ..."

"François, no! For Henri's sake! Don't you see? I was expecting that fly; I was hoping it would find me here but it couldn't know what had become of me. What else could it do but go to others it loves, to Henri, to you ... you who might know and understand what was to be done!"

Was she really mad, or was she simulating again? But mad or not, she was cornered. Wondering how to follow up and how to land the knockout blow without running the risk of seeing her slip away out of reach, I said very quietly:

"Tell me all, Hélène. I can then protect your boy."

"Protect my boy from what? Don't you understand that if I am here, it is merely so that Henri won't be the son of a woman who was guillotined for having murdered his father? Don't you understand that I would by far prefer the guillotine to the living death of this lunatic asylum?"

"I understand, Hélène, and I'll do my best for the boy whether you tell me or not. If you refuse to tell me, I'll still do the best I can to protect Henri, but you must understand that the game will be out of my hands, because Commissaire Charas will have the fly."

"But why must you know?" said, rather than asked, my sister-in-law, struggling to control her temper.

"Because I must and will know how and why my brother died, Hélène."

"All right. Take me back to the . . . house. I'll give you what your commissaire would call my 'confession.' "

"Do you mean to say that you have written it!"

"Yes. It was not really meant for you, but more likely for *your friend,* the commissaire. I had foreseen that, sooner or later, he would get too close to the truth."

"You then have no objection to his reading it?"

"You will act as you think fit, François. Wait for me a minute."

Leaving me at the door of the parlour, Hélène ran upstairs to her room. In less than a minute she was back with a large brown envelope.

"Listen, François; you are not nearly as bright as was your poor brother, but you are not unintelligent. All I ask is that you read this alone. After that, you may do as you wish."

"That I promise you, Hélène," I said, taking the precious envelope. "I'll read it tonight and although tomorrow is not a visiting day, I'll come down to see you."

"Just as you like," said my sister-in-law without even saying goodbye as she went back upstairs.

It was only on reaching home, as I walked from the garage to the house, that I read the inscription on the envelope:

TO WHOM IT MAY CONCERN
(Probably Commissaire Charas)

Having told the servants that I would have only a light supper, to be served immediately in my study, and that I was not to be disturbed after, I ran upstairs, threw Hélène's envelope on my desk and made another careful search of the room before closing the shutters and drawing the curtains. All I could find was a long-since-dead mosquito stuck to the wall near the ceiling.

Having motioned to the servant to put her tray down on a table by the fireplace, I poured myself a glass of wine and locked the door behind her. I then disconnected the telephone—I always did this now at night—and turned out all the lights but the lamp on my desk.

Slitting open Hélène's fat envelope, I extracted a thick wad of closely written pages. I read the following lines neatly centered in the middle of the top page:

This is not a confession because, although I killed my husband, I am not a murderess. I simply and very faithfully carried out his last wish by crushing his head and right arm under the steam hammer at his brother's factory.

Without even touching the glass of wine by my elbow, I turned the page and started reading.

For very nearly a year before his death *(the manuscript began),* my husband had told me of some of his experiments. He knew full well that his colleagues of the Air Ministry would have forbidden some of them as too dangerous, but he was keen on obtaining positive results before reporting his discovery.

Whereas only sound and pictures had been, so far, transmitted through space by radio and television, André claimed to have discovered a way of transmitting matter. Matter, any solid object, placed in his "transmitter" was instantly disintegrated and reintegrated in a special receiving set.

André considered his discovery as perhaps the most important since that of the wheel sawn off the end of a tree trunk. He reckoned that the transmission of matter by instantaneous "disintegration-reintegration" would completely change life as we had known it so far. It would mean the end of all means of transport, not only of goods including food, but also of human beings. André, the practical scientist who never allowed theories or daydreams to get the better of him, already foresaw the time when there would no longer be any aeroplanes, ships, trains, or cars and, therefore, no longer any roads or railway lines, ports, airports, or stations. All that would be replaced by matter transmitting-and receiving-stations throughout the world. Travellers and goods would be placed in special cabins and, at a given signal, would simply disappear and reappear almost immediately at the chosen receiving station.

André's receiving set was only a few feet away from his transmitter, in an adjoining room of his laboratory, and he at first ran into all sorts of snags. His first successful experiment was carried out with an ashtray taken from his desk, a souvenir we had brought back from a trip to London.

That was the first time he told me about his experiments and I had no idea of what he was talking about the day he came dashing into the house and threw the ashtray in my lap.

"Hélène, look! For a fraction of a second, a bare ten-millionth of a second, that ashtray has been completely disintegrated. For one little moment it no longer existed! Gone! Nothing left, absolutely nothing! Only atoms travelling through space at the speed of light! And the moment after, the atoms were once more gathered together in the shape of an ashtray!"

"André, please . . . please! What on earth are you raving about?"

He started sketching all over a letter I had been writing. He laughed at my wry face, swept all my letters off the table and said:

"You don't understand? Right? Let's start all over again. Hélène, do you remember I once read you an article about the mysterious flying stones that seem to come from nowhere in particular, and which are said occasionally to fall in certain houses in India? They come flying in as though thrown from outside, in spite of closed doors and windows."

"Yes, I remember. I also remember that Professor Augier, your friend of the Collège de France, who had come down for a few days, remarked that if there was no trickery about it, the only possible explanation was that the stones had been disintegrated after having been thrown from outside, come through the walls, and then been reintegrated before hitting the floor or the opposite walls."

"That's right. And I added that there was, of course, one other possibility, namely the momentary and partial disintegration of the walls as the stone or stones came through."

"Yes, André. I remember all that, and I suppose you also remember that I failed to understand, and that you got quite annoyed. Well, I still do not understand why and how, even disintegrated, stones should be able to come through a wall or a closed door."

"But it is possible, Hélène, because the atoms that make up matter are not close together like the bricks of a wall. They are separated by relative immensities of space."

"Do you mean to say that you have disintegrated that ashtray and then put it together again after pushing it through something?"

"Precisely, Hélène. I projected it through the wall that separates my transmitter from my receiving set."

"And would it be foolish to ask how humanity is to benefit from ashtrays that can go through walls?"

André seemed quite offended, but he soon saw that I was only teasing and again waxing enthusiastic, he told me of some of the possibilities of his discovery.

"Isn't it wonderful, Hélène?" he finally gasped, out of breath.

"Yes, André. But I hope you won't ever transmit me; I'd be too much afraid of coming out at the other end like your ashtray."

"What do you mean?"

"Do you remember what was written under that ashtray?"

"Yes, of course: Made in Japan. That was the great joke of our typically British souvenir."

"The words are still there André; but . . . look!"

He took the ashtray out of my hands, frowned, and walked over to the window. Then he went quite pale, and I knew that he had seen what had proved to me that he had indeed carried out a strange experiment.

The three words were still there, but reversed and reading:

nɒqɒႱ ni ɘbɒM

Without a word, having completely forgotten me, André rushed off to his laboratory. I only saw him the next morning, tired and unshaven after a whole night's work.

A few days later, André had a new reverse which put him out of sorts and made him fussy and grumpy for several weeks. I stood it patiently enough for a while, but being myself bad-tempered one evening, we had a silly row over some futile thing, and I reproached him for his moroseness.

"I'm sorry, *chérie*. I've been working my way through a maze of problems and have given you all a very rough time. You see, my very first experiment with a live animal proved a complete fiasco."

"André! You tried that experiment with Dandelo, didn't you?"

"Yes. How did you know?" he answered sheepishly. "He disintegrated perfectly, but he never reappeared in the receiving set."

"Oh, André! What became of him then?"

"Nothing . . . there is just no more Dandelo; only the dispersed atoms of a cat wandering, God knows where, in the universe."

Dandelo was a small white cat the cook had found one morning in the garden and which we had promptly adopted. Now I knew how it had disappeared and was quite angry about the whole thing, but my husband was so miserable over it all that I said nothing.

I saw little of my husband during the next few weeks. He had most of his meals sent down to the laboratory. I would often wake up in the morning and find his bed unslept in. Sometimes, if he had come in very late, I would find that storm-swept appearance which only a man can give a bedroom by getting up very early and fumbling around in the dark.

One evening he came home to dinner all smiles, and I knew that his troubles were over. His face dropped, however, when he saw I was dressed for going out.

"Oh. Were you going out, Hélène?"

"Yes, the Drillons invited me for a game of bridge, but I can easily phone them and put it off."

"No, it's all right."

"It isn't all right. Out with it, dear!"

"Well, I've at last got everything perfect and I wanted you to be the first to see the miracle."

"*Magnifique,* André! Of course I'll be delighted."

Having telephoned our neighbours to say how sorry I was and so forth, I ran down to the kitchen and told the cook that she had exactly ten minutes in which to prepare a "celebration dinner."

"An excellent idea, Hélène," said my husband when the maid appeared with the champagne after our candlelight dinner. "We'll celebrate with reintegrated champagne!" and taking the tray from the maid's hands, he led the way down to the laboratory.

"Do you think it will be as good as before its disintegration?" I asked, holding the tray while he opened the door and switched on the lights.

"Have no fear. You'll see! Just bring it here, will you," he said, opening the door of a telephone call box he had bought and which had been transformed into what he called a transmitter. "Put it down on that now," he added, putting a stool inside the box.

Having carefully closed the door, he took me to the other end of the room and handed me a pair of very dark sunglasses. He put on another pair and walked back to a switchboard by the transmitter.

"Ready, Hélène?" said my husband, turning out all the lights. "Don't remove your glasses till I give the word."

"I won't budge, André, go on," I told him, my eyes fixed on the tray which I could just see in a greenish shimmering light through the glass-panelled door of the telephone booth.

"Right," said André, throwing a switch.

The whole room was brilliantly illuminated by an orange flash. Inside the cabin I had seen a crackling ball of fire and felt its heat on my face, neck, and hands. The whole thing lasted but a fraction of a second, and I found myself blinking at green-edged black holes like those one sees after having stared at the sun.

"*Et voilà!* You can take off your glasses, Hélène."

A little theatrically perhaps, my husband opened the door of the cabin. Though André had told me what to expect, I was astonished to find that the champagne, glasses, tray, and stool were no longer there.

André ceremoniously led me by the hand into the next room in a corner of which stood a second telephone booth. Opening the door wide, he triumphantly lifted the champagne tray off the stool.

Feeling somewhat like the good-natured kind-member-of-the-audience that has been dragged onto the music hall stage by the magician, I repressed from saying, "All done with mirrors," which I knew would have annoyed my husband.

"Sure it's not dangerous to drink?" I asked as the cork popped.

"Absolutely sure, Hélène," he said, handing me a glass. "But that was nothing. Drink this off and I'll show you something much more astounding."

We went back into the other room.

"Oh, André! Remember poor Dandelo!"

"This is only a guinea pig, Hélène. But I'm positive it will go through all right."

He set the furry little beast down on the green enamelled floor of the booth and quickly closed the door. I again put on my dark glasses and saw and felt the vivid crackling flash.

Without waiting for André to open the door, I rushed into the next room where the lights were still on and looked into the receiving booth.

"Oh, André! *Chéri!* He's there all right!" I shouted excitedly, watching the little animal trotting round and round. "It's wonderful, André. It works! You've succeeded!"

"I hope so, but I must be patient. I'll know for sure in a few weeks' time."

"What do you mean? Look! He's as full of life as when you put him in the other cabin."

"Yes, so he seems. But we'll have to see if all his organs are intact, and that will take some time. If that little beast is still full of life in a month's time, we then consider the experiment a success."

I begged André to let me take care of the guinea pig.

"All right, but don't kill it by overfeeding," he agreed with a grin for my enthusiasm.

Though not allowed to take Hop-la—the name I had given the guinea pig—out of its box in the laboratory, I had tied a pink ribbon round its neck and was allowed to feed it twice a day.

Hop-la soon got used to its pink ribbon and became quite a tame little pet, but that month of waiting seemed a year.

And then one day, André put Miquette, our cocker spaniel, into his "transmitter." He had not told me beforehand, knowing full well that I would never have agreed to such an experiment with our dog. But when he did tell me, Miquette had been successfully transmitted half-a-dozen times and seemed to be enjoying the operation thoroughly; no sooner was she let out of the "reintegrator" than she dashed madly into the next room, scratching at the "transmitter" door to have "another go," as André called it.

I now expected that my husband would invite some of his colleagues and Air Minisitry specialists to come down. He usually did this when he had finished a research job and, before handing them long detailed reports which he always typed himself, he would carry out an experiment or two before them. But this time, he just went on working. One morning I finally asked him when he intended throwing his usual "surprise party," as we called it.

"No, Hélène; not for a long while yet. This discovery is much too important. I have an awful lot of work to do on it still. Do you realize that there are some parts of the transmission proper which I do not yet myself fully understand? It works all right, but you see, I can't just say to all these eminent professors that I do this and that and, poof, it works! I must be able to explain how and why it works. And what is even more important, I must be ready and able to refute every destructive argument they will not fail to trot out, as they usually do when faced with anything really good."

I was occasionally invited down to the laboratory to witness some new experiment, but I never went unless André invited me, and only talked about his work if he broached the subject first. Of course it never occurred to me that he would, at that stage at least, have tried an experiment with a human being; though, had I thought about it—

knowing André—it would have been obvious that he would never have allowed anyone into the "transmitter" before he had been through to test it first. It was only after the accident that I discovered he had duplicated all his switches inside the disintegration booth, so that he could try it out by himself.

The morning André tried this terrible experiment, he did not show up for lunch. I sent the maid down with a tray, but she brought it back with a note she had found pinned outside the laboratory door: "Do not disturb me, I am working."

He did occasionally pin such notes on his door and, though I noticed it, I paid no particular attention to the unusually large handwriting of his note.

It was just after that, as I was drinking my coffee, that Henri came bouncing into the room to say that he had caught a funny fly, and would I like to see it. Refusing even to look at his closed fist, I ordered him to release it immediately.

"But, Maman, it has such a funny white head!"

Marching the boy over to the open window, I told him to release the fly immediately, which he did. I knew that Henri had caught the fly merely because he thought it looked curious or different from other flies, but I also knew that his father would never stand for any form of cruelty to animals, and that there would be a fuss should he discover that our son had put a fly in a box or a bottle.

At dinnertime that evening, André had still not shown up and, a little worried, I ran down to the laboratory and knocked at the door.

He did not answer my knock, but I heard him moving around and a moment later he slipped a note under the door. It was typewritten:

HÉLÈNE, I AM HAVING TROUBLE. PUT THE BOY TO BED AND COME BACK IN AN HOUR'S TIME. A.

Frightened, I knocked and called, but André did not seem to pay any attention and, vaguely reassured by the familiar noise of his type-writer, I went back to the house.

Having put Henri to bed, I returned to the laboratory where I found another note slipped under the door. My hand shook as I picked it up because I knew by then that something must be radically wrong. I read:

HÉLÈNE, FIRST OF ALL I COUNT ON YOU NOT TO LOSE YOUR NERVE OR DO
ANYTHING RASH BECAUSE YOU ALONE CAN HELP ME. I HAVE HAD A SERIOUS AC-
CIDENT. I AM NOT IN ANY PARTICULAR DANGER FOR THE TIME BEING THOUGH IT
IS A MATTER OF LIFE AND DEATH. IT IS USELESS CALLING TO ME OR SAYING ANY-
THING. I CANNOT ANSWER, I CANNOT SPEAK. I WANT YOU TO DO EXACTLY AND
VERY CAREFULLY ALL THAT I ASK. AFTER HAVING KNOCKED THREE TIMES TO SHOW
THAT YOU UNDERSTAND AND AGREE, FETCH ME A BOWL OF MILK LACED WITH RUM.
I HAVE HAD NOTHING ALL DAY AND CAN DO WITH IT.

Shaking with fear, not knowing what to think and repressing a furious
desire to call André and bang away until he opened the door, I knocked
three times as requested and ran all the way home to fetch what he
wanted.

In less than five minutes I was back. Another note had been slipped
under the door:

HÉLÈNE, FOLLOW THESE INSTRUCTIONS CAREFULLY. WHEN YOU KNOCK I'LL
OPEN THE DOOR. YOU ARE TO WALK OVER TO MY DESK AND PUT DOWN THE BOWL
OF MILK. YOU WILL THEN GO INTO THE OTHER ROOM WHERE THE RECEIVER IS.
LOOK CAREFULLY AND TRY TO FIND A FLY WHICH OUGHT TO BE THERE BUT WHICH
I AM UNABLE TO FIND. UNFORTUNATELY I CANNOT SEE SMALL THINGS VERY EASILY.

BEFORE YOU COME IN YOU MUST PROMISE TO OBEY ME IMPLICITY. DO NOT
LOOK AT ME AND REMEMBER THAT TALKING IS QUITE USELESS. I CANNOT ANSWER.
KNOCK AGAIN THREE TIMES AND THAT WILL MEAN I HAVE YOUR PROMISE. MY LIFE
DEPENDS ENTIRELY ON THE HELP YOU CAN GIVE ME.

I had to wait a while to pull myself together, and then I knocked
slowly three times.

I heard André shuffling behind the door, then his hand fumbling
with the lock, and the door opened.

Out of the corner of my eye, I saw that he was standing behind the
door, but without looking round, I carried the bowl of milk to his
desk. He was evidently watching me and I had to at all costs appear
calm and collected.

"*Chéri,* you can count on me," I said gently, and putting the bowl
down under his desk lamp, the only one alight, I walked into the next
room where all the lights were blazing.

My first impression was that some sort of hurricane must have blown
out of the receiving booth. Papers were scattered in every direction,

a whole row of test tubes lay smashed in a corner, chairs and stools were upset and one of the window curtains hung half torn from its bent rod. In a large enamel basin on the floor a heap of burned documents was still smouldering.

I knew that I would not find the fly André wanted me to look for. Women know things that men only suppose by reasoning and deduction; it is a form of knowledge very rarely accessible to them and which they disparagingly call intuition. I already knew that the fly André wanted was the one which Henri had caught and which I had made him release.

I heard André shuffling around in the next room, and then a strange gurgling and sucking as though he had trouble in drinking his milk.

"André, there is no fly here. Can you give me any sort of indication that might help? If you can't speak, rap or something . . . you know: once for yes, twice for no."

I had tried to control my voice and speak as though perfectly calm, but I had to choke down a sob of desperation when he rapped twice for "no."

"May I come to you, André? I don't know what can have happened, but whatever it is, I'll be courageous, dear."

After a moment of silent hesitation, he tapped once on his desk.

At the door I stopped aghast at the sight of André standing with his head and shoulders covered by the brown velvet cloth he had taken from a table by his desk, the table on which he usually ate when he did not want to leave his work. Suppressing a laugh that might easily have turned to sobbing, I said:

"André, we'll search thoroughly tomorrow, by daylight. Why don't you go to bed? I'll lead you to the guest room if you like, and won't let anyone else see you."

His left hand tapped the desk twice.

"Do you need a doctor, André?"

"No," he rapped.

"Would you like to call up Professor Augier? He might be of more help . . . ."

Twice he rapped "no" sharply. I did not know what to do or say. And then I told him:

"Henri caught a fly this morning which he wanted to show me, but I made him release it. Could it have been the one you are looking for? I didn't see it, but the boy said its head was white."

André emitted a strange metallic sigh, and I just had time to bite my fingers fiercely in order not to scream. He had let his right arm drop, and instead of his long-fingered muscular hand, a gray stick with little buds on it like the branch of a tree hung out of his sleeve almost down to his knee.

"André, *mon chéri,* tell me what happened. I might be of more help to you if I knew, André . . . oh, it's terrible!" I sobbed, unable to control myself.

Having rapped once for yes, he pointed to the door with his left hand.

I stepped out and sank down crying as he locked the door behind me. He was typing again and I waited. At last he shuffled to the door and slid a sheet of paper under it.

HÉLÈNE, COME BACK IN THE MORNING. I MUST THINK AND WILL HAVE TYPED OUT AN EXPLANATION FOR YOU. TAKE ONE OF MY SLEEPING TABLETS AND GO STRAIGHT TO BED. I NEED YOU FRESH AND STRONG TOMORROW, MA PAUVRE CHÉRIE. A.

"Do you want anything for the night, André?" I shouted through the door.

He knocked twice for no, and a little later I heard the typewriter again.

The sun full on my face woke me up with a start. I had set the alarm clock for five but had not heard it, probably because of the sleeping tablets. I had indeed slept like a log, without a dream. Now I was back in my living nightmare and crying like a child I sprang out of bed. It was just on seven!

Rushing into the kitchen, without a word for the startled servants, I rapidly prepared a trayload of coffee, bread, and butter with which I ran down to the laboratory.

André opened the door as soon as I knocked and closed it again as I carried the tray to his desk. His head was still covered, but I saw from his crumpled suit and his open camp bed that he must have at least tried to rest.

On his desk lay a typewritten sheet for me which I picked up. André opened the other door, and taking this to mean that he wanted to be left alone, I walked into the next room. He pushed the door to, and I heard him pouring out the coffee as I read:

DO YOU REMEMBER THE ASHTRAY EXPERIMENT? I HAVE HAD A SIMILAR ACCI-
DENT. I TRANSMITTED MYSELF SUCCESSFULLY THE NIGHT BEFORE LAST. DURING A
SECOND EXPERIMENT YESTERDAY A FLY WHICH I DID NOT SEE MUST HAVE GOT
INTO THE DISINTEGRATOR. MY ONLY HOPE IS TO FIND THAT FLY AND GO THROUGH
AGAIN WITH IT. PLEASE SEARCH FOR IT CAREFULLY SINCE, IF IT IS NOT FOUND, I
SHALL HAVE TO FIND A WAY OF PUTTING AN END TO ALL THIS.

If only André had been more explicit! I shuddered at the thought
that he must be terribly disfigured and then cried softly as I imagined
his face inside-out, or perhaps his eyes in place of his ears, or his
mouth at the back of his neck, or worse!

André must be saved! For that, the fly must be found!

Pulling myself together, I said:

"André, may I come in?"

He opened the door.

"André, don't despair; I am going to find that fly. It is no longer in
the laboratory, but it cannot be very far. I suppose you're disfigured,
perhaps terribly so, but there can be no question of putting an end to
all this, as you say in your note; that I will never stand for. If necessary,
if you do not wish to be seen, I'll make you a mask or a cowl so that
you can go on with your work until you get well again. If you cannot
work, I'll call Professor Augier, and he and all your other friends will
save you, André."

Again I heard that curious metallic sigh as he rapped violently on
his desk.

"André, don't be annoyed; please be calm. I won't do anything
without first consulting you, but you must rely on me, have faith in me
and let me help you as best I can. Are you terribly disfigured, dear?
Can't you let me see your face? I won't be afraid . . . . I am your wife
you know."

But my husband again rapped a decisive "no" and pointed to the
door.

"All right. I am going to search for the fly now, but promise me
you won't do anything foolish; promise you won't do anything rash or
dangerous without first letting me know all about it!"

He extended his left hand, and I knew I had his promise.

I will never forget that ceaseless daylong hunt for a fly. Back home,
I turned the house inside out and made all the servants join in the
search. I told them that a fly had escaped from the Professor's laboratory

and that it must be captured alive, but it was evident they already thought me crazy. They said so to the police later, and that day's hunt for a fly most probably saved me from the guillotine later.

I questioned Henri, and as he failed to understand right away what I was talking about, I shook him and slapped him and made him cry in front of the round-eyed maids. Realizing that I must not let myself go, I kissed and petted the poor boy and at last made him understand what I wanted of him. Yes, he remembered, he had found the fly just by the kitchen window; yes, he had released it immediately as told to.

Even in summertime we had very few flies because our house is on the top of a hill and the slightest breeze coming across the valley blows round it. In spite of that, I managed to catch dozens of flies that day. On all the window sills and all over the garden I had put saucers of milk, sugar, jam, meat—all the things likely to attract flies. Of all those we caught, and many others which we failed to catch but which I saw, none resembled the one Henri had caught the day before. One by one, with a magnifying glass, I examined every unusual fly, but none had anything like a white head.

At lunchtime, I ran down to André with some milk and mashed potatoes. I also took some of the flies we had caught, but he gave me to understand that they could be of no possible use to him.

"If that fly has not been found by tonight, André, we'll have to see what is to be done. And this is what I propose: I'll sit in the next room. When you can't answer by the yes-no method of rapping, you'll type out whatever you want to say and then slip it under the door. Agreed?"

"Yes," rapped André.

By nightfall we had still not found the fly. At dinnertime, as I prepared André's tray, I broke down and sobbed in the kitchen in front of the silent servants. My maid thought that I had had a row with my husband, probably about the mislaid fly, but I learned later that the cook was already quite sure that I was out of my mind.

Without a word, I picked up the tray and then put it down again as I stopped by the telephone. That this was really a matter of life and death for André, I had no doubt. Neither did I doubt that he fully intended committing suicide, unless I could make him change his mind, or at least put off such a drastic decision. Would I be strong enough? He would never forgive me for not keeping a promise, but under the circumstances, did that really matter? To the devil with promises and honour! At all costs André must be saved! And having thus made up my mind, I looked up and dialled Professor Augier's number.

"The professor is away and will not be back before the end of the week," said a polite neutral voice at the other end of the line.

That was that! I would have to fight alone and fight I would. I would save André come what may.

All my nervousness had disappeared as André let me in and, after putting the tray of food down on his desk, I went into the other room, as agreed.

"The first thing I want to know," I said as he closed the door behind me, "is what happened exactly. Can you please tell me, André?"

I waited patiently while he typed an answer which he pushed under the door a little later.

HÉLÈNE, I WOULD RATHER NOT TELL YOU. SINCE GO I MUST, I WOULD RATHER YOU REMEMBER ME AS I WAS BEFORE. I MUST DESTROY MYSELF IN SUCH A WAY THAT NONE CAN POSSIBLY KNOW WHAT HAS HAPPENED TO ME. I HAVE OF COURSE THOUGHT OF SIMPLY DISINTEGRATING MYSELF IN MY TRANSMITTER, BUT I HAD BETTER NOT BECAUSE, SOONER OR LATER, I MIGHT FIND MYSELF REINTEGRATED. SOMEDAY, SOMEWHERE, SOME SCIENTIST IS SURE TO MAKE THE SAME DISCOVERY. I HAVE THEREFORE THOUGHT OF A WAY WHICH IS NEITHER SIMPLE NOR EASY, BUT YOU CAN AND WILL HELP ME.

For several minutes I wondered if André had not simply gone stark raving mad.

"André," I said at last, "whatever you may have chosen or thought of, I cannot and will never accept such a cowardly solution. No matter how awful the result of your experiment or accident, you are alive, you are a man, a brain . . . and you have a soul. You have no right to destroy yourself. You know that!"

The answer was soon typed and pushed under the door.

I AM ALIVE ALL RIGHT, BUT I AM ALREADY NO LONGER A MAN. AS TO MY BRAIN OR INTELLIGENCE, IT MAY DISAPPEAR AT ANY MOMENT. AS IT IS, IT IS NO LONGER INTACT. AND THERE CAN BE NO SOUL WITHOUT INTELLIGENCE . . . AND YOU KNOW THAT!

"Then you must tell the other scientists about your discovery. They will help you and save you, André!"

I staggered back frightened as he angrily thumped the door twice.

"André . . . Why? Why do you refuse the aid you know they would give you with all their hearts?"

A dozen furious knocks shook the door and made me understand that my husband would never accept such a solution. I had to find other arguments.

For hours, it seemed, I talked to him about our boy, about me, about his family, about his duty to us and to the rest of humanity. He made no reply of any sort. At last I cried:

"André . . . do you hear me?"

"Yes," he knocked very gently.

"Well, listen then. I have another idea. You remember your first experiment with the ashtray? . . . Well, do you think that if you had put it through again a second time, it might possibly have come out with the letters turned back the right way?"

Before I had finished speaking, André was busily typing and a moment later I read his answer:

I HAVE ALREADY THOUGHT OF THAT, AND THAT IS WHY I NEEDED THE FLY. IT HAS GOT TO GO THROUGH WITH ME. THERE IS NO HOPE OTHERWISE.

"Try all the same, André. You never know!"

I HAVE TRIED SEVEN TIMES ALREADY, was the typewritten reply I got to that.

"André! Try again, please!"

The answer this time gave me a flutter of hope, because no woman has ever understood, or will ever understand, how a man about to die can possibly consider anything funny.

I DEEPLY ADMIRE YOUR DELICIOUS FEMININE LOGIC. WE COULD GO ON DOING THIS EXPERIMENT UNTIL DOOMSDAY. HOWEVER, JUST TO GIVE YOU THAT PLEASURE, PROBABLY THE VERY LAST I SHALL EVER BE ABLE TO GIVE YOU, I WILL TRY ONCE MORE. IF YOU CANNOT FIND THE DARK GLASSES, TURN YOUR BACK TO THE MACHINE AND PRESS YOUR HANDS OVER YOUR EYES. LET ME KNOW WHEN YOU ARE READY.

"Ready, André!" I shouted without even looking for the glasses and following his instructions.

I heard him moving around and then opening and closing the door of his "disintegrator." After what seemed a very long wait, but probably was not more than a minute or so, I heard a violent crackling noise and perceived a bright flash through my eyelids and fingers.

I turned around as the cabin door opened.

His head and shoulders still covered with the brown velvet carpet, André was gingerly stepping out of it.

"How do you feel, André? Any difference?' I asked, touching his arm.

He tried to step away from me and caught his foot in one of the stools which I had not troubled to pick up. He made a violent effort to regain his balance, and the velvet cloth slowly slid off his shoulders and head as he fell heavily backwards.

The horror was too much for me, too unexpected. As a matter of fact, I am sure that, even had I known, the horror impact could hardly have been less powerful. Trying to push both hands into my mouth to stifle my screams and although my fingers were bleeding, I screamed again and again. I could not take my eyes off him, I could not even close them, and yet I knew that if I looked at the horror much longer, I would go on screaming for the rest of my life.

Slowly, the monster, the thing that had been my husband, covered its head, got up and groped its way to the door and passed it. Though still screaming, I was able to close my eyes.

I who had ever been a true Catholic, who believed in God and another, better life hereafter, have today but one hope: that when I die, I really die, and that there may be no afterlife of any sort because, if there is, then I shall never forget! Day and night, awake or asleep, I see it, and I know that I am condemned to see it forever, even perhaps into oblivion!

Until I am totally extinct, nothing can, nothing will ever make me forget that dreadful white hairy head with its low flat skull and its two pointed ears. Pink and moist, the nose was also that of a cat, a huge cat. But the eyes! Or rather, where the eyes should have been were two brown bumps the size of saucers. Instead of a mouth, animal or human, there was a long hairy vertical slit from which hung a black quivering trunk that widened at the end, trumpetlike, and from which saliva kept dripping.

I must have fainted, because I found myself flat on my stomach on the cold cement floor of the laboratory, staring at the closed door behind which I could hear the noise of André's typewriter.

Numb, numb and empty, I must have looked as people do immediately after a terrible accident, before they fully understand what has happened. I could only think of a man I had once seen on the platform of a railway station, quite conscious, and looking stupidly at his leg still on the line where the train had just passed.

My throat was aching terribly, and that made me wonder if my vocal cords had not perhaps been torn, and whether I would ever be able to speak again.

The noise of the typewriter suddenly stopped and I felt I was going to scream again as something touched the door and a sheet of paper slid from under it.

Shivering with fear and disgust, I crawled over to where I could read it without touching it:

NOW YOU UNDERSTAND. THAT LAST EXPERIMENT WAS A NEW DISASTER, MY POOR HÉLÈNE. I SUPPOSE YOU RECOGNIZED PART OF DANDELO'S HEAD. WHEN I WENT INTO THE DISINTEGRATOR JUST NOW, MY HEAD WAS ONLY THAT OF A FLY. I NOW ONLY HAVE ITS EYES AND MOUTH LEFT. THE REST HAS BEEN REPLACED BY PARTS OF THE CAT'S HEAD. POOR DANDELO WHOSE ATOMS HAD NEVER COME TOGETHER. YOU SEE NOW THAT THERE CAN ONLY BE ONE POSSIBLE SOLUTION, DON'T YOU? I MUST DISAPPEAR. KNOCK ON THE DOOR WHEN YOU ARE READY AND I SHALL EXPLAIN WHAT YOU HAVE TO DO.

Of course he was right, and it had been wrong and cruel of me to insist on a new experiment. And I knew that there was now no possible hope, that any further experiments could only bring about worse results.

Getting up dazed, I went to the door and tried to speak, but no sound came out of my throat . . . so I knocked once!

You can of course guess the rest. He explained his plan in short typewritten notes, and I agreed, I agreed to everything!

My head on fire, but shivering with cold, like an automaton, I followed him into the silent factory. In my hand was a full page of explanation: what I had to know about the steam hammer.

Without stopping or looking back, he pointed to the switchboard that controlled the steam hammer as he passed it. I went no farther and watched him come to a halt before the terrible instrument.

He knelt down, carefully wrapped the cloth round his head, and then stretched out flat on the ground.

It was not difficult. I was not killing my husband. André, poor André, had gone long ago, years ago it seemed. I was merely carrying out his last wish . . . and mine.

Without hesitating, my eyes on the long still body, I firmly pushed the "stroke" button right in. The great metallic mass seemed to drop slowly. It was not so much the resounding clang of the hammer that made me jump as the sharp cracking which I had distinctly heard at the same time. My hus . . . the thing's body shook a second and then lay still.

It was then I noticed that he had forgotten to put his right arm, his flyleg, under the hammer. The police would never understand but the scientists would, and they must not! That had been André's last wish, also!

I had to do it and quickly, too; the night watchman must have heard the hammer and would be round any moment. I pushed the other button and the hammer slowly rose. Seeing but trying not to look, I ran up, leaned down, lifted and moved forward the right arm which seemed terribly light. Back at the switchboard, again I pushed the red button, and down came the hammer a second time. Then I ran all the way home.

You know the rest and can now do whatever you think right.

So ended Hélène's manuscript.

The following day I telephoned Commissaire Charas to invite him to dinner.

"With pleasure, Monsieur Delambre. Allow me, however, to ask: is it the commissaire you are inviting, or just Monsieur Charas?"

"Have you any preference?"

"No, not at the present moment."

"Well then, make it whichever you like. Will eight o'clock suit you?"

Although it was raining, the commissaire arrived on foot that evening.

"Since you did not come tearing up to the door in your black Citroen, I take it you have opted for Monsieur Charas, off duty?"

"I left the car up a side street," mumbled the commissaire with a grin as the maid staggered under the weight of his raincoat.

"Merci," he said a minute later as I handed him a glass of Pernod into which he tipped a few drops of water, watching it turn the golden amber liquid to pale blue milk.

"You heard about my poor sister-in-law?"

"Yes, shortly after you telelphoned me this morning. I am sorry, but perhaps it was all for the best. Being already in charge of your brother's case, the inquiry automatically comes to me."

"I suppose it was suicide."

Without a doubt. Cyanide the doctors say quite rightly; I found a second tablet in the unstitched hem of her dress."

"Monsieur est servi," announced the maid.

"I would like to show you a very curious document afterwards, Charas."

"Ah, yes. I heard that Madame Delambre had been writing a lot, but we could find nothing beyond the short note informing us that she was committing suicide."

During our tête-à-tête dinner, we talked politics, books and films, and the local football club of which the commissaire was a keen supporter.

After dinner, I took him up to my study where a bright fire—a habit I had picked up in England during the war—was burning.

Without even asking him, I handed him his brandy and mixed myself what he called "crushed-bug juice in soda water"—his appreciation of whisky.

"I would like you to read this, Charas; first because it was partly intended for you and, secondly, because it will interest you. If you think Commissaire Charas has no objection, I would like to burn it after."

Without a word, he took the wad of sheets Hélène had given me the day before and settled down to read them.

"What do you think of it all?" I asked some twenty minutes later as he carefully folded Hélène's manuscript, slipped it into the brown envelope, and put it into the fire.

Charas watched the flames licking the envelope from which wisps of grey smoke were escaping, and it was only when it burst into flames that he said, slowly raising his eyes to mine:

"I think it proves very definitely that Madame Delambre was quite insane."

For a long while we watched the fire eating up Hélène's "confession."

"A funny thing happened to me this morning, Charas. I went to the cemetery, where my brother is buried. It was quite empty and I was alone."

"Not quite, Monsieur Delambre. I was there, but I did not want to disturb you."

"Then you saw me...."

"Yes, I saw you bury a matchbox."

"Do you know what was in it?"

"A fly, I suppose."

"Yes, I had found it early this morning, caught in a spider's web in the garden."

"Was it dead?"

"No, not quite. I... crushed it... between two stones. Its head was ... white ... all white."

FREAKS

(1932)

SPURS
TOD ROBBINS

When MGM wünderkind Irving Thalberg hired Tod
Browning (who had made a number of Lon Chaney classics and scored a major hit in 1931 with the original Bela
Lugosi *Dracula*) to direct the studio's next thriller, he
supposedly said, "I want something that out-horrors *Fran-
kenstein.*" What he got with *Freaks* was more than he,
and certainly more than the audiences of the day, had
bargained for. When it opened in New York in July, 1932,
the stunned critics were cautious, but the public responded with outright shock and revulsion. Across the
U.S., distributors refused to touch the film, and in Great
Britain it was summarily banned until more than thirty
years after its release. Among the film's most unsettling
aspects is the fact that the "monsters" it depicts are not
the creations of studio makeup wizards but *actual* circus
freaks—midgets, pinheads, Siamese twins, hermaphrod-
ites, and limbless wonders—and the final wedding scene
in which they transform the malicious trapeze artist and
her strongman lover into specimens of their own kind is
one of the most grisly moments in horror film history.
Equally disturbing is the contrast between the relative
innocence and humanity of the freaks and the petty vi-
ciousness of the so-called "normal" human beings. Thal-

berg tried to re-release the film a year later under the title *Nature's Mistakes* as a sort of sociological document that included a serious academic prologue, but this exploitive attempt proved futile as well. Until recent years, *Freaks* existed as one of Hollywood's nearly lost films.

CLARENCE AARON "TOD" ROBBINS (1888–1949) was an American-born writer whose novel *The Unholy Three* was also translated to the screen by Browning in both silent and sound versions, in 1925 and 1930 respectively.

FREAKS

Released: 1932
Production: MGM
Direction: Tod Browning
Screenplay: Willis Goldbeck and Leon Gordon, with dialogue by Edgar Allan Woolf and Al Boasberg
Cinematography: Merritt B. Gerstad
Editing: Basil Wrangell
Running time: 64 minutes

Principal characters:

Phroso	Wallace Ford
Venus	Lelia Hyams
Cleopatra	Olga Baclanova
Roscoe	Roscoe Ates
Hans	Harry Earles
Frieda	Daisy Earles
Hercules	Henry Victor
Bearded Lady	Olga Roderick

Jácques Courbé was a romanticist. He measured only twenty-eight inches from the soles of his diminutive feet to the crown of his head; but there were times, as he rode into the arena on his gallant charger, St. Eustache, when he felt himself a doughty knight of old about to do battle for his lady.

What matter that St. Eustache was not a gallant charger except in his master's imagination—not even a pony, indeed, but a large dog of a nondescript breed, with the long snout and upstanding ears of a wolf? What matter that Monsieur Courbé's entrance was invariably greeted with shouts of derisive laughter and bombardments of banana skins and orange peel? What matter that he had no lady and that his daring deeds were severely curtailed to a mimicry of the bareback riders who preceded him? What mattered all these things to the tiny man who lived in dreams and who resolutely closed his shoe-button eyes to the drab realities of life?

The dwarf had no friends among the other freaks in Copo's Circus. They considered him ill-tempered and egotistical, and he loathed them for their acceptance of things as they were. Imagination was the armor that protected him from the curious glances of a cruel, gaping world, from the stinging lash of ridicule, from the bombardments of banana skins and orange peel. Without it, he must have shrivelled up and died. But these others? Ah, they had no armor except their own thick hides! The door that opened on the kingdom of imagination was closed and locked to them; and although they did not wish to open this door, although they did not miss what lay beyond it, they resented and mistrusted anyone who possessed the key.

Now it came about, after many humiliating performances in the arena, made palatable only by dreams, that love entered the circus tent and beckoned commandingly to Monsieur Jacques Courbé. In an instant the dwarf was engulfed in a sea of wild, tumultuous passion.

Mademoiselle Jeanne Marie was a daring bareback rider. It made Monsieur Jacques Courbé's tiny heart stand still to see her that first night of her appearance in the arena, performing brilliantly on the broad back of her aged mare, Sappho. A tall, blonde woman of the amazon type, she had round eyes of baby blue which held no spark of her avaricious peasant's soul, carmine lips and cheeks, large white teeth which flashed continually in a smile, and hands which, when doubled up, were nearly the size of the dwarf's head.

Her partner in the act was Simon Lafleur, the Romeo of the circus tent—a swarthy, Herculean young man with bold black eyes and hair that glistened with grease like the back of Solon, the trained seal.

From the first performance Monsieur Jacques Courbé loved Mademoiselle Jeanne Marie. All his tiny body was shaken with longing for her. Her buxom charms, so generously revealed in tights and spangles, made him flush and cast down his eyes. The familiarities allowed to Simon Lafleur, the bodily acrobatic contacts of the two performers, made the dwarf's blood boil. Mounted on St. Eustache, awaiting his turn at the entrance, he would grind his teeth in impotent rage to see Simon circling round and round the ring, standing proudly on the back of Sappho and holding Mademoiselle Jeanne Marie in an ecstatic embrace, while she kicked one shapely bespangled leg skyward.

"Ah, the dog!" Monsieur Jacques Courbé would mutter. "Some day I shall teach this hulking stable-boy his place! *Ma foi,* I will clip his ears for him!"

St. Eustache did not share his master's admiration for Mademoiselle Jeanne Marie. From the first he evinced his hearty detestation for her by low growls and a ferocious display of long, sharp fangs. It was little consolation for the dwarf to know that St. Eustache showed still more marked signs of rage when Simon Lafleur approached him. It pained Monsieur Jacques Courbé to think that his gallant charger, his sole companion, his bedfellow, should not also love and admire the splendid giantess who each night risked life and limb before the awed populace. Often, when they were alone together, he would chide St. Eustache on his churlishness.

"Ah, you devil of a dog!" the dwarf would cry. "Why must you always growl and show your ugly teeth when the lovely Jeanne Marie condescends to notice you? Have you no feelings under your tough hide? Cur, she is an angel and you snarl at her! Do you not remember how I found you, a starving puppy in a Paris gutter? And now you must threaten the hand of my princess! So this is your gratitude, great hairy pig!"

Monsieur Jacques Courbé had one living relative—not a dwarf, like himself, but a fine figure of a man, a prosperous farmer living just outside the town of Roubaix. The elder Courbé had never married and so one day, when he was found dead from heart failure, his tiny nephew—for whom, it must be confessed, the farmer had always felt an instinctive aversion—fell heir to a comfortable property. When the tidings were brought to him, the dwarf threw both arms about the shaggy neck of St. Eustache and cried out:

"Ah, now we can retire, marry, and settle down, old friend! I am worth many times my weight in gold!"

That evening, as Mademoiselle Jeanne Marie was changing her gaudy costume after the performance, a light tap sounded on the door.

"Enter!" she called, believing it to be Simon Lafleur, who had promised to take her that evening to the Sign of the Wild Boar for a glass
of wine to wash the sawdust out of her throat. "Enter, *mon chéri!*"

The door swung slowly open and in stepped Monsieur Jacques
Courbé, very proud and upright, in the silks and laces of a courtier,
with a tiny gold-hilted sword swinging at his hip. Up he came, his shoe-
button eyes all a-glitter to see the more than partially revealed charms
of his robust lady. Up he came to within a yard of where she sat, and
down on one knee he went and pressed his lips to her red-slippered
foot.

"Oh, most beautiful and daring lady," he cried, in a voice as shrill
as a pin scratching on a window-pane, "will yo not take mercy on the
unfortunate Jacques Courbé? He is hungry for your smiles, he is starving
for your lips! All night long he tosses on his couch and dreams of
Jeanne Marie!"

"What play-acting is this, my brave little fellow?" she asked, bending
down with the smile of an ogress. "Has Simon Lafleur sent you to tease
me?"

"May the black plague have Simon!" the dwarf cried, his eyes seeming to flash blue sparks. "I am not play-acting. It is only too true that
I love you, mademoiselle, that I wish to make you my lady. And now
that I have a fortune, now that—" He broke off suddenly and his face
resembled a withered apple. "What is this, mademoiselle?" he said, in
the low, droning tone of a hornet about to sting. "Do you laugh at my
love? I warn you, mademoiselle—do not laugh at Jacques Courbé!"

Mademoiselle Jeanne Marie's large, florid face had turned purple
from suppressed merriment. Her lips twitched at the corners. It was
all she could do not to burst out into a roar of laughter.

Why, the ridiculous little manikin was serious in his love-making!
This pocket-sized edition of a courtier was proposing marriage to her!
He, this splinter of a fellow, wished to make her his wife! Why, she
could carry him about on her shoulder like a trained marmoset!

What a joke this was—what a colossal, corset-creaking joke! Wait
till she told Simon Lafleur! She could fairly see him throw back his
sleek head, open his mouth to its widest dimensions and shake with
silent laughter. But *she* must not laugh—not now. First she must
listen to everything the dwarf had to say, draw all the sweetness out
of this bonbon of humor before she crushed it under the heel of
ridicule.

"I am not laughing," she managed to say. "You have taken me by surprise. I never thought, I never even guessed—"

"That is well, mademoiselle," the dwarf broke in. "I do not tolerate laughter. In the arena I am paid to make laughter, but these others pay to laugh at *me*. I always make people pay to laugh at me!"

"But do I understand you aright, Monsieur Courbé? Are you proposing an honorable marriage?"

The dwarf rested his hand on his heart and bowed. "Yes, mademoiselle, an honorable marriage, and the wherewithal to keep the wolf from the door. A week ago my uncle died and left me a large estate. We shall have a servant to wait on our wants, a horse and carriage, food and wine of the best, and leisure to amuse ourselves. And you? Why, you will be a fine lady! I will clothe that beautiful big body of yours with silks and laces! You will be as happy, mademoiselle, as a cherry tree in June!"

The dark blood slowly receded from Mademoiselle Jeanne Marie's full cheeks, her lips no longer twitched at the corners, her eyes had narrowed slightly. She had been a bareback rider for years and she was weary of it. The life of the circus tent had lost its tinsel. She loved the dashing Simon Lafleur, but she knew well enough that this Romeo in tights would never espouse a dowerless girl.

The dwarf's words had woven themselves into a rich mental tapestry. She saw herself a proud lady, ruling over a country estate, and later welcoming Simon Lafleur with all the luxuries that were so near his heart. Simon would be overjoyed to marry into a country estate. These pygmies were a puny lot. They died young! She would do nothing to hasten the end of Jacques Courbé. No, she would be kindness itself to the poor little fellow, but, on the other hand, she would not lose her beauty mourning for him.

"Nothing that you wish shall be withheld from you as long as you love me, mademoiselle," the dwarf continued. "Your answer?"

Mademoiselle Jeanne Marie bent forward and, with a single movement of her powerful arms, raised Monsieur Jacques Courbé and placed him on her knee. For an ecstatic instant she held him thus, as if he were a large French doll, with his tiny sword cocked coquettishly out behind. Then she planted on his cheek a huge kiss that covered his entire face from chin to brow.

"I am yours!" she murmured, pressing him to her ample bosom. "From the first I loved you, Monsieur Jacques Courbé!"

2

The wedding of Mademoiselle Jeanne Marie was celebrated in the town of Roubaix, where Copo's Circus had taken up its temporary quarters. Following the ceremony, a feast was served in one of the tents, which was attended by a whole galaxy of celebrities.

The bridegroom, his dark little face flushed with happiness and wine, sat at the head of the board. His chin was just above the tablecloth, so that his head looked like a large orange that had rolled off the fruit-dish. Immediately beneath his dangling feet, St. Eustache, who had more than once evinced by deep growls his disapproval of the proceedings, now worried a bone with quick, sly glances from time to time at the plump legs of his new mistress. Papa Copo was on the dwarf's right, his large round face as red and benevolent as a harvest moon. Next to him sat Griffo, the giraffe boy, who was covered with spots, and whose neck was so long that he looked down on all the rest, including Monsieur Hercule Hippo, the giant. The rest of the company included Mademoiselle Lupa, who had sharp white teeth of an incredible length, and who growled when she tried to talk; the tiresome Monsieur Jejongle, who insisted on juggling fruit, plates, and knives, although the whole company was heartily sick of his tricks; Madame Samson, with her trained baby boa constrictors coiled about her neck and peeping out timidly, one above each ear; Simon Lafleur and a score of others.

The bareback rider had laughed silently and almost continually ever since Jeanne Marie had told him of her engagement. Now he sat next to her in his crimson tights. His black hair was brushed back from his forehead and so glistened with grease that it reflected the lights over-head, like a burnished helmet. From time to time he tossed off a brimming goblet of burgundy, nudged the bride in the ribs with his elbow, and threw back his sleek head in another silent outburst of laughter.

"And you are sure that you will not forget me, Simon?" she whis-pered. "It may be some time before I can get the little ape's money."

"Forget you, Jeanne?" he muttered. "By all the dancing devils in champagne, never! I will wait as patiently as Job till you have fed that mouse some poisoned cheese. But what will you do with him in the meantime, Jeanne? You must allow him no liberties. I grind my teeth to think of you in his arms!"

The bride smiled and regarded her diminutive husband with an appraising glance. What an atom of a man! And yet life might linger in his bones for a long time to come. Monsieur Jacques Courbé had allowed himself only one glass of wine and yet he was far gone in intoxication. His tiny face was suffused with blood and he stared at Simon Lafleur belligerently. Did he suspect the truth?

"Your husband is flushed with wine!" the bareback rider whispered. *"Ma foi,* madame, later he may knock you about! Possibly he is a dangerous fellow in his cups. Should he maltreat you, Jeanne, do not forget that you have a protector in Simon Lafleur."

"You clown!" Jeanne Marie rolled her large eyes roguishly and laid her hand for an instant on the bareback rider's knee. "Simon, I could crack his skull between my finger and thumb, like this hickory nut!" She paused to illustrate her example, and then added reflectively: "And, perhaps, I shall do that very thing, if he attempts any familiarities. Ugh! The little ape turns my stomach!"

By now the wedding guests were beginning to show the effects of their potations. This was especially marked in the case of Monsieur Jacques' associates in the side-show.

Griffo, the giraffe boy, had closed his large brown eyes and was swaying his small head languidly above the assembly, while a slightly supercilious expression drew his lips down at the corners. Monsieur Hercule Hippo, swollen out by his libations to even more colossal proportions, was repeating over and over: "I tell you I am not like other men. When I walk, the earth trembles!" Mademoiselle Lupa, her hairy upper lip lifted above her long white teeth, was gnawing at a bone, growling unintelligible phrases to herself and shooting savage, suspicious glances at her companions. Monsieur Jejongle's hands had grown unsteady and, as he insisted on juggling the knives and plates of each new course, broken bits of crockery littered the floor. Madame Samson, uncoiling her necklace of baby boa constrictors, was feeding them lumps of sugar soaked in rum. Monsieur Jacques Courbé had finished his second glass of wine and was surveying the whispering Simon Lafleur through narrowed eyes.

There can be no genial companionship among great egotists who have drunk too much. Each one of these human oddities thought that he or she alone was responsible for the crowds that daily gathered at Copo's Circus; so now, heated with the good burgundy, they were not slow in asserting themselves. Their separate egos rattled angrily together, like so many pebbles in a bag. Here was gunpowder which needed only a spark.

"I am a big—a very big man!" Monsieur Hercule Hippo said sleepily. "Women love me. The pretty little creatures leave their pygmy husbands, so that they may come and stare at Hercule Hippo of Copo's Circus. Ha, and when they return home, they laugh at other men always! 'You may kiss me again when you grow up,' they tell their sweethearts."

"Fat bullock, here is one woman who has no love for you!" cried Mademoiselle Lupa, glaring sidewise at the giant over her bone. "That great carcass of yours is only so much food gone to waste. You have cheated the butcher, my friend. Fool, women do not come to see *you!* As well might they stare at the cattle being led through the street. Ah, no, they come from far and near to see one of their own sex who is not a cat!"

"Quite right," cried Papa Copo in a conciliatory tone, smiling and rubbing his hands together. "Not a cat, mademoiselle, but a wolf. Ah, you have a sense of humor! How droll!"

"I *have* a sense of humor," Mademoiselle Lupa agreed, returning to her bone, "and also sharp teeth. Let the erring hand not stray too near!"

"You, Monsieur Hippo and Mademoiselle Lupa, are both wrong," said a voice which seemed to come from the roof. "Surely it is none other than me whom the people come to stare at!"

All raised their eyes to the supercilious face of Griffo, the giraffe boy, which swayed slowly from side to side on its long, pipe-stem neck. It was he who had spoken, although his eyes were still closed.

"Of all the colossal impudence!" cried the matronly Madame Samson. "As if my little dears had nothing to say on the subject!" She picked up the two baby boa constrictors, which lay in drunken slumber on her lap, and shook them like whips at the wedding guests. "Papa Copo knows only too well that it is on account of these little charmers, Mark Antony and Cleopatra, that the sideshow is so well attended!"

The circus owner, thus directly appealed to, frowned in perplexity. He felt himself in a quandary. These freaks of his were difficult to handle. Why had he been fool enough to come to Monsieur Jacques Courbe's wedding feast? Whatever he said would be used against him.

As Papa Copo hesitated, his round, red face wreathed in ingratiating smiles, the long deferred spark suddenly alighted in the powder. It all came about on account of the carelessness of Monsieur Jejongle, who had become engrossed in the conversation and wished to put in a word for himself. Absent-mindedly juggling two heavy plates and a spoon, he said in a petulant tone: "You all appear to forget *me!*"

Scarcely were the words out of his mouth when one of the heavy plates descended with a crash on the thick skull of Monsieur Hippo, and Monsieur Jejongle was instantly remembered. Indeed, he was more than remembered, for the giant, already irritated to the boiling-point by Mademoiselle Lupa's insults, at this new affront struck out savagely past her and knocked the juggler head-over-heels under the table.

Mademoiselle Lupa, always quick-tempered and especially so when her attention was focused on a juicy chicken bone, evidently considered her dinner companion's conduct far from decorous and promptly inserted her sharp teeth in the offending hand that had administered the blow. Monsieur Hippo, squealing from rage and pain like a wounded elephant, bounded to his feet, overturning the table.

Pandemonium followed. Every freak's hands, teeth, feet, were turned against the others. Above the shouts, screams, growls, and hisses of the combat, Papa Copo's voice could be heard bellowing for peace:

"Ah, my children, my children! This is no way to behave! Calm yourselves, I pray you! Mademoiselle Lupa, remember that you are a lady as well as a wolf!"

There is no doubt that Monsieur Jacques Courbé would have suffered most in this undignified fracas had it not been for St. Eustache, who had stationed himself over his tiny master and who now drove off all would-be assailants. As it was, Griffo, the unfortunate giraffe boy, was the most defenseless and therefore became the victim. His small, round head swayed back and forth to blows like a punching bag. He was bitten by Mademoiselle Lupa, buffeted by Monsieur Hippo, kicked by Monsieur Jejongle, clawed by Madame Samson, and nearly strangled by both the baby boa constrictors, which had wound themselves about his neck like hangmen's nooses. Undoubtedly he would have fallen a victim to circumstances had it not been for Simon Lafleur, the bride, and half a dozen of her acrobatic friends, whom Papa Copo had implored to restore peace. Roaring with laughter, they sprang forward and tore the combatants apart.

Monsieur Jacques Courbé was found sitting grimly under a fold of the tablecloth. He held a broken bottle of wine in one hand. The dwarf

was very drunk and in a towering rage. As Simon Lafleur approached
with one of his silent laughs, Monsieur Jacques Courbé hurled the
bottle at his head.

"Ah, the little wasp!" the bareback rider cried, picking up the dwarf
by his waistband. "Here is your fine husband, Jeanne! Take him away
before he does me some mischief. *Parbleu,* he is a blood-thirsty fellow
in his cups!"

The bride approached, her blonde face crimson from wine and
laughter. Now that she was safely married to a country estate she took
no more pains to conceal her true feelings.

"Oh, la, la!" she cried, seizing the struggling dwarf and holding him
forcibly on her shoulder. "What a temper the little ape has! Well, we
shall spank it out of him before long!"

"Let me down!" Monsieur Jacques Courbé screamed in a paroxysm
of fury. "You will regret this, madame! Let me down, I say!"

But the stalwart bride shook her head. "No, no my little one!" she
laughed. "You cannot escape your wife so easily! What, you would fly
from my arms before the honeymoon!"

"Let me down!" he cried again. "Can't you see that they are laughing
at me?"

"And why should they not laugh, my little ape? Let them laugh, if
they will, but I will not put you down. No, I will carry you thus, perched
on my shoulder, to the farm. It will set a precedent which brides of
the future may find a certain difficulty in following!"

"But the farm is quite a distance from here, my Jeanne," said Simon
Lafleur. "You are as strong as an ox and he is only a marmoset, still, I
will wager a bottle of burgundy that you set him down by the roadside."

"Done, Simon!" the bride cried, with a flash of her strong white
teeth. "You shall lose your wager, for I swear that I could carry my
little ape from one end of France to the other!"

Monsieur Jacques Courbé no longer struggled. He now sat bolt
upright on his bride's broad shoulder. From the flaming peaks of blind
passion he had fallen into an abyss of cold fury. His love was dead,
but some quite alien emotion was rearing an evil head from its ashes.

"So, madame, you could carry me from one end of France to the
other!" he droned in a monotonous undertone. "From one end of
France to the other! I will remember that always, madame!"

"Come!" cried the bride suddenly. "I am off. Do you and the others,
Simon, follow to see me win my wager."

They all trooped out of the tent. A full moon rode the heavens and showed the road, lying as white and straight through the meadows as the parting in Simon Lafleur's black, oily hair. The bride, still holding the diminutive bridegroom on her shoulder, burst out into song as she strode forward. The wedding guests followed. Some walked none too steadily. Griffo, the giraffe boy, staggered pitifully on his long, thin legs. Papa Copo alone remained behind.

"What a strange world!" he muttered, standing in the tent door and following them with his round blue eyes. "Ah, these children of mine are difficult at times—very difficult!"

3

A year had rolled by since the marriage of Mademoiselle Jeanne Marie and Monsieur Jacques Courbé. Copo's Circus had once more taken up its quarters in the town of Roubaix. For more than a week the country people for miles around had flocked to the side-show to get a peep at Griffo, the giraffe boy; Monsieur Hercule Hippo, the giant; Mademoiselle Lupa, the wolf lady; Madame Samson, with her baby boa constrictors; and Monsieur Jejongle, the famous juggler. Each was still firmly convinced that he or she alone was responsible for the popularity of the circus.

Simon Lafleur sat in his lodgings at the Sign of the Wild Boar. He wore nothing but red tights. His powerful torso, stripped to the waist, glistened with oil. He was kneading his biceps tenderly with some strong-smelling fluid.

Suddenly there came the sound of heavy, laborious footsteps on the stairs. Simon Lafleur looked up. His rather gloomy expression lifted, giving place to the brilliant smile that had won for him the hearts of so many lady acrobats.

"Ah, this is Marcelle!" he told himself. "Or perhaps it is Rose, the English girl; or, yet again, little Francesca, although she walks more lightly. Well, no matter—whoever it is, I will welcome her!"

But now the lagging, heavy footfalls were in the hall and, a moment later, they came to a halt outside the door. There was a timid knock.

Simon Lafleur's brilliant smile broadened. "Perhaps some new admirer who needs encouragement," he told himself. But aloud he said: "Enter, mademoiselle!"

The door swung slowly open and revealed the visitor. She was a tall, gaunt woman dressed like a peasant. The wind had blown her hair into her eyes. Now she raised a large, toil-worn hand, brushed it back across her forehead and looked long and attentively at the bareback rider.

"You do not remember me?" she said at length.

Two lines of perplexity appeared above Simon Lafleur's Roman nose; he slowly shook his head. He, who had known so many women in his time, was now at a loss. Was it a fair question to ask a man who was no longer a boy and who had lived? Women change so in a brief time! Now this bag of bones might at one time have appeared desirable to him.

Parbleu! Fate was a conjurer! She waved her wand and beautiful women were transformed into hags, jewels into pebbles, silks and laces into hempen cords. The brave fellow who danced tonight at the prince's ball might tomorrow dance more lightly on the gallows tree. The thing was to live and die with a full belly. To digest all that one could—that was life!

"You do not remember me?" she said again.

Simon Lafleur once more shook his sleek, black head. "I have a poor memory for faces, madame," he said politely. "It is my misfortune, when there are such beautiful faces."

"Ah, but you should have remembered, Simon!" the woman cried, a sob rising up in her throat. "We were very close together, you and I. Do you not remember Jeanne Marie?"

"Jeanne Marie!" the bareback rider cried. "Jeanne Marie, who married a marmoset and a country estate? Don't tell me, madame, that you—"

He broke off and stared at her, open-mouthed. His sharp black eyes wandered from the wisps of wet, straggling hair down her gaunt person till they rested at last on her thick cowhide boots, encrusted with layer on layer of mud from the countryside.

"It is impossible!" he said at last.

"It is indeed Jeanne Marie," the woman answered, "or what is left of her. Ah, Simon, what a life he has led me! I have been merely a beast of burden! There are no ignominies which he has not made me suffer!"

"To whom do you refer?" Simon Lafleur demanded. "Surely you cannot mean that pocket edition husband of yours—that dwarf, Jacques Courbé?"

"Ah, but I do, Simon! Alas, he has broken me!"

"He—that toothpick of a man?" the bareback rider cried, with one of his silent laughs. "Why, it is impossible! As you once said yourself, Jeanne, you could crack his skull between finger and thumb like a hickory nut!"

"So I thought once. Ah, but I did not know him then, Simon! Because he was small, I thought I could do with him as I liked. It seemed to me that I was marrying a manikin. 'I will play Punch and Judy with this little fellow,' I said to myself. Simon, you may imagine my surprise when he began playing Punch and Judy with me!"

"But I do not understand, Jeanne. Surely at any time you could have slapped him into obedience!"

"Perhaps," she assented wearily, "had it not been for St. Eustache. From the first that wolf dog of his hated me. If I so much as answered his master back, he would show his teeth. Once, at the beginning, when I raised my hand to cuff Jacques Courbé, he sprang at my throat and would have torn me limb from limb had not the dwarf called him off. I was a strong woman, but even then I was no match for a wolf!"

"There was poison, was there not?" Simon Lafleur suggested.

"Ah, yes, I, too, thought of poison, but it was of no avail. St. Eustache would eat nothing that I gave him and the dwarf forced me to taste first of all food that was placed before him and his dog. Unless I myself wished to die, there was no way of poisoning either of them."

"My poor girl!" the bareback rider said, pityingly. "I begin to understand, but sit down and tell me everything. This is a revelation to me, after seeing you stalking homeward so triumphantly with your bridegroom on your shoulder. You must begin at the beginning."

"It was just because I carried him thus on my shoulder that I have had to suffer so cruelly," she said, seating herself on the only other chair the room afforded. "He has never forgiven me the insult which he says I put upon him. Do you remember how I boasted that I could carry him from one end of France to the other?"

"I remember. Well, Jeanne?"

"Well, Simon, the little demon has figured out the exact distance in leagues. Each morning, rain or shine, we sally out of the house—he on my back, the wolf dog at my heels—and I tramp along the dusty roads till my knees tremble beneath me from fatigue. If I so much as slacken my pace, if I falter, he goads me with his cruel little golden spurs, while, at the same time, St. Eustache nips my ankles. When we return home, he strikes so many leagues off a score which he says is the number of leagues from one end of France to the other. Not half that distance has been covered and I am no longer a strong woman, Simon. Look at these shoes!"

She held up one of her feet for his inspection. The sole of the cowhide boot had been worn through; Simon Lafleur caught a glimpse of bruised flesh caked with the mire of the highway.

"This is the third pair that I have had," she continued hoarsely. "Now he tells me that the price of shoe leather is too high, that I shall have to finish my pilgrimage barefooted."

"But why do you put up with all this, Jeanne?" Simon Lafleur asked angrily. "You, who have a carriage and a servant, should not walk at all!"

"At first there was a carriage and a servant," she said, wiping the tears from her eyes with the back of her hand, "but they did not last a week. He sent the servant about his business and sold the carriage at a near-by fair. Now there is no one but me to wait on him and his dog."

"But the neighbors?" Simon Lafleur persisted. "Surely you could appeal to them?"

"We have no near neighbors, the farm is quite isolated. I would have run away many months ago if I could have escaped unnoticed, but they keep a continual watch on me. Once I tried, but I hadn't travelled more than a league before the wolf dog was snapping at my ankles. He drove me back to the farm and the following day I was compelled to carry the little fiend till I fell from sheer exhaustion."

"But tonight you got away?"

"Yes," she said, with a quick, frightened glance at the door. "Tonight I slipped out while they were both sleeping and came here to you. I knew that you would protect me, Simon, because of what we have been to each other. Get Papa Copo to take me back in the circus and I will work my fingers to the bone! Save me, Simon!"

Jeanne Marie could no longer suppress her sobs. They rose in her throat, choking her, making her incapable of further speech.

"Calm yourself, Jeanne," Simon Lafleur said soothingly. "I will do what I can for you. I shall have a talk with Papa Copo tomorrow. Of course, you are no longer the same woman that you were a year ago. You have aged since then, but perhaps our good Papa Copo could find you something to do."

He broke off and eyed her intently. She had stiffened in the chair, her face, even under its coat of grime, had gone a sickly white.

"What troubles you, Jeanne?" he asked a trifle breathlessly.

"Hush!" she said, with a finger to her lips. "Listen!"

Simon Lafleur could hear nothing but the tapping of the rain on the roof and the sighing of the wind through the trees. An unusual silence seemed to pervade the Sign of the Wild Boar.

"Now don't you hear it?" she cried with an inarticulate gasp. "Simon, it is in the house—it is on the stairs!"

At last the bareback rider's less sensitive ears caught the sound his companion had heard a full minute before. It was a steady *pit-pat, pit-pat,* on the stairs, hard to dissociate from the drip of the rain from the eaves, but each instant it came nearer, grew more distinct.

"Oh, save me, Simon, save me!" Jeanne Marie cried, throwing herself at his feet and clasping him about the knees. "Save me! It is St. Eustache!"

"Nonsense, woman!" the bareback rider said angrily, but nevertheless he rose. "There are other dogs in the world. On the second landing there is a blind fellow who owns a dog. Perhaps it is he you hear."

"No, no—it is St. Eustache's step! My God, if you had lived with him a year, you would know it, too! Close the door and lock it!"

"That I will not," Simon Lafleur said contemptuously. "Do you think I am frightened so easily? If it is the wolf dog, so much the worse for him. He will not be the first cur I have choked to death with these two hands!"

Pit-pat, pit-pat—it was on the second landing. *Pit-pat, pit-pat*—now it was in the corridor, and coming fast. *Pit-pat*—all at once it stopped.

There was a moment's breathless silence and then into the room trotted St. Eustache. Monsieur Jacques Courbé sat astride the dog's broad back, as he had so often done in the circus ring. He held a tiny drawn sword, his shoe-button eyes seemed to reflect its steely glitter.

The dwarf brought the dog to a halt in the middle of the room and took in, at a single glance, the prostrate figure of Jeanne Marie. St. Eustache, too, seemed to take silent note of it. The stiff hair on his back rose up, he showed his long white fangs hungrily and his eyes glowed like two live coals.

"So I find you *thus,* madame!" Monsieur Jacques Courbé said at last. "It is fortunate that I have a charger here who can scent out my enemies as well as hunt them down in the open. Without him, I might have had some difficulty in discovering you. Well, the little game is up. I find you with your lover!"

"Simon Lafleur is not my lover!" she sobbed. "I have not seen him once since I married you until tonight! I swear it!"

"Once is enough," the dwarf said grimly. "The impudent stable-boy must be chastised!"

"Oh, spare him!" Jeanne Marie implored. "Do not harm him, I beg of you! It is not his fault that I came! I—"

But at this point Simon Lafleur drowned her out in a roar of laughter.

"Ho, ho!" he roared, putting his hands on his hips. "You would chastise me, eh? *Nom d'un chien!* Don't try your circus tricks on *me!* Why, hop-o-my thumb, you who ride on a dog's back like a flea, out of this room before I squash you! Begone, melt, fade away!" He paused, expanded his barrel-like chest, puffed out his cheeks and blew a great breath at the dwarf. "Blow away, insect," he bellowed, "lest I put my heel on you!"

Monsieur Jacques Courbé was unmoved by this torrent of abuse. He sat very upright on St. Eustache's back, his tiny sword resting on his tiny shoulder.

"Are you done?" he said at last, when the bareback rider had run dry of invectives. "Very well, monsieur! Prepare to receive cavalry!" He paused for an instant, then added in a high, clear voice: "Get him, St. Eustache!"

The dog crouched and, at almost the same moment, sprang at Simon Lafleur. The bareback rider had no time to avoid him and his tiny rider. Almost instantaneously the three of them had come to death grips. It was a gory business.

Simon Lafleur, strong man as he was, was bowled over by the wolf dog's unexpected leap. St. Eustache's clashing jaws closed on his right arm and crushed it to the bone. A moment later the dwarf, still clinging to his dog's back, thrust the point of his tiny sword into the body of the prostrate bareback rider.

Simon Lafleur struggled valiantly, but to no purpose. Now he felt the fetid breath of the dog fanning his neck and the wasp-like sting of the dwarf's blade, which this time found a mortal spot. A convulsive tremor shook him and he rolled over on his back. The circus Romeo was dead.

Monsieur Jacques Courbé cleansed his sword on a kerchief of lace, dismounted and approached Jeanne Marie. She was still crouching on the floor, her eyes closed, her head held tightly between both hands. The dwarf touched her imperiously on the broad shoulder which had so often carried him.

"Madame," he said, "we now can return home. You must be more careful hereafter. *Ma foi,* it is an ungentlemanly business cutting the throats of stable-boys!"

She rose to her feet, like a large trained animal at the word of command.

"You wish to be carried?" she said between livid lips.

"Ah, that is true, madame," he murmured. "I was forgetting our little wager. Ah, yes! Well, you are to be congratulated, madame—you have covered nearly half the distance."

"Nearly half the distance," she repeated in a lifeless voice.

"Yes, madame," Monsieur Jacques Courbé continued. "I fancy that you will be quite a docile wife by the time you have done." He paused and then added reflectively: "It is truly remarkable how speedily one can ride the devil out of a woman—with spurs!"

Papa Copo had been spending a convivial evening at the Sign of the Wild Boar. As he stepped out into the street he saw three familiar figures preceding him—a tall woman, a tiny man and a large dog with upstanding ears. The woman carried the man on her shoulder, the dog trotted at her heels.

The circus owner came to a halt and stared after them. His round eyes were full of childish astonishment.

"Can it be?" he murmured. "Yes, it is! Three old friends! And so Jeanne Marie still carries him! Ah, but she should not poke fun at Monsieur Jacques Courbé! He is so sensitive; but, alas, they are the kind that are always henpecked!"

GUYS & DOLLS

(1955)

THE IDYLL OF MISS SARAH BROWN
DAMON RUNYON

Originally a very successful Broadway musical, the film of *Guys & Dolls* cost a reported $6,000,000 in production and literary fees. It tells the story of a veteran gambler who makes a bet that he can romance a pretty young Salvation Army worker. While the picture suffered a bit in the casting—Marlon Brando is not the ideal song-and-dance man—it nonetheless captures all the color and verve of Runyon's world of endearing sharks, con men, and hoofers.

DAMON RUNYON (1880–1946) has been called "the prose laureate of the semi-literate American" and even today the term "Runyonesque" is used to describe characters whose speech and style reflect the street-wise cool of urban—specifically New York—life. Born in Manhattan, Kansas, Runyon moved to its Eastern namesake in 1911. He began sportswriting there and later became a war correspondent for the Hearst papers during World War I. His stories began to appear in the early 1930s, and many quickly found their way to the movies, the most notable being Frank Capra's *Lady for a Day* (1933) and *Little Miss Marker* (1934), the picture that launched Shirley Temple's career.

GUYS & DOLLS

Released: 1955
Production: Sam Goldwyn/MGM
Direction: Joseph L. Mankiewicz
Screenplay: Joseph L. Mankiewicz; musical book by Abe Burrows & Jo Swerling
Cinematography: Harry Stradling, Sr.
Editing: Daniel Mandell
Costume design: Irene Sharaff
Music and Lyrics: Frank Loesser
Choreography: Michael Kidd
Running time: 150 minutes

PRINCIPAL CHARACTERS:

Sky Masterson	Marlon Brando
Sarah Brown	Jean Simmons
Nathan Detroit	Frank Sinatra
Miss Adelaide	Vivian Blaine
Lt. Brannigan	Robert Keith
Nicely-Nicely Johnson	Stubby Kaye
Big Jule	B.S. Pully
Harry the Horse	Sheldon Leonard
Arvide Abernathy	Regis Toomey

Of all the high players this country ever sees, there is no doubt but that the guy they call The Sky is the highest. In fact, the reason he is called The Sky is because he goes so high when it comes to betting on any proposition whatever. He will bet all he has, and nobody can bet any more than this.

His right name is Obadiah Masterson, and he is originally out of a little town in southern Colorado where he learns to shoot craps, and play cards, and one thing and another, and where his old man is a very well-known citizen, and something of a sport himself. In fact, The

Sky tells me that when he finally cleans up all the loose scratch around his home town and decides he needs more room, his old man has a little private talk with him and says to him like this:

"Son," the old guy says, "you are now going out into the wide, wide world to make your own way, and it is a very good thing to do, as there are no more opportunities for you in this burg. I am only sorry," he says, "that I am not able to bankroll you to a very large start, but," he says, "not having any potatoes to give you, I am now going to stake you to some very valuable advice, which I personally collect in my years of experience around and about, and I hope and trust you will always bear this advice in mind.

"Son," the old guy says, "no matter how far you travel, or how smart you get, always remember this: Some day, somewhere," he says, "a guy is going to come to you and show you a nice brand-new deck of cards on which the seal is never broken, and this guy is going to offer to bet you that the jack of spades will jump out of this deck and squirt cider in your ear. But, son," the old guy says, "do not bet him, for as sure as you do you are going to get an ear full of cider."

Well, The Sky remembers what his old man says, and he is always very cautious about betting on such propositions as the jack of spades jumping out of a sealed deck of cards and squirting cider in his ear, and so he makes few mistakes as he goes along. In fact, the only real mistake The Sky makes is when he hits St. Louis after leaving his old home town, and loses all his potatoes betting a guy St. Louis is the biggest town in the world.

Now of course this is before The Sky ever sees any bigger towns, and he is never much of a hand for reading up on matters such as this. In fact, the only reading The Sky ever does as he goes along through life is in these Gideon Bibles such as he finds in the hotel rooms where he lives, for The Sky never lives anywhere else but in hotel rooms for years.

He tells me that he reads many items of great interest in these Gideon Bibles, and furthermore The Sky says that several times these Gideon Bibles keep him from getting out of line, such as the time he finds himself pretty much frozen-in over in Cincinnati, what with owing everybody in town except maybe the mayor from playing games of chance of one kind and another.

Well, The Sky says he sees no way of meeting these obligations and he is figuring the only thing he can do is to take a run-out powder, when he happens to read in one of these Gideon Bibles where it says like this:

"Better is it," the Gideon Bible says, "that thou shouldest not vow, than that thou shouldest vow and not pay."

Well, The Sky says he can see that there is no doubt whatever but that this means a guy shall not welsh, so he remains in Cincinnati until he manages to wiggle himself out of the situation, and from that day to this, The Sky never thinks of welshing.

He is maybe thirty years old, and is a tall guy with a round kisser, and big blue eyes, and he always looks as innocent as a little baby. But The Sky is by no means as innocent as he looks. In fact, The Sky is smarter than three Philadelphia lawyers, which makes him very smart, indeed, and he is well established as a high player in New Orleans, and Chicago, and Los Angeles, and wherever else there is any action in the way of card-playing, or crap-shooting, or horse-racing, or betting on the baseball games, for The Sky is always moving around the country following the action.

But while The Sky will bet on anything whatever, he is more of a short-card player and a crap-shooter than anything else, and furthermore he is a great hand for propositions, such as are always coming up among citizens who follow games of chance for a living. Many citizens prefer betting on propositions to anything you can think of, because they figure a proposition gives them a chance to out-smart somebody, and in fact I know citizens who will sit up all night making up propositions to offer other citizens the next day.

A proposition may be only a problem in cards, such as what is the price against a guy getting aces back-to-back, or how often a pair of deuces will win a hand in stud, and then again it may be some very daffy proposition, indeed, although the daffier any proposition seems to be, the more some citizens like it. And no one ever sees The Sky when he does not have some proposition of his own.

The first time he ever shows up around this town, he goes to a baseball game at the Polo Grounds with several prominent citizens, and while he is at the ball game, he buys himself a sack of Harry Stevens' peanuts, which he dumps in a side pocket of his coat. He is eating these peanuts all through the game, and after the game is over and he is walking across the field with the citizens, he says to them like this:

"What price," The Sky says, "I cannot throw a peanut from second base to the home plate?"

Well, everybody knows that a peanut is too light for anybody to throw it this far, so Big Nig, the crap shooter, who always likes to have a little the best of it running for him, speaks as follows:

"You can have 3 to 1 from me, stranger," Big Nig says.

"Two C's against six," The Sky says, and then he stands on second base, and takes a peanut out of his pocket, and not only whips it to the home plate, but on into the lap of a fat guy who is still sitting in the grand stand putting the zing on Bill Terry for not taking Walker out of the box when Walker is getting a pasting from the other club.

Well, naturally, this is a most astonishing throw, indeed, but afterwards it comes out that The Sky throws a peanut loaded with lead, and of course it is not one of Harry Stevens' peanuts, either, as Harry is not selling peanuts full of lead at a dime a bag, with the price of lead what it is.

It is only a few nights after this that The Sky states another most unusual proposition to a group of citizens sitting in Mindy's restaurant when he offers to bet a C note that he can go down into Mindy's cellar and catch a live rat with his bare hands and everybody is greatly astonished when Mindy himself steps up and takes the bet, for ordinarily Mindy will not bet you a nickel he is alive.

But it seems that Mindy knows that The Sky plants a tame rat in the cellar, and this rat knows The Sky and loves him dearly, and will let him catch it any time he wishes, and it also seems that Mindy knows that one of his dish washers happens upon his rat, and not knowing it is tame, knocks it flatter than a pancake. So when The Sky goes down into the cellar and starts trying to catch a rat with his bare hands he is greatly surprised how inhospitable the rat turns out to be, because it is one of Mindy's personal rats, and Mindy is around afterwards saying he will lay plenty of 7 to 5 against even Strangler Lewis being able to catch one of his rats with his bare hands, or with boxing gloves on.

I am only telling you all this to show you what a smart guy The Sky is, and I am only sorry I do not have time to tell you about many other very remarkable propositions that he thinks up outside of his regular business.

It is well-known to one and all that he is very honest in every respect, and that he hates and despises cheaters at cards, or dice, and furthermore The Sky never wishes to play with any the best of it himself, or anyway not much. He will never take the inside of any situation, as many gamblers love to do, such as owning a gambling house, and having the percentage run for him instead of against him, for always The Sky is strictly a player, because he says he will never care to settle down in one spot long enough to become the owner of anything.

In fact, in all the years The Sky is drifting around the country, nobody ever knows him to own anything except maybe a bank roll, and when he comes to Broadway the last time, which is the time I am now speaking of, he has a hundred G's in cash money, and an extra suit of clothes, and this is all he has in the world. He never owns such a thing as a house, or an automobile, or a piece of jewelry. He never owns a watch, because The Sky says time means nothing to him.

Of course some guys will figure a hundred G's comes under the head of owning something, but as far as The Sky is concerned, money is nothing but just something for him to play with and the dollars may as well be doughnuts as far as value goes with him. The only time The Sky ever thinks of money as money is when he is broke, and the only way he can tell he is broke is when he reaches into his pockct and finds nothing there but his fingers.

Then it is necessary for The Sky to go out and dig up some fresh scratch somewhere, and when it comes to digging up scratch, The Sky is practically supernatural. He can get more potatoes on the strength of a telegram to some place or other than John D. Rockefeller can get on collateral, for everybody knows The Sky's word is as good as wheat in the bin.

Now one Sunday evening The Sky is walking along Broadway, and at the corner of Forty-ninth Street he comes upon a little bunch of mission workers who are holding a religious meeting, such as mission workers love to do of a Sunday evening, the idea being that they may round up a few sinners here and there, although personally I always claim the mission workers come out too early to catch any sinners on this part of Broadway. At such an hour the sinners are still in bed resting up from their sinning of the night before, so they will be in good shape for more sinning a little later on.

There are only four of these mission workers, and two of them are old guys, and one is an old doll, while the other is a young doll who is tootling on a cornet. And after a couple of ganders at this young doll, The Sky is a goner, for this is one of the most beautiful young dolls anybody ever sees on Broadway, and especially as a mission worker. Her name is Miss Sarah Brown.

She is tall, and thin, and has a first-class shape, and her hair is a light brown, going on blond, and her eyes are like I do not know what, except that they are one-hundred-per-cent eyes in every respect. Furthermore, she is not a bad cornet player, if you like cornet players, although at this spot on Broadway she has to play against a scat band in a chop-suey joint near by, and this is tough competition, although at that many citizens believe Miss Sarah Brown will win by a large score if she only gets a little more support from one of the old guys with her who has a big bass drum, but does not pound it hearty enough.

Well, The Sky stands there listening to Miss Sarah Brown tootling on the cornet for quite a spell, and then he hears her make a speech in which she puts the blast on sin very good, and boosts religion quite some, and says if there are any souls around that need saving the owners of same may step forward at once. But no one steps forward, so The Sky comes over to Mindy's restaurant where many citizens are congregated, and starts telling us about Miss Sarah Brown. But of course we already know about Miss Sarah Brown, because she is so beautiful, and so good.

Furthermore, everybody feels somewhat sorry for Miss Sarah Brown, for while she is always tootling the cornet, and making speeches, and looking to save any souls that need saving, she never seems to find any souls to save, or at least her bunch of mission workers never gets any bigger. In fact, it gets smaller, as she starts out with a guy who plays a very fair sort of trombone, but this guy takes it on the lam one night with the trombone, which one and all consider a dirty trick.

Now from this time on, The Sky does not take any interest in anything but Miss Sarah Brown, and any night she is out on the corner with the other mission workers, you will see The Sky standing around looking at her, and naturally after a few weeks of this, Miss Sarah Brown must know The Sky is looking at her, or she is dumber than seems possible. And nobody ever figures Miss Sarah Brown dumb, as she is always on her toes, and seems plenty able to take care of herself, even on Broadway.

Sometimes after the street meeting is over, The Sky follows the mission workers to their headquarters in an old storeroom around in Forty-eighth Street where they generally hold an indoor session, and

I hear The Sky drops many a large coarse note in the collection box while looking at Miss Sarah Brown, and there is no doubt these notes come in handy around the mission, as I hear business is by no means so good there.

It is called the Save-a-Soul Mission, and it is run mainly by Miss Sarah Brown's grandfather, an old guy with whiskers, by the name of Arvide Abernathy, but Miss Sarah Brown seems to do most of the work, including tootling the cornet, and visiting the poor people around and about, and all this and that, and many citizens claim it is a great shame that such a beautiful doll is wasting her time being good.

How The Sky ever becomes acquainted with Miss Sarah Brown is a very great mystery, but the next thing anybody knows, he is saying hello to her, and she is smiling at him out of her one-hundred-per-cent eyes, and one evening when I happen to be with The Sky we run into her walking along Forty-ninth Street, and The Sky hauls off and stops her, and says it is a nice evening, which it is, at that. Then The Sky says to Miss Sarah Brown like this:

"Well," The Sky says, "how is the mission dodge going these days? Are you saving any souls?" he says.

Well, it seems from what Miss Sarah Brown says the soul-saving is very slow, indeed, these days.

"In fact," Miss Sarah Brown says, "I worry greatly about how few souls we seem to save. Sometimes I wonder if we are lacking in grace."

She goes on up the street, and The Sky stands looking after her, and he says to me like this:

"I wish I can think of some way to help this little doll," he says, "especially," he says, "in saving a few souls to build up her mob at the mission. I must speak to her again, and see if I can figure something out."

But The Sky does not get to speak to Miss Sarah Brown again, because somebody weighs in the sacks on him by telling her he is nothing but a professional gambler, and that he is a very undesirable character, and that his only interest in hanging around the mission is because she is a good-looking doll. So all of a sudden Miss Sarah Brown plays plenty of chill for The Sky. Furthermore, she sends him word that she does not care to accept any more of his potatoes in the collection box, because his potatoes are nothing but ill-gotten gains.

Well, naturally, this hurts The Sky's feelings no little, so he quits standing around looking at Miss Sarah Brown, and going to the mission, and takes to mingling again with the citizens in Mindy's, and showing some interest in the affairs of the community, especially the crap games.

Of course the crap games that are going on at this time are nothing much, because practically everybody in the world is broke, but there is a head-and-head game run by Nathan Detroit over a garage in Fifty-second Street where there is occasionally some action, and who shows up at this crap game early one evening but The Sky, although it seems he shows up there more to find company than anything else.

In fact, he only stands around watching the play, and talking with other guys who are also standing around and watching, and many of these guys are very high shots during the gold rush, although most of them are now as clean as a jaybird, and maybe cleaner. One of these guys is a guy by the name of Brandy Bottle Bates, who is known from coast to coast as a high player when he has anything to play with, and who is called Brandy Bottle Bates because it seems that years ago he is a great hand for belting a brandy bottle around.

This Brandy Bottle Bates is a big, black-looking guy, with a large beezer, and a head shaped like a pear, and he is considered a very immoral and wicked character, but he is a pretty slick gambler, and a fast man with a dollar when he is in the money.

Well, finally The Sky asks Brandy Bottle why he is not playing and Brandy laughs, and states as follows:

"Why," he says, "in the first place I have no potatoes, and in the second place I doubt if it will do me much good if I do have any potatoes the way I am going the past year. Why," Brandy Bottle says, "I cannot win a bet to save my soul."

Now this crack seems to give The Sky an idea, as he stands looking at Brandy Bottle very strangely, and while he is looking, Big Nig, the crap shooter, picks up the dice and hits three times hand-running, bing, bing, bing. Then Big Nig comes out on a six and Brandy Bottle Bates speaks as follows:

"You see how my luck is," he says. "Here is Big Nig hotter than a stove, and here I am without a bob to follow him with, especially," Brandy says, "when he is looking for nothing but a six. Why," he says, "Nig can make sixes all night when he is hot. If he does not make this six, the way he is, I will be willing to turn square and quit gambling forever."

"Well, Brandy," The Sky says, "I will make you a proposition. I will lay you a G note Big Nig does not get his six. I will lay you a G note against nothing but your soul," he says. "I mean if Big Nig does not get his six, you are to turn square and join Miss Sarah Brown's mission for six months."

"Bet!" Brandy Bottle Bates says right away, meaning the proposition is on, although the chances are he does not quite understand the pro-position. All Brandy understands is The Sky wishes to wager that Big Nig does not make his six, and Brandy Bottle Bates will be willing to bet his soul a couple of times over on Big Nig making his six, and figure he is getting the best of it, at that, as Brandy has great confidence in Nig.

Well, sure enough, Big Nig makes the six, so The Sky weeds Brandy Bottle Bates a G note, although everybody around is saying The Sky makes a terrible over-lay of the natural price in giving Brandy Bottle a G against his soul. Furthermore, everybody around figures the chances are The Sky only wishes to give Brandy an opportunity to get in action, and nobody figures The Sky is on the level about trying to win Brandy Bottle Bates' soul, especially as The Sky does not seem to wish to go any further after paying the bet.

He only stands there looking on and seeming somewhat depressed as Brandy Bottle goes into action on his own account with the G note, fading other guys around the table with cash money. But Brandy Bottle Bates seems to figure what is in The Sky's mind pretty well, because Brandy Bottle is a crafty old guy.

It finally comes his turn to handle the dice, and he hits a couple of times, and then he comes out on a four, and anybody will tell you that a four is a very tough point to make, even with a lead pencil. Then Brandy Bottle turns to The Sky and speaks to him as follows:

"Well, Sky," he says, "I will take the odds off you on this one. I know you do not want my dough," he says. "I know you only want my soul for Miss Sarah Brown, and," he says, "without wishing to be fresh about it, I know why you want it for her. I am young once myself," Brandy Bottle says. "And you know if I lose to you, I will be over there in Forty-eighth Street in an hour pounding on the door, for Brandy always settles.

"But, Sky," he says, "now I am in the money, and my price goes up. Will you lay me ten G's against my soul I do not make this four?"

"Bet!" The Sky says, and right away Brandy Bottle hits with a four.

Well, when word goes around that The Sky is up at Nathan Detroit's crap game trying to win Brandy Bottle Bates' soul for Miss Sarah Brown, the excitement is practically intense. Somebody telephones Mindy's, where a large number of citizens are sitting around arguing about this and that, and telling one another how much they will bet in support of their arguments, if only they have something to bet, and Mindy himself is almost killed in the rush for the door.

One of the first guys out of Mindy's and up to the crap game is Regret, the horse player, and as he comes in Brandy Bottle is looking for a nine, and The Sky is laying him twelve G's against his soul that he does not make this nine, for it seems Brandy Bottle's soul keeps getting more and more expensive.

Well, Regret wishes to bet his soul against a G that Brandy Bottle gets his nine, and is greatly insulted when The Sky cannot figure his price any better than a double saw, but finally Regret accepts this price, and Brandy Bottle hits again.

Now many other citizens request a little action from The Sky, and if there is one thing The Sky cannot deny a citizen it is action, so he says he will lay them according to how he figures their word to join Miss Sarah Brown's mission if Brandy Bottle misses out, but about this time The Sky finds he has no more potatoes on him, being now around thirty-five G's loser, and he wishes to give markers.

But Brandy Bottle says that while ordinarily he will be pleased to extend The Sky this accommodation, he does not care to accept markers against his soul, so then The Sky has to leave the joint and go over to his hotel two or three blocks away, and get the night clerk to open his damper so The Sky can get the rest of his bank roll. In the meantime the crap game continues at Nathan Detroit's among the small operators, while the other citizens stand around and say that while they hear of many a daffy proposition in their time, this is the daffiest that ever comes to their attention, although Big Nig claims he hears of a daffier one, but cannot think what it is.

Big Nig claims that all gamblers are daffy anyway, and in fact he says if they are not daffy they will not be gamblers, and while he is arguing this matter back comes The Sky with fresh scratch, and Brandy Bottle Bates takes up where he leaves off, although Brandy says he is accepting the worst of it, as the dice have a chance to cool off.

Now the upshot of the whole business is that Brandy Bottle hits thirteen licks in a row, and the last lick he makes is on a ten, and it is for twenty G's against his soul, with about a dozen other citizens getting anywhere from one to five C's against their souls, and complaining bitterly of the price.

And as Brandy Bottle makes his ten, I happen to look at The Sky and I see him watching Brandy with a very peculiar expression on his face, and furthermore I see The Sky's right hand creeping inside his coat where I know he always packs a Betsy in a shoulder holster, so I can see something is wrong somewhere.

But before I can figure out what it is, there is quite a fuss at the door, and loud talking, and a doll's voice, and all of a sudden in bobs nobody else but Miss Sarah Brown. It is plain to be seen that she is all steamed up about something.

She marches right up to the crap table where Brandy Bottle Bates and The Sky and the other citizens are standing, and one and all are feeling sorry for Dobber, the doorman, thinking of what Nathan Detroit is bound to say to him for letting her in. The dice are still lying on the table showing Brandy Bottles Bates' last throw, which cleans The Sky and gives many citizens the first means they enjoy in several months.

Well, Miss Sarah Brown looks at The Sky, and The Sky looks at Miss Sarah Brown, and Miss Sarah Brown looks at the citizens around and about, and one and all are somewhat dumbfounded, and nobody seems to be able to think of much to say, although The Sky finally speaks up as follows:

"Good evening," The Sky says. "It is a nice evening," he says. "I am trying to win a few souls for you around here, but," he says, "I seem to be about half out of luck."

"Well," Miss Sarah Brown says, looking at The Sky most severely out of her hundred-per-cent eyes, "you are taking too much upon yourself. I can win any souls I need myself. You better be thinking of your own soul. By the way," she says, "are you risking your own soul, or just your money?"

Well, of course up to this time The Sky is not risking anything but his potatoes, so he only shakes his head to Miss Sarah Brown's question, and looks somewhat disorganized.

"I know something about gambling," Miss Sarah Brown says, "especially about crap games. I ought to," she says. "It ruins my poor papa and my brother Joe. If you wish to gamble for souls, Mister Sky, gamble for your own soul."

Now Miss Sarah Brown opens a small black leather pocketbook she is carrying in one hand, and pulls out a two-dollar bill, and it is such a two-dollar bill as seems to have seen much service in its time, and holding up this deuce, Miss Sarah Brown speaks as follows:

"I will gamble with you, Mister Sky," she says. "I will gamble with you," she says, "on the same terms you gamble with these parties here. This two dollars against your soul, Mister Sky. It is all I have, but," she says, "it is more than your soul is worth."

Well, of course anybody can see that Miss Sarah Brown is doing this because she is very angry, and wishes to make The Sky look small, but right away The Sky's duke comes from inside his coat, and he picks up the dice and hands them to her and speaks as follows:

"Roll them," The Sky says, and Miss Sarah Brown snatches the dice out of his hand and gives them a quick sling on the table in such a way that anybody can see she is not a professional crap shooter, and not even an amateur crap shooter, for all amateur crap shooters first breathe on the dice, and rattle them good, and make remarks to them, such as "Come on, baby!"

In fact, there is some criticism of Miss Sarah Brown afterwards on account of her haste, as many citizens are eager to string with her to hit, while others are just as anxious to bet she misses, and she does not give them a chance to get down.

Well, Scranton Slim is the stick guy, and he takes a gander at the dice as they hit up against the side of the table and bounce back, and then Slim hollers, "Winner, winner, winner," as stick guys love to do, and what is showing on the dice as big as life, but a six and a five, which makes eleven, no matter how you figure, so The Sky's soul belongs to Miss Sarah Brown.

She turns at once and pushes through the citizens around the table without even waiting to pick up the deuce she lays down when she grabs the dice. Afterwards a most obnoxious character by the name of Red Nose Regan tries to claim the deuce as a sleeper and gets the heave-o from Nathan Detroit, who becomes very indignant about this, stating that Red Nose is trying to give his joint a wrong rap.

Naturally, The Sky follows Miss Brown, and Dobber, the doorman, tells me that as they are waiting for him to unlock the door and let them out, Miss Sarah Brown turns on The Sky and speaks to him as follows:

"You are a fool," Miss Sarah Brown says.

Well, at this Dobber figures The Sky is bound to let one go, as this seems to be most insulting language, but instead of letting one go, The Sky only smiles at Miss Sarah Brown and says to her like this:

"Why," The Sky says, "Paul says 'If any man among you seemeth to be wise in this world, let him become a fool, that he may be wise.' I love you, Miss Sarah Brown," The Sky says.

Well, now, Dobber has a pretty fair sort of memory, and he says that Miss Sarah Brown tells The Sky that since he seems to know so much about the Bible, maybe he remembers the second verse of the Song of Solomon, but the chances are Dobber muffs the number of the verse, because I look the matter up in one of these Gideon Bibles, and the verse seems a little too much for Miss Sarah Brown, although of course you never can tell.

Anyway, this is about all there is to the story, except that Brandy Bottle Bates slides out during the confusion so quietly even Dobber scarcely remembers letting him out, and he takes most of The Sky's potatoes with him, but he soon gets batted in against the faro bank out in Chicago, and the last anybody hears of him he gets religion all over again, and is preaching out in San Jose, so The Sky always claims he beats Brandy for his soul, at that.

I see The Sky the other night at Forty-ninth Street and Broadway, and he is with quite a raft of mission workers, including Mrs. Sky, for it seems that the soul-saving business picks up wonderfully, and The Sky is giving a big bass drum such a first-class whacking that the scat band in the chop-suey joint can scarcely be heard. Furthermore, The Sky is hollering between whacks, and I never see a guy look happier, especially when Mrs. Sky smiles at him out of her hundred-per-cent eyes. But I do not linger long, because The Sky gets a gander at me, and right away he begins hollering:

"I see before me a sinner of deepest dye," he hollers. "Oh, sinner, repent before it is too late. Join with us, sinner," he hollers, "and let us save your soul."

Naturally, this crack about me being a sinner embarrasses me no little, as it is by no means true, and it is a good thing for The Sky there is no copper in me, or I will go to Mrs. Sky, who is always bragging about how she wins The Sky's soul by outplaying him at his own game, and tell her the truth.

And the truth is that the dice with which she wins The Sky's soul, and which are the same dice with which Brandy Bottle Bates wins all his potatoes, are strictly phony, and that she gets into Nathan Detroit's just in time to keep The Sky from killing old Brandy Bottle.

THE HEARTBREAK KID

(1972)

A CHANGE OF PLAN
BRUCE JAY FRIEDMAN

The Heartbreak Kid combined the talents of four comedic geniuses: Elaine May as director, Neil Simon as script-writer, Bruce Jay Friedman as original writer, and new-comer Charles Grodin as an utterly outrageous leading man. The result was a work of unrelentingly nerve-wrack-ing modern comedy that can be matched only by the films of Woody Allen or Albert Brooks. The story details the odyssey of a young Jewish newlywed honeymooning in Florida who, two days into his marriage, dumps his frumpy wife (played by Elaine May's real-life daughter Jeannie Berlin) and sets off to conquer a young Minnesota blonde (Cybill Shepherd) he meets at the hotel pool. The ensuing clash between the worlds of the middle-class Jew and the high-brow WASP is doggedly hilarious. If one were to require a cinematic definition of *chutzpah, The Heartbreak Kid* would be it.

Often labelled a "black humorist" (a term he is credited with coining), BRUCE JAY FRIEDMAN was born in the Bronx,

N.Y., in 1930. In his many novels, short stories and plays, Friedman chronicles both the humor and pathos of the Jewish-American experience. His novel, *The Lonely Guy's Guide to Life,* was made into the film *The Lonely Guy* in 1984, and starred Steve Martin and Charles Grodin.

THE HEARTBREAK KID

Released: 1972
Production: Edgar J. Scherick for Palomar
Direction: Elaine May
Screenplay: Neil Simon
Cinematography: Owen Roizman
Editing: John Carter
Art Direction: Richard Sylbert
Music: Garry Sherman
Running Time: 104 minutes

PRINCIPAL CHARACTERS:

Lenny Cantrow	Charles Grodin
Lila Kolodny	Jeannie Berlin
Kelly Corcoran	Cybill Shepherd
Mr. Corcoran	Eddie Albert
Mrs. Corcoran	Audra Lindley

And so finally, after four years of drift, they had found all exits barricaded and gotten married in a sudden spurt, bombing their parents with the news. A Justice had been rounded up, also uncles in the area. After the ceremony, Cantrow's new father-in-law had taken him around and said, "It's going to be great, isn't it."

"How can you say that," said a stray uncle, wandering by. "Which one of us knows such things. Maybe it will. Then again, maybe it won't." That night there was a need to get away, to sail as quickly as possible into the eye of the marriage, and off they went, south, driving in a frenzy, all that afternoon, all that night. Once, bleary-eyed, they had gone through a Southern town with two wheels up on a sidewalk.

Later, moving through a misted patch of farmland, Cantrow spotted a monster turkey, his first live one, and gunned the motor, thinking it was a dreaded hawk. Only once had they stopped, for chocolate frosteds, Cantrow tipping his into her lap. With soaked shorts, she broke into laughter, then chuckled her way through five more towns. This is the kind of sense of humor she has, Cantrow thought. And I didn't even catch that.

Curling from side to side, as though the car itself were drunk, they were somehow blessed, missing head-on collisions; at the hotel, Cantrow told the clerk, "We're not bums," and got a room. Upstairs, zombielike, they made a feeble pass at sex, wanting to try it married, but collapsed instead into sleep. Two hours later, hardly fresh, Cantrow awoke and stared at his bride's slack form. So that's what I've got, he thought. Maybe for forty-seven years.

Down below, at poolside, the lifeguard winked and said, "Ho, ho, ho," a standard greeting to honeymooners. The pool water slapped Cantrow awake; so did a blonde girl, sitting at the edge. She had a nice fleshiness, a good hundred thirty pounds to his bride's hundred four. He caught her scent, too, just like honey. He had never really smelled honey, but guessed it must be in that family.

"I didn't know they allowed big puppies in pools," she said. And now there was her voice, crushed, feminine for a change. At a club, once, he had introduced his bride to a football-star friend of his. "She's okay," the friend had said privately, "but I could never live with those pipes of hers."

Cantrow fished himself out of the water and sat by the girl's side. She was eighteen, from Minnesota, vacationing between semesters. These were her folks, at the terrace bar, the heavyset man and the handsome woman in the white silk dress. Cantrow and the girl kidded around, wound up tickling each other. Then the shadow of the hotel seemed to fall on his back like a heavy beam. "You probably know I'm married," he said. "Just since yesterday. Down here on my honeymoon."

"And what else is new," she said. Cheered on, Cantrow told her some jokes; they teased each other. But there was a whisper of difference. Before it became a roar, Cantrow suddenly panicked, took her arm and said, "Look, this is crazy, but I've got to see you one more time and find out something. I really have to." Their glances met, combined, turned soft together.

"We don't stay here," she said. "At the Regent."

"I'll be there at six," he said. "I'll work it out. For cocktails."

"Guess who I met at the pool," he told his bride, later, in the room. "Crazy guy from school, Blaum, always wore a tooth around his neck, called it the Sacred Tooth of Mickasee. Didn't care what you did to him, beat him up, anything, long as you didn't touch his tooth. 'Fool with my tooth and you're in trouble,' he'd say to you. Anyway, I told him I'd meet him later tonight for a drink. No girls, though. He's not himself when any are around and I want to see him carry on about that tooth again." He hurried on. "I'll just have a quick one with him and then I'll come back and we can really start."

In the early evening, he dressed carefully, getting his hair just right, one loop down over the eye, with feigned carelessness, for extra appeal. At the Regent, she sat with her folks at a table, but joined him immediately at the bar. He liked the size of her in heels, the weight of her, the bounce of her hair, the honeyed look. A combo began to work in a deep beat; he gathered her in, made it once around the floor, then put his nose in her hair and said, "That did it. Over to your folks we go."

The parents were pushed back from the table, comfortable, expectant, as though waiting for a curtain to part. Cantrow stood before them and began to speak, then said, "Hold it a second," and unbuckled his belt for comfort. "Okay, sir," he said, "I've just made one helluva mistake, about the biggest one a guy can make. But I met your daughter and I'm undoing it, not matter what it takes. You see, I got married yesterday and I'm down here on my honeymoon, but it was a bad idea from the beginning. There wasn't a damned thing in the world between us and I just got married because it seemed like the only way out. Anyway, I met your daughter and she's the one I want. I know it's crazy, but I could tell in a second. You should see the difference between them. There's no comparison. I just had to be with her a few minutes and I saw all the things I was really after. She's easier, more feminine, just real comfortable to be with. I don't know exactly what I expect from you. What I'd like, really, is for you to study the look in my eyes and know that I've never been more sincere in my life and that I'm not fooling around and that I'm the right guy for her. I'm getting out of the thing and then I'm coming after your daughter, but I just wanted to lay it out on the table and see how it struck you, whether you were with me or against me."

The father yawned, drummed his fingers on the table and said, "Not if they stripped me naked and dragged me four times around the world. Over the desert, through the jungle, under the seven seas."

"Okay," said Cantrow. "Long as we're clear. But you don't know me, sir. You don't know what I can do. I'm coming after her anyway. Once I make up my mind on something, that's it.

"First thing I've got to do is get out of it," he said, with a bow to the parents. "You take it easy, honey," he said, pecking her on the cheek.

"But I listen to my father," she said, as he walked to the door.

"Another thing about you that turns me on."

Pale and angular, Cantrow's bride slapped on pancake before a mirror. "Hold it, hold it," he said, tearing into the room. "Whoa. We're not going out tonight. Any night, for that matter, unless we meet some day later on as platonic friends, and I'm not even really sure of that. There was no Blaum and no tooth. That is, there *is* a Blaum and the tooth part was no lie either, but I didn't just meet him. It's a new girl I ran into at the pool. I don't see any point in describing what went on, because that would be just like waving a red flag in your face. What's important is us and how flat it's always been when you take away those first few weeks, just one, if you really want to be strict about it. Look, I'm pulling out. I admit, I shouldn't have gone this far, but I didn't see it clearly until just before at the pool. There's a whole other way. With us, it would be one long downhill ride. Get yourself someone else. I admit, I'll be a little shaky on that issue if I stop and think about it, but I can stand it. Meanwhile, I'm on my way."

"And I'm supposed to just listen to that."

"Oh, we can kick it around if you like," said Cantrow, packing, "but how'd you like to lift this hotel on your back and move it across the street. That's roughly what you'd be up against trying to talk me out of this thing I've got in my head. Look, here's three hundred dollars for openers. I'm throwing in the car and just holler if you think that's not generous. The funny thing is, as we're making this break, I'm starting to like you more already.

"Maybe," he said, slamming shut his suitcase, "years later, when the sting is out of it for both of us, we really *can* meet for dinner."

That night, Cantrow flew north and woke up Wenger, his attorney-cousin, at midnight. "Cantrow with an emergency," he said. "Remember that marriage I told you about? I've got to get out of it now. We were just hitched for the shortest time you can imagine and then the whole thing blew up. Anyway, I'm actually out of it already since there isn't anything—tornadoes, nuclear war, you name it—that could get me back in. So you just take care of the legal part. I've got five grand from the service and believe me it wasn't easy to save. Cut down on everything, meals included, to get it together. Anyway, use the whole bundle if you need to and keep the change. Just get me out."

"If we weren't cousins, you wouldn't call me at this hour."

"I'll stick around one week, in case there are papers. Then I'm getting into something else."

"Hi, Mom," said Cantrow at his folks' apartment. "The entire marriage is down the drain, but don't worry, I'm in good health and got out clean."

"I saw the whole thing coming," said Cantrow's mother. "If you'd asked me, I could have recited the entire story before it happened. Okay, how about a trip to Europe, all expenses for a month. To clear your head."

"No, Mom, I'm bunking in here for a week, then I've got to go out to the Midwest on something."

"I knew it," she said. "Another little winner. One wasn't enough for my son. I can tell you the end of this story, too, if you want to sit and listen."

With great crankiness, Wenger gave the go-ahead and Cantrow took a plane west, then tracked the girl down to a small teachers' college of Episcopal persuasion. Off-campus she lived with her folks and came home for meals. His first night in town, Cantrow announced his presence to her mother at the door. "Hi, you probably remember me from the resort hotel. I don't expect you to let me see your daughter right off, but I thought I'd let you know I'm here and that wasn't a wild story I'd made up when I saw you at the bar."

"My daughter's preparing for bed," said the mother, easing the door shut. "She studies very hard and needs her sleep."

Later that night, Cantrow asked around and smoked out his one rival, a fair-skinned fellow of strange, shifting sexuality. Sliding in beside him at a bleakly lit campus hangout, Cantrow ordered the local special, beer and braunschweiger sandwiches, and said, "Hi, I've just gotten down here and what I'm after is Sue Ellen Parker. Now look, we can do this like gentlemen, you just tapering off with another date or two to save face, or else we can go to muscle. You look pretty well set up, but the point is, if we fight, it doesn't matter how it goes. If you take me boxing, I'll bring in karate and if you know that, I'll go to guns."

"Would you really do all those things," said the fellow with a wet stare, kaleidoscopically shifting sexes before Cantrow's very eyes.

The road partially clear, Cantrow called the girl herself. "I'd be teasing if I pretended not to be flattered, but it's just so completely out of the question," she said. "I mean with Mother and Dad. And me, sort of." Undismayed, driven, Cantrow hung on, peppered her with calls, nourished himself on her great phone voice. One night that honeyed blonde fragrance seemed to trickle through the wire. She said she would sneak out and meet him on the corner. Cantrow hired a car, scooped her up and off they drove in silence to a wooded place she knew. Thin, towering Minnesota trees, crowded together, stripped and haunted. "I won't sleep with you tonight," she said, as they left the car, "but let's take off our clothes and run through there, as far as we can go."

"Suits me," said Cantrow, knowing instantly he'd been right about her.

And so they began. All the things he had missed. Nude walks and swims. Hours of savoring honeyed flesh. Sudden love, almost anywhere, under stairwells, beneath a tree. Giving everything. Wonder of wonders. Getting back. "I knew I wasn't crazy," he told her one night, bewitched, at some lake's edge. "It must have been a hell of a jolt to all concerned, but I knew I was on the right track."

A month later she phoned, out of breath. "Dad's calling a truce. From now on, it's the front door for us, darling." Legitimate now, Cantrow arrived that night in a suit and tie. "I never thought I'd see the day I'd be doing this," said her father. "But let's have us a handshake. You Eastern fellows sure are determined. Well, more power to you, son."

Later that night, passion undiminished, they made love in the parlor. The next night in her very room. Pacing himself, Cantrow waited another week, then told her, "Look, I haven't been fooling around."

"I know, darling, I feel the same way. I've already said something and the folks' answer is, of course, anything we want."

With blurred speed, the wedding plans were made. Cantrow's folks declined, but Wenger, the lawyer, came west with the final papers. Soon Cantrow, who had always dreamed of tails, stood erect in them and watched strange blonde people with great Scandinavian profiles mill around him at the church. Mr. Parker came over, cuffed him in friendliness and said, "Now this is one for the books, isn't it. The first time you came up to us and now here we are. I think it's great though, kind of thing you see in the movies." He disappeared in a swirl of guests. Mrs. Parker took his place. Solid, tanned gold, an easeful ripened version of her daughter. She took his arm and said, "I want you to know how warming I find all of this. And I have a confession to make. Even at the hotel I just knew. There was something so profound about the cast of your neck and shoulders."

"And how about how I feel," said Cantrow. "I get sick when I think of how I could have let the whole thing slide and muffed the chance of a lifetime. Sue Ellen. Being here in Minnesota. The things that have happened. Mr. Parker. You. Even the way you just said that. That it was all so warming. And what was that word you used about my neck and shoulders. You know once in a while I'd check myself in mirrors and there really was something about them, although I guess I'd be the last one to say it about myself. But what was that you called them? *Profound.*"

"Oh, Jesus, look," he said covering her hand. "I wonder if we could just talk for a second. I'll talk and you don't say a word till I'm finished."

HIGH NOON

(1952)

THE TIN STAR
JOHN M. CUNNINGHAM

When producer Stanley Kramer released *High Noon* in 1952, the Western film was at the apex of its popularity, and the picture has rightly come to be regarded as a terse and beautifully executed example of the genre. In addition to its Western setting, it is also a masterful work of suspense. After years as town sheriff, Will Kane (portrayed in an Academy Award-winning performance by Gary Cooper) has turned in his badge to marry a young Quaker girl (Grace Kelly). Word arrives that a ruthless killer Kane helped to sentence years before is returning to seek revenge that day at noon. While many details of the story and resultant film differ (Cunningham's Sheriff Doane is an arthritic widower with no real future ahead), the basic themes remain intact: the abandonment of a man by his community, and his decision to confront evil through a sense of personal justice and commitment. In many ways, *High Noon* can be viewed as an existential Western. Directed by Fred Zinnemann, who created such diverse classics as *The Member of the Wedding* (1953), *From Here to Eternity* (1953), and *A Man for All Seasons* (1966), *High Noon* was praised by *The New York Times* as "a Western to challenge *Stagecoach* for the all-time championship."

———

JOHN M. CUNNINGHAM was born in Montana in 1915. He began writing Western fiction in 1946 and is the author of many short stories and three novels. He presently lives in Oregon and is at work on a new novel.

————

HIGH NOON

Released: 1952
Production: Stanley Kramer for Stanley Kramer Productions; released by United Artists
Direction: Fred Zinnemann
Screenplay: Carl Foreman
Cinematography: Floyd Crosby
Editing: Elmo Williams and Harry Gerstad (Academy Award)
Music: Dmitri Tiomkin (Academy Award)
Song: Dmitri Tiomkin and Ned Washington, "High Noon" (Academy Award)
Running time: 84 minutes

PRINCIPAL CHARACTERS:

Will Kane	Gary Cooper (Academy Award)
Jonas Henderson	Thomas Mitchell
Harvey Pell	Lloyd Bridges
Helen Ramirez	Katy Jurado
Amy Kane	Grace Kelly
Percy Mettrick	Otto Kruger
Frank Miller	Ian MacDonald

————

Sheriff Doane looked at his deputy and then down at the daisies he had picked for his weekly visit, lying wrapped in newspaper on his desk. "I'm sorry to hear you say that, Toby. I was kind of counting on you to take over after me."

"Don't get me wrong, Doane," Toby said, looking through the front window. "I'm not afraid. I'll see you through this shindig. I'm not afraid of Jordan or young Jordan or any of them. But I want to tell you now. I'll wait till Jordan's train gets in. I'll wait to see what he does. I'll see you through whatever happens. After that, I'm quitting."

Doane began kneading his knuckles, his face set against the pain as he gently rubbed the arthritic, twisted bones. He said nothing.

Toby looked around, his brown eyes troubled in his round, olive-skinned face. "What's the use of holding down a job like this? Look at you. What'd you ever get out of it? Enough to keep you eating. And what for?"

Doane stopped kneading his arthritic hands and looked down at the star on his shirt front. He looked from it to the smaller one on Toby's. "That's right," he said. "They don't even hang the right ones. You risk your life catching somebody, and the damned juries let them go so they can come back and shoot at you. You're poor all your life, you got to do everything twice, and in the end they pay you off in lead. So you can wear a tin star. It's a job for a dog, son."

Toby's voice did not rise, but his eyes were a little wider in his round, gentle face. "Then why keep on with it? What for? I been working for you for two years—trying to keep the law so sharp-nosed money-grabbers can get rich, while we piddle along on what the county pays us. I've seen men I used to bust playing marbles going up and down this street on four-hundred-dollar-saddles, and what've I got? Nothing. Not a damned thing."

There was a little smile around Doane's wide mouth. "That's right, Toby. It's all for free. The headaches, the bullets, and everything, all for free. I found that out long ago." The mock-grave look vanished. "But somebody's got to be around and take care of things." He looked out of the window at the people walking up and down the crazy boardwalks. "I like it free. You know what I mean? You don't get a thing for it. You've got to risk everything. And you're free inside. Like the larks. You know the larks? How they get up in the sky and sing when they want to? A pretty bird. A very pretty bird. That's the way I like to feel inside."

Toby looked at him without expression. "That's the way you look at it. I don't see it. I've only got one life. You talk about doing it all for nothing, and that gives you something. What? What've you got now, waiting for Jordan to come?"

"I don't know yet. We'll have to wait and see."

Toby turned back to the window. "All right, but I'm through. I don't see any sense in risking your neck for nothing."

"Maybe you will," Doane said, beginning to work on his hands again.

"Here comes Mettrick. I guess he don't give up so easy. He's still got that resignation in his hand."

"I guess he doesn't," Doane said. "But I'm through listening. Has young Jordan come out of the saloon yet?"

"No," Toby said, and stepped aside as the door opened. Mettrick came in. "Now listen, Doane," he burst out, "for the last time—"

"Shut up, Percy," Doane said. "Sit down over there and shut up or get out."

The flare went out of the mayor's eyes. "Doane," he moaned, "you are the biggest—"

"Shut up," Doane said. "Toby, has he come out yet?"

Toby stood a little back from the window, where the slant of golden sunlight, swarming with dust, wouldn't strike his white shirt.

"Yes. He's got a chair. He's looking this way, Doane. He's still drinking. I can see a bottle on the porch beside him."

"I expected that. Not that it makes much difference." He looked down at the bunch of flowers.

Mettrick, in the straight chair against the wall, looked up at him, his black eyes scornful in his long, hopeless face.

"Don't make much difference? Who the hell do you think you are, Doane? God? It just means he'll start the trouble without waiting for his stinking brother, that's all it means." His hand was shaking, and the white paper hanging listlessly from his fingers fluttered slightly. He looked at it angrily and stuck it out at Doane. "I gave it to you. I did the best I could. Whatever happens, don't be blaming me, Doane. I gave you a chance to resign, and if—" he left off and sat looking at the paper in his hand as though it were a dead puppy of his that somebody had run a buggy over.

Doane, standing with the square, almost chisel-pointed tips of his fingers just touching the flowers, turned slowly, with the care of movement he would have used around a crazy horse. "I know you're my friend, Percy. Just take it easy, Percy. If I don't resign, it's not because I'm ungrateful."

"Here comes Staley with the news," Toby said from the window. "He looks like somebody just shot his grandma."

Percy Mettrick laid his paper on the desk and began smoothing it out ruefully. "It's not as though it were dishonorable, Doane. You should have quit two years ago, when your hands went bad. It's not dishonorable now. You've still got time."

He glanced up at the wall clock. "It's only three. You've got an hour before he gets in, you can take your horse . . ." As he talked to himself, Doane looking slantwise at him with his little smile, he grew more cheerful. "Here." He jabbed a pen out at Doane. "Sign it and get out of town."

The smile left Doane's mouth. "This is an elective office. I don't have to take orders, even if you are mayor." His face softened. "It's simpler than you think, Percy. When they didn't hang Jordan, I knew this day would come. Five years ago, I knew it was coming, when they gave him that silly sentence. I've been waiting for it."

"But not to commit suicide," Mettrick said in a low voice, his eyes going down to Doane's gouty hands. Doane's knobby, twisted fingers closed slowly into fists, as though hiding themselves; his face flushed slightly. "I may be slow, but I can still shoot."

The mayor stood up and went slowly over to the door.

"Good-bye, Doane."

"I'm not saying good-bye, Percy. Not yet."

"Good-bye," Mettrick repeated, and went out of the door.

Toby turned from the window. His face was tight around the mouth. "You should have resigned like he said, Doane. You ain't a match for one of them alone, much less two of them together. And if Pierce and Frank Colby come, too, like they was all together before—"

"Shut up, shut up," Doane said. "For God's sake, shut up." He sat down suddenly at the desk and covered his face with his hands. "Maybe the pen changes a man." He was sitting stiff, hardly breathing.

"What are you going to do, Doane?"

"Nothing. I can't do anything until they start something. I can't do a thing. . . . Maybe the pen changes a man. Sometimes it does. I remember—"

"Listen, Doane," Toby said, his voice, for the first time, urgent. "It maybe changes some men, but not Jordan. It's already planned, what they're going to do. Why else would young Jordan be over there, watching? He's come three hundred miles for this."

"I've seen men go in the pen hard as rock and come out peaceful and settle down. Maybe Jordan—"

Toby's face relapsed into dullness. He turned back to the window listlessly. Doane's hands dropped.

"You don't think that's true, Toby?"

Toby sighed. "You know it isn't so, Doane. He swore he'd get you. That's the truth."

Doane's hands came up again in front of his face, but this time he was looking at them, his big gray eyes going quickly from one to the other, almost as though he were afraid of them. He curled his fingers slowly into fists, and uncurled them slowly, pulling with all his might, yet slowly. A thin sheen on his face reflected the sunlight from the floor. He got up.

"Is he still there?" he asked.

"Sure, he's still there."

"Maybe he'll get drunk. Dead drunk."

"You can't get a Jordan that drunk."

Doane stood with feet apart, looking at the floor, staring back and forth along one of the cracks. "Why didn't they hang him?" he asked the silence in the room.

"Why didn't they hang him?" he repeated, his voice louder.

Toby kept his post by the window, not moving a muscle in his face, staring out at the man across the street. "I don't know," he said. "For murder, they should. I guess they should, but they didn't."

Doane's eyes came again to the flowers, and some of the strain went out of his face. Then suddenly his eyes closed and he gave a long sigh, and then, luxuriously, stretched his arms. "Good God!" he said, his voice easy again. "It's funny how it comes over you like that." He shook his head violently. "I don't know why it should. It's not the first time. But it always does."

"I know," Toby said.

"It just builds up and then it busts."

"I know."

"The train may be late."

Toby said nothing.

"You never can tell," Doane said, buckling on his gun belt. "Things may have changed with Jordan. Maybe won't even come. You never can tell. I'm going up to the cemetery as soon as we hear from Staley."

"I wouldn't. You'd just tempt young Jordan to start something."

"I've been going up there every Sunday since she died."

"We'd best both just stay in here. Let them make the first move."

Feet sounded on the steps outside and Doane stopped breathing for a second. Staley came in, his face pinched, tight and dead, his eyes on the floor. Doane looked him over carefully.

"Is it on time?" he asked steadily.

Staley looked up, his faded blue eyes distant, pointed somewhere over Doane's head. "Mr. Doane, you ain't handled this thing right. You should of drove young Jordan out of town." His hand went to his chest and he took off the deputy's badge.

"What are you doing?" Doane asked sharply.

"If you'd of handled it right, we could have beat this," Staley said, his voice louder.

"You know nobody's done nothing yet," Toby said softly, his gentle brown eyes on Staley. "There's nothing we can do until they start something."

"I'm quitting, Mr. Doane," Staley said. He looked around for some-place to put the star. He started for the desk, hesitated, and then awk-wardly, with a peculiar diffidence, laid the star gently on the window sill.

Doane's jaw began to jut a little. "You still haven't answered my question. Is the train on time?"

"Yes. Four ten. Just on time." Staley stood staring at Doane, then swallowed. "I saw Frank Colby. He was in the livery putting up his horse. He'd had a long ride on that horse. I asked him what he was doing in town—friendly like." He ducked his head and swallowed again. "He didn't know I was a deputy, I had my star off." He looked up again. "They're all meeting together, Mr. Doane. Young Jordan, and Colby and Pierce. They're going to meet Jordan when he comes in. The same four."

"So you're quitting," Doane said.

"Yes, sir. It ain't been handled right."

Toby stood looking at him, his gentle eyes dull. "Get out," he said, his voice low and tight.

Staley looked at him, nodded and tried to smile, which was too weak to last. "Sure."

Toby took a step toward him. Staley's eyes were wild as he stood against the door. He tried to back out of Toby's way.

"Get out," Toby said again, and his small brown fist flashed out. Staley stepped backward and fell down the steps in a sprawling heap,

scrambled to his feet and hobbled away. Toby closed the door slowly.
He stood rubbing his knuckles, his face red and tight.

"That didn't do any good," Doane said softly.

Toby turned on him. "It couldn't do no harm," he said acidly, throwing the words into Doane's face.

"You want to quit, too?" Doane asked, smiling.

"Sure, I want to quit," Toby shot out. "Sure. Go on to your blasted
cemetery, go on with your flowers, old man—" He sat down suddenly
on the straight chair. "Put a flower up there for me, too."

Doane went to the door. "Put some water on the heater, Toby. Set
out the liniment that the vet gave me. I'll try it again when I get back.
It might do some good yet."

He let himself out and stood in the sunlight on the porch, the flowers
drooping in his hand, looking against the sun across the street at the
dim figure under the shaded porch.

Then he saw the two other shapes hunkered against the front of
the saloon in the shade of the porch, one on each side of young Jordan,
who sat tilted back in a chair. Colby and Pierce. The glare of the sun
beat back from the blinding white dust and fought shimmering in the
air.

Doane pulled the brim of his hat farther down in front and stepped
slowly down to the board sidewalk, observing carefully from squinted
eyes, and just as carefully avoiding any pause which might be interpreted as a challenge.

Young Jordan had the bottle to his lips as Doane came out. He held
it there for a moment motionless, and then, as Doane reached the
walk, he passed the bottle slowly sideward to Colby and leaned forward,
away from the wall, so that the chair came down softly. He sat there,
leaning forward slightly, watching while Doane untied his horse. As
Doane mounted, Jordan got up. Colby's hand grabbed one of his arms.
He shook it off and untied his own horse from the rail.

Doane's mouth tightened and his eyes looked a little sad. He turned
his horse, and holding the flowers so the jog would not rattle off the
petals, headed up the street, looking straight ahead.

The hoofs of his horse made soft, almost inaudible little plops in
the deep dust. Behind him he heard a sudden stamping of hoofs and
then the harsh splitting and crash of wood. He looked back. Young
Jordan's horse was up on the sidewalk, wild-eyed and snorting, with

young Jordan leaning forward half out of the saddle, pushing himself back from the horse's neck, back off the horn into the saddle, swaying insecurely. And as Jordan managed the horse off the sidewalk Doane looked quickly forward again, his eyes fixed distantly ahead and blank.

He passed men he knew, and out of the corner of his eye he saw their glances slowly follow him, calm, or gloomy, or shrewdly speculative. As he passed, he knew their glances were shifting to the man whose horse was softly coming behind him. It was like that all the way up the street. The flowers were drooping markedly now.

The town petered out with a few Mexican shacks, the road dwindled to broad ruts, and the sage was suddenly on all sides of him, stretching away toward the heat-obscured mountains like an infinite multitude of gray-green sheep. He turned off the road and began the slight ascent up the little hill whereon the cemetery lay. Grasshoppers shrilled invisibly in the sparse, dried grass along the track, silent as he came by, and shrill again as he passed, only to become silent again as the other rider came.

He swung off at the rusty barbed wire Missouri gate and slipped the loop from the post, and the shadow of the other slid tall across his path and stopped. Doane licked his lips quickly and looked up, his grasp tightening on the now sweat-wilted newspaper. Young Jordan was sitting his horse, open-mouthed, leaning forward with his hands on the pommel to support himself, his eyes vague and dull. His lips were wet and red, and hung in a slight smile.

A lark made the air sweet over to the left, and then Doane saw it, rising into the air. It hung in the sun, over the cemetery. Moving steadily and avoiding all suddenness, Doane hung his reins over the post.

"You don't like me, do you?" young Jordan said. A long thread of saliva descended from the corner of his slackly smiling mouth.

Doane's face set into a sort of blank preparedness. He turned and started slowly through the gate, his shoulders hunched up and pulled backward.

Jordan got down from the saddle, and Doane turned toward him slowly. Jordan came forward straight enough, with his feet apart, braced against staggering. He stopped three feet from Doane, bent forward, his mouth slightly open.

"You got any objections to me being in town?"

"No," Doane said, and stood still.

Jordan thought that over, his eyes drifting idly sideways for a moment. Then they came back, to a finer focus this time, and he said, "Why not?" hunching forward again, his hands open and held away from the holsters at his hips.

Doane looked at the point of his nose. "You haven't done anything, Jordan. Except get drunk. Nothing to break the law."

"I haven't done nothing," Jordan said, his eyes squinting away at one of the small, tilting tombstones. "By God, I'll do something. Whadda I got to do?" He drew his head back, as though he were farsighted, and squinted. "Whadda I got to do to make you fight, huh?"

"Don't do anything," Doane said quietly, keeping his voice even. "Just go back and have another drink. Have a good time."

"You think I ain't sober enough to fight?" Jordan slipped his right gun out of its holster, turning away from Doane. Doane stiffened. "Wait, mister," Jordan said.

He cocked the gun. "See that bird?" He raised the gun into the air, squinting along the barrel. The bright nickel of its finish gleamed in the sun. The lark wheeled and fluttered. Jordan's arm swung unsteadily in a small circle.

He pulled the trigger and the gun blasted. The lark jumped in the air, flew away about twenty feet, and began circling again, catching insects.

"Missed 'im," Jordan mumbled, lowering his arm and wiping sweat off his forehead. "Damn it, I can't see!" He raised his arm again. Again the heavy blast cracked Doane's ears. Down in the town, near the Mexican huts, he could see tiny figures run out into the street.

The bird didn't jump this time, but darted away out of sight over the hill.

"Got him," Jordan said, scanning the sky. His eyes wandered over the graveyard for a moment, looking for the bird's body. "Now you see?" he said, turning to Doane, his eyes blurred and watering with the sun's glare. "I'm going down and shoot up the damned town. Come down and stop me, you old—"

He turned and lurched sideways a step, straightened himself out and walked more steadily toward his horse, laughing to himself. Doane turned away, his face sick, and trudged slowly up the hill, his eyes on the ground.

He stopped at one of the newer graves. The headstone was straight on this one. He looked at it, his face changing expression. "Here lies Cecelia Doane, born 1837, died 1885, the loyal wife..."

He stooped and pulled a weed from the side of the grave, then pulled a bunch of withered stems from a small green funnel by the headstone, and awkwardly took the fresh flowers out of the newspaper. He put the flowers into the funnel, wedging them firmly down into the bottom, and let it down again. He stood up and moved back, wiping sweat from his eyes.

A sudden shout came from the gate, and the sharp crack of a quirt. Doane turned with a befuddled look.

Jordan was back on his horse, beating Doane's. He had looped the reins over its neck so that it would run free. It was tearing away down the slope heading back for town.

Doane stood with his hat in his hand, his face suddenly beet red. He took a step after Jordan, and then stood still, shaking a little. He stared fixedly after him, watching him turn into the main road and toward the main street again. Then, sighing deeply, he turned back to the grave. Folding the newspaper, he began dusting off the heavy slab, whispering to himself. "No, Cissie. I could have gone. But, you know— it's my town."

He straightened up, his face flushed, put on his hat, and slapping the folded paper against his knee, started down the path. He got to the Missouri gate, closed it, and started down the ruts again.

A shot came from the town, and he stopped. Then there were two more, sharp spurts of sound coming clear and definite across the sage. He made out a tiny figure in a blue shirt running along a sidewalk.

He stood stock-still, the grasshoppers singing in a contented chorus all around him in the bright yellow glare. A train whistle came faint from off the plain, and he looked far across it. He made out the tiny trailed plume of smoke.

His knees began to quiver very slightly and he began to walk, very slowly, down the road.

Then suddenly there was a splatter of shots from below. The train whistle came again, louder, a crying wail of despair in the burning, brilliant, dancing air.

He began to hurry, stumbling a little in the ruts. And then he stopped short, his face open in fear. "My God, my empty horse, those shots— Toby, no!" He began to run, shambling, awkward and stumbling, his face ashen.

From the end of the street, as he hobbled panting past the tight-shut Mexican shanties, he could see a blue patch in the dust in front of the saloon, and shambled to a halt. It wasn't Toby, whoever it was, lying there face down: face buried in the deep, pillowing dust, feet still on the board sidewalk where the man had been standing.

The street was empty. None of the faces he knew looked at him now. He drew one of his guns and cocked it and walked fast up the walk, on the saloon side.

A shot smashed ahead of him and he stopped, shrinking against a store front. Inside, through the glass door, he could see two pale faces in the murk. Blue powder smoke curled out from under the saloon porch ahead of him.

Another shot smashed, this time from his office. The spurt of smoke, almost invisible in the sunlight, was low down in the doorway. Two horses were loose in the street now, his own, standing alert up past the saloon, and young Jordan's, half up on the boardwalk under one of the porches.

He walked forward, past young Jordan's horse, to the corner of the saloon building. Another shot slammed out of his office door, the bullet smacking the window ahead of him. A small, slow smile grew on his mouth. He looked sideways at the body in the street. Young Jordan lay with the back of his head open to the sun, crimson and brilliant, his bright nickel gun still in his right hand, its hammer still cocked, unfired.

The train whistle moaned again, closer.

"Doane," Toby called from the office door, invisible. "Get out of town." There was a surge of effort in the voice, a strain that made it almost a squeal. "I'm shot in the leg. Get out before they get together."

A door slammed somewhere. Doane glanced down between the saloon and the store beside it. Then he saw, fifty yards down the street, a figure come out of another side alley and hurry away down the walk toward the station. From the saloon door another shot slammed across the street. Toby held his fire.

Doane peered after the running figure, his eyes squinting thoughtfully. The train's whistle shrieked again like the ultimatum of an approaching conqueror at the edge of town, and in a moment the ground under his feet began to vibrate slightly and the hoarse roar of braking wheels came up the street.

He turned back to young Jordan's horse, petted it around the head a moment and then took it by the reins close to the bit. He guided it across the street, keeping its body between him and the front of the

saloon, without drawing fire, and went on down the alley beside his
office. At the rear door he hitched the horse and went inside.

Toby was on the floor, a gun in his hand, his hat beside him, peering
out across the sill. Doane kept low, beneath the level of the window,
and crawled up to him. Toby's left leg was twisted peculiarly and blood
leaked steadily out from the boot top onto the floor. His face was
sweating and very pale, and his lips were tight.

"I thought he got you," Toby said, keeping his eyes on the saloon
across the street. "I heard those shots and then your horse came buck-
eting back down the street. I got Jordan. Colby got me in the leg before
I got back inside."

"Never mind about that. Come on, get on your feet if you can and
I'll help you on the horse in back. You can get out of town and I'll
shift for myself."

"I think I'm going to pass out. I don't want to move. It won't hurt
no worse getting killed than it does now. The hell with the horse! Take
it yourself."

Doane looked across the street, his eyes moving over the door and
the windows carefully, inch by inch.

"I'm sorry I shot him," Toby said. "It's my fault. And it's my fight
now, Doane. Clear out."

Doane turned and scuttled out of the back. He mounted the horse
and rode down behind four stores. He turned up another alley, dashed
across the main street, down another alley, then back up behind the
saloon.

He dismounted, his gun cocked in his hand. The back door of the
place was open and he got through it quickly, the sound of his boot
heels dimmed under the blast of a shot from the front of the saloon.
From the dark rear of the room, he could see Pierce, crouched behind
the bar, squinting through a bullet hole in the stained-glass bottom
half of the front window.

There was a bottle of whisky standing on the bar beside Pierce; he
reached out a hand and tilted the bottle up to his mouth, half turning
toward Doane as he did so. Pierce kept the bottle to his lips, pretending
to drink, and, with his right hand invisible behind the bar, brought his
gun into line with Doane.

The tip of Pierce's gun came over the edge of the bar, the rest of
him not moving a hair, and Doane, gritting his teeth, squeezed slowly
and painfully on his gun trigger. The gun flamed and bucked in his

hand, and he dropped it, his face twisting in agony. The bottle fell out of Pierce's hand and spun slowly on the bar. Pierce sat there for a moment before his head fell forward and he crashed against the edge of the bar and slipped down out of sight.

Doane picked up his gun with his left hand and walked forward to the bar, holding his right hand like a crippled paw in front of him. The bottle had stopped revolving. Whisky inside it, moving back and forth, rocked it gently. He righted it and took a short pull at the neck, and in a moment the pain lines relaxed in his face. He went to the batwing doors and pushed one of them partly open.

"Toby!" he called.

There was no answer from across the street, and then he saw the barrel of a revolver sticking out of his office door, lying flat, and behind it one hand, curled loosely and uselessly around the butt.

He looked down the street. The train stood across it. A brakeman moved along the cars slowly, his head down. There was nobody else in sight.

He started to step out, and saw then two men coming up the opposite walk, running fast. Suddenly one of them stopped, grabbing the other by the arm, and pointed at him. He stared back for a moment, seeing Jordan clearly now, the square, hard face unchanged except for its pallor, bleak and bony as before.

Doane let the door swing to and continued to watch them over the top of it. They talked for a moment. Then Colby ran back down the street—well out of effective range—sprinted across it and disappeared. Down the street the engine, hidden by some building, chuffed angrily, and the cars began to move again. Jordan stood still, leaning against the front of a building, fully exposed, a hard smile on his face.

Doane turned and hurried to the back door. It opened outward. He slammed and bolted it, then hurried back to the front and waited, his gun ready. He smiled as the back door rattled, turned, fired a shot at it and listened. For a moment there was no sound. Then something solid hit it, bumped a couple of times and silence came again.

From the side of the building, just beyond the corner where Pierce's body lay, a shot crashed. The gun in the office door jumped out of the hand and spun wildly. The hand lay still.

He heard Jordan's voice from down the street, calling, the words formed slowly, slightly spaced.

"Is he dead?"

"Passed out," Colby called back.

"I'm going around back to get him. Keep Doane inside." Jordan turned and disappeared down an alley.

Doane leaned across the bar, knocked bottles off the shelves of the back bar and held his pistol on the corner of the wall, about a foot above the floor.

"Pierce," he said.

"Throw out your guns," Pierce answered.

Doane squinted at the corner, moved his gun slightly and fired. He heard a cry of pain, then curses; saw the batwing doors swing slightly. Then he turned and ran for the back door. It wouldn't give. He threw back the bolt and pushed on the door. It wouldn't give. He threw himself against it. It gave a little at the bottom. Colby had thrown a stake up against it to keep him locked in.

He ran back to the front.

Across the street, he could see somebody moving in his office, dimly, beyond the window. Suddenly the hand on the floor disappeared.

"Come on out, you old—" Pierce said, panting. "You only skinned me." His voice was closer than before, somewhere between the door and the corner of the building, below the level of the stained glass.

Then Doane saw Toby's white shirt beyond the window opposite. Jordan was holding him up, and moving toward the door. Jordan came out on the porch, hugging Toby around the chest, protecting himself with the limp body. With a heave he sent Toby flying down the steps, and jumped back out of sight. Toby rolled across the sidewalk and fell into the street, where he lay motionless.

Doane looked stupidly at Toby, then at young Jordan, still lying with his feet cocked up on the sidewalk.

"He ain't dead, Doane," Jordan called. "Come and get him if you want him alive." He fired through the window. Dust jumped six inches from Toby's head. "Come on out, Doane, and shoot it out. You got a chance to save him." The gun roared again, and dust jumped a second time beside Toby's head, almost in the same spot.

"Leave the kid alone," Doane called. "This fight's between you and me."

"The next shot kills him, Doane."

Doane's face sagged white and he leaned against the side of the door. He could hear Pierce breathing heavily in the silence, just outside. He pushed himself away from the door and drew a breath through

clenched teeth. He cocked his pistol and strode out, swinging around.
Pierce fired from the sidewalk, and Doane aimed straight into the blast
and pulled as he felt himself flung violently around by Pierce's bullet.

Pierce came up from the sidewalk and took two steps toward him,
opening and shutting a mouth that was suddenly full of blood, his eyes
wide and wild, and then pitched down at his feet.

Doane's right arm hung useless, his gun at his feet. With his left
hand he drew his other gun and stepped out from the walk, his mouth
wide open, as though he were gasping for breath or were about to
scream, and took two steps toward Toby as Jordan came out of the
office door, firing. The slug caught Doane along the side of his neck,
cutting the shoulder muscle, and his head fell over to one side. He
staggered on, firing. He saw Toby trying to get up, saw Jordan fall back
against the building, red running down the front of his shirt, and the
smile gone.

Jordan stood braced against the building, holding his gun in both
hands, firing as he slid slowly down. One bullet took Doane in the
stomach, another in the knee. He went down, flopped forward and
dragged himself up to where Toby lay trying to prop himself up on
one elbow. Doane knelt there like a dog, puking blood into the dust,
blood running out of his nose, but his gray eyes almost indifferent, as
though there were one man dying and another watching.

He saw Jordan lift his gun with both hands and aim it toward Toby,
and as the hammer fell, he threw himself across Toby's head and took
it in the back. He rolled off onto his back and lay staring into the sky.

Upside down, he saw Toby take his gun and get up on one elbow,
level it at Jordan and fire, and then saw Toby's face, over his, looking
down at him as the deputy knelt in the street.

They stayed that way for a long moment, while Doane's eyes grew
more and more dull and the dark of his blood in the white dust grew
broader. His breath was coming hard, in small sharp gasps.

"There's nothing in it, kid," he whispered. "Only a tin star. They
don't hang the right ones. You got to fight everything twice. It's a job
for a dog."

"Thank you, Doane."

"It's all for free. You going to quit, Toby?"

Toby looked down at the gray face, the mouth and chin and neck
crimson, the gray eyes dull. Toby shook his head. His face was hard
as a rock.

Doane's face suddenly looked a little surprised, his eyes went past Toby to the sky. Toby looked up. A lark was high above them, circling and fluttering, directly overhead. "A pretty bird," Doane mumbled. "A very pretty bird."

His head turned slowly to one side, and Toby looked down at him and saw him as though fast asleep.

He took Doane's gun in his hand, and took off Doane's star, and sat there in the street while men slowly came out of stores and circled about them. He sat there unmoving, looking at Doane's half-averted face, holding the two things tightly, one in each hand, like a child with a broken toy, his face soft and blurred, his eyes unwet.

After a while the lark went away. He looked up at the men, and saw Mettrick.

"I told him he should have resigned," Mettrick said, his voice high. "He could have taken his horse—"

"Shut up," Toby said. "Shut up or get out." His eyes were sharp and his face placid and set. He turned to another of the men. "Get the doc," he said. "I've got a busted leg. And I've got a lot to do."

The man looked at him, a little startled, and then ran.

IT HAPPENED ONE NIGHT

(1934)

NIGHT BUS
SAMUEL HOPKINS ADAMS

Frank Capra first read "Night Bus" in a Palm Springs barbershop. "It had the smell of novelty," said Capra, who bought the piece for $5,000 and then promptly forgot about it. After being shunted back and forth between the Columbia and MGM studios on a couple of aborted projects, Capra returned to Columbia and started pushing what would become *It Happened One Night* into production. It was perhaps the biggest "sleeper" in the history of American filmmaking—indeed, the picture was almost never made at all. For starters, producer Harry Cohn was against the idea of a "bus picture" based on the history of two similar films that had stiffed the previous year; leading man Clark Gable, on loan from MGM, resented being forced into what he felt was a chump role; and the script went to four possible leading ladies before Claudette Colbert relented with the proviso that her base salary of $25,000 be doubled and the shooting completed in four weeks. Amazingly, Capra succeeded in finishing the film on schedule and within budget (a mere $325,000) and upon her arrival in Sun Valley for the Christmas picture in the world." Nobody, least of all the cast and crew, could have been prepared for what happened on the night of the Academy Award ceremonies in 1935. *It Happened One Night* won all five major awards: Best Picture, Best Director, Best Actor, Best Actress, and Best Writer—a sweep that only one other film, *One Flew Over the Cuckoo's Nest* (1975), has ever achieved. For Depression-era audiences, the film offered a slice of escapist fantasy grounded in characters and plot that were still within the experience of the average movie-goer. The picture has endured as a classic of romantic comedy.

Novelist, short story writer, and investigative reporter, SAMUEL HOPKINS ADAMS (1871–1958) was raised in Rochester, N.Y. Among his many works of reportage, a series in *Collier's* on quackery in patent medicine is credited with furthering the passage of the first Pure Food and Drug Act. Many of his novels were also exposés of civic corruption. About his life as a writer, Adams said, "It permits freedom of thought, action, and mode of existence, and this is an era when individual choice, threatened as it is, has never been so precious." In nearly half a century of literary output, only two of Adams's stories went unsold.

IT HAPPENED ONE NIGHT

Released: 1934
Production: Harry Cohn for Columbia (Academy Award)
Direction: Frank Capra (Academy Award)
Screenplay: Robert Riskin and Frank Capra (uncredited) (Academy Award)
Cinematography: Joseph Walker
Editing: Gene Havlick
Running time: 105 minutes

PRINCIPAL CHARACTERS:

Peter Warne	Clark Gable (Academy Award)
Ellie Andrews	Claudette Colbert (Academy Award)
Alexander Andrews	Walter Connolly
Mr. Shapeley	Roscoe Karns
King Westley	Jameson Thomas
Bus Driver	Ward Bond

Through the resonant cave of the terminal, a perfunctory voice boomed out something about Jacksonville, points north, and New York. The crowd at the rail seethed. At the rear, Mr. Peter Warne hoisted the battered weight of his carryall, resolutely declining a porter's aid. Too bad he hadn't come earlier; he'd have drawn a better seat. Asperities of travel, however, meant little to his seasoned endurance.

Moreover, he was inwardly fortified by what the advertisement vaunted as "The Best Fifteen-cent Dinner in Miami; Wholesome, Clean and Plentiful." The sign knew. Appetite sated, ticket paid for, a safe if small surplus in a secure pocket; on the whole, he was content with life.

Behind him stood and, if truth must be told, shoved, a restive girl. Like him she carried her own luggage, a dressing case, small and costly. Like him she had paid for her ticket to New York. Her surplus, however, was a fat roll of high-caste bills. Her dinner at the ornate Seafoam Club had cost somebody not less than ten dollars. But care sat upon her somber brow, and her expression was a warning to all and sundry to keep their distance. She was far from being content with life.

All chairs had been filled when Peter Warne threaded the aisle, having previously tossed his burden into an overhead bracket. Only the rear bench, stretching the full width of the car, offered any space. Three passengers had already settled into it; there was accommodation for two more, but the space was piled full of baled newspapers.

"Hi!" said the late arrival cheerfully to the uniformed driver, who stood below on the pavement looking bored. "I'd like one of these seats."

The driver turned a vacant gaze upon him and turned away again.

"Have this stuff moved, won't you?" requested the passenger, with unimpaired good humor.

The official offered a fair and impartial view of a gray-clad back.

Mr. Warne reflected. "If you want a thing well done, do it yourself," he decided. Still amiable, he opened the window and tossed out four bundles in brisk succession.

Upon this, the occupant of the uniform evinced interest. "Hey! What d'you think you're doin'?" He approached, only to stagger back under the impact of another bale which bounded from his shoulder. With a grunt of rage, he ran around to the rear door, yanked it open and pushed his way in, his face red and threatening.

Having, meantime, disposed of the remainder of the papers, Mr. Warne turned, thrust his hand into his rear pocket, and waited. The driver also waited, lowering but uncertain. Out popped the hand, grasping nothing more deadly than a notebook.

"Well, come ahead," said its owner.

"Come ahead with what?"

"You were figuring to bust me in the jaw, weren't you?"

"Yes; and maybe I *am* goin' to bust you in the jor."

"Good!" He made an entry in the book. "I need the money."

The other goggled. "What money?"

"Well, say ten thousand dollars' damages. Brutal and unprovoked assault upon helpless passenger. It ought to be worth that. Eh?"

The official wavered, torn between caution and vindictiveness. A supercilious young voice in the aisle behind Peter Warne said: "Do you mind moving aside?"

Peter Warne moved. The girl glided into the corner he had so laboriously cleared for himself. Peter raised his cap.

"Take my seat, madam," he invited, with empressement. She bestowed upon him a faintly speculative glance, indicating that he was of a species unknown to her, and turned to the window. He sat down in the sole remaining place.

The bus started.

Adjustment to the motion of ten tons on wheels is largely a matter of technique and experience. Toughened traveler as he was, Peter Warne sat upright, swaying from the hips as if on well-oiled hinges. Not so the girl at his side. She undertook to relax into her corner with a view to forgetting her troubles in sleep. This was a major error. She was shuttled back and forth between the wall and her neighbor until her exasperation reached the point of protest.

"Tell that man to drive slower," she directed Peter.

"It may surprise you, but I doubt if he'd do it for me."

"Oh, of course! You're afraid of him. I could see that." Leaning wearily away, she said something not so completely under her breath but that Peter caught the purport of it.

"I suspect," he observed unctuously and with intent to annoy, "that you are out of tune with the Infinite."

Unwitherable though his blithe spirit was, it felt the scorch of her glare. Only too obviously he was, at that moment, the focal point for a hatred which included the whole universe. Something must have seriously upset a disposition which, he judged, was hardly inured to accepting gracefully the contrarieties of a maladjusted world.

She looked like that. Her eyes were dark and wide beneath brows that indicated an imperious temper. The long, bold sweep of the cheek was deeply tanned and ended in a chin which obviously expected to have its own way. But the mouth was broad, soft and generous. Peter wondered what it would look like when, as, and if it smiled. He didn't think it likely that he would find out.

Beyond Fort Lauderdale the bus was resuming speed when the feminine driver of a sports roadster, disdaining the formality of a signal, took a quick turn and ran the heavier vehicle off the road. There was a bump, a light crash, a squealing of brakes, the bus lurched to a stop with a tire ripped loose. After a profane inspection, the driver announced a fifteen-minute wait.

They were opposite that sign manual of Florida's departed boom days, a pair of stone pillars leading into a sidewalked wilderness and flanked by two highly ornamental lamp-posts without glass or wiring. The girl got out for a breath of air, set her dressing case at her feet and leaned against one of the monuments to perishable optimism. As she disembarked, her neighbor, in a spirit of unappreciated helpfulness, had advised her to walk up and down; it would save her from cramps later on.

Just for that she wouldn't do it. He was too officious, that young man. Anyway, the fewer human associations she suffered, the better she would like it. She had a hate on the whole race. Especially men. With a total lack of interest, she observed the parade of her fellow wayfarers up and down the road, before shutting them out from her bored vision.

A shout startled her. The interfering stranger on the opposite side of the road had bounded into the air as if treacherously stabbed from behind, and was now racing toward her like a bull at full charge. At the same time she was aware of a shadow moving away from her elbow and dissolving into the darkness beyond the gates. Close to her, the sprinter swerved, heading down the deserted avenue. Beyond him she heard a crash of brush. His foot caught in a projecting root and he went headlong, rising to limp forward a few yards and give it up with a ruefully shaken head.

"Lost him," he said, coming opposite her.

"I don't know why that should interest me." She hoped that she sounded as disagreeable as she felt. And she did.

"All right," he replied shortly, and made as if to go on, but changed his mind. "He got your bag," he explained.

"Oh!" she ejaculated, realizing that that important equipment was indeed missing. "Who?" she added feebly.

"I don't know his name and address. The thin-faced bird who sat in front of you."

"Why didn't you catch him?" she wailed. "What'll I do now?"

"Did it have much in it?"

"All my things."

"Your money and ticket?"

"Not my ticket; I've got that."

"You can wire for money from Jacksonville, you know."

"Thank you. I can get to New York all right," she returned, with deceptive calm, making a rapid calculation based on the six or eight dollars which she figured (by a considerable overestimate) were still left her.

"Shall I report your loss at the next stop?"

"Please don't." She was unnecessarily vehement. One might almost suppose the suggestion had alarmed her.

Joining the others, she climbed aboard. The departed robber had left a chair vacant next the window. One bit of luck, anyway; now she could get away from that rear seat and her friendly neighbor. She transferred herself, only to regret the change bitterly before ten miles had been covered. For she now had the chair above the curve of the wheel, which is the least comfortable of bus seats. In that rigorously enforced distortion of the body she found her feet asleep, her legs cramped. Oh, for the lesser torments of the place she had so rashly abandoned!

Twisting her stiffening neck, she looked back. The seat was still vacant. The chatty young man seemed asleep.

Lapsing into the corner, she prepared for a night of heroism. The bus fled fast through the dark and wind. Exigencies of travel she had known before; once she had actually slept in the lower berth of a section, all the drawing-rooms and compartments being sold out. But that was less cramped than her present seat. Just the same, she would have stood worse rather than stay at home after what had happened!

If only she had brought something to read. She surveyed her fellow passengers, draped in widely diverse postures. Then the miracle began to work within her. She grew drowsy. It was not so much sleep as the reflex anaesthetic of exhaustion. Consciousness passed from her.

Sun rays struck through the window upon her blinking lids. White villas slid by. A milk cart rattled past. Stiff and dazed, she felt as if her legs had been chilled into paralysis, but all the upper part of her was swathed in mysterious warmth. What were these brown, woolly folds?

The tanned, quick-fingered hands explored, lifted a sleeve which flopped loose, discovered a neatly darned spot; another; a third. It had seen hard service, that garment which wrapped her. She thought, with a vague pleasure of the senses, that it had taken on a sturdy personality of its own connected with tobacco and wood smoke and strong soap; the brisk, faintly troubling smell of clean masculinity. She liked it, that sweater.

From it, her heavy eyes moved to her neighbor who was still asleep. By no stretch of charity could he be called an ornament to the human species. His physiognomy was blunt, rough and smudgy with bristles; his hair reddish and uncompromisingly straight.

Nevertheless, a guarded approval might be granted to the setting of the eyes under a freckled forehead, and the trend of the mouth suggested strong, even teeth within. Nose and chin betokened a careless good humor. As for the capable hands, there was no blinking the stains upon them.

His clothing was rough and baggy, but neat enough except for a gaping rent along one trouser leg which he had come by in chasing her thief. For the first time in her life, she wished that she knew how to sew. This surprised her when she came to consider it later.

For the moment she only smiled. It was a pity that Peter Warne could not have waked up at the brief, warm interval before her lips drooped back to weariness.

Nearly an hour later he roused himself at the entrance to Jacksonville where a change of lines was due, and his first look rested upon a wan and haggard face.

"Breakfast!" said he, with energy and anticipation.

The face brightened. "The Windsor is a good place," stated its owner.

"I wouldn't doubt it for a minute. So is Hungry Joe's."

"Do you expect me to eat at some horrid beanery?"

"Beans have their virtue. But oatmeal and coffee give you the most for your money."

"Oh, money! I'd forgotten about money."

"If you want to change your mind and wire for it—"

"I don't. I want to eat."

"With me?"

She speculated as to whether this might be an invitation; decided that it probably wasn't. "If the place is clean."

"It's cleaner than either of us at the present moment of speaking," he grinned.

Thus recalled to considerations of femininity, she said: "I'll bet I look simply *terrible!*"

"Well, I wouldn't go as far as that," was the cautious reply.

"Anyhow, there's one thing I've got to have right away."

"What's that?"

"If you must know, it's a bath."

"Nothing doing. Bus leaves in fifty minutes."

"We can tell the driver to wait."

"Certainly, we can tell him. But there's just a possibility that he might not do it."

This was lost upon her. "Of course he'll do it. People always wait for me," she added with sweet self-confidence. "If they didn't, I'd never get anywhere."

"This is a hard-boiled line," he explained patiently. "The man would lose his job if he held the bus, like as not."

She yawned. "He could get another, couldn't he?"

"Oh, of course! Just like that. You haven't happened to hear of a thing called unemployment, have you?"

"Oh, that's just socialistic talk. There are plenty of jobs for people who really want to work."

"Yes? Where did you get that line of wisdom?"

She was bored and showed it in her intonation. "Why, everybody knows that. Bill was saying the other day that most of these people are idle because they're just waiting for the dole or something."

"Who's Bill?"

"My oldest brother."

"Oh! And I suppose Bill works?"

"We-ell, he plays polo. Almost every day."

Mr. Warne made a noise like a trained seal.

"What did you say?"

"I said, 'here's the eatery.' Or words to that effect."

The place was speckless. Having a heatlhy young appetite, the girl disdained to follow the meager example of her escort, and ordered high, wide and handsome. Directing that his fifteen-cent selection be held for five minutes, Peter excused himself with a view to cleaning up. He returned to find his companion gone.

"At the Windsor, having my bath," a scrawl across the bill of fare enlightened him. "Back in half an hour."

That, he figured after consultation of his watch, would leave her just four minutes and twenty seconds to consume an extensive breakfast and get around the corner to the terminal, assuming that she lived up to her note, which struck him as, at the least, doubtful. Well, let the little fool get out of it as best she could. Why bother?

Peter ate slowly, while reading the paper provided free for patrons. At the end of twenty-five minutes, he was craning his neck out of the window. A slight figure turned the corner. Relief was in the voice which bade the waiter rush the order. The figure approached—and passed. Wrong girl. Peter cursed.

Time began to race. Less than five minutes to go now. Half of that was the minimum allowance for getting to the starting place. Peter bore his grip to the door, ready for a flying take-off, in case she appeared. In case she didn't. . . . People always waited for her, did they? Well, he'd be damned if he would! In one short minute he would be leaving. Thirty seconds; twenty; fifteen; five. Sister Ann, do you see anything moving? *Malbrouck s'en va-t'en guerre*. No dust along the road? We're off!

Such was the intention. But something interfered; an intangible something connected with the remembrance of soft contours on a young, sleeping face, of wondering eyes slowly opened. Peter dashed his valise upon the floor, kicked it, cast himself into a chair and sulked. His disposition was distinctly tainted when the truant made triumphal entrance. She was freshened and groomed and radiant, a festal apparition. Up rose then Mr. Warne, uncertain where to begin. She forestalled him.

"Why, how nice you look!" By virtue of his five minutes, the freedom of the washroom, and a pocket kit, he had contrived to shave, brush up, and make the best of a countenance which, if by strict standards unbeautiful, did not wholly lack points. "How much time have I for breakfast?"

"Plenty," barked Peter.

"Swell! I'm starving. I *did* hurry."

"Did you?" he inquired, between his teeth.

"Of course I did. Didn't you just say I had plenty of time?"

"You certainly have. All day."

She set down her coffee cup. "Why, I thought our bus—"

"Our bus is on its way to New York. The next one leaves at eight tonight."

"I do think you might have telephoned them to wait," she protested. A thought struck her impressionable mind. "Why, you missed it, too!"

"So I did. Isn't that extraordinary!"

"Because you were waiting for me?"

"Something of the sort."

"It was awfully nice of you. But why?"

"Because the poor damfool just didn't have the heart to leave a helpless little hick like you alone," he explained.

"I believe you're sore at me."

"Oh, not in the least! Only at myself for getting involved in such a mix-up."

"Nobody asked you to miss the old bus," she stated warmly. "Why did you?"

"Because you remind me of my long-lost angel mother, of course. Don't you ever go to the movies? Now, do you still want to go to New York?"

"We-ell; I've got my ticket. I suppose that's still good."

"Up to ten days. At this rate, it'll take us all of that to get there. The thing is to figure out what to do now."

"Let's go to the races," said she.

"On what?" he inquired.

"I've got some money left."

"How much?"

She examined her purse. "Why, there's only a little over four dollars," she revealed in disappointed accents.

"How far d'you think that'll take you?"

"I could bet it on the first race. Maybe I'd win."

"Maybe you'd lose, too."

"I thought you had that kind of disposition the minute I set eyes on you," she complained. "Pessimist!"

"Economist," he corrected.

"Just as bad. Anyway, we've got a whole day to kill. What's your dashing idea of the best way to do it?"

"A park bench."

"What do you do on a park bench?"

"Sit."

"It sounds dumb."

"It's cheap."

"I hate cheap things, but just to prove I'm reasonable I'll try it for a while."

He led her a block or so to the area of palms and flowers facing the Windsor where they found a bench vacant and sat down. Peter slouched restfully. His companion fidgeted.

"Maybe the band will play by and by," said he encouragingly.

"Wouldn't that be nah-ice!" murmured the girl, and Peter wondered whether a hard slap would break her beyond repair.

"How old are you, anyway?" he demanded. "Fifteen?"

"I'm twenty-one, if you want to know."

"And I suppose it cost your family a bunch of money to bring you to your present fine flower of accomplished womanhood."

"You shouldn't try to be poetic. It doesn't, somehow, go with your face."

"Never mind my face. If I take you to the station and buy you a ticket to Miami—day coach, of course," he interpolated, "will you go back, like a sensible girl?"

"No, I won't. Think how silly I'd look, sneaking back after having—"

"You'd look sillier trying to get to New York at your present rate of expenditure," he warned, as she failed to complete her objection.

"If you can put up the price of a ticket to Miami," said she, with a luminous thought, "you might better lend me the money. I'll pay you back—twice over."

"Tha-anks."

"Meaning you won't?"

"Your powers of interpretation are positively uncanny."

"I might have known you wouldn't." She turned upon him an offended back.

"My name," he said to the back, "is Peter Warne."

A shrug indicated her total indifference to this bit of information. Then she rose and walked away.

He called after her: "I'll be here at six-thirty. Try not to keep me waiting *more* than half an hour."

Just for that—thought the girl—I'll be an hour late.

But she was not. It annoyed her to find how a day could drag in a town where she knew nobody. She went to a movie. She lunched. She went to another movie. She took a walk. Still, it was not yet six o'clock.

At six thirty-one she started for the park. At six thirty-four she was at the spot, or what she had believed to be the spot, but which she decided couldn't be, since no Peter Warne was visible. Several other benches were in sight of the vacant band stand. She made the rounds of all. None was occupied by the object of her search. Returning to the first one, she sat down in some perturbation: perhaps something had happened to Peter Warne. Nothing short of an accident could explain his absence.

There she sat for what seemed like the better part of an hour, until an ugly suspicion seeped into her humiliated mind that she had been left in the lurch. And by a man. A clock struck seven. She rose uncertainly.

"Oh!" she said, in a long exhalation.

Peter Warne was strolling around the corner of the stand.

"Where have you been?" she demanded, like an outraged empress.

He remained unstricken. "You were late," he observed.

"I wasn't. What if I was? Only a minute."

"Nearer five."

"How do you know? You must have been watching. You were here all the time. And you let me think you'd gone away. Oh! Oh! *Oh!*"

"You're pretty casual about keeping other people waiting, you know."

"That's different." She spoke with a profound conviction of privilege.

"I'm not going to argue that with you. Have you any money left?"

"A dollar and four cents," she announced, after counting and recounting.

Coolly he took her purse, transferred the coins to his pocket, and handed it back. "Confiscated for the common necessity," he stated, and she refrained from protest. "Come along."

She fell into step with him. "Could I please have something to eat?"

"Such is the idea. We'll try Hungry Joe's again."

This time he did the ordering for both of them: soup, hash, thick, pulpy griddle cakes and coffee. Total, sixty-five cents. Fortified by this unfamiliar but filling diet, she decided to give Mr. Peter Warne a more fitting sense of their relative status. Some degree of respect was what her soul demanded to bolster her tottering self-confidence. She had heard that a married woman was in a better position to assert herself than a girl. On that basis she would impress Peter.

"You've been treating me like a child," she complained. "You may as well understand right now that I'm not. I'm a married woman. I'm Mrs. Corcoran Andrews." She had selected this name because Corcoran, who was her third or fourth cousin, had been pestering her to marry him for a year. So he wouldn't mind. The effect was immediate.

"Huh?" jerked out the recipient of the information. "I thought Corker Andrews married a pink chorine."

"They're divorced. Do you *know* Corker?"

"Sure I know Corker."

"You're not a *friend* of his?" The implication of her surprise was unflattering.

"I didn't say that." He grinned. "The fact is, I blacked his boots once for three months."

"What did you do that for?"

"What does a man black boots for? Because I had to. So you're Cor—Mr. Andrews' wife." His regard rested upon her small, strong, deeply browned left hand. She hastily pulled it away.

"My ring's in the bag that was stolen."

"Of course," he remarked. (What did he mean by that?) "Time to be moving."

They emerged into a droning pour of rain. "Can't you get a taxi?" she asked.

"We walk," was the uncompromising reply, as he tucked his hand beneath her arm. They caught the bus with little to spare, and again drew the rear seat.

Outside, someone was saying: "Since Thursday. Yep; a hundred miles up the road. There'll be bridges out."

Feeling sleepy and indifferent, she paid no heed. She lapsed into a doze which, beginning bumpily against the wall, subsided into the unrealized comfort of his shoulder.

Water splashing on the floor boards awakened her; it was followed by the whir of the wheels, spinning in reverse.

"Got out by the skin of our teeth," said Peter Warne's lips close to her ear.

"What is it?"

"Some creek or other on the rampage. We'll not make Charleston this night."

He went forward, returning with dreary news. "We're going to stay in the nearest village. It looks like a night in the bus for us."

"Oh, no! I can't stand this bus any longer. I want to go to bed," she wailed.

He fetched out his small notebook and fell to figuring. "It'll be close reckoning," he said, scowling at the estimate. "But if you feel that way about it—" To the driver he shouted: "Let us off at Dake's place."

"What's that?"

"Tourist camp."

"Aren't they awful places? They look it."

"The Dake's chain are clean and decent enough for anybody," he answered in a tone so decisive that she followed him meekly out into the night.

Leading her to a sort of waiting room, he vanished into an office, where she could hear his voice in colloquy with an unseen man. The latter emerged with a flashlight and indicated that they were to follow. Her escort said to her, quick and low: "What's your name?"

"I told you," she returned, astonished. "I'm Mrs. Cor—"

"Your first name."

"Oh. Elspeth. Why? What's the matter?" She regarded him curiously.

"I had to register as Mr. and Mrs.," he explained nervously. "It's usual for a husband to know his wife's first name."

She asked coldly: "What is the idea?"

"Do you mind," he urged, "talking it over after we get inside?"

Their guide opened the door of a snug cabin, lighted a light and gave Elspeth a shock by saying: "Good night, Mrs. Warne. Good night, Mr. Warne. I hope you find everything comfortable."

Elspeth looked around upon the bare but neat night's lodging: two bunks separated by a scant yard of space, a chair, four clothes hooks, a shelf with a mirror above it. Peter set down his carryall and sat at the head of a bunk.

"Now," said he, "you're free to come or go."

"Go where?" she asked blankly.

"Nowhere, I hope. But it's up to you. You're a lot safer here with me," he added, "than you would be by yourself."

"But why did you have to register that way? To save appearances?"

"To save two dollars," was his grim correction, "which is more to the point. That's the price of a cabin."

"But *you're* not going to stay *here*."

"Now, let me explain this to you in words of one syllable. We've got darn little money at best. The family purse simply won't stand separate establishments. Get that into your head. And I'm not spending the night outside in this storm!"

"But I—I don't know anything about you."

"All right. Take a look." He held the lamp up in front of what developed into a wholly trustworthy grin.

"I'm looking." Her eyes were wide, exploring, steady, and—there was no doubt about it in his mind—innocent.

"Well; do I look like the villain of the third act?"

"No; you don't." She began to giggle. "You look like a plumber. A nice, honest, intelligent, high-principled plumber."

"The washroom," he stated in the manner of a guidebook, "will be found at the end of this row of shacks."

While she was gone, he extracted a utility kit from his bag, tacked two nails to the end walls, fastened a cord to them and hung a spare blanket, curtain-wise, upon it.

"The walls of Jericho," was his explanation, as she came in. "Solid porphyry and marble. Proof against any assault."

"Grand! What's this?" She recoiled a little from a gaudy splotch ornamenting the foot of her bed.

"Pajamas. My spare set. Hope you can sleep in them."

"I could sleep," she averred with conviction, "in a straitjacket." She had an impulse of irrepressible mischief. "About those walls of Jericho, Peter. You haven't got a trumpet in that big valise of yours, have you?"

"Not even a mouth organ."

"I was just going to tell you not to blow it before eight o'clock."

"Oh, shut up and go to sleep."

So they both went to sleep.

Something light and small, falling upon her blanket, woke Elspeth. "Wha'za'?" she murmured sleepily.

"Little present for you," answered Peter.

"Oh-h-h-h-h-h!" It was a rapturous yawn. "I never slept so hard in my *whole* life. What time is it?"

"Eight o'clock, and all's well before the walls of Jericho."

She ripped the small package open, disclosing a toothbrush. "What a snappy present! Where did it come from?"

"Village drug store. I'm just back."

"Now nice of you! But can we afford it?" she asked austerely.

"Certainly not. It's a wild extravagance. But I'm afraid to cut you off from all luxuries too suddenly. Now, can you get bathed and dressed in twenty minutes?"

"Don't be silly! I'm not even up yet."

"One—two—three—four—"

"What's the count about?"

"On the stroke of ten I'm going to break down the wall, drag you out and dress you myself if neces—"

"Why, you big bum! I believe you wou—"

"—five—six—seven—"

"Wait a *minute!*"

"—eight—ni-i-i-i—"

A blanket-wrapped figure dashed past him and down to the showers. After a record bath she sprinted back to find him squatted above a tiny double grill which he had evidently extracted from that wonder-box of a valise.

"What we waste on luxuries we save on necessities," he pointed out. "Two eggs, one nickel. Two rolls, three cents. Tea from the Warne storehouse. Accelerate yourself, my child."

Odors, wafted from the cookery to her appreciative nostrils, stimulated her to speed. Her reward was a nod of approval from her companion and the best egg that had ever caressed her palate.

"Now you wash up the dishes while I pack. The bus is due in ten minutes."

"But they're greasy," she shuddered.

"That's the point. Get 'em clean. Give 'em a good scraping first."

He vanished within. Well, she would try. Setting her teeth, she scraped and scrubbed and wiped and, at the end, invited his inspection, confident of praise. When, with a pitying glance, he silently did over two plates and a cup before stacking and packing them, she was justifiably hurt. "There's no suiting some people," she reflected aloud and bitterly.

Flood news from the northward, they learned on boarding the bus, compelled a re-routing far inland. Schedules were abandoned. If they made Charleston by nightfall they'd do pretty well, the driver said. Elspeth, refreshed by her long sleep, didn't much care. Peter would bring them through, she felt. . . .

Yellow against the murk of the night sky shone the lights of Charleston. While Peter was at the terminal office making inquiries, Elspeth, on the platform, heard her name pronounced in astonishment. From a group of company chauffeurs a figure was coming toward her.

"Andy Brinkerhoff! What are you doing in that uniform?"

"Working. Hello, Elspie! How's things?"

"Working? For the bus company?"

"Right," he chirped. "This being the only job in sight and the family having gone bust, I grabbed it. What-ho!"

"How awful!"

"Oh, dunno. I'd rather be the driver than a passenger. What brought you so low, Elspie?"

"Sh! I've beat it from home."

"Gee! Alone?"

"Yes. That is—yes. Oh, Andy! I never dreamed how awful this kind of travel could be."

"Why don't you quit it, then?"

"No money."

The lad's cherubic face became serious. "I'll raise some dough from the bunch. You could catch the night plane back."

For a moment she wavered. In the distance she sighted Peter Warne scanning the place. There was a kind of expectant brightness on his face. She couldn't quite picture him going on alone in the bus with that look still there. She flattered herself that she had something to do with its presence.

"I'll stick," she decided to herself, but aloud: "Andy, did you ever hear of a man named Peter Warne?"

"Warne? No. What about him?"

"Nothing. What's a telegram to Miami cost?"

"How much of a telegram?"

"Oh, I don't know. Give me a dollar." And then she wrote out a message:

Mr. Corcoran D. Andrews, Bayside Place, Miami Beach, Fla.
  Who what and why is Peter Warne Stop Important I should know Stop On my way somewhere and hope to get there some time Stop

This is strictly confidential so say nothing to nobody Stop Having a belluva-ruff time and liking it Stop Wire Bessie Smith, Western Union, Raleigh, N.C.

El"

"Oh, here you are," said Peter, barely giving her time to smuggle the paper into Brinkerhoff's hand. "We're going on. Think you can stand it?"

"I s'pose I've got to," replied Elspeth.

Incertitude had discouraged about half the passengers. Consequently, the pair secured a window chair apiece. At the moment of starting there entered a spindly young male all aglow with self-satisfaction which glossed him over from his cocky green hat to his vivid spats.

By the essential law of his being it was inevitable that, after a survey of the interior, he should drop easily into a seat affording an advantageous view of the snappy-looking girl who seemed to be traveling alone. He exhumed a magazine from his grip and leaned across.

"Pardon *me*. But would you care to look at this?"

Elspeth wouldn't but she looked at Mr. Horace Shapley with attention which he mistook for interest. He transferred himself with suitable preliminaries to the vacant chair at her side and fell into confidential discourse.

His line, so Elspeth learned, was typewriter supplies and he hailed from Paterson, New Jersey. Business was punk but if you knew how to make yourself solid with the girl behind the machine (and that was his specialty, believe *him)*, you could make expenses and a little bit on the side.

Elspeth glanced across at Peter to see how he regarded this development. Peter was asleep. All right, then; if he wanted to leave her unprotected against the advances of casual strangers. Unfamiliar with this particular species, she was mildly curious about its hopeful antics.

She smiled politely, asked a question or two, and Mr. Shapley proceeded to unfold romantic adventures and tales of life among the typewriters. The incidents exhibited a similarity of climax: "And did *she* fall for me! Hot momma!"

"It must be a fascinating business," commented his listener.

"And how! I'll bet," said Mr. Shapley, with arch insinuation, "you

could be a naughty little girl yourself, if nobody was lookin'." He offered
her a cigarette. She took it with a nod and tossed it across the aisle,
catching the somnolent Peter neatly in the neck. He woke up.

"Hi!"

"Come over here, Peter." He staggered up. "I want you to know"
(with a slight emphasis on the word) "Mr. Shapley."

"Pleezetomeetcha," mumbled that gentleman in self-refuting accents.

"He thinks," pursued Elspeth, "that I'm probably a naughty little
girl. Am I?"

"You can't prove it by me," said Peter.

"Say, what's the idea?" protested the puzzled Mr. Shapley.

"I don't like him; he nestles," stated Elspeth.

"Aw, now, sister! I was just nicin' you along and—"

"Nicing me along!" Elspeth repeated the phrase with icy disfavor.
"Peter; what are you going to do about this?"

Peter ruminated. "Change seats with you," he said brightly.

"Oh!" she choked as she rose. As she stepped across her neighbor
to gain the aisle, he gave a yelp and glared savagely, though it was
presumably an accident that her sharp, high heel had landed upon the
most susceptible angle of his shin. After a moment's consideration,
Peter followed her to her new position.

So entered discord into that peaceful community. Mr. Shapley sulked
in his chair. Elspeth gloomed in hers. Discomfort invaded Peter's amiable soul. He perceived that he had fallen short in some manner.

"What did you expect me to do about that bird?" he queried.

"Nothing."

"Well, that's what I did."

"I should say you did. If it had been me, I'd have punched his nose."

"And got into a fight. I never could see any sense in fighting unless
you have to," he argued. "What happens? You both get arrested. If I
got arrested and fined here, how do we eat? If they jug me, what
becomes of you? Be sensible."

"Oh, you're sensible enough for both of us." It was plain, however,
to the recipient of this encomium, that it was not intended as a compliment. "Never mind. What are we stopping for?"

The halt was occasioned by evil reports of the road ahead, and the
chauffeur's unwillingness to risk it in darkness.

"I'll do a look-see," said Peter, and came back, pleased, to announce that there was a cheap camp around the turn. Without formality, the improvised Warne family settled in for the night.

Silence had fallen upon the little community when an appealing voice floated across the wall of their seventy-five-cent Jericho. "Peter. Pe-*ter!*"

"Mmpff."

"You're not a very inquisitive person, Peter. You haven't asked me a single question about myself."

"I did. I asked you your name."

"Because you had to. In self-protection."

"Do you want me to think up some more questions?"

She sniffed. "You might show a *little* human interest. You know, I don't like you much, Peter. But I could talk to you, if you'd let me, as freely as if you were—well, I don't know how to put it."

"Another species of animal."

"No-o-o-o. You mustn't belittle yourself," said she kindly.

"I wasn't. And I didn't say an inferior species."

It took her a moment to figure this out, and then she thought she must have got it wrong. For how could his meaning possibly be that her species was the inferior? . . . Better pass that and come to her story. She began with emphasis:

"If there's one thing I can't stand, it's unfairness."

"I thought so."

"You thought *what?*"

"Somebody's been interfering with your having your own sweet way, and so you walked out on the show. What was the nature of this infringement upon the rights of American womanhood?"

"Who's making this stump speech; you or me?" she retorted. "It was about King Westley, if you want to know."

"The headline aviator?"

"Yes. He and I have been playing around together."

"How does friend husband like that?"

"Huh? Oh! Why, he's away, you see. Cruising. I'm staying with Dad."

"Then he's the one to object?"

"Yes. Dad doesn't understand me."

"Likely enough. Go ahead."

"I'll bet you're going to be dumb about this, too. Anyway, it was all right till King got the idea of finding the lost scientific expedition in South America. Venezuela, or somewhere. You know."

"Professor Schatze's? South of the Orinoco. I've read about it."

"King wants to fly down there and locate them."

" 'S all right by me. But where does he figure he'll land?"

"Why, on the prairie or the pampas."

"Pampas, my glass eye! There isn't any pampas within a thousand miles of the Orinoco."

"What do you know about it?"

"I was there myself, five years ago."

"You were! What doing?"

"Oh, just snooping around."

"Maybe it wasn't the same kind of country we were going to."

"*We?*" She could hear a rustle and judged that he was sitting upright. She had him interested at last,

"Of course. I was going with him. Why, if we'd found the expedition I'd be another Amelia Earhart."

Again the cot opposite creaked. Its occupant had relaxed. "I guess your family needn't have lost any sleep."

"Why not?" she challenged.

"Because it's all a bluff," he returned. "Westley never took a chance in his life outside of newspaper headlines."

"I think you're positively septic. The family worried, all right. They tried to keep me from seeing him. So he took to nosing down across our place and dropping notes in the swimming pool, and my father had him arrested and grounded for reckless flying. Did you ever hear anything like that?"

"Not so bad," approved Peter.

"Oh-h-h-h! I might know you'd side against me. I suppose you'd have had me sit there and let Dad get away with it."

"Mmmmm. I can't exactly see you doing it. But why take a bus?"

"All the cars were locked up. I had to sneak out. I knew they'd watch the airports and the railroad stations, but they wouldn't think of the bus. Now you've got the whole story, do you blame me?"

"Yes."

"I do think you're unbearable. You'd probably expect me to go back."

"Certainly."

"Maybe you'd like to send me back."

"You wouldn't go. I did try, you know."

"Not alive, I wouldn't! Of *course* you wouldn't think of doing any-thing so improper. as helping me any more."

"Sure, I will," was the cheerful response. "If you've got your mind set on getting to New York, I'll do my best to deliver you there intact. And may God have mercy on your family's soul! By the way, I suppose you left some word at home so they won't worry too much."

"I did not! I hope they worry themselves into convulsions."

"You don't seem to care much about your family," he remarked.

"Oh, dad isn't so bad. But he always wants to boss everything. I—I expect I didn't think about his worrying. D'you think he will—much?" The query terminated in a perceptible quaver.

"Hm. I wonder if you're really such a hard-boiled little egg as you make out to be. Could you manage with a bag of pecans for dinner tomorrow?"

"Ouch! Do I have to?"

"To wire your father would come to about the price of two dinners."

"Wire him? And have him waiting in New York for me when we get there? If you do, I'll jump through the bus window and you'll never see me again."

"I see. Westley is meeting you. You don't want any interference. Is that it?"

"I left him a note," she admitted.

"Uh-huh. Now that you've got everything movable off your mind, what about a little sleep?"

"I'm for it."

Silence settled down upon the Warne menage.

Sunup brought Peter out of his bunk. From beyond the gently un-dulant blanket he could hear the rhythm of soft breathing. Stealthily he dressed. As he opened the door, a gust of wind twitched down the swaying screen. The girl half turned in her sleep. She smiled. Peter stood, bound in enchantment.

In something like panic he bade himself listen to sense and reason. That's a spoiled child, Peter. Bad medicine. Willful, self-centered—and sweet. (How had that slipped in?) Impractical, too. Heaven pity the bird that takes her on! Too big a job for you, Peter, my lad, even if you could get the contract. So don't go fooling with ideas, you poor boob.

Breakfast necessities took him far afield before he acquired at a bargainer's price what he needed. Elspeth had already fished the cooking kit out of the bag and made ready in the shelter of the shack. Not a word did she say about the fallen blanket. This made Peter self-conscious. They breakfasted in some restraint.

A wild sky threatened renewal of the storm. Below the hill a shallow torrent supplanted the road for a space. Nevertheless, the bus was going on. Elspeth washed the dishes—clean, this time.

"You get out and stretch your legs while I pack," advised Peter.

As she stepped from the shack, the facile Mr. Shapley confronted her.

"The cream off the milk to you, sister," said he, with a smile which indicated that he was not one to bear a grudge. "I just want to square myself with you. If I'd known you was a married lady—"

"I'm not," returned Elspeth absently.

Mr. Shapley's eyes shifted from her to the shack. Peter's voice was raised within: "Where are your pajamas, Elspeth?"

"Airing out. I forgot 'em." She plucked them from a bush and tossed them in at the door.

"*Oh*-oh!" lilted Mr. Shapley, with the tonality of cynical and amused enlightenment. He went away, cocking his hat.

Warning from the bus horn brought out Peter with his bag. They took their seats and were off.

The bus's busy morning was spent mainly in dodging stray watercourses. They made Cheraw toward the middle of the afternoon. There Peter bought two pounds of pecans; a worthy nut and one which satisfies without cloying. They were to be held in reserve, in case. In case of what? Elspeth wished to be informed. Peter shook his head and said, darkly, that you never could tell.

North of Cheraw, the habits of the bus became definitely amphibian. The main route was flowing in a northeasterly direction, and every side road was a contributory stream. A forested rise of land in the distance held out hope of better things, but when they reached it they found cars parked all over the place, waiting for a road-gang to strengthen a doubtful bridge across the swollen river.

"Let's have a look at this neck of the woods," Peter suggested to Elspeth.

To determine their geographical circumstances was not difficult. Rising waters had cut off from the rest of the world a ridge, thinly oval in shape, of approximately a mile in length, and hardly a quarter of a

mile across. On this were herded thirty or forty travelers, including
the bus passengers.

There was no settlement of any sort within reach; only a ramshackle
farmhouse surrounded by a discouraged garden. Peter, however, ne-
gotiated successfully for a small box of potatoes, remarking to his
companion that there was likely to be a rise in commodity prices before
the show was over.

A sound of hammering and clinking, interspersed with rugged pro-
fanity, led them to a side path. There they found a well-equipped
housekeeping van, the engine of which was undergoing an operation
by its owner while his motherly wife sat on the steps watching.

"Cussin' never done you any good with that machine, Abner," said
she. "It ain't like a mule."

"It is like a mule. Only meaner." Abner sighted Peter. "Young man,
know anything about this kind of critter?"

"Ran one once," answered Peter. He took off his coat, rolled up his
sleeves, and set to prodding and poking in a professional manner.
Presently the engine lifted up its voice and roared.

Elspeth, perched on a log, reflected that Peter seemed to be a useful
sort of person to other people. Why hadn't he done better for himself
in life? Maybe that was the reason. This was a new thought and gave
her something to mull over while he worked. From the van she borrowed a basin of water, a bar of soap and a towel, and was standing
by when he finished the job.

"What do I owe you, young man?" called Abner Braithe, from the
van.

"Noth-*uh!*" Elspeth's well-directed elbow had reached its goal in
time.

"Don't be an idiot!" she adjured him.

A conference took place.

"You see," said Peter at its close, "my—uh—wife doesn't sleep well
outdoors. If you had an extra cot, now—"

"Why, we can fix that," put in Mrs. Braithe. "We haven't got any cot,
but if you can sleep in a three-quarter bed—"

"We can't," said both hastily.

"We're used to twin beds," explained Elspeth.

"My wife's quite nervous," put in Peter, "and—and I snore."

"You don't," contradicted Elspeth indignantly, and got a dirty look
from him.

It was finally arranged that, as payment for Peter's services, the Braithes were to divide the night into two watches; up to and after one A.M., Elspeth occupying the van bed for the second spell while Peter roosted in the bus. This being settled, the young pair withdrew to cook a three-course dinner over a fire coaxed by Peter from wet brush and a newspaper; first course, thick potato soup; second course, boiled potatoes with salt; dessert, five pecans each.

"We've been Mr. and Mrs. for pretty near three days now, Peter," remarked the girl suddenly, "and I don't know the first darn thing about you."

"What do you want to know?"

"What have you got in the line of information?"

"Not much that's exciting."

"That's too bad. I hoped you were an escaped con or something, traveling incog."

"Nothing so romantic. Just a poor but virtuous specimen of the half-employed."

"Who employs you?"

"I do. I'm a rotten employer."

"Doing what? Besides blacking boots."

"Oh, I've nothing as steady as that since. If you want to know, I've been making some experiments in the line of vegetable chemistry; pine tar, to be exact. I'm hoping to find some sucker with money to take it up and subsidize me and my process. That's what I'm going to New York to see about. Meantime," he grinned, "I'm traveling light."

"What'll the job be worth if you do get it?"

"Seven or eight thousand a year to start with," said he, with pride.

"Is *that* all?" She was scornful.

"Well, I'll be—look here, Elspeth, I said per year."

"I heard you. My brother Bill says he can't get along on ten thousand. And," she added thoughtfully, "he's single."

"So am I."

"You didn't tell me that before. Not that it matters, of course. Except that your wife might misunderstand if she knew we'd been sl—traveling together."

"I haven't any wife, I tell you."

"All right; all *right!* Don't bark at me about it. It isn't my fault."

"Anything else?" he inquired with careful politeness.

"I think it's going to rain some more."

They transferred themselves to the bus and sat there until one
o'clock, when he escorted her to the Braithe van. He returned to join
his fellow passengers, leaving her with a sensation of lostness and
desertion.

Several small streams, drunk and disorderly on spring's strong liquor, broke out of bounds in the night, came crawling down the hills
and carried all before them, including the bridge whereby the ma-
rooned cars had hoped to escape.

"I don't care," said Elspeth, when the morning's news was broken
to her. She was feeling gayly reckless.

"I do," returned Peter soberly.

"Oh, you're worrying about money again. What's the use of money
where there's nothing to buy? We're out of the world, Peter. I like it,
for a change. What's that exciting smell?"

"Fish." He pointed with pride to his fire, over which steamed a pot.
Dishing up a generous portion he handed it to her on a plate. "Guaranteed fresh this morning. How do you like it?"

She tasted it. "It—it hasn't much personality. What kind of fish is
it?"

"They call it mudfish, I believe. It was flopping around in a slough
and I nailed it with a stick. I thought there'd be enough for dinner,
too," said he, crestfallen by her lack of appreciation.

"Plenty," she agreed. "Peter, could I have four potatoes? Raw ones."

"What for?"

"I'm going marketing."

"Barter and exchange, eh? Look out that these tourists don't gyp
you."

"Ma feyther's name is Alexander Bruce MacGregor Andrews," she
informed him in a rich Scottish accent. "Tak' that to heart, laddie."

"I get it. You'll do."

Quenching his fire, he walked to the van. A semicircle of men and
women had grouped about the door. Circulating among them, Abner
Braithe was taking up a collection. Yet, it was not Sunday. The explanation was supplied when the shrewd Yankee addressed his audience.

"The morning program will begin right away. Any of you folks whose
money I've missed, please raise the right hand. Other news and musical
ee-vents will be on the air at five-thirty this P.M. and eight tonight. A
nickel admission each, or a dime for the three perfomances."

Having no nickel to waste on frivolities, Peter moved on. Elspeth, triumphant, rejoined him with her booty.

Item: a small parcel of salt.

Item: a smaller parcel of pepper.

Item: a half pound of lard.

Item: two strips of fat bacon.

Item: six lumps of sugar.

"What d'ye ken about that?" she demanded. "Am I no the canny Scawtswumman?"

"You're a darn bonny one," returned Peter, admiring the flushed cheeks and brilliant eyes.

"Is this the first time you've noticed that?" she inquired impudently.

"It hadn't struck in before," he confessed.

"And now it has? Hold the thought. I can't hurt you." (He felt by no means so sure about that.) "Now Mr. Shapley"—her eyes shifted to the road up which that gentleman was approaching—"got it right away. I wonder what's his trouble."

Gratification, not trouble, signalized his expression as he sighted them. His bow to Elspeth was gravely ceremonious. He then looked at her companion.

"Could I have a minute's conversation apart with you?"

"Don't mind me," said Elspeth, and the two men withdrew a few paces.

"I don't want to butt into your and the lady's private affairs," began Mr. Shapley, "but this is business. I want to know if that lady is your wife."

"She is. Not that it's any concern of yours."

"She said this morning that she wasn't married."

"She hadn't got used to the idea yet," returned Peter, with great presence of mind. "She's only been that way a few days. Honeymoon trip."

"That's as may be," retorted the other. "Even if it's true, it wouldn't put a crimp in the reward."

"What's this?" demanded Peter, eying him in surprise. "Reward? For what?"

"Come off. You heard the raddio this morning, didn'cha?"

"No."

"Well, is that lady the daughter of Mr. A. B. M. Andrews, the yachting millionaire, or ain't she? 'Cause I know she is."

"Oh! You know that, do you! What of it?"

"Ten grand of it. That's what of it," rejoined Mr. Shapley. "For information leadin' to the dis—"

"Keep your voice down."

"Yeah. I'll keep my voice down till the time comes to let it loose. Then I'll collect on that ten thou'. They think she's kidnaped."

"What makes you so sure of your identification?"

"Full description over the air. When the specifications came across on the raddio I spotted the garments. Used to be in ladies' wear," he explained.

"If you so much as mention this to Mi—to Mrs. Warne, I'll—" began Peter.

"Don't get rough, now, brother," deprecated the reward-hunter. "I ain't lookin' for trouble. And I'm not sayin' anything to the little lady, just so long as you and me understand each other."

"What do you want me to understand?"

"That there's no use your tryin' to slip me after we get out of this place. Of course, you can make it hard or easy for me. So, if you want to play in with me and be nice, anyway—I'm ready to talk about a little cut for you. . . . No? Well, suit yourself, pal. See you in the mornin'."

He chuckled himself away. Peter, weighing the situation, discovered in himself a violent distaste at the thought of Mr. Horace Shapley collecting Elspeth's family's money for the delivering up of Elspeth. In fact, it afflicted him with mingled nausea and desire for manslaughter. Out of this unpromising combination emerged an idea. If he, Peter, could reach a wire before the pestilent Shapley, he could get in his information first and block the reward.

Should he tell Elspeth about the radio? Better not, he concluded.

It was characteristic of her and a big credit mark in his estimate of her, that she put no questions as to the interview with Shapley. She did not like that person; therefore, practically speaking, he did not exist. But the mudfish did. With a captivating furrow of doubt between her eyes, she laid the problem before her partner: could it be trusted to remain edible overnight?

"Never mind the fish. Can you swim?"

She looked out across the brown turbulence of the river, more than two hundred yards now to the northern bank. "Not across that."

"But you're used to water?"

"Oh, yes!"

"I've located an old boat in the slough where I killed the fish. I think I can patch her up enough to make it."

"Okay by me; I wouldn't care to settle here permanently. When do we start?"

"Be ready about ten."

"In the dark?"

"We-ell, I don't exactly want the public in on this. They might try to stop us. You know how people are."

"Come clean, Peter. We're running away from something. Is it that Shapley worm?"

"Yes. He thinks he's got something on me." This explanation which he had been at some pains to devise, he hoped would satisfy her. But she followed it to a conclusion which he had not foreseen.

"Is it because he knows we're not married?"

"He doesn't know ex—"

"I told him we weren't. Before I thought how it would look."

"I told him we were."

"Did he believe you?"

"Probably not."

"Then he thinks you're abducting me. Isn't that priceless!"

"Oh, absolutely. What isn't so funny is that there are laws in some states about people—er—traveling as man and wife if they're not married."

She stared at him, wide-eyed. "But so long as—Oh, Peter! I'd *hate* it if I got you into any trouble."

"All we have to do is slip Shapley. Nobody else is on." He sincerely hoped that was true.

The intervening time he occupied in patching up the boat as best he might. He had studied the course of various flotsam and thought that he discerned a definite set of the current toward the northern bank which was their goal. With bailing they ought to be able to keep the old tub afloat.

Through the curtain of the rushing clouds the moon was contriving to diffuse a dim light when they set out. The opposite bank was visible only as a faint, occasional blur. Smooth with treachery, the stream at their feet sped from darkness into darkness.

Peter thrust an oar into Elspeth's hand, the only one he had been able to find, to be used as a steering paddle. For himself he had fashioned a pole from a sapling. The carryall he disposed aft of amidships. Bending over Elspeth as she took the stern seat, he put a hand on her shoulder.

"You're not afraid?"

"No." Just the same, she would have liked to be within reach of that firm grasp through what might be coming.

"Stout fella! All set? Shove!"

The river snatched at the boat, took it into its secret keeping—and held it strangely motionless. But the faintly visible shore slipped backward and away and was presently visible no more. Peter, a long way distant from her in the dimness, was active with his pole, fending to this side and that. It was her job to keep them on the course with her oar. She concentrated upon it.

The boat was leaking profusely now. "Shall I bail?" she called.

"Yes. But keep your oar by you."

They came abreast of an island. As they neared the lower end, an uprooted swamp maple was snatched outward in the movement of the river. Busy with her pan, Elspeth did not notice it until a mass of leafy branches heaved upward from the surface, hovered, descended, and she was struggling in the grasp of a hundred tentacles.

"Peter!" she shrieked.

They had her, those wet, clogging arms. They were dragging her out into the void, fight them as she would in her terror and desperation. Now another force was aiding her; Peter, his powerful arms tearing, thrusting, fending against this ponderous invasion. The boat careened. The water poured inboard. Then, miraculously, they were released as the tree sideslipped, turning again, freeing their craft. Elspeth fell back, bruised and battered.

"Are you all right?"

"Yes. It t-t-tried to drag me overboard!"

"I know." His voice, too, was unsteadied by that horror.

"Don't go away. Hold me. Just for a minute."

The skiff, slowly revolving like a ceremonious dancer in the performance of a solo waltz, proceeded on its unguided course. The girl sighed.

"Where's my oar?" It was gone.

"It doesn't matter now. There's the shore. We're being carried in."

They scraped and checked as Peter clutched at a small sapling, growing at the edge of a swampy forest. From trunk to trunk he guided the course until there was a solid bump.

"Land ho!" he shouted, and helped his shipmate out upon the bank. "What do we do now?"

"Walk until we find a road and a roost."

Valise on shoulder, he set out across the miry fields, Elspeth plodding on behind. It was hard going. Her breath labored painfully after the first half-mile, and she was agonizingly sleepy.

Now Peter's arm was around her; he was murmuring some encouraging foolishness to her who was beyond courage, fear, hope, or any other emotion except the brutish lust for rest.... Peter's voice, angry and harsh, insisting that she throw more of her weight on him and *keep* moving. How silly! She hadn't any weight. She was a bird on a bough. She was a butterfly, swaying on a blossom. She was nothing. . . .

Broad daylight, spearing through a paneless window, played upon her lids, waking her. Where was the shawl of Jericho? In its place were boards, a raw wall. Beneath her was fragrant hay. She was actually alive and rested. She looked about her.

"Why, it's a barn!" she exclaimed. She got up and went to the door. Outside stood Peter.

"How do you like the quarters?" he greeted her. "Room"—he pointed to the barn—"and bath." He indicated a huge horse trough fed by a trickle of clear water. "I've just had mine."

She regarded him with supefaction. "And now you're *shaving*. Where's the party?"

"Party?"

"Well, if not, why the elaborate toilet?"

"Did you ever travel on the thumb?"

She looked her incomprehension. He performed a digital gesture which enlightened her.

"The first rule of the thumb," explained Peter, "is to look as neat and decent as you can. It inspires confidence in the passing motorist's breast."

"Is that the way we're going to travel?"

"If we're lucky."

"Without eating?" she said wistfully.

"Tluck-tluck!" interposed a young chicken from a near-by hedge, the most ill-timed observation of its brief life.

A handy stick, flung deftly, checked its retreat. Peter pounced. "Breakfast!" he exulted.

"Where do we go now?" inquired his companion, half an hour later, greatly restored.

"The main highways," set forth Peter, thinking of the radio alarm and the state police, "are not for us. Verdant lanes and bosky glens are more in our line. We'll take what traffic we can."

Hitch-hiking on sandy side roads in the South means slow progress. Peter finally decided that they must risk better-traveled roads, but select their transportation cautiously. It was selected for them. They had not footed it a mile beside Route 1, when a touring car, battered but serviceable, pulled up and a ruddy face emitted welcome words.

"Well, well, well! Boys *and* girls! Bound north?"

"Yes." It was a duet, perfect in accord.

"Meet Thad Banker, the good old fatty. Throw in the old trunk."

"What's the arrangement?" queried Peter, cautious financier that he was.

"Free wheeling," burbled the fat man. "You furnish the gas and I furnish the spark." They climbed in with the valise. "Any special place?" asked the obliging chauffeur.

"Do we go through Raleigh?" asked the girl, and upon receiving an affirmative, added to Peter: "There may be a wire there for me."

Which reminded that gentleman that he had something to attend to. At the next town he got a telegraph blank and a stamped envelope. After some cogitation, he produced this composition, addressed to Mr. A. B. M. Andrews, Miami Beach, Fla.

"Daughter taking trip for health and recreation. Advise abandonment of effort to trace which can have no good results and may cause delay. Sends love and says not to worry. Undersigned guarantees safe arrival in New York in a few days. Pay no reward to any other claimant as this is positively first authentic information.
Peter Warne"

To this he pinned a dollar bill and mailed it for transmission to Western Union, New Orleans, Louisiana, by way of giving the pursuit, in case one was instituted, a pleasant place to start from. Five cents more of his thin fortune went for a newspaper. Reports from the southward were worth the money; there was no let-up in the flood. Competition from Mr. Shapley would be delayed at least another day.

Mr. Thad Banker was a card. He kept himself in roars of laughter with his witty sallies. Peter, in the rear seat, fell peacefully asleep. Elspeth had to act as audience for the conversational driver.

At Raleigh she found the expected telegram from Corcoran, which she read and thrust into her purse for future use. Shortly after, a traffic light held them up and the policeman on the corner exhibited an interest in the girl on the front seat quite disturbing to Peter.

The traffic guardian was sauntering toward them when the green flashed on. "Step on it," urged Peter.

Mr. Banker obliged. A whistle shrilled.

"Keep going!" snapped Peter.

Mr. Banker still obliged, slipping into a maze of side streets. It did not occur to Peter that their driver's distaste for police interference was instinctive. Also successful, it began to appear; when a motor cop swung around unexpectedly and headed them to the curb. The license was inspected and found in order.

"Who's the lady?" the officer began.

"My niece," said Mr. Banker, with instant candor.

"Is that right, ma'am?"

"Yes, of course it is." (Peter breathed again.)

"And this man behind?"

"Search me."

"He thumbed us and Uncle Thad stopped for him." (Peter's admiration became almost more than he could bear.)

"Have you got a traveling bag with you, ma'am?" (So the radio must have laid weight on the traveling bag, now probably in some Florida swamp.)

"No. Just my purse."

The cop consulted a notebook. "The dress looks like it," he muttered. "And the description sort of fits. Got anything on you to prove who you are, ma'am?"

"No; I'm afraid—Yes; of course I have." She drew out the yellow envelope. "Is that enough?"

"Miss Bessie Smith," he read. "I reckon that settles it. Keep to your right for Greensboro at Morrisville."

"Greensboro, my foot! Us for points east," announced the fat man, wiping his brow as the motorcycle chugged away. "Phe-e-ew! What's it all about? Been lootin' a bank, you two?"

"Eloping," said Peter. "Keep it under your shirt."

"Gotcha." He eyed the carryall. "All your stuff in there?"

"Yes."

"How about a breath of pure, country air? I'm not so strong for all this public attention."

They kept to side roads until long after dark, bringing up before a restaurant in Tarboro. There the supposed elopers consulted and announced that they didn't care for dinner. "Oh, on me!" cried Mr. Banker. "Mustn't go hungry on your honeymoon."

He ordered profusely. While the steak was cooking, he remarked, he'd just have a look at the car; there was a rattle in the engine that he didn't like. As soon as he had gone, Elspeth said:

"Wonder what the idea is. I never heard a sweeter-running engine for an old car. What's more, he's got two sets of license cards. I saw the other one when that inquiring cop—"

But Peter was halfway to the door, after slamming some money on the table and snapping out directions for her to wait, no matter how long he took. Outside, she heard a shout and the rush of a speeding engine. A car without lights sped up the street.

With nothing else to do, Elspeth settled down to leisurely eating. . . .

At nine-thirty, the waiter announced the closing hour as ten, sharp. Beginning to be terrified for Peter and miserable for herself, she ordered more coffee. The bill and tip left her a dollar and fifteen cents.

At nine-fifty, the wreckage of Peter entered the door. Elspeth arose and made a rush upon him, but recoiled.

"Peter! You've been fighting."

"Couldn't help it."

"You've got a black eye."

"That isn't all I've got," he told her.

"No; it isn't. What an *awful*-looking ear!"

"That isn't all I've got, either." His grin was bloody, but unbowed.

"Then it must be internal injuries."

"Wrong. It's a car."

"Whose car?"

"Ours now, I expect. I had to come home in something."

"Where's the fat man?"

The grin widened. "Don't know exactly. Neither does he, I reckon. That big-hearted Samaritan, my child, is a road-pirate. He picks people up, plants 'em, and beats it with their luggage. Probably does a little holdup business on the side."

"Tell me what happened, Peter. Go on and eat first."

Between relishing mouthfuls, he unfolded his narrative. "You didn't put me wise a bit too quick. He was moving when I got out but I landed aboard with a flying tackle. Didn't dare grab him for fear we'd crash. He was stepping on it and telling me that when he got me far enough away he was going to beat me up and tie me to a tree. That was an idea! So when he pulled up on some forsaken wood road in a swamp, I beat him up and tied him to a tree."

"Why, Peter! He's twice as big as you."

"I can't help that. It wasn't any time for half measures. It took me an hour to find my way. But here we are."

"I'm glad," she said with a new note in her voice.

"Jumping Jehoshaphat! Is *that* all we've got left?" Aghast, he stared at the sum she put in his hands. "And it's too cold to sleep out tonight. It's an open car, anyhow. Oh, well; our transportation's going to be cheap from now on. What price one more good night's rest? Torney's Haven for Tourists is three miles up the highway. Let's get going."

Torney's provided a cabin for only a dollar. Before turning in, Peter returned to the car, parked a few roads away against a fence, to make a thorough inspection. His companion was in bed on his return.

"I've changed the plates to another set that I found under the seat. Indiana, to match the other set of licenses. It'll be safer in case our friend decides to report the loss, after he gets loose from his tree. There's a nice robe, too. We've come into property. And by the way, Elspeth; you're Mrs. Thaddeus Banker till further notice."

Elspeth pouted. "I'd rather be Mrs. Peter Warne. I'm getting used to that."

"We've got to live up to our new responsibilities." Seated on his cot, he had taken off his shoes, when he started hastily to resume them.

"Where are you going?" she asked plaintively. "Looking for more trouble?"

"Walls of Jericho. I forgot. I'll get the robe out of the car."

"Oh, darn the robe! Why bother? It's pouring, too. Let it go. I don't mind if you don't." All in a perfectly matter-of-fact tone. She added: "You can undress outside. I'm going to sleep."

As soon as he withdrew she got out Corcoran's reply to "Miss Bessie Smith," and read it over again before tearing it into fragments. It ran as follows:

"What's all this about P.W.? Watch out for that bird. Dangerous corner, blind road, and all that sorta thing. At any given moment he might be running a pirate fleet or landing on the throne of the Kingdom of Boopa-doopia. Ask him about the bet I stuck him on in college, and then keep your guard up. I'm off for a week on the Keys so you can't get me again until then. Better come back home and be a nice little girl or papa spank. And how!

Cork

The scraps she thrust beneath her pillow and was asleep almost at once. But Peter lay, wakeful, crushing down thoughts that made him furious with himself. At last peace came, and dreams. . . . One of them so poignant, so incredibly dear, that he fought bitterly against its turning to reality.

Yet reality it was; the sense of warmth and softness close upon him; the progress of creeping fingers across his breast, of seeking lips against his throat. His arms drew her down. His mouth found the lips that, for a dizzying moment, clung to his, then trembled aside to whisper:

"No, Peter. I didn't mean—Listen!"

Outside sounded a light clinking.

"Somebody's stealing the car!"

Elspeth's form, in the lurid pajamas, slid away from Peter like a ghost. He followed to the window. Silent as a shadow the dim bulk of the Banker automobile moved deliberately along under a power not its own. Two other shadows loomed in its rear, propelling it by hand.

"Shall I scream?" whispered the girl.

He put a hand on her mouth. "Wait."

Another of his luminous ideas had fired the brain of Peter Warne. In his role of Thad Banker, he would let the robbers get away, then report the theft to the police and, allowing for reasonable luck, get back his property (né Mr. Banker's) with the full blessing of the authorities.

"I'm going to let 'em get away with it," he murmured. "As soon as they really start, I'll telephone the road patrol."

The dwindling shadow trundled out on the pike, where the engine struck up its song and the car sped southward. Simultaneously Peter made a rush for the camp office. It was all right, he reported, on getting back. He'd been able to get the police at once.

"But suppose they don't catch 'em."

"That'll be just too bad," admitted Peter. He yawned.

"You're sleepy again. You're always sleepy."

"What do you expect at three o'clock in the morning?"

"I'm wide awake," complained Elspeth.

Something had changed within her, made uncertain and uneasy, since she had aroused Peter and found herself for one incendiary moment in his arms. She didn't blame him; he was only half awake at the time. But she had lost confidence in him. Or could it be herself in whom she had lost confidence? In any case, the thought of sharing the same room with him the rest of that night had become too formidable.

"Please go outside again, Peter. I'm going to get dressed. I'm restless."

"Oh, my gosh!" he sighed. "Can't you count some sheep or something?"

"No; I can't." A brilliant idea struck her. "How'd you expect me to sleep when they may be back with the car any minute?"

"And then again, they may not be back till morning."

But Elspeth had a heritage of the immovable Scottish obstinacy. In a voice all prickly little italics she announced that she was *going to get up*. And she was going to walk off her nervousness. It needn't make any difference to Peter. He could go back to bed.

"And let you wander around alone in this blackness? You might not come back."

"What else could I do?"

The forlorn lack of alternative for her struck into his heart. Absolute dependence upon a man of a strange breed in circumstances wholly new. What a situation for a girl like her! And how gallantly, on the whole, she was taking it! How sensible it would be for him to go back to that telephone; call up her father (reverse charges, of course) and tell him the whole thing. *And* get himself thoroughly hated for it.

No; he couldn't throw Elspeth down. Not even for her own good. Carry on. There was nothing else for it, especially now that luck was favoring them. The car, if they got it back, was their safest obtainable method of travel. Her dress was the weak spot and would be more of a danger point after Horace Shapley contributed his evidence to the hunt. Couldn't something be done about that? . . . The dress appeared in the doorway, and Peter went in to array himself for the vigil.

The two state police found the pair waiting at the gate. Apologetically they explained that the thieves had got away into the swamp. Nothing could have suited Peter better, since there would now be no question of his being held as complaining witness. To satisfy the authorities of his ownership was easy. They took his address (fictitious), wished him and his wife good luck, and were off.

"Now we can go back to bed," said Peter.

"Oh, dear! Can't we start on?"

"At this hour? Why, I suppose we could, but—"

"Let's, then." In the turmoil of her spirit she wanted to be quit forever of Torney's Haven for Tourists and its atmosphere of unexpected emotions and disconcerting impulses. Maybe something of this had trickled into Peter's mind, too, for presently he said:

"Don't you know it's dangerous to wake a sound sleeper too suddenly?"

"So I've heard."

"You can't tell what might happen. I mean, a man isn't quite responsible, you know, before he comes quite awake."

So he was apologizing. Very proper.

"Let's forget it."

"Yes," he agreed quietly. "I'll have quite a little to forget."

"So will I," she thought, startled at the realization.

They packed, and chugged out, one cylinder missing. "I hope the old junk-heap holds together till we reach New York," remarked Peter.

"Are we going all the way in this?"

"Unless you can think of a cheaper way."

"But it isn't ours. It's the fat man's."

"I doubt it. Looks to me as if it had been stolen and gypped up with new paint and fake numbers. However, we'll leave it somewhere in Jersey if we get that far, and write to both license numbers to come and get it. How does that set on an empty conscience?"

"Never mind my conscience. That isn't the worst emptiness I'm suffering from. What's in the house for breakfast? It's nearly sunup."

"Potatoes. Pecans." He investigated their scanty store and looked up. "There are only three spuds left."

"Is that all?"

Something careless in her reply made him scan her face sharply. "There ought to be five. There are two missing. You had charge of the larder. Well?"

"I took 'em. You see—"

"Without saying a word about it to me? You must have pinched them out when we were on the island and cooked them for yourself while I was working on the boat," he figured somberly. Part of this was true, but not all of it. The rest she was saving to confound him with. "Do you, by any chance, still think that this is a picnic?"

Now she *wouldn't* tell him! She was indignant and hurt. He'd be sorry! When he came to her with a potato now, she would haughtily decline it—if her rueful stomach didn't get the better of her wrathful fortitude.

In resentment more convincing than her own, he built the wayside fire, boiled the water and inserted one lone potato; the smallest at that. He counted out five pecans, added two more, and handed the lot to her. He then got out his pocketknife, opened it, and prodded the bubbling tuber. Judging it soft enough, he neatly speared it out upon a plate. Elspeth pretended a total lack of interest. She hoped she'd have the resolution to decline her half with hauteur. She didn't get the chance.

Peter split the potato, sprinkled on salt, and ate it all.

With difficulty, Elspeth suppressed a roar of rage. That was the kind of man he was, then! Selfish, greedy, mean, tyrannical, unfair, smug, bad-tempered, uncouth—her stock ran thin. How idiotically she had overestimated him! Rough but noble; that had been her formula for his character. And now look at him, pigging down the last delicious fragments while she was to be content with a handful of nuts. Nuts! She rose in regal resentment, flung her seven pecans into the fire, and stalked back to the car.

Somewhere in the vicinity of Emporia, eighty miles north of their breakfast, he spoke. "No good in sulking, you know."

"I'm *not* sulking." Which closed that opening.

Nevertheless, Elspeth was relieved. An oppressive feeling that maybe his anger would prove more lasting than her own had tainted her satisfaction in being the injured party. One solicitude, too, he exhibited. He kept tucking her up in the robe.

This would have been less reassuring had she understood its genesis. He was afraid her costume might be recognized. He even thought of suggesting that she might effect a trade in some secondhand store. In her present state of childish petulance, however, he judged it useless to suggest this. Some other way must be found.

Some money was still left to them. Elspeth saw her companion shaking his head over it when their gas gave out, happily near a filling station. His worried expression weakened her anger, but she couldn't bring herself to admit she was sorry. Not yet.

"There's a cheap camp seventy miles from here," he said. "But if we sleep there we can't have much of a dinner."

"Potatoes," said the recalcitrant Elspeth. She'd teach him!

They dined at a roadside stand which, in ordinary conditions, she would have considered loathsome. Every odor of it now brought prickly sensations to her palate.

The night presented a problem troubling to her mind. No shared but unpartitioned cabin for her! Last night's experience had been too revelatory. What made things difficult was that she had told him she needed no more walls of Jericho to insure peaceful sleep. Now if she asked him to put up the curtain, what would he think?

Pursuant to his policy of avoiding large cities and the possible interest of traffic cops, Peter had planned their route westward again, giving Richmond a wide berth. They flashed without stop through towns with hospitable restaurants only to pull up at a roadside stand of austere menu, near Sweet Briar.

Never had Elspeth seen the important sum of twenty-five cents laid out so economically as by Peter's method. Baked beans with thick, fat, glorious gollups of pork; a half-loaf of bread, and bitter coffee. To say that her hunger was appeased would be overstatement. But a sense of returned well-being comforted her. She even felt that she could face the morning's potato, if any, with courage. Meantime, there remained the arrangements for the night.

Peter handled that decisively, upon their arrival at the camp. Their cabin was dreary, chill, and stoveless. When he brought in the robe from the car, she hoped for it over her bunk. Not at all; out came his little tool kit; up went the separating cord, and over it was firmly pinned the warm fabric.

With a regrettable though feminine want of logic, Elspeth nursed a grievance; he needn't have been at such pains to raise that wall again without a request from the person most interested. She went to sleep crossly but promptly.

In the morning the robe was tucked snugly about her. How long had that been there? She looked around and made a startling discovery. Her clothes were gone. So was Peter. Also, when she looked out, the car. The wild idea occurred to her that he had stolen her outfit and run away, *à la* Thad Banker. One thing was certain: to rise and wander forth clad in those grotesque pajamas was out of the question. Turning over, she fell asleep again.

Some inner sensation of his nearness awoke her, or perhaps it was, less occultly, his footsteps outside, approaching, pausing. She craned upward to bring her vision level with the window. Peter was standing with his side face toward her, a plump bundle beneath his arm. Her clothes, probably, which he had taken out to clean. How nice of him!

He set down his burden and took off his belt. With a knife he slit the stitches in the leather, carefully prying something from beneath the strips. It was a tight-folded bill.

So he had been holding out on her! Keeping her on a gnat's diet. Letting her go hungry while he gorged himself on boiled potato and salt, and gloated over his reserve fund. Beast! This knowledge, too, she would hold back for his ultimate discomfiture. It was a composed and languid voice which responded to his knock on the door.

"Hello! How are you feeling, Elspeth?"

"Very well, thank you. Where have you been?

"Act two, scene one of matrimonial crisis," chuckled Peter. "Hubby returns early in the morning. Wife demands explanation. Husband is ready with it: 'You'd be surprised.' " There was a distinct trace of nervousness in his bearing.

"Well, surprise me," returned Elspeth, with hardly concealed hostility. "Where are my clothes?"

"That's the point. They're—uh—I—er—well, the fact is, I pawned 'em. In Charlottesville?"

"You—pawned—my—clothes! Where's the money?" If that was the bill in the belt, she proposed to know it.

"I spent most of it. On other clothes. You said your feet hurt you."

"When we were walking. We don't have to walk any more."

"How do you know? We aren't out of the woods yet. And you don't need such a fancy rig, traveling with me. And we do need the little bit extra I picked up on the trade."

Stern and uncompromising was the glare which she directed upon his bundle. "Let me see."

Her immediate reaction to the dingy, shoddy, nondescript outfit he disclosed was an involuntary yip of distress.

"Don't you like 'em?" he asked.

"They're terrible! They're ghastly!"

"The woman said they were serviceable. Put 'em on. I'll wait outside."

It would have taken a sturdier optimism than Peter's to maintain a sun-kissed countenance in the face of the transformation which he presently witnessed. Hardly could he recognize her in that horrid misfit which she was pinning here, adjusting there.

"Hand me the mirror, please."

"Perhaps you'd better not—"

"Will you be so good as to do as I ask?"

"Oh, all *right!*"

She took one long, comprehensive survey and burst into tears.

"Don't, Elspeth," he protested, appalled. "What's the difference? There's no one to see you."

"There's me," she gulped. "And there's you."

"I don't mind." As if he were bearing up courageously under an affliction.

"I'm a *sight,*" she wailed. "I'm hideous! Go and get my things back."

"It can't be done."

"I won't go out in these frightful things. I won't. I won't. I *won't!*"

"Who's going to pay the rent if you stay?"

Obtaining no reply to this pertinent inquiry, he sighed and went out. Down the breeze, there presently drifted to Elspeth's nostrils the tang of wood smoke. Her face appeared in the window.

"About those missing potatoes," said she. (How mean she was going to make him feel in a minute!) "Are you interested in knowing what became of them?"

"It doesn't matter. They're gone."

"They're gone where they'll do the most good," she returned with slow impressiveness. "I gave them away."

"Without consulting me?"

"Do I have to consult you about everything I do?"

"We-ell, some people might figure that I had an interest in those potatoes."

"Well, I gave them to a poor old woman who needed them. She was hungry."

"Umph! Feeling sure, I suppose, that your generosity would cost you nothing, as I'd share the remainder with you. Error Number One."

"Peter, I wouldn't have thought anyone could be so des-des-despicable!"

This left him unmoved. "Who was the starving beneficiary? I'll bet it was that old creature with the black bonnet and gold teeth in the bus."

"How did you know?"

"She's the sort you would help. In case you'd like to know, that old hoarder had her bag half full of almond chocolates. I saw her buy 'em at Charleston."

"Hoarder, yourself!" Enraged at the failure of her bombshell, she fell back on her last ammunition. "What did you take out of your belt this morning?"

"Oh, you saw that, did you? Watchful little angel!"

"I'm not! I just happened to see it. A bill. A big one, I'll bet. You had it all the time. And you've starved me and bullied me and made me walk miles and sleep in barns, while you could just as well have—"

"Hired a special train. On ten dollars."

"Ten dollars is a lot of money." (Ideas change.)

"Now, I'll tell you about that ten dollars," said he with cold precision. "It's my backlog. It's the last resort. It's the untouchable. It's the dead line of absolute necessity."

"You needn't touch it on my account." (Just like a nasty-tempered little brat, she told herself.) "Of course, starvation isn't absolute necessity."

"Can you do simple arithmetic?"

"Yes. I'm not quite an idiot, even if you do think so, Peter."

"Try this one, then. We've got something over five hundred miles to go. Gas will average us seventeen cents. This old mudcart of Banker's won't do better than twelve miles on a gallon. Now, can any bright little girl in this class tell me how much over that leaves us to eat, sleep and live on, not counting oil, ferry charge, and incidentals?"

"I can't. And I don't want to," retorted Elspeth, very dispirited. A long, dull silence enclosed them like a globe. She shattered it. "Peter!"

"What?"

"D'you know why I hate you?"

"I'll bite," said he, wearily. "Why?"

"Because, darn you! you're always right and I'm always wrong. Peter! Peter, dear! A potato, Peter. Please, Peter; one potato. Just one. The littlest. I know I don't deserve it, but—"

"Oh, what's the *use!*" vociferated Peter, throwing up both hands in abject and glad surrender. And that quarrel drifted on the smoke of their fire down to the limbo of things become insignificant, yet never quite to be forgotten.

Two young people, haggard, gaunt, shabby, bluish with the chill of an April storm, drove their battered car aboard the Fort Lee ferry as the boat pulled out. They were sharing a bag of peanuts with the conscientious exactitude of penury: one to you; one to me. Quarter of the way across, both were asleep. At the halfway distance the whistle blared and they woke up.

"We're nearly there," observed the girl without any special enthusiasm.

"Yes," said the man with still less.

A hiatus of some length. "Why didn't you tell me about blacking Corker's boots?"

"What about it?"

"It was on a bet, wasn't it?"

"Yes. In college. I picked the wrong team. If I'd won, the Corker would have typed my theses for the term. What put you on?"

"A telegram from Cork."

"Oh! The one to Bessie Smith that saved our lives in Raleigh?"

She nodded. "Anyway, I knew all the time you weren't a valet," she asserted.

He cocked a mild, derisive eye at her. "You're not building up any rosy picture of me as a perfect gentleman, are you?"

"No-o. I don't know what you are."

"Don't let it worry you. Go back to sleep."

"You're always telling me to go to sleep," she muttered discontentedly. She rubbed her nose on his shoulder. "Peter."

He sighed and kissed her.

"You needn't be so solemn about it."

"I'm not feeling exactly sprightly."

"Because we're almost home? But we'll be seeing each other soon."

"I thought that headliner of the air was waiting to fly you somewhere."

"Who? Oh-h-h-h, King." She began to laugh. "Isn't that funny! I'd absolutely forgotten about King. He doesn't matter. When am I going to see you?" As he made no reply, she became vaguely alarmed. . . . "You're not going right back?"

"No. I've got that possible contract to look after. Down in Jersey."

"But you'll be in town again. And I'll see you then."

"No."

"Peter! Why not?"

"Self-preservation," he proclaimed oracularly, "is the first law of nature."

"You don't want to see me again?"

"Put it any way you like," came the broad-minded permission, "just so the main point gets across."

"But I think that's absolutely lousy!" Another point occurred to her. "There's no reason why you shouldn't if it's because—well, that business about my being married was a good deal exaggerated. If that makes any difference."

"It does. It makes it worse."

"Oh! . . . You don't seem surprised, though."

"Me? I should say not! I've known from the first that was all bunk."

"Have you, Smarty? How?"

"You tried to put it over that you'd been wearing a wedding ring. But there was no band of white on the tan of your finger."

"Deteckative! I haven't had a bit of luck trying to fool you about anything, have I, Peter? Not even putting across the superior-goddess idea. And now you're the one that's being snooty."

"I'm not. I'm being sensible. See here, Elspeth. It may or may not have been called to your attention that you're a not wholly unattractive young person—and that I myself am not yet beyond the age of—"

"Consent," broke in the irrepressible Elspeth.

"—damfoolishness," substituted Peter, with severity. "So," he concluded, with an effect of logic, "we may as well call it a day."

"Not to mention several nights." She turned the brilliance of mirthful eyes upon him. "Wouldn't it be funny if you fell in love with me, Peter?"

"Funny for the spectators. Painful for the bear."

"Then don't mention it, Bear!" Another idea occurred to her. "How much money have you got left?"

"Forty-odd cents."

"Now that you're in New York you can get more, of course."

"Yes? Where?"

"At the bank, I suppose. Where does one get money?"

"That's what I've always wanted to know," he grinned.

"I can get all I want tomorrow. I'll lend you a hundred dollars. Or more if you want it."

"No; thank you."

"But I borrowed yours!" she cried. "At least, you paid for me."

"That's different."

"I don't see how." Of course she did see, and inwardly approved. "But—but I owe you money!" she cried. "I'd forgotten all about that. You'll let me pay that back, of course."

If she expected him to deprecate politely the idea she was swiftly undeceived. "The sooner, the better," said Peter cheerfully.

"I'll bet you've got it all set down in that precious notebook of yours."

"Every cent." He tore out a leaf which he handed to her.

"Where can I send it?"

He gave her an address on a street whose name she had never before heard; Darrow, or Barrow, or some such matter.

In the splendor of the great circular court off Park Avenue, the bedraggled automobile looked impudently out of place. The door-keeper almost choked with amazement as the luxurious Miss Elspeth Andrews, clad in such garments as had never before affronted those august portals, jumped out, absently responding to his greeting.

"I think your father is expecting you, miss," said he.

"Oh, Lord!" exclaimed Elspeth. "Now, what brought him here?"

Peter could have told her, but didn't. He was looking straight through the windshield. She was looking at him with slightly lifted brows.

"Good-bye, Elspeth," said he huskily.

"Good-bye, Peter. You've been awfully mean to me. I've loved it."

Why, thought Peter as he went on his way, did she have to use that particular word in that special tone at that unhappy moment?

Between Alexander Bruce MacGregor Andrews and his daughter, Elspeth, there existed a lively and irritable affection of precarious status, based upon a fundamental similarity of character and a prevalent lack of mutual understanding. That she should have willfully run away from home and got herself and him on the front pages of the papers, seemed to him an outrage of the first order.

"But it was your smearing the thing all over the air that got us into the papers," pointed out Elspeth, which didn't help much as a contribution to the *entente cordiale*. Both sulked for forty-eight hours.

Meantime, there arrived by special delivery a decidedly humid shoebox addressed in an uncompromisingly straight-up-and-down hand—just exactly the kind one would expect, thought the girl, knowing whose it was at first sight—full of the freshest, most odorous bunch of arbutus she had ever beheld. Something about it unmistakably defined it as having been picked by the sender.

Elspeth searched minutely for a note; there was none. She carried the box to her room and threw three clusters of orchids and a spray of gardenias into the scrapbasket. After that she went to a five-and-ten-cent store, made a purchase at the toy counter, had it boxed, and herself mailed it to the address given her by Peter Warne. The shipment did not include the money she owed him. That detail had escaped her mind.

"Scotty, dear." She greeted her father in the style of their companionable moods. "Do let's be sensible."

Mr. Andrews grunted suspiciously. "Suppose you begin."

"I'm going to. Drink your cocktail first." She settled down on the arm of his chair.

"Now what devilment are you up to?" demanded the apprehensive parent.

"Not a thing. I've decided to tell you about my trip."

Having her narrative all duly mapped out, she ran through it smoothly enough, hoping that he would not notice a few cleverly glossed passages. Disapproval in the paternal expression presently yielded to amused astonishment.

"Nervy kid!" he chuckled. "I'll bet it did you good."

"It didn't do me any harm. And I certainly found out a few things I'd never known before."

"Broadening effect of travel. Who did you say this young man was that looked after you?"

"I'm coming to that. The question is, what are you going to do for him?"

"What does he want?"

"I don't know that he exactly wants anything. But he's terribly poor, Scotty. Why, just think! He had to reckon up each time how much he could afford to spend on a meal!"

"Yes? I'm told there are quite a few people in this country in the same fix," observed Mr. Andrews dryly. "How much'll I make out the check for?"

"That's the trouble. I don't believe he'd take it. He's one of these inde-be-goshdarn-pendent birds. Wouldn't listen to my lending him some money."

"Humph! That probably means he's fallen for your fair young charms. Be funny if he hadn't."

"I'll tell you what would be funnier."

"What?"

"If I'd fallen for him," was the brazen response.

"Poof! You're always imagining you're in love with the newest hero in sight. Remember that young Danish diplo—"

"Yes; I do. What of it? I always get over it, don't I? And I'll get over this. You'd think he was terrible, dad. He's sure rough. You ought to have seen Little Daughter being bossed around by him and taking it."

"Is that so?" said her father, spacing his words sardonically. "Bossed you, did he? He and who else?"

"Oh, Peter doesn't need any help."

The grin was wiped off the Andrews face. "Who?"

"Peter. That's his name. Peter Warne."

"What?"

"Gracious! Don't yell so. Do you know him?"

"I haven't that pleasure as yet. Just let me make sure about this." He went into the adjoining room, whence he emerged with a sheaf of papers. "Peter Warne. So he's poor, is he?"

"Desperately."

"Well, he won't be, after tomorrow."

"Oh, Scotty! How do you know? Is he going to get some money? I'm so glad!"

"Some money is correct. Ten thousand dollars, to be exact."

"From his tar-pine or something process? How did *you* know about it?"

"From me. I don't know anything about—"

"From you?" Her lips parted; her eyes were wide and alarmed. "What for?"

"Information leading to the discovery and return of Elspeth, daughter of—"

"The reward? For me? Peter? I don't believe it. Peter wouldn't do such a thing. Take money for—"

"He has done it. Put in his claim for the reward. Do you want to see the proof?"

"I wouldn't believe it anyway."

Alexander Andrews studied her defiant face with a concern that became graver. This looked serious. Selecting a letter and a telegram from his dossier, he put them into her reluctant hand. At sight of the writing her heart sank. It was unmistakably that of the address on the box of arbutus. The note cited the writer's telegram of the fourteenth ("That's the day after we got off the island," thought Elspeth. "He was selling me out then.") and asked for an appointment.

"He's coming to my office at ten-thirty Thursday morning."

"Are you going to give him the money?"

"It looks as if I'd have to."

"He certainly worked hard enough for it," she said bitterly. "And I expect he needs it."

"I might be able to work a compromise," mused the canny Scot. "Though I'm afraid he's got the material for a bothersome lawsuit. If any of the other claimants"—he indicated the sheaf of letters and telegrams—"had a decent case, we could set off one against the other. The most insistent is a person named Shapley."

"Don't let him have it," said the girl hastily. "I'd rather Peter should get it, though I'd never have believed—Sold down the river!" She forced a laugh. "I brought a price, anyway."

"I've a good mind to give him a fight for it. It would mean more publicity, though."

"Oh, no!" breathed Elspeth.

"Enough's enough, eh? Though it couldn't be worse than what we've had."

"It could. Much worse. If you're going to see Pe—Mr. Warne, I'd better tell you something, Father. I've been traveling as Mrs. Peter Warne."

"Elspeth!"

"It isn't what you think. Purely economy—with the accent on the 'pure.' But it wouldn't look pretty in print. Oh, damn!" Her voice broke treacherously. "I thought Peter was so straight."

Her father walked up and down the room several times. He then went over and put his arm around his daughter's shoulders. "It's all right, dautie. We'll get you out of it. And we'll find a way to keep this fellow's mouth shut. I'm having a detectaphone set up in my office, and if he makes one slip we'll have him by the short hairs for blackmail."

"Peter doesn't make slips," returned his daughter. "It's his specialty not to. Oh, well, let's go in to dinner, Scotty."

Resolutely, she put the arbutus out of her room when she went up to bed that night. But the spicy odor from far springtime woodlands clung about the place like a plea for the absent.

Stern logic of the morning to which she sorrowfully awoke filled in the case against Peter. Nevertheless and notwithstanding, "I don't believe it," said Elspeth's sore heart. "And I won't believe it until—until—"

Severe as were the fittings of Mr. Alexander Bruce MacGregor Andrews' spacious office, they were less so than the glare which apprised Peter Warne, upon his entry, that this spare, square man did not like him and probably never would. That was all right with Peter. He was prepared not to like Mr. Andrews, either. On this propitious basis the two confronted each other.

After a formidable silence which the younger man bore without visible evidence of discomposure, his host barked:

"Sit down."

"Thank you," said Peter. He sat down.

"You have come about the money, I assume."

"Yes."

"Kindly reduce your claim to writing."

"You'll find it there." He handed over a sheet of paper. "Itemized."

"What's this?" Mr. Andrews' surprised eye ran over it.

"Traveling expenses. Elsp—your daughter's."

The father gave the column of figures his analytical attention. "Boat, twenty dollars," he read. "You didn't take my daughter to Cuba, did you?"

"I had to steal a boat to get through the flood. The owner ought to be reimbursed. If you think that's not a fair charge, I'll assume half of it. Everything else is split."

"Humph! My daughter's share of food, lodging, and gasoline, excluding the—er—alleged boat, seems to figure up to eighteen dollars and fifty-six cents. Where did you lodge?"

"Wherever we could."

With the paper before him, Mr. Andrews began to hammer his desk. "You have the temerity, the impudence, the effrontery, the—the— anyway, you come here to hold me up for ten thousand dollars and on top of that you try to spring a doctored expense account on me!"

"Doctored!" echoed Peter. "Maybe you think you could do it for less?"

Taken aback, Mr. Andrews ceased his operations on the desk. "We'll pass that for the main point," he grunted. "Upon what do you base your claim for the ten thousand dollars?"

"Nothing," was the placid reply. "I made no claim."

"Your telegram. Your letter—"

"You couldn't have read them. I simply warned you against paying anybody else's claim. You had others, I suppose."

"Others! A couple of hundred!"

"One signed Horace Shapley?"

"I believe so."

"I don't like him," observed Peter, and explained.

"Then your idea," interposed Mr. Andrews, "was to get in first merely to block off this other person. Is that it?"

"Yes."

"And you aren't claiming any part of the reward?"

"No."

"You're crazy," declared the other. "Or maybe I am. What *do* you want?"

Peter gently indicated the expense account. Mr. Andrews went over it again.

"You mean to tell me that you kept my daughter for five days and more on a total of eighteen dollars and fifty-six cents?"

"There are the figures."

Mr. Andrews leaned forward. "Did she kick much?"

Peter's grin was a bit rueful. "There were times when—"

"You'd have liked to sock her. I know. Why didn't you present your bill to her?"

"I did. I reckon she just forgot it."

"She would! . . . Have a cigar." As the young fellow lighted up, his entertainer was writing and entering a check.

"As a matter of correct business, I ought to have Elspeth's OK on this bill. However, I'll pass it, including the boat. Receipt here, please." The amount was $1,038.56.

Shaking his head, Peter pushed the check across the desk. "Thank you, but I can't take this, Mr. Andrews."

"Bosh! Elspeth told me you were broke."

"I am. . . . No; I'm not, either. I forgot. I've just made a deal on a new process of mine. Anyway, I couldn't take that—that bonus."

"That's funny. If you're no longer broke, I should think you'd be above bringing me a trifling expense account for—er—entertaining my daughter."

"It's a matter of principle," returned Peter firmly.

Mr. Andrews rose and smote his caller on the shoulder. "I begin to see how you made that little spitfire of mine toe the mark. More than I've been able to do for the past ten years. Eighteen dollars and fifty-six cents, huh?" He sank back in his chair and laughed. "See here, my boy; I like you. I like your style. Will you take that money as a present from me?"

"Sorry, sir, but I'd rather not."

The older man stared him down. "Because I'm Elspeth's father, eh? You're in love with her, I suppose."

Peter grew painfully red. "God forbid!" he muttered.

"What do you mean, God forbid?" shouted the magnate. "Better men than you have been in love with her."

"All right, Mr. Andrews," said Peter in desperation. "Then I am, too. I have been from the first. Now, you tell me—you're her father— what's the sense of it with a girl like Elspeth? I'm going back to Florida with a contract for eight thousand a year, to complete my process."

"That's more than I was making at your age."

"It's more than I expect to be making at yours," said Peter with candor. "But how far would that go with her? Look me over, sir. Even if I had a chance with Elspeth, would you advise a fellow like me to try to marry her?"

"No, I wouldn't!" roared the father. "You're too darn good for her."

"Don't talk like a fool," snapped Peter.

"Just for that," reflected Mr. Andrews as his caller withdrew, jamming a substituted check into his pocket, "I'll bet you'll have little enough to say about it when the time comes."

He sent for Elspeth and left her alone with the detectaphone. What that unpoetic cylinder spouted forth rang in her heart like the music of the spheres with the morning and evening stars in the solo parts. So *that* was how Peter felt about it.

Memory obligingly supplied the number on Darrow or Farrow or Barrow or whatever strange street it was. The taxi man whom she hailed earned her admiration by knowing all about it.

Peter said: "Come in," in a spiritless manner. With a totally different vocal effect he added: "What are *you* doing *here?*" and tacked onto that "You oughtn't to be here at all."

"Why not?" Elspeth sat down.

He muttered something wherein the word "proper" seemed to carry the emphasis, and in which the term "landlady" occurred.

"Proper!" jeered his visitor. "You talk to me about propriety after we've been traveling together and sharing the same room for nearly a week!"

"But this is New York," he pointed out.

"And you're packing up to leave it. When?"

"Tonight."

"Without the ten thousand dollar reward?"

"How did you know about that? Your fath—"

"I've just come from his office. You might better have taken the check."

"Don't want it."

"That's silly. What," she inquired reasonably, "have you got to get married on?"

"Eight thousand a ye—I'm not going to get married," he interrupted himself with needless force.

"Not after compromising a young and innocent—"

"I haven't compromised anyone." Sulkily and doggedly.

"Peter! I suppose registering me as your wife all over the map isn't compromising. Did you ever hear of the Mann Act?"

"B-b-b-but—"

"Yes; I know all about that 'but.' It's a great big, important 'but,' but there's another bigger 'but' to be considered. We know what happened and didn't happen on our trip, *but* nobody else would ever believe it in this world. I certainly wouldn't."

"Nor I," he agreed. "Unless," he qualified hastily, "the girl was you."

"Or the man was you."

They laughed with dubious heartiness. When they had done laughing, there seemed to be nothing to follow, logically. Elspeth got up slowly.

"Where are you going?" demanded Peter, in a panic.

"If you don't like me any more"—she put the slightest possible stress on the verb, leaving him to amend it if he chose—"I'm sorry I came."

To this rueful observation, Peter offered no response.

"You did like me once, you know. You as much as admitted it."

Peter swore.

"Did you or did you not tell my father that you would never get over it?"

"It?"

"Well—me."

"Your father," said Peter wrathfully, "is a human sieve."

"No; he isn't. There was a detectaphone listening in on everything you said. I got it all from that."

"In that case," said the now desperate and reckless Peter, "I may as well get it off my chest." And he repeated what he had earlier said about his feelings, with a fervor that wiped the mischief from Elspeth's face.

"Oh-h-h-h!" she murmured, a little dazed. "That's the way you feel."

"No, it isn't. It isn't half of it."

"Where do we go from here?" thought the girl. The atmosphere of sprightly combat and adventure had changed. She was not breathing quite so easily. Her uncertain look fell upon an object at the top of the half-packed carryall. "Oh!" she exlaimed. "You got my present."

"Yes; I got it."

"I hope you liked it." Politely.

"Not particularly."

Her eyes widened. "Why not?"

"Well, I may be oversensitive where you're concerned, but I don't care so much about being called a tinhorn sport, because—well, I don't know, but I suppose it's because I let you pay back the money for our trip. What do I know about the way girls look at those things, anyway?" he concluded morosely.

One girl was looking at him with a mixture of contempt, amusement, pity, and something stronger than any of these. "Oh, you boob!" she breathed. "That isn't a tinhorn. That's a trumpet."

"A *trumpet?*"

"The kind What's-his-name blew before the walls of Jericho, if you have to have a diagram. Oh, *Pee*-ter; you're such a dodo!" sighed Elspeth. "What am I ever going to do about you? Would you like to kiss me, Peter?"

"Yes," said Peter. And he did.

"This means," he informed her presently, and dubiously, "our having to live in a Florida swamp—"

"On eighteen dollars and fifty-six cents?"

"On eight thousand a year. That isn't much more, to you. You'll hate it."

"I'll love it. D'you know where I'd like to land on our wedding trip, Peter?"

"Yes. Dake's Two-dollar Cabins; Clean; Comfortable; Reasonable."

"*And* respectable. You're too clever, Peter, darling."

"Because that's exactly what I'd like. Social note: Mr. and Mrs. Peter Warne are stopping in Jaw-jaw on their return trip South."

"Let's go," said Elspeth joyously.

Mrs. Dake, in the wing off the tourist-camp office, yawned herself awake of an early May morning and addressed her husband. "That's a funny couple in Number Seven, Tim. Do you reckon they're respectable?"

"I should worry. They registered all right, didn't they?"

"Uh-huh. Wouldn't take any other cabin but Seven. And wanted an extra blanket. This hot night."

"Well, we could spare it."

"That isn't the only queer thing about 'em. After you was asleep, I looked out and there was the young fellah mopin' around. By and by he went in, and right soon somebody blew a horn. Just as plain as you ever heard. What do you think about that, Tim?"

Mr. Dake yawned. "What they do after they're registered and paid up is their business, not our'n."

Which is the proper and practical attitude for the management of a well-conducted tourist camp.

IT'S A WONDERFUL LIFE

(1946)

THE GREATEST GIFT
PHILIP VAN DOREN STERN

Returning to Hollywood from World War II in 1945, Frank Capra was a decorated Army colonel who for the previous three years had produced a series of patriotic propaganda films for the War Department. Eager to get going on a commerical project with his newly formed Liberty Films, an independent film production company founded with fellow-directors William Wyler and George Stevens, Capra set about searching for an idea to launch the fledgling operation. At the suggestion of a colleague, he chose "The Greatest Gift," a short story that writer-historian Philip Van Doren Stern had sent out as a Christmas card to personal friends. Although *It's a Wonderful Life* did not win a single Academy Award—Wyler's *The Best Years of Our Lives* all but swept the major kudos at the 1947 ceremonies—it is probably Capra's best-loved and most typical film. Chronicling the life of George Bailey (Jimmy Stewart), a small-town savings and loan man passed over by both wealth and glory, the film is a perfect distillation of Capra's theme of the travail and moral triumph of the common man. James Agee called it "one of the most efficient sentimental pieces since 'A Christmas Carol,' " and along with myriad Dickens adaptations and *Miracle on 34th Street* (1947), it has become a classic of Christmas holiday fables.

Novelist, Civil War aficionado, and anthologist, PHILIP VAN DOREN STERN (1900–1984) worked for many years as a book designer for the publishers Alfred A. Knopf and Simon & Schuster. In addition to editing the papers of Abraham Lincoln, he served as general manager for Editions for the Armed Services, a non-profit organization that issued 122,000,000 paperback books for troops overseas during World War II.

IT'S A WONDERFUL LIFE

Released: 1946
Production: Frank Capra for Liberty Films; released by RKO/Radio
Direction: Frank Capra
Screenplay: Fances Goodrich, Albert Hackett, and Frank Capra, with
    additional scenes by Jo Swerling
Cinematography: Joseph Walker and Joseph Biroc
Editing: William Hornbeck
Sound: Richard Van Hessen, Clem Portman, and John Aalberg
Music: Dmitri Tiomkin
Running time: 129 minutes

PRINCIPAL CHARACTERS:

George Bailey	James Stewart
Mary Hatch	Donna Reed
Mr. Potter	Lionel Barrymore
Uncle Billy	Thomas Mitchell
Clarence	Henry Travers
Mrs. Bailey	Beulah Bondi
Violet Bick	Gloria Grahame
Mr. Gower	H. B. Warner
Bert	Ward Bond
Ernie	Frank Faylan
Pa Bailey	Samuel S. Hinds
Cousin Tilly	Mary Treen
Bodyguard	Frank Hagney
Nick	Sheldon Leonard

The little town straggling up the hill was bright with colored Christmas lights. But George Pratt did not see them. He was leaning over the railing of the iron bridge, staring down moodily at the black water. The current eddied and swirled like liquid glass, and occasionally a bit of ice, detached from the shore, would go gliding downstream to be swallowed up in the shadows under the bridge.

The water looked paralyzingly cold. George wondered how long a man could stay alive in it. The glassy blackness had a strange, hypnotic effect on him. He leaned still farther over the railing. . . .

"I wouldn't do that if I were you," a quiet voice beside him said.

George turned resentfully to a little man he had never seen before. He was stout, well past middle age, and his round cheeks were pink in the winter air as though they had just been shaved.

"Wouldn't do what?" George asked sullenly.

"What you were thinking of doing."

"How do you know what I was thinking?"

"Oh, we make it our business to know a lot of things," the stranger said easily.

George wondered what the man's business was. He was a most unremarkable little person, the sort you would pass in a crowd and never notice. Unless you saw his bright blue eyes, that is. You couldn't forget them, for they were the kindest, sharpest eyes you ever saw. Nothing else about him was noteworthy. He wore a moth-eaten old fur cap and a shabby overcoat that was stretched tightly across his paunchy belly. He was carrying a small black satchel. It wasn't a doctor's bag—it was too large for that and not the right shape. It was a salesman's sample kit, George decided distastefully. The fellow was probably some sort of peddler, the kind who would go around poking his sharp little nose into other people's affairs.

"Looks like snow, doesn't it?" the stranger said, glancing up appraisingly at the overcast sky. "It'll be nice to have a white Christmas. They're getting scarce these days—but so are a lot of things." He turned to face George squarely. "You all right now?"

"Of course I'm all right. What made you think I wasn't? I—"

George fell silent before the stranger's quiet gaze.

The litle man shook his head. "You know you shouldn't think of such things—and on Christmas Eve of all times! You've got to consider Mary—and your mother, too."

George opened his mouth to ask how this stranger could know his wife's name, but the fellow anticipated him. "Don't ask me how I know such things. It's my business to know 'em. That's why I came along this way tonight. Lucky I did too." He glanced down at the dark water and shuddered.

"Well, if you know so much about me," George said, "give me just one good reason why I should be alive."

The little man made a queer chuckling sound. "Come, come, it can't be that bad. You've got your job at the bank. And Mary and the kids. You're healthy, young, and—"

"And sick of everything!" George cried. "I'm stuck here in this mudhole for life, doing the same dull work day after day. Other men are leading exciting lives, but I—well, I'm just a small-town bank clerk that even the Army didn't want. I never did anything really useful or interesting, and it looks as if I never will. I might just as well be dead. I might better be dead. Sometimes I wish I were. In fact, I wish I'd never been born!"

The little man stood looking at him in the growing darkness. "What was that you said?" he asked softly.

"I said I wish I'd never been born," George repeated firmly. "And I mean it too."

The stranger's pink cheeks glowed with excitement. "Why that's wonderful! You've solved everything. I was afraid you were going to give me some trouble. But now you've got the solution yourself. You wish you'd never been born. All right! Okay! You haven't!"

"What do you mean?" George growled.

"You haven't been born. Just that. You haven't been born. No one here knows you. You have no responsibilities—no job—no wife—no children. Why, you haven't even a mother. You couldn't have, of course. All your troubles are over. Your wish, I am happy to say, has been granted—officially."

"Nuts!" George snorted and turned away.

The stranger ran after him and caught him by the arm.

"You'd better take this with you," he said, holding out his satchel. "It'll open a lot of doors that might otherwise be slammed in your face."

"What doors in whose face?" George scoffed. "I know everybody in this town. And besides, I'd like to see anybody slam a door in my face."

"Yes, I know," the little man said patiently. "But take this anyway. It can't do any harm and it may help." He opened the satchel and displayed a number of brushes. "You'd be surprised how useful these brushes can be as an introduction—especially the free ones. These, I mean." He hauled out a plain little handbrush. "I'll show you how to use it." He thrust the satchel into George's reluctant hands and began. "When the lady of the house comes to the door you give her this and then talk fast. You say: 'Good evening, madam. I'm from the World Cleaning Company, and I want to present you with this handsome and useful brush absolutely free—no obligation to purchase anything at all.' After that, of course, it's a cinch. Now you try it." He forced the brush into George's hand.

George promptly dropped the brush into the satchel and fumbled with the catch, finally closing it with an angry snap. "Here," he said, and then stopped abruptly, for there was no one in sight.

The little stranger must have slipped away into the bushes growing along the river bank, George thought. He certainly wasn't going to play hide and seek with him. It was nearly dark and getting colder every minute. He shivered and turned up his coat collar.

The street lights had been turned on, and Christmas candles in the windows glowed softly. The little town looked remarkably cheerful. After all, the place you grew up in was the one spot on earth where you could really feel at home. George felt a sudden burst of affection even for crotchety old Hank Biddle whose house he was passing. He remembered the quarrel he had had when his car had scraped a piece of bark out of Hank's big maple tree. George looked up at the vast spread of leafless branches towering over him in the darkness. The tree must have been growing there since Indian times. He felt a sudden twinge of guilt for the damage he had done. He had never stopped to inspect the wound, for he was ordinarily afraid to have Hank catch him even looking at the tree. Now he stepped out boldly into the roadway to examine the huge trunk.

Hank must have repaired the scar or painted it over, for there was no sign of it. George struck a match and bent down to look more closely. He straightened up with an odd, sinking feeling in his stomach. There wasn't any scar. The bark was smooth and undamaged.

He remembered what the little man at the bridge had said. It was all nonsense, of course, but the non-existent scar bothered him.

When he reached the bank, he saw that something was wrong. The building was dark, and he knew he had turned the vault light on. He noticed, too, that someone had left the window shades up. He ran around to the front. There was a battered old sign fastened on the door. George could just make out the words:

FOR RENT OR SALE.

Apply   JAMES SILVA, *Real Estate.*

Perhaps it was some boys' trick, he thought wildly. Then he saw a pile of ancient leaves and tattered newspapers in the bank's ordinarily immaculate doorway. And the windows looked as though they hadn't been washed in years. A light was still burning across the street in Jim Silva's office. George dashed over and tore the door open.

Jim looked up from his ledgerbook in surprise. "What can I do for you, young man?" he said in the polite voice he reserved for potential customers.

"The bank," George said breathlessly. "What's the matter with it?"

"The old bank building?" Jim Silva turned around and looked out of the window. "Nothing that I can see. Wouldn't like to rent or buy it, would you?"

"You mean—it's out of business?"

"For a good ten years. Went bust during the depression. Stranger 'round these parts, ain't you?"

George sagged against the wall. "I was here some time ago," he said weakly. "The bank was all right then. I even knew some of the people who worked there."

"Didn't know a feller named Marty Jenkins, did you?"

"Marty Jenkins! Why, he—" George was about to say that Marty had never worked at the bank—couldn't have, in fact, for when they had both left school they had applied for a job there and George had gotten it. But now, of course, things were different. He would have to be careful. "No, I didn't know him," he said slowly. "Not really, that is. I'd heard of him."

"Then maybe you heard how he skipped out with fifty thousand dollars. That's why the bank went broke. Pretty near ruined everybody around here." Silva was looking at him sharply. "I was hoping for a minute maybe you'd know where he is. I lost plenty in that crash myself. We'd like to get our hands on Marty Jenkins."

"Didn't he have a brother? Seems to me he had a brother named Arthur."

"Art? Oh, sure. But he's all right. He don't know where his brother went. It's had a terrible effect on him, too. Took to drink, he did. It's too bad—and hard on his wife. He married a nice girl."

George felt the sinking feeling in his stomach again. "Who did he marry?" he demanded hoarsely. Both he and Art had courted Mary.

"Girl named Mary Thatcher," Silva said cheerfully. "She lives up on the hill just this side of the church—Hey! Where are you going?"

But George had bolted out of the office. He ran past the empty bank building and turned up the hill. For a moment he thought of going straight to Mary. The house next to the church had been given them by her father as a wedding present. Naturally Art Jenkins would have gotten it if he had married Mary. George wondered whether they had any children. Then he knew he couldn't face Mary—not yet anyway. He decided to visit his parents and find out more about her.

There were candles burning in the windows of the little weather-beaten house on the side street, and a Christmas wreath was hanging on the glass panel of the front door. George raised the gate latch with a loud click. A dark shape on the porch jumped up and began to growl. Then it hurled itself down the steps, barking ferociously.

"Brownie!" George shouted. "Brownie, you old fool, stop that! Don't you know me?" But the dog advanced menacingly and drove him back behind the gate. Th porch light snapped on, and George's father stepped outside to call the dog off. The barking subsided to a low, angry growl.

His father held the dog by the collar while George cautiously walked past. He could see that his father did not know him. "Is the lady of the house in?" he asked.

His father waved toward the door. "Go on in," he said cordially. "I'll chain this dog up. She can be mean with strangers."

His mother, who was waiting in the hallway, obviously did not recognize him. George opened his sample kit and grabbed the first brush that came to hand. "Good evening, ma'am," he said politely.

"I'm from the World Cleaning Company. We're giving out a free sample brush. I thought you might like to have one. No obligation. No obligation at all. . . ." His voice faltered.

His mother smiled at his awkwardness. "I suppose you'll want to sell me something. I'm not really sure I need any brushes."

"No'm. I'm not selling anything," he assured her. "The regular salesman will be around in a few days. This is just—well, just a Christmas present from the company."

"How nice," she said. "You people never gave such good brushes away before."

"This is a special offer," he said. His father entered the hall and closed the door.

"Won't you come in for a while and sit down?" his mother said. "You must be tired walking so much."

"Thank you, ma'am. I don't mind if I do." He entered the little parlor and put his bag down on the floor. The room looked different somehow, although he could not figure out why.

"I used to know this town pretty well," he said to make conversation. "Knew some of the townspeople. I remember a girl named Mary Thatcher. She married Art Jenkins, I heard. You must know them."

"Of course," his mother said. "We know Mary well."

"Any children?" he asked casually.

"Two—a boy and a girl."

George sighed audibly. "My, you must be tired," his mother said. "Perhaps I can get you a cup of tea."

"No'm, don't bother," he said. "I'll be having supper soon." He looked around the little parlor, trying to find out why it looked different. Over the mantelpiece hung a framed photograph which had been taken on his kid brother Harry's sixteenth birthday. He remembered how they had gone to Potter's studio to be photographed together. There was something queer about the picture. It took him a full minute to realize what it was. It showed only one figure—Harry's.

"That your son? he asked.

His mother's face clouded. She nodded but said nothing.

"I think I met him, too," George said hesitantly. "His name's Harry, isn't it?"

His mother turned away, making a strange choking noise in her throat. Her husband put his arm clumsily around her shoulder. His voice, which was always mild and gentle, suddenly became harsh. "You couldn't have met him," he said. "He's been dead a long while. He was drowned the day that picture was taken."

George's mind flew back to the long-ago August afternoon when he and Harry had visited Potter's studio. On their way home they had gone swimming. Harry had been seized with a cramp, he remembered. He had pulled him out of the water and had thought nothing of it. But suppose he hadn't been there!

"I'm sorry," he said miserably. "I guess I'd better go. I hope you like the brush. And I wish you both a very Merry Christmas." There, he had put his foot in it again, wishing them a Merry Christmas when they were thinking about their dead son.

Brownie tugged fiercely at her chain as George went down the porch steps and accompanied his departure with a hostile, rolling growl.

He wanted desperately now to see Mary. He wasn't sure he could stand not being recognized by her, but he had to see her.

The lights were on in the church, and the choir was making last-minute preparations for Christmas vespers. The organ had been practicing "Holy Night" evening after evening until George had become thoroughly sick of it. But now the music almost tore his heart out.

He stumbled blindly up the path to his own house. The lawn was untidy, and the flower bushes he had kept carefully trimmed were neglected and badly sprouted. Art Jenkins could hardly be expected to care for such things.

When he knocked at the door there was a long silence, followed by the shout of a child. Then Mary came to the door.

At the sight of her, George's voice almost failed him. "Merry Christmas, ma'am," he managed to say at last. His hand shook as he tried to open the satchel.

"Come in," Mary said indifferently. "It's cold out."

When George entered the living room, unhappy as he was, he could not help noticing with a secret grin that the too-high-priced blue sofa they often had quarreled over was there. Evidently Mary had gone through the same thing with Art Jenkins and had won the argument with him, too.

George got his satchel open. One of the brushes had a bright blue handle and vari-colored bristles. It was obviously a brush not intended to be given away, but George didn't care. He handed it to Mary. "This would be fine for your sofa," he said.

"My, that's a pretty brush," she exclaimed. "You're giving it away free?"

He nodded solemnly. "Special introductory offer. It's one way for the company to keep excess profits down—share them with its friends."

She stroked the sofa gently with the brush, smoothing out the velvety nap. "It *is* a nice brush. Thank you. I—" There was a sudden scream from the kitchen, and two small children rushed in. A little, homely-faced girl flung herself into her mother's arms, sobbing loudly as a boy of seven came running after her, snapping a toy pistol at her head. "Mommy, she won't die," he yelled. "I shot her a hunert times, but she won't die."

He looks just like Art Jenkins, George thought. Acts like him too. The boy suddenly turned his attention to him. "Who're you?" he demanded belligerently. He pointed his pistol at George and pulled the trigger. "You're dead!" he cried. "You're dead. Why don't you fall down and die?"

There was a heavy step on the porch. The boy looked frightened and backed away. George saw Mary glance apprehensively at the door.

Art Jenkins came in. He stood for a moment in the doorway, clinging to the knob for support. His eyes were glazed, and his face was very red. "Who's this?" he demanded thickly.

"He's a brush salesman," Mary tried to explain. "He gave me this brush."

"Brush salesman!" Art sneered. "Well, tell him to get outa here. We don't want no brushes." Art hiccoughed violently and lurched across the room to the sofa where he sat down suddenly. "An' we don't want no brush salesmen neither."

"You'd better go," Mary whispered to George. "I'm sorry."

The boy edged toward George. "G'wan, go 'way. We don't want no brushes. An' we don't want no ole brush salesmen neither."

George looked despairingly at Mary. Her eyes were begging him to go. Art had lifted his feet up on the sofa and was sprawling out on it, muttering unkind things about brush salesmen. George went to the door, followed by Art's son who kept snapping his pistol at him and saying: "You're dead—dead—dead!"

Perhaps the boy was right, George thought when he reached the porch. Maybe he was dead, or maybe this was all a bad dream from which he might eventually awake. He wanted to find the little man on the bridge again and try to persuade him to cancel the whole deal.

He hurried down the hill and broke into a run when he neared the river. George was relieved to see the little stranger standing on the bridge. "I've had enough," he gasped. "Get me out of this—you got me into it."

The stranger raised his eyebrows. "I got you into it! I like that! You were granted your wish. You got everything you asked for. You're the freest man on earth now. You have no ties. You can go anywhere— do anything. What more can you possibly want?"

"Change me back," George pleaded. "Change me back—please. Not just for my sake but for others too. You don't know what a mess this town is in. You don't understand. I've got to get back. They need me here."

"I understand right enough," the stranger said slowly. "I just wanted to make sure you did. You had the greatest gift of all conferred upon you—the gift of life, of being a part of this world and taking a part in it. Yet you denied that gift." As the stranger spoke, the church bell high up on the hill sounded, calling the townspeople to Christmas vespers. Then the downtown church bell started ringing.

"I've got to get back," George said desperately. "You can't cut me off like this. Why, it's murder!"

"Suicide rather, wouldn't you say?" the stranger murmured. "You brought it on yourself. However, since it's Christmas Eve—well, anyway, close your eyes and keep listening to the bells." His voice sank lower. "Keep listening to the bells. . . ."

George did as he was told. He felt a cold, wet snowdrop touch his cheek—and then another and another. When he opened his eyes, the snow was falling fast, so fast that it obscured everything around him. The little stranger could not be seen, but then neither could anything else. The snow was so thick that George had to grope for the bridge railing.

As he started toward the village, he thought he heard someone saying: "Merry Christmas," but the bells were drowning out all rival sounds, so he could not be sure.

When he reached Hank Biddle's house he stopped and walked out into the roadway, peering down anxiously at the base of the big maple tree. The scar was there, thank Heaven! He touched the tree affectionately. He'd have to do something about the wound—get a tree surgeon or something. Anyway, he'd evidently been changed back. He was himself again. Maybe it was all a dream, or perhaps he had been hypnotized by the smooth-flowing black water. He had heard of such things.

At the corner of Main and Bridge Streets he almost collided with a hurrying figure. It was Jim Silva, the real estate agent. "Hello, George," Jim said cheerfully. "Late tonight, ain't you? I should think you'd want to be home early on Christmas Eve."

George drew a long breath. "I just wanted to see if the bank is all right. I've got to make sure the vault light is on."

"Sure it's on. I saw it as I went past."

"Let's look, huh?" George said, pulling at Silva's sleeve. He wanted the assurance of a witness. He dragged the surprised real estate dealer around to the front of the bank where the light was gleaming through the falling snow. "I told you it was on," Silva said with some irritation.

"I had to make sure," George mumbled. "Thanks—and Merry Christmas!" Then he was off like a streak, running up the hill.

He was in a hurry to get home, but not in such a hurry that he couldn't stop for a moment at his parents' house, where he wrestled with Brownie until the friendly old bulldog waggled all over with delight. He grasped his startled brother's hand and wrung it frantically, wishing him an almost hysterical Merry Christmas. Then he dashed across the parlor to examine a certain photograph. He kissed his mother, joked with his father, and was out of the house a few seconds later, stumbling and slipping on the newly fallen snow as he ran on up the hill.

The church was bright with light, and the choir and the organ were going full tilt. George flung the door to his home open and called out at the top of his voice: "Mary! Where are you? Mary! Kids!"

His wife came toward him, dressed for going to church, and making gestures to silence him. "I've just put the children to bed," she protested. "Now they'll—" But not another word could she get out of her mouth, for he smothered it with kisses, and then he dragged her up to the children's room, where he violated every tenet of parental behavior by madly embracing his son and his daughter and waking them up thoroughly.

It was not until Mary got him downstairs that he began to be coherent. "I thought I'd lost you. Oh, Mary, I thought I'd lost you!"

"What's the matter, darling?" she asked in bewilderment.

He pulled her down on the sofa and kissed her again. And then, just as he was about to tell her about his queer dream, his fingers came in contact with something lying on the seat of the sofa. His voice froze.

He did not even have to pick the thing up, for he knew what it was. And he knew that it would have a blue handle and vari-colored bristles.

THE JAZZ SINGER

(1927)

THE DAY OF ATONEMENT
SAMSON RAPHAELSON

Although it was not the first "sound" picture per se, (earlier Vitaphone releases, including *Don Juan* (1926), made effective use of synchronized soundtracks), *The Jazz Singer* was the first real "talkie" and is generally considered to be the film that irrevocably established the sound film as Hollywood's industry standard. Combining spoken dialogue with classical music and popular songs—"My Gal Sal", "Toot Toot Tootsie", and, the film's signature song, "Mammy"—it was received upon its release with almost unqualified acclaim. *The Jazz Singer* charts the life of Jakie Rabinowitz, a boy in New York's Jewish ghetto, who forsakes the family profession of cantor to become an immensely popular jazz singer. The inspiration for the original story came to the young writer Samson Raphaelson when he saw Al Jolson perform in Chicago in the early 1920s and was struck by the similarity of his vocal style to that of an Orthodox Jewish cantor's. Ironically, Jolson himself (who went on to star in the film) had entered show business against the wishes of his cantor father.

A successful playwright and screenwriter, SAMSON RAPHAELSON (1896–1983) was born on the Lower East Side of New York and later raised in Chicago. During the 1930s and '40s, he wrote many of director Ernst Lubitsch's sophisticated comedies including *Trouble in Paradise* (1932), *The Shop around the Corner* (1940), and *Heaven Can Wait* (1943) as well as Alfred Hitchcock's thriller, *Suspicion* (1941). At the time of his death, he was Professor of Film and Drama at Columbia University.

THE JAZZ SINGER

Released: 1927
Production: Jack L. Warner for Warner Bros. and the Vitaphone
   Corporation (Special Academy Award)
Direction: Alan Crosland
Screenplay: Alfred A. Cohn
Cinematography: Hal Mohr
Editing: Harold McCord
Music direction: Louis Silvers
Title design: Jack Jarmuth
Running time: 88 minutes

PRINCIPAL CHARACTERS:

Jakie Rabinowitz (Jack Robin)	Al Jolson
Jakie Rabinowitz (younger)	Bobby Gordon
Mary Dale	May McAvoy
Cantor Rabinowitz	Warner Oland
Sara Rabinowitz	Eugenie Besserer
Cantor Josef Rosenblatt	Himself

What Jack Robin needs," said David Lee, who owns some of the whitest of Broadway's white lights, "is a wife."

"What our Jakie needs," said Jack Robin's father, old Cantor Rabinowitz, of the Hester Street Synagogue, "is a God."

"What I need," said Jack Robin, "is a song-number with a kick in it. The junk that Tin Pan Alley is peddling these days is rusty—that's all— *rusty.*"

And the sum and substance of it was a sober-faced Jack, engaged fitfully in experiments with pleasure, a worried but watchful David Lee, and a tragically lonely household on Hester Street, where dwelt the aged cantor and his wife.

For Jack was no ordinary singer of ragtime. Those dark eyes of his might have been the ecstatic eyes of a poet in the days when the Chosen People lived sedately in the land of Canaan. They might have been prophetic eyes, stern and stirring, in the years of Zedekiah, son of Josiah, King of Judah, when Jerusalem "knew not its God." They might have been deep wells of lamentation even one generation ago had his lyric voice been born to cry the sorrows of Israel in a Russian synagogue.

But he lived in New York, and his slender, well-set-up figure was draped in perfectly fitting suits of Anglo-Saxon severity, and his dark hair was crisply trimmed and parted after the fashion of young America, and the black eyes in his thin, handsome face were restless, cynical, and without joy.

That bewilderment, brooding and fitful, which was now so palpable, had vaguely begun to propel Jack in the days when, as Jakie Rabinowitz, he had drifted with a gang of Hester Street hoodlums. He was twelve then, rather tall and sturdy for his age, and for an exciting few weeks he enjoyed the thrills of looting fruit stands, of stealing milk bottles and of openly shooting craps. But the bliss of these few weeks came to a hysterical termination when he violated the code of the gang, and it was not until ten years later, when he knew Amy Prentiss, that he felt such happiness again.

The gang's code regarded certain acts of loyalty as religion, and certain epithets could be avenged only in blood—the blood of a bleeding nose or a lacerated lip. Foremost among the firebrand epithets was the term "sheeny." If someone called you a sheeny, only one thing could properly ensue—violent fistic battle. But Jakie, traversing Cherry Street, the Irish domain, received the stigma with indifference.

He and nine-year-old Hymie Cohen were on their way home from an East River saltwater swimming-shack, where for a dime they had received the use of faded trunks and the privileges of a moldy wooden tank. A barefoot young "mick," slighter than Jakie but of truculent demeanor, had united ten fingers with his nose in a trestle of vilification and cried: "Yah! Lookit the sheeny! Go back where yah came from, yah sheeny!"

Jakie shrugged his shoulders and passed on. Neither righteous indignation nor the tremors of fear had risen within him.

Little Hymie told his brother Joe of the humiliating incident, and that night Joe asked Jakie about it.

"Yah didn't fight, did yah?" he demanded. "Yah didn't do nothin'?"

"Why should I fight? I wasn't mad."

Joe stepped close to Jakie.

"You're yeller! Yah got a yeller streak a mile wide right t'rough to your liver! Yah can't hang around wit' de gang no more. Go 'way before I paste yah one on the jaw!"

This was disturbing. Jakie was not minded to obedient alacrity. He responded with a show of spirit,

"I'll go when I feel like it!"

Joe's response was a contemptuous slap over the eyes—a slap which stung and infuriated. Sobbing and seeing red, he fell upon Joe and blindly pommeled away with his fists.

After it was over and Jakie lay on the curb with a "shiner," a bleeding nose, and a perforated dental display, sobbing breathlessly and cursing in richly filthy East Side *argot,* Joe came up to him.

"I take it back, Jakie," he said, proffering his hand. "Y'ain't yeller. I—"

"Go to hell," Jakie panted, "you dirty sheeny!"

Jakie went directly home that night and endured stoically his father's scolding and his mother's running fire of questions. Dwelling in a passion of hatred for the complete order of things, his parents exasperated him into a seething calm beyond the point of articulate resentment. The next day he played truant from Hebrew school.

The *melammed,* who was receiving a dollar a month extra for teaching the cantor's son, anxious to prepare him magnificently for the *bar mitzvah* recitative and speech in the synagogue, went out in search of the boy. He found Jakie playing basketball in the Hester Street playgrounds, dragged him back to the small, ill-smelling, gas-lit room where a few of the older boys still were singsonging the cadenced subtleties of *"Baba Kama,"* and flogged him until his body was purple.

Jakie came home that night somewhat terrified by the decision he had made, yet completely set in his determination. He was acute enough to speak to his mother first.

"Mamma, that *rebi*—he ain't no good. He's so *dirty,* and he's always hollering, and, anyways, none of us kids ever learns anything. And he nearly killed me today, mamma, with a big strap— Look how sore my back is—and I never did nothing at all!"

"I'll tell papa," said his mother, busily applying goose-grease to his tortured back, "and he'll speak to the *rebi* he shouldn't hit you no more."

"I don't wanna go to *chaidar,*" Jakie announced, with low-voiced intensity.

"Jakie! Your papa shouldn't hear you speak like this! How could you ever be a *chazon*—a cantor in a big fancy synagogue—if you don't know good your Hebrew? I'll speak to papa he should find you a new *chaidar* and a new *rebi.*"

"I don't want no new *chaidar,* and I don't want to be a *chazon* when I grow up!"

"Jakie! Eat your supper and don't speak it another word like this! Lucky your papa he's ain't home, or he would kill you."

The boy did not move toward the table. He raised a blazing face to his mother.

"If papa kills me," he said, "then I'll run away from home."

The old cantor did whip Jakie. It had long been a matter of profound distress to the cantor that a youth with so nimble a mind should be so diffident in the presence of the great culture of the noblest of all peoples. For ten generations, in Russia and now in America, the name "Rabinowitz" had stood for devout, impassioned *chazonoth,* and Jakie's father was animated by the one desire that his son should become even a greater cantor than himself.

"I can see it comes a day when the Children of Israel will need it more *chazonim,*" the old father had said once to his young son. "It's too good here in America—too much money—too much telephones and trains and ragtime. A little bit more God ain't a bad thing, Jakie. Music is God's voice, and you make it your papa and mamma happy, Jakie, if you grow up to be a great *chazon* like your grandfather in Vilna *olav-hasholom.*"

"Aw, gee," Jakie had responded; "I wish the *rebi* would comb his whiskers onct in a while!"

Fervently considering his God, the cantor had beaten Jakie soberly, and the boy had been inclined after that to listen in silence, if with resentment, to his pleas and homilies. That beating a year ago was the first Jakie had suffered from his father. The present belaboring was the second and last. That night, while his parents slept, Jakie, true to his word, did run away from home.

A policeman found him, two days later, white with hunger and dragging his feet with weariness. His parents, who had become panic-stricken, overfed him, and put him tenderly to bed. In the next few days they argued and pleaded with him, and, before they admitted defeat, wept before him.

"I'll sing in the choir every Sabbath," he said then. "But, honest, pa, *honest,* I'd quicker die than go every day to a *chaidar.*"

His father had to find comfort during the several years that followed in hearing the liquid golden tones of Jakie's alto voice in the choir only on Sabbath and on holy days.

"Maybe," he said to his wife, "maybe when he gets older, he'll see how beautiful is *Yiddishkeit.* Maybe he would stop hanging around music places and singing these ragtime songs what all the bums they sing."

"I'm afraid, Yosele; I'm afraid," she sighed. "When he grows older, a job he'll get it—in a tailor shop, maybe—and right away with a girl he'll be running around."

"Better he should never marry," the cantor cried, "than with one of these peek-a-boo-waist girls with paint on the faces! Oy, Rivka mine, why ain't it here in America good healthy girls like you was?"

But girls were not in Jakie's mind. The few who moved through his life had laughed too much and listened too little. They were shrill creatures, made for anything but love. They were haughty when they should have been humbly eager, and they greedily mimicked things they should austerely have left alone.

He might have sunk to a Russian kind of morbidness if he had not been caught up in the stream of highly seasoned folk song which poured constantly from Tin Pan Alley.

By the time he was eighteen he moved in an unreal, syncopated world of his own. If he had a sentimental grief, what better relief than sitting in the dark of his bedroom in the tiny Hester Street flat and howling dolefully the strains of "Down by the Old Mill Stream"? If the joys of being alive smote him, what could more sweetly ease the ache of happiness than the plaintive blare of "Alexander's Ragtime Band"?

So he haunted the motion picture shows.

Then one night he got a job singing popular songs in the Great

Alcazar Palace on Grand Street—one of the new movie-houses with
rococo modeling in front, a house penetrating into the bowels of the
building to a greater depth than its rickety, makeshift predecessors.
And later that night his father told him never to show his face in the
Hester Street home again.

"Better I shouldn't have it no son at all. Your loafer's talk stabs me
in my heart. I couldn't bear to see your face no more—bum! In a
synagogue you don't even put your head. For ten generations was every
Rabinowitz a God-fearing *chazon,* and you—my only son—street-songs
you are singing! Go! Be a ragtime singer with the bums!"

How could the old cantor, or, for that matter, Jakie himself, understand that instead of being sinful and self-indulgent, loose and lazy,
this grave-eyed boy with the ways of the street was sincerely carrying
on the tradition of plaintive, religious melody of his forefathers—
carrying on that tragic tradition disguised ironically with the gay trap-
pings of Broadway and the rich vulgarity of the East Side? Instinctively
the East Side responded to it, for people came hours early to the Great
Alcazar Palace and stood in line twenty deep to hear Jakie, now Jack
Robin, sing "Lovey Joe" or "When Dat Midnight Choo-Choo Leaves for
Alabam'."

"Chee, but that baby can rag!" they said, as they swayed, hypnotized,
to the caressing quavers of his voice. They knew only that he caught
at their heartstrings. They failed to perceive that Jakie was simply translating the age-old music of the cantors—that vast loneliness of a race
wandering "between two worlds, one dead, the other powerless to be
born"—into primitive and passionate Americanese.

One year Jakie spent thus, and then David Lee, on a periodical
scouting expedition, drifted into the Great Alcazar Palace. A short, fat
man with cold blue eyes in a round pink face, Lee slipped unnoticed
into the dark of the last row. He heard Jack Robin render "Underneath
the Sugar Moon" with swifter, more potent tunefulness than a certain
black-face comedian whom he was paying a thousand a week for singing
the same song on Broadway. As a result, Jack Robin found himself
booked on the great Keats vaudeville circuit.

"It's up to you," David Lee told him. "If you can put it over in
vaudeville for a year or two, I'll place you on Broadway in electric
lights."

With money and comfort and prestige tossed into his lap, a certain
change came slowly over Jack. The clouds, lifting away, did not reveal

sunshine, but a gray void. The clouds had been grim, inexplicable, tormenting—but they had inspired. The present void was reflected by emptiness in Jack. He was singing badly when he encountered Amy Prentiss, who was billed by the Keats people as "The World-Famous Dancer of Joyous Dances."

It was in San Francisco. Her act preceded his, and he stood in the wings, waiting his turn. Slender, dark-haired, blue-eyed, she had none of the Oriental instinct for undulation which Jack had understood so easily and to which he was so casually indifferent. Her open, frankly gay movements, her girlishly graceful fluttering pricked him to a breathless interest. She was baffingly foreign to him—everything about her. Elusive, infinitely desirable to his naturally complex nature because of her simplicity, *she* was seeing the sunshine which for him did not exist. As he stood there watching, Henrietta Mooney, of the Mooney Ballet, joined him.

Henrietta's name offstage was Sadie Rudnick. Jack had seen her performance several times in the past few years, and, while it was skilful and had its charm, its qualities were no mystery to him. Nor was Henrietta herself a mystery, for with one glance Jack knew her as baldly as he would a sister. "A clever Grand Street kid—in her second youth."

Henrietta listened in the wings at his Monday matinée while Jack went through his performance. She was there when he came off, and came directly up to him, saying without preliminaries,

"Kiddo, I heard you last September in Chicago, and you're losing the wallop."

Jack smiled without replying.

"What's wrong?" the girl persisted. "Booze?"

Jack shook his head amiably.

"Is it a skirt?"

"No; and it isn't an off day, either," he said wearily. "Guess I'm just getting tired of the game."

"Bunk!" was her scornful response. "You were born to the profession."

With the easy fellowship of the stage, they became chummy during the week. They would stand idly in the wings during the greater part of the performances, exchanging comments and gossip. Jack liked Henrietta's sturdy honesty, her slangy sophistication. Saturday evening, as he was hungrily following the fairylike movements of Amy Prentiss, Henrietta said,

"That girl's got your goat!"

"Do you think so?"

"Say—do I *think* so? I *know* it!"

"I wonder why," he mused audibly.

Henrietta looked him squarely in the eyes.

"You wonder why? She's a *shiksa;* that's why! I've seen Jewish boys fall that way before. It ain't new to me." There was bitterness in her voice.

"But why?" Jack repeated, more to himself than to her. "Why?"

"You come from the ghetto, and she studied fancy dancing in a private school. You're the son of a poor old *chazon,* and she's the daughter of a Boston lawyer. You're— Aw, you make me sick!"

Abruptly Henrietta left him, and during the one remaining day of their stay in San Francisco she avoided him. But her words stayed with him; they pried brutally into his apathy; they jeered him from afar; they came terribly close and stung him. The thought of approaching this lovely dancer with the quiet eyes and the gentle mouth frightened him a little; but his fear angered him. As she came out into the wings Saturday night, she found him in her path.

"Say—" he began. She stopped, smiling uncertainly. Jack, to her, was a pleasingly debonair figure with a handsome face, glowing eyes. His manner she hadn't the time or the gift to analyze.

"I have to hand it to you," he went on, self-consciously, flushing to the roots of his hair. "You—you dance with more real class—I mean to say—you're darn good—" He paused, floundering.

It is a curious fact that often the only signs of yearning, of sincere and painful humbleness, of profound anxiety to express fine things consist of awkwardness—of a stilted nonchalance. His confusion served simply to embarrass her. She strove, not in vain, for poise to cover her embarrassment. Her only resource was to smile vaguely and say, "Glad you liked—uh—" And then, fearing that he might gurgle more badly still, she passed on.

Jack hated her for having made it so hard for him.

"I know she don't care a damn about me," he told himself savagely.

"But she didn't have to make a fool of me. She could have said a few civil words, even if I don't mean anything in her life."

In San Diego, in Dallas, in San Antonio, in New Orleans and in the other cities he made on the long swing back to New York, his eyes seemed to seek morbidly for further evidences of the simple, unruffled Anglo-Saxon quality of temperament. He found plenty of them, and as the weeks passed, they served to beat him down into a soothing numbness, which was bad for the audiences, who sat stonily through his performances. Henrietta's words would constantly drum into his ears: "You come from the ghetto, and she's the daughter of a Boston lawyer."

It was slowly, because he was fundamentally temperate, that he learned to seek self-respect in barrooms. No one else would have called it that. It had too little of the nature of peace. It brought back the invigorating uncertainty, the inspiring restlessness of his adolescent days. It eliminated, for the moment, this new numbness which had come upon him, this queer sensation of being softly strangled. And, since it substituted his old *Weltschmerz* for the feeling of being slowly buried into a grave of inarticulateness by the Amy Prentisses of the world, his ragtime singing got back some of its old lilting plaintiveness.

Jack saw his parents occasionally. His mother's furtive pride in the adulation which younger Hester Street gave to her son had even begun to reflect itself in a way in the old cantor.

"Every actor he's ain't a loafer, Yosele," she would say. "Look—is Jacob Adler a loafer? A finer man you couldn't find it if you should search a whole lifetime."

"But he's a *Yiddisher* actor, *leben*. He feels the *Yiddishe* heart. And our Jakie sings ragtime—like a *shagetz!*"

"I know—I know," she soothed him. "But he's an American boy. And he's a good boy. He's sending you and me presents only last month from New Haven. He lives a clean life, Yosele. Maybe soon he makes enough money and he goes into business and gets married and comes regular every Sabbath and holy day to the synagogue."

When he visited them in the summer, Jack's dumb unhappiness became apparent to them. They took it for a good sign—for indication of a new, more mature thoughtfulness. His booking for the year ended, he took a month's vacation and spent two weeks of it in New York. For two consecutive Sabbath days he attended the synagogue, and the old cantor, singing from the pulpit, exulted in the conviction that his son was returning to his God.

Indeed, Jack himself found a certain solace in it. As he sat on the old familiar wooden bench, clothed in the silk *talis*—the prayer-shawl which his father had so solemnly presented to him on the occasion of his *bar mitzvah*—with good old Yudelson, the cobbler, on one side of him, and stout, hearty, red-bearded Lapinsky, the butcher, on the other, he felt a singular warmth and sweetness. And the voice of his father, still clear and lyric, rising in the intricacies of the familiar old lamenting prayers—prayers which he remembered perfectly, which he would never forget—the dissonant rumble of response from the congregation, the restive shufflings of youngsters—all these were to him blessedly familiar and blissful.

In the murmurous peacefulness of those two weeks his father talked to him constantly of the austere beauties of the ancient ways of his people, and it began to appeal to Jack that there was indeed something to be said for them. He could not and did not dismiss his father's world as he used to—with a sneer and the words: "Dead! I tell you that stuff's behind the times." For he began to feel that if it was a dead or a dying world, still it possessed some reality, an orderly nobility; while the world he was alive to was chaotic, crassly unreal.

During the two weeks which followed in Atlantic City he thought a good deal on this, but the nearness of violins and cocktails, the flash of women and the glamour of moonlight on the sea made it easy for him to decide arbitrarily that it was rather an abstract problem.

In Buffalo, where he opened with his act, he began committing the unforgivable sin in the theatrical world—he began missing performances. He had lost all vital interest in his work.

By the time he was playing in Chicago, reports of his derelictions had reached David Lee, who, after long pondering, wrote a severe note.

"What Jack Robin needs," Lee said to Harry Anthony, his partner, "is a wife." In his note he said:

If I can't depend on a performer being steadily on the job, no matter if he has the genius of Booth and the popularity of George Cohan, I will not have him in my employ. I don't know what's ailing you, but whatever it is, you must steady down. There isn't a producer or booking-office in New York that will gamble on you if you're not completely dependable, and we're no exception.

Jack smiled crookedly when he read this. It came at a most unfortunate time, for, having arrived in Chicago that morning, Jack had discovered that the sixth number on the bill with him at the Majestic was "The World-Famous Dancer of Joyous Dances."

And this discovery was sending him sauntering, blithely bitter, to Righeimer's bar.

It was two in the afternoon. His act went on at three. The act of the girl whose unseen nearness possessed the power to slash him into bewilderment would begin at four. If he left the theatre promptly after his act, most likely he could avoid seeing her. And, with a comforting cargo of Righeimer's product on board, he felt he would be able to give an account of himself on the stage.

To make doubly sure that the sense of Amy's nearness would not cause his heart to sink before the footlights, he took three or four extra drinks. They more than achieved their purpose. The world became an insignificant turmoil underneath his feet, and he strolled, his smile growing steadily more crooked, down Clark Street toward Madison, where at the Morrison bar they could mix the finest Tom Collins in the world. The words of David Lee's letter came into his mind. " 'Completely dependable'—that's me! I'll drink all the Tom Collinses Jerry can mix—to the great god Dependability."

He halted in the crush of traffic on the corner, and, not two feet away from him, jammed by a fat woman on one side and grabbed at on the other by two sticky children, he saw Amy Prentiss. As his eyes glimpsed her proud little head, brown-toqued, quaintly half veiled, his lips compressed into a straight line and he turned sharply away. But the crowd began to move; Amy had seen him, and she was already edging her way toward him. Her face smiled a friendly greeting, and involuntarily Jack looked behind him to see if it were not some one else she was addressing.

"Why, Mr. Robin!" she was saying. "I was just going to the house early to see your turn."

Jack was dumb. They crossed Madison Street together in the surge of the released crowd.

"How did you happen to recognize me?" he blurted.

"You recognized *me,* didn't you?"

"Oh, I recognized you, all right." Jack paused. He longed for an hour in solitude, so that he could think. "This gets me," he confessed.

"Your knowing me so quickly, and your actually going early to see my act."

"You're funny. Hasn't anybody let you in on the secret that you're one of the few real rag singers in America? As for remembering you, how could I ever forget your genuine little compliment on my act out on the coast?"

They had turned the corner at Monroe Street and were at the entrance to the Majestic. Jack looked hurriedly at his watch.

"Listen," he said; "I have to speed like the deuce to make it. I want to see you—talk to you some more. Meet me after your turn."

His mind raced in zigzags as he hastened to his dressing-room. He searched his memory for the exact wording of Amy's remark that Saturday in San Francisco, for her expression. He tried to see and hear again the outward things and to give a new, inner meaning to them. But all he could recall was the bitterness in him, the significant and fateful words of Henrietta, and Amy's vagueness, which turned the knife in his wounded vanity. And now she had voluntarily talked to him; she was deliberately coming to see him perform; she had been pleasant, approachable, inviting. His mind could find no place for such a manifestation from this girl.

His performance that matinée was discouragingly poor. Amy made no comment on it when they met.

"Let's have dinner somewhere," Jack suggested. "That is"—a flicker of his old wretchedness returning—"that is, if you haven't made any other arrangements, and—and if—"

"I should be glad to."

They dined at the Café Lafayette, which has a sedate lower floor and an upper floor with an orchestra for dancing. It had been in Jack's mind to avoid the beat of syncopated music, but by the time they reached the restaurant, the sweet poise of the girl had filled him with unreasoning dismay at himself. The old familiar bewildered sinking of the heart followed. And so he led her upstairs. A violin was weaving a slim pattern of simple melody, which was being tortured into savage bedlam by the bullet-like spitting of the drum and by the saxophone's gusts of passionate whining.

He felt instinctively that liquor was not on the cards. But he was tense, strung up, dreadfully nervous.

"Let's dance," he said.

The music was sending forth a one-step, and Jack gave himself to it hungrily. He seemed, somehow, to make of the simple steps a wild, heart-breaking aria, a mad pounding on the doors of heaven.

Back at the table they sat a while in silence. Amy studied his face. She said,

"You dance differently from any one I know."

Jack flushed.

"I don't suppose I dance very well. I—I wish I could dance standing straight and moving sort of—well, evenly and correctly, if you know what I mean. Like that fellow, for instance." He indicated a tall, stolid-looking youth who was soberly and skilfully maneuvering a sleek young creature about the polished floor.

"That's funny," Amy remarked. "I'm crazy about the way you dance. I never quite liked any one's dancing so well. You danced tonight the way you used to sing—the way you sang when I first heard you in New York."

"You *like* my dancing?" Jack leaned to her, unbelieving. His voice came huskily. "*You* don't dance that way—even on the stage. You dance more like that fellow. I don't mean stiff as him—not that. But you're his kind, if you know what I mean. I'm—I'm crazy about that quality in you. I'd give anything if I could have it—that careless, happy— Guess I'm talking like a fool," he ended lamely.

But Amy, her eyes aglow, was leaning to him.

"You're the *funniest* person! I've been crazy about the very thing in you that you're deprecating. I wish I had it. I'd give *anything* to have it. It—it hurt me a lot to find your performance today lacking in it."

They dined and danced together every day that week. There was no making of appointments after that evening; tacitly they met after Amy's turn and went out together. Jack went about in an unreal world. He tried to think, but his mind persisted in substituting the turn of Amy's wrist, the curve of her cheek, the gay animation of her eyes, the little liquid turns in her voice.

Each day he grew more afraid of her while she was with him and more desolate while she was not. His only interludes were when they danced. The blare of the orchestra had somehow for him become Music—a glorious substitute for tears, a gleaming speedway for a breathless race hand in hand with grief. Sunday evening—the last of the week they would have together—he found himself holding Amy crushingly close, and he relaxed sharply, dancing badly after that.

Back at the table, sitting side by side on an upholstered bench against the wall, Amy chattered happily until she became aware that Jack was not listening. His food untouched, he was staring with undisguised misery before him. Amy placed her hand lightly over his on the seat.

"What is it?" she asked.

He withdrew his hand, afraid. For a moment he was silent, and Amy repeated her question.

"I—I suppose you think I'm out of my head, but—I—I'm crazy about you."

"I'm crazy about you, too," said Amy promptly.

Jack looked at her then, a puzzled, imploring look.

"You don't know what I mean."

"What do you mean?"—with a flicker of a smile.

He breathed deeply.

"I mean that I love you—that I want to marry you."

"That," said Amy, "is what I thought you meant."

Late that night, in his room at the hotel Jack scribbled a note to David Lee and one to his mother. To Lee he wrote:

> You needn't worry any longer about my dependability. I'm engaged to be married. . . . She's the kind of a girl who could no more understand my not being on the job than she could understand quitting of any kind. I'm going to work my head off. If it's in me at all, I'll be on Broadway in a year.

To his mother he wrote briefly that he was to be married, mentioning the girl's name, Amy Prentiss.

His letters brought two prompt results. David Lee offered him a part in the coming "Frivolities" and instructed him to leave for New York at once for rehearsals. And old Cantor Rabinowitz, not so strong as he used to be, had a nervous collapse.

"A *shiksa!*" he repeated over and over as he lay in his bed. "A *shiksa!* Our Jakie should marry a *shiksa!* God in heaven, why do you let me live to suffer like this?"

His white-haired wife, broken-hearted, tried to console him.

"What could you tell it from a name, Yosele! A name, it ain't nothing. Look—our Jakie he goes by the name Jack Robin. Amy Prentiss—it could be she's a *Yiddishe* girl. Look—Jenny Levy from Ludlow Street is her name on the stage Genevieve Leeds. Wait we should hear from Jakie some more."

"It's a *shiksa*," her husband insisted. "If it was a *Yiddishe* girl, he would have written it in the letter. I feel it—I know it—it's a *shiksa*. *Gott im Himmel,* help me to live out my last years!"

The next Tuesday evening Jack came unexpectedly. As he stepped into the spotless flat, his father, who was sitting before the kitchen table in his shirtsleeves, a skullcap on his white head, reading loudly to himself from the *Mishna,* looked up mildly over his glasses and spoke the question he must have rehearsed scores of times to himself.

"To a *shiksa* you're engaged, ain't it?"

Jack hesitated. The calmness of his father he sensed at once as being anything but indifference. He suddenly was swept with shame for not having thought more about what his engagement would mean to them.

The old man had turned back to the *Mishna.* Apparently, Jack's hesitation had replied adequately. And now his mother came into the kitchen from the narrow, dark corridor of the tenement. Jack kissed her wrinkled cheek. It was the first time in years that he had kissed her, and it thrilled the old woman. But in a moment she had observed the portentous absorption of her husband in his book of the Talmud.

"Yosele, don't you see our Jakie is here?"

The cantor continued with the low-murmured singsong as if he had not heard her. She turned to Jack, who gave her a queer smile and an almost imperceptible shrug of the shoulders.

"Then it's a *shiksa?*" she whispered. Briskly she moved to the kitchen stove. "You'll stay for supper, Jakie?" she asked over her shoulder. "Sit down. I'll have it quick ready. The soup is already on the stove—*borsht,* red beets soup, Jakie—and tonight we got it cucumbers in sour cream, and cheese *blintzes,* too."

The old cantor joined them at the table, but beyond the various ritual prayers he and Jack mumbled together, he did not utter a word. The old woman, pathetically striving to eke out some harmony from the situation, made not the slightest attempt to get Jack to talk of his *fiancée.*

"You are coming to the synagogue next Sabbath?"

"I'm sorry, ma. I'm going to be terribly busy. You see, this is my one big chance. Lee has been fine, and it's up to me to repay him. He's one of these men who doesn't do things halfway. Either he backs you to the limit or he drops you. He's watching me closely, and I have to prove I can be relied upon. He's not giving me a star part, but I'm a principal, and if I make a hit, I'll rise fast with David Lee. This is the first time, ma, that my future has meant anything to me, and I'm going to give all I have to rehearsals."

When the meal was cleared off the table, the old cantor moved with his tome to the smaller kitchen table, where he went on with his low-toned recitative of the Talmud. Jack and his mother sat in silence at the larger table. Then Jack placed his hand tenderly over hers.

"Ma, it's a funny thing, but I'm just beginning to appreciate what you and pa mean to me. I never realized it until suddenly last week. I—"

"Do you hear what our Jakie is saying, Yosele? He's saying that now he's grown up and he knows how good it is a papa and a mamma. He's saying—"

It was as if the old man had not heard.

They talked on softly, rapidly at first, exchanging ideas and comments, and then peaceful silences crept between them. After a rather long pause in the talk, his mother said, with a casual air:

"You know, Jakie, I was just thinking the other day—I was thinking that if a *Yiddishe* girl marries a *goyisher* boy, then it's bad, because you know how it is in a house—everything is like the father wants. But if a *Yiddisher* boy marries a *goyishe* girl, then it ain't so terrible. She could be learned to buy *kosher* meat and to have two kinds of dishes, for *fleischige* and for *milchige*—and the children could be brought up like *Yiddishe* children; they could be sent to a *chaidar*—I was just thinking like this only yesterday, Jakie. Ain't it funny I should think of it?"

Jack's hand tightened over hers.

"You're sweet, ma," he said slowly. "I'm afraid it can't be. I was brought up that way, ma, and I've been unhappy all my life. And Amy was brought up the other way, and she's been happy from the day she was a baby. I'll want my children to be happy like Amy is."

The sharp sound of a book snapping shut twisted their attention to the cantor. He had risen, and, eyes blazing, was pointing a shaking finger at Jack.

"Go out!" he cried. "Go out from my house—bum! Go!" A fit of coughing seized him, and he sank to his chair. They hastened to his side. The old man was unable to speak, but his eyes glared so that Jack stepped back. His mother turned, tragic-eyed, to him and said,

"Maybe you better go, Jakie."

There are few tasks more absorbing and exacting than that of re-hearsing for the "Frivolities," and the days which followed for Jack were so full that he found time only to telephone his mother. As there was no connection directly to the flat on Hester Street, Jack had to call the drug store on the corner. He succeeded in getting her but twice in the five times he called. His father was well, she told him cheerfully, but naturally getting old and feeble. She doubted whether he would be able to continue as cantor for very many more years, but thanked God that he would be able to lead in the services for the coming holy day, Yom Kippur—the Day of Atonement. "Maybe you will come to the synagogue then, and fast the whole day?" she asked wistfully.

"Ma, I don't see how I can possibly come. It's the fifteenth, and our show opens on Broadway the same evening. I—I'd give anything, ma, to be able to come. I'd do it for my own sake as well as for papa's and yours. It's beginning to mean something to me—Yom Kippur. You see how it is, don't you, ma?"

"Yes," his mother sighed; "I see."

The second time, she brought up the subject again.

"Your papa he's ain't feeling so good, Jakie. Maybe this will be his last Yom Kippur. He talks about you. He is all the time talking about you. He says God has punished him enough for his sins that he should be the last Rabinowitz in ten generations to sing *chazonoth* in a *shool*. He don't *say* you should come on Yom Kippur—he didn't talk about that. But I think in his heart he means it, Jakie."

"I'll tell you what I'll do, ma," he replied, after some thought. "We open Monday night, and there probably will be a lot of changes made in the special rehearsal on Tuesday. But I'll try to dodge that Tuesday rehearsal and come to the synagogue for the morning and most of the afternoon."

"You're a good boy, Jakie."

Amy, who had swung West on the vaudeville circuit, was in Denver at this time. Jack wrote her every day—love letters, almost childish in their outpouring of longing, full of high resolve, glowing with the miracle of the new insight he felt he was getting into life.

I realize that with me it isn't a question of ability, but of character. I've seen enough of this show to believe that I can put my songs over so big that Lee will have to star me. But I must be unswervingly steady. I have to be as good at the end of the season as on the opening night. I have to be on hand all of the time. My health must be guarded as well as my impulses. I don't even want to miss a performance with illness as an excuse. I can see that some of them are a bit leery of me—they're not dead-sure they can depend on me. Lee is the only one who's different. He's like a rock. I'd rather break a leg than fail him. But your wonderful confidence and my own resolution make me smile at them. I know I'll come through.

Swiftly the last month of rehearsal went by, and then the great day came. At two Monday afternoon, David Lee, who had attended the dress rehearsal, called a halt.

"That's all," he said. "Take it easy until tonight. Robin, I want to see you."

He took Jack aside in a corner of the shadowy theatre.

"You're a winner if you can come through. Not exactly a world-beater—Frank Binney and Hal Bolton and Eddie Loren and Helen Kennedy still have something you haven't got. I don't know what it is, but you have the *capacity* to get it. I've seen it show suddenly in talented performers, sometimes overnight. But you'll make the electric lights, and I'm behind you. Now beat it, and be sure to take it easy."

At three in the afternoon, Jack, in his suite at the family hotel on Seventy-ninth Street, was busily writing a letter to Amy, who was in Salt Lake City. He had taken a hot bath, intending to sleep off some of his nervousness after this note to his sweetheart. He finished the letter and had just sunk beneath the covers of his bed when the telephone bell rang. It was old Chiam Yudelson, friend and neighbor of his parents, to tell him that his father had just died.

When Jack's taxicab drew up before his home in Hester Street, a harassed policeman was swinging his club in the effort to disperse the crowd in front of the tenement where the beloved cantor lay dead. Jack elbowed his way through. He was recognized, and a pathway was instantly made for him.

In the tiny flat were his mother, the *shamas* of the synagogue, old Chiam Yudelson and his wife, and Lawyer Feldman, the friend of all Hester Street. Greater perhaps than her grief at the loss of the man who had loved her and his God with equal fervor for sixty years was Mrs. Rabinowitz's panic at the thought that it was Yom Kippur eve and that the lyric voice of a Rabinowitz would not be raised in supplication to wipe out the sins of the Chosen People before their Creator. When Jack crowded his way through the friends and neighbors who packed the dark, narrow corridor, she was clinging to the hand of Lawyer Feldman.

"Look, Mr. Feldman," she was saying; "it's only two hours to Yom Kippur. It's got to be a good *chazon* to sing. The last words my Yosele he said to me, he said, 'Rivka, get our Jakie.' So low he says it, Mr. Feldman, I couldn't hardly hear him. His face was white like a *yahrzeit* candle, and he says to me: 'Rivka, God will forgive our Jakie if he will sing *"Kol Nidre"* for me tonight. Maybe my dying,' he says, 'will make a *chazon* from our Jakie. Tell him, Rivka,' he says. Look, Mr. Feldman; Jakie is maybe coming here. Maybe you could talk to him. In his heart he's a good boy. Tell him—tell him—his father is dead—tell him— oh, Mr. Feldman, my heart is breaking in pieces—I—I can't talk no more—"

"Here's Jakie!" Chaim Yudelson broke in.

The next moment his mother was in his arms. Lawyer Feldman drew her gently away, and she turned into the other room—the bedroom where her dead husband lay. Silence followed. Nervously Jack went after her, fearing that silence.

It was an immaculately clean room—so clean that every rip in the wallpaper, every stain on the plastered ceiling stared at them, hollow-eyed, terrible in nakedness. The bed, a thing of iron tubing, whose green paint had long since scaled off, stood head against an ancient oak bookcase, crammed with old-fashioned mahogany-colored books of the Talmud, the *Chumesh,* the various prayer books, and a mass of huge music portfolios filled with note-scribbled sheets. On the bed lay his father's body. It had been covered completely with a white sheet, but his mother, flung across it, had drawn the sheet off so that the waxlike face and one thin old shoulder were revealed. Jack looked long at his father's face. It was beautiful in death. Every line in it spoke of a brave, poetic fight, of deep, fierce religious faith. His mother's body shuddered, and Jack reached over to take her hand.

She rose from the bed then, and son and mother stood alone.

"I—I came as soon as I—heard," Jack said.

His mother's hand rested lightly against his coat.

"He—he died this morning. It was a quarter to twelve. Yesterday he got sick. He talked about you—all the time about you, Jakie. At a quarter to twelve he died—a quarter to twelve. He just closed his eyes—like a baby, Jakie—and he said—he said: 'Rivka,' he said, 'God will forgive our Jakie if he will sing *"Kol Nidre"* for me tonight. Maybe,' he said, 'maybe—maybe—' Oh, Jakie, I— Jakie, *mein Kind,* your father is dead—I can't stand it—"

She was again in his arms. Lawyer Feldman appeared in the doorway.

"Better take her out of that room," he suggested. "It isn't doing her any good. Has she spoken to you about—"

Jack nodded. He gently led his mother toward the kitchen. As they passed him, the lawyer asked in a low tone,

"Are you going to do it?"

Jack placed his mother in a chair, where she sat blankly, looking first at the friends gathered in the kitchen, then out of the window where the crowds were still pushing and surging noisily, and then, in a most pathetic and forlorn way, down at her hands folded so helplessly in her lap.

The *shamas,* who was there, mainly for the purpose of finding out whether Jack would serve as cantor that evening and the next day or whether he would have to step into the breach himself, was becoming nervous and impatient. He approached Jack, who looked unseeingly at him.

It was four-thirty. If he appeared in the show that evening, singing ragtime songs while his father lay dead—while the Hester Street Synagogue went cantorless for the first Day of Atonement in forty years—while his mother struggled under an unbearable double grief—

He turned to the *shamas.*

"My father's *talis,* it is at the synagogue?"

"Yes; everything is in the *shool,* Mr. Rabinowitz," the *shamas* replied eagerly.

"The tunes—the *genigen*—of the choir—are they the same my father used ten, fifteen years ago?"

"The same *genigen,* exactly."

"All right. I'll be there at six o'clock."

As Jack took his mother in his arms to sit out the next hour with her and to comfort her, the tears for the first time since her husband died flowed from her eyes, and she said over and over to him:

"In your heart you're a good boy. I always told him that in your heart you're a good boy."

———

News travels like lightning in the East Side. "Jack Robin—the vaudeville headliner—is singing as cantor at the Hester Street Synagogue this Yom Kippur!" It might have been a newspaper scare headline, for by six-thirty that evening the slowly arriving members of the Hester Street Synagogue congregation had almost to fight their way through the mob that packed the street up to the corners of both Norfolk and Essex Streets. Wealthy East Siders, who had paid their ten and twelve dollars for pews in the much larger Beth Medresh Hagadol, neglected that comparatively splendid house of prayer to stand in the crammed lobby of the Hester Street Synagogue and listen to the golden notes of this young singer of ragtime as he rendered *"Kol Nidre"* with a high, broken sobbing which, they insisted critically, surpassed his father's in his best days.

Every twist and turn of his father's had been branded unforgettably in Jack's memory from childhood days, but he sang the grief-laden notes with a lyric passion that was distinctly his own. The low-hanging rafters of the old synagogue, the cheap, shiny chandeliers of painted gold, the faded velvet hangings on the holy vault where the parchments of the Old Testament stood, the gold-fringed, worn white-silk cloth that covered the stand in the pulpit where he prayed—these called to something surging and powerful in him, something which made his whole life since his boyhood seem blurred and unreal.

When, with the congregation standing and swaying in humility before their Creator, he uttered that refrain which asks forgiveness for every sin of mankind from evil thoughts to murder, rising from a low singsong into a quivering, majestic wail and then breaking into incoherent plaintiveness, the sobs choked his throat.

His mother sat in the small gallery at the back reserved for women, and he saw her when, after marching slowly forward with the choir, he had flung open the hangings before the holy vault and turned to face the congregation as he led in the appeal that the "prayers of this evening shall come before the Divine Presence in the morning and by nightfall bring redemption for all sins."

When he finished the high melodious strains of his triumphant yet humble and supplicating piece, there was a low murmur of approbation throughout the synagogue.

The rabbi, a rotund little man in the front pews, turned to his neighbor and remarked:

"Even Rosenblatt, when I heard him in Moscow, didn't give a *'Yaaleh'* like this. *Aza Singen nehmt by die Harz!"*

When the time came for *Kaddish,* the prayer uttered only by those in mourning for their dead, the whole congregation rose in silence in honor of the cantor who was dead and his son and wife. The other mourners subdued their customary loud recital, and the voices of Jack and his mother, the one flowing and resonant, the other high and broken with sobs, were heard clearly.

Crowds followed the couple as they slowly walked the half block to the tenement house that evening. As they paused on the stoop, Jack turned to the gathering people and in a low voice asked them to be good enough to leave his mother and himself alone with their grief. Instantly a cry was raised:

"Beat it!"

"Go home, bums, loafers! Ain't you got no respect for the *chazon?"*

"G'wan! Can't you leave some peace be even on Yom Kippur— *paskudniks!"*

The crowd dispersed.

Jack sat up until midnight that night with his mother, and then, completely weary, he fell asleep, to dream fitfully of Amy and of David Lee, of David Lee and of Amy, until morning.

David Lee slept fitfully also that night. Jack's failure at the last moment to appear on the opening night had ruined three numbers and had made two others awkward, and Lee had a difficult job ahead of him in the next twenty-four hours. He wasted no time thinking about the delinquent. *"He's* going to do the worrying, not me," he said grimly to Harry Anthony. He stayed up until four in the morning, telephoning and telegraphing in the effort to get a substitute so much better than Jack that the reviews of Tuesday, probably derogatory, would be reversed on Wednesday morning.

His efforts did not meet with success, and he left word with his man to wake him early Tuesday. When his man called him, he asked for the morning papers.

He was about to turn to the theatrical page, when his eye was caught by a headline on the front sheet. Sitting on the edge of the bed, he read, and, as he read, a low whistle escaped him. He dropped the first paper and took another. He swore softly.

"That damn kid!" he murmured gleefully. "That damn kid! Stevens, tell Herman to have the car out in a half-hour."

He had to slip a crisp green banknote into the hand of the policeman before room was made for him to stand in the crush in the narrow lobby of the Hester Street Synagogue. Jack Robin, swathed in the folds of a great black-striped linen *talis,* an elaborate and stiff black plush skullcap on his head, his think, handsome face deadly white, his dark eyes afire, was singing that splendid aria of his father's—*"Hamelech,"* "The King"—and as the majesty of it rolled forth, broke, and narrowed into rivulets of humility, David Lee pinched himself to see if he were asleep.

Then, after a few moments of quick rattling recitative, Jack went on into a clear, low-toned series of sound which had the effect of musical talking, of superbly self-contained remonstrance. This speech gradually rose to a fluttering uncertainty, a bewildered pleading, and then the climax came—a flood of confession.

Excitedly Lee elbowed his way out of the crowd.

"Where's the nearest telephone?" he asked the policeman.

"Right on the corner—the drug store, sir."

In five minutes Harry Anthony was on the wire.

"Harry," said Lee, "do you want to hear the greatest ragtime singer in America in the making? A wonder, Harry, a wonder! Got Hal Bolton mopped off the boards. Come down right away. It's a dirty little hole down on the East Side called the Hester Street Synagogue. I'll meet you on the corner of Hester and Norfolk."

MR. BLANDINGS BUILDS HIS DREAM HOUSE

(1948)

MR. BLANDINGS BUILDS HIS CASTLE
ERIC HODGINS

A delightful satire on the postwar exodus of city dwellers to suburbia. *Mr. Blandings Builds His Dream House* was cited by critic James Agee as "a bull's-eye for middle-class middlebrows." The film plays perfectly on the ironic contrasts between big-city hustle and rural bliss; Cary Grant and Myrna Loy are perfect as the couple who aspire to the peace of country life and are nearly driven to bankruptcy and mental breakdown by the endless problems that beset the building of their idyllic retreat. Melvyn Douglas is also excellent as the stock "friend of the-family." More recent renderings of a similar theme include *The Money Pit* (1986) and Albert Brooks's wild *Lost In America* (1985), where the dream house becomes a souped-up camper van.

Novelist ERIC HODGINS (1899–1971) was for many years an editor at *Fortune* magazine and was one of the founders of *The New Yorker*. It was in a special architectural issue of *Fortune* that the short story "Mr. Blandings Builds His Castle" first appeared. Later, Hodgins expanded it into the novel from which the film was made. Of this work, Hodgins said, "It made me pots of money. Twenty years later it is still well remembered and will probably go on my tombstone."

MR. BLANDINGS BUILDS HIS DREAM HOUSE

Released: 1948
Production: Norman Panama and Melvin Frank for RKO/Radio
Direction: H. C. Potter
Screenplay: Norman Panama and Melvin Frank
Cinematography: James Wong Howe
Editing: Harry Marker
Running time: 94 minutes

PRINCIPAL CHARACTERS:

Jim Blandings	Cary Grant
Muriel Blandings	Myrna Loy
Bill Cole	Melvyn Douglas
Joan Blandings	Sharyn Moffett
Betsy Blandings	Connie Marshall
Gussie	Louise Beavers
Henry Simms	Reginald Denny

---

he sweet old farmhouse burrowed into the upward slope of the land so that you could enter either its bottom or middle floor at ground level. Its window trim was delicate and the lights in its sash were a bubbly amethyst. Its rooftree seemed to sway a little against the sky, and the massive chimney that rose out of it tilted a little to the south. Where the white paint was flecking off on the siding, there showed the blush of what must once have been a coat of rich, dense red.

In front of it, rising and spreading along the whole length of the house, was the vastest lilac tree that Mr. and Mrs. Blandings had ever seen. When the house was new, the lilac must have been a shrub planted in the dooryard—and house and shrub had gone on together, side by side, since then. That was a hundred and seventy years ago this April.

Using a penknife as a key, the real estate man unlocked a lower door. As it swung back, the top hinge gave way and splashed in a red powder on the floor. The door lurched against Mr. Blandings and gave him a sharp crack on the forehead, but the damage was repaired in an instant and Mr. Blandings, a handkerchief at his temple and his wife by his side, stood looking through one of the misty amethyst window-lights at an arc of beauty that made them both cry out. The land rushed downward to the river valley a mile away; then it rose again, layer after layer, plane after plane of hills and higher hills lighter beyond them. The air was luminous and there were twenty shades of browns and greens in the plowed and wooded and folded earth.

"On a clear day you can see the Catskills," said the real estate man.

Mr. and Mrs. Blandings were not such fools as to exclaim at this revelation. Mrs. Blandings flicked a glove in which a cobweb and spider had become entangled; Mr. Blandings, his lips pursed and his eyes half-closed, was a picture of controlled reserve. By the way the two of them said "Uh-hum?" with a rising inflection in perfect unison, the real estate man knew that his sale was made. Not today, of course; the offer might not come for a fortnight. But it would come; it would come with all the certainty of the equinox. He computed five per cent of $10,275 rapidly in his head and turned to the chimney footing.

"You'd have to do a little pointing up here," he said, indicating a compact but disorderly pile of stone, in which a blackened hollow suggested a fireplace that had been in good working order at the time of the Treaty of Ghent. Mrs. Blandings, looking at the rubble, saw instead the kitchen of the Wayside Inn: a distaff plump with flax lying idly on the polished hearth; a tempered scale of copper pans and skillets near the oven wall; a bootjack in the corner; a shoat glistening on the spit.

What Mr. Blandings saw broke through into speech: "With a flagstone floor in here it would be a nice place for a beer party on a Saturday night. You'd put the keg right in that corner."

"You could at that," said the real estate man, as if he had just heard a brilliant revision of atomic theory. He quickly did five per cent of $11,550 in his head; aloud, he said: "Let's go upstairs and then take a look at your orchard. There's a very interesting story connected with . . ."

The effect of the plural possessive pronoun was as a fiery liquor in Mr. and Mrs. Blandings' veins.

Thus it came about that Mr. and Mrs. Blandings bought—for $11,550— the old Halleck place, the old house and the gorgeous acres surrounding it. But it would be a year, at least, before the Blandings' would "build." Mr. Blandings had stated, unequivocally, that you wouldn't catch him building until prices were "right." The forces that were to make prices right in the residential-construction industry were not known to Mr. Blandings, but he did not know that he did not know them. Mr. Blandings' eventual cost of building when prices were right was somewhat in excess, by a percentage only an astrologer could calculate, of what it would have been had he built when they were not so right. But the excess percentage was removed from Mr. Blandings at a later time, when he was numb from shock and scarcely felt a thing.

"Let's say your land'll cost you $10,000, round numbers," the real estate man had said in the days before it had actually cost $11,550. "And let's say it'll cost you $10,000 to restore that farmhouse. So you've made a $20,000 investment that'll stand you all the rest of your life, to say nothing of having a home to live in, and the benefit of what your friend Mr. Grover calls 'the indescribable charm' of the place." This lyric passage had served the Blandings' in lieu of thought for several months until, one evening, Mrs. Blandings had looked up from her mending.

"Do you suppose it's worth our while to remodel that old house?" she had asked in a faraway voice.

If she had flatly announced the illegitimacy of the two Blandings children she could scarcely have had a more thunderous effect upon her husband.

"I only mean," she went on in an effort to silence him, "that maybe someone should look at it besides Mr. Funkhauser."

Mr. Funkhauser was a young architect to whom Mr. Blandings had taken a shine. Working mostly from photographs, plus some measurements taken one rainy day on Bald Mountain, he had been covering reams of sketch tissue with the graceful swashes of a 6-B pencil, and making of the old Halleck farmhouse something quite else again. The Blandings' had found the results enchanting.

"What's the matter with Funkhauser?" asked Mr. Blandings.

"I only mean," said Mrs. Blandings, "that he's so enthusiastic about everything that sometimes I think he gets carried away. I'd like to have some other sort of person look at the old house before we get too far along—an engineer, or somebody."

Eventually Mr. Blandings came to believe that he himself had had this prudent idea. He asked his lawyer friend Bill Cole to dig him up an engineer—a good practical fellow who wouldn't be carried away by *anything*. As a result, Mr. Giobatta Appolonio, engineer, did indeed visit the old Halleck place with Mr. and Mrs. Blandings some days later. In his black shoes, dark business suit, and derby he made an odd picture among the roaming hills, particularly compared with Mr. Blandings in his slightly aggressive rural tweeds.

Mrs. Blandings had expected Mr. Appolonio to bring a bag of instruments along like a physician, and perhaps to practice the physician's rites of auscultation or palpation on her dwelling. But Mr. Appolonio's only instrument was a foot rule, and far from palpating her house, he did not even seem to want to go near it. He merely stood looking at it for five minutes from about a hundred feet away. He then went up to it and kicked it on one corner. Mr. and Mrs. Blandings winced in unison when something unidentified fell off. Mr. Appolonio returned to his clients and spoke to them in a soft voice.

"You should ought to tear it down," said he.

"That stinking roughneck has simply no feeling for antiquity," said Mr. Blandings, taking a spastic gulp out of his glass.

"I wish you wouldn't drink when you're upset," said Mrs. Blandings. She and her husband were back in their city apartment. The train trip home with Mr. Appolonio had been very trying. Once home, Mr. Blandings had written out a check for his $50 fee and mailed it to him instantly with a curt, correct note. But now Mr. Blandings was alone with God and Mrs. Blandings, and there was no concealing from either one that Mr. Blandings had paid a considerable sum, above land cost alone, for a structure that he had now been advised (for $50 more) to destroy. In Mr. Blandings' view, his wife was an accessory before the fact, and God stood convicted of the grossest sort of contributory negligence—but condemn them as he might, he could see no recourse from either of them, or from the real estate man, or from Ephemus W. Halleck.

There remained, however, the luckless Mr. Funkhauser, still doodling happily on his sketch tissue, dreaming towers and battlements, spires and turrets, onto a lousy old wreck of a farmhouse that had neither sills nor chimney to support its present crumbling weight. Him Mr. Blandings fired with a vicious suddenness that left, as one residue, a folder in the files of the American Institute of Architects, labeled "Funkhauser-Blandings Grievance Case." After an eventual chilly interchange, Mr. Blandings paid Mr. Funkhauser's bill of $635 for "Preliminary Plans of Restored Blandings Residence," and received the blueprints thereof. They were cold comfort. So was the report of Mr. Joe Perlasky, a local house wrecker and junkyard proprietor. Mr. Blandings had consulted him on the sly, in the hope of presenting to Mrs. Blandings the happy news that they could realize perhaps $2,000 out of the materials salvaged from the razing of the structure that was to have been the home of their children's children. Mr. Perlasky had figured for fifteen minutes and then announced that he would take the house down, leave everything neat and clean around the foundation, and not charge Mr. Blandings a penny more than $850. *"Charge?"* cried Mr. Blandings. "Atsa right," said Mr. Perlasky, explaining his modest figure by saying that he might just possibly be able to use some of the beams on another job.

It was at this point that Mr. Blandings' stout heart failed him. After a painful discussion, the entire Blandings' Building Project was put by to await a new and happier time. In calculation one evening, Mr. Blandings came face to face with the figure that in land cost, surveys, Mr. Appolonio's fee, legal expenses (so far), Mr. Funkhauser's blueprints, demolition estimates, and a dozen other items all small in themselves, he had so far spent or obligated himself to a total of $13,881.34, and not the rasp of one saw or the blow of one hammer had yet been heard on Bald Mountain.

"Don't act surprised when the children grow up to be guttersnipes, hearing words like that in their own living room," said Mrs. Blandings.

We can fix up that old house," said Mr. Simms, the new architect. "Of course we can. But it'll cost you as much as building a new house, or more, and you won't have what you want. My advice, if you'll let me be frank, is to start afresh."

Starting afresh sounded to Mr. and Mrs. Blandings like what they wanted most in all the world to do.

The Blandings' had begun their home-building career with the assumption that they had $20,000 to spend. When the real estate man had pointed out to them that $10,000 for land and the old house, plus $10,000 for "restoration" came to this precise figure, the logic and arithmetic had seemed very simple indeed. It was somewhat more clouded now, but not hopelessly so—not hopelessly so by a long shot, Mr. Blandings kept saying to himself. Manifestly, with some $14,000 invested so far, you couldn't skimp on the building by putting up a mere $6,000 bungalow. No—the house the Blandings' would have to build was that $10,000 house they had in mind from the beginning. Prices were somewhat higher now, of course, so an adjusted figure would probably be something nearer $12,500. That was the figure to shoot at anyway; it might come out a little on the high side, but still . . . And suppose it even turned out to be $15,000, when you included every-thing, as of course it wouldn't. . . .

The Blandings' began to spend their weekends in a rented cottage not far from their mountaintop, and Mr. Simms used to drop in on them almost every Saturday or Sunday afternoon. He developed a really charming habit of bringing his drawing board, T square, and triangles along with him, and in the sweet vernal afternoons he and the Bland-ings' would confer and plan together. Things went swimmingly. Mr. Blandings had only one complaint. "Simms makes things too small," he said. "I think he's got wonderfully ingenious ideas, but my God, if there's one thing I don't want in the country, it's to feel *cramped.*"

To this criticism Mr. Simms replied that he was watching the cubage. The Blandings' had never heard of cubage before; it was, Mr. Simms explained, merely the over-all cubic contents that the walls and roof enclosed, and a rough rule of thumb was to figure that the sort of house the Blandings' wanted would cost about 45 to 50 cents a cubic foot. This sounded dirt cheap to Mr. and Mrs. Blandings, neither of whom were conscious of the traps held for the unwary by an expo-nential equation of no higher than the third power. Mr. Simms, they felt (and told him), was holding a little too tight a rein on the cubage, good fault though it was. Mr. Simms sighed a little. "It's getting to look more like an $18,000 house every day," he said to the Blandings', who made noises of mild deprecation but did not pause for long.

What the Blandings' wanted was simple enough: a two-story house in quiet, modern good taste; frame and whitewashed brick veneer, to blend with the older architectural examples that dotted the hills about them. They wanted a good-sized living room, a dining room, and kitchen on the first floor; four bedrooms and accompanying baths on the second; a roomy cellar, a good attic, plenty of closets, and a couple of nice porches. And that was all.

The Blandings' soon discovered they had overlooked the servant problem. With thirty-one acres to look after, they'd have to have "a couple"—he to do the outdoor work, she to cook. To get them space for a small living room, bedroom, and bath off the kitchen called for some ingenuity, but Mr. Simms supplied it after adding twelve more feet to the house's long dimension. Mrs. Blandings' closet proposal (on which she would not retreat one inch) called for two per bedroom, one in every hallway, plus one broom closet, three kitchen closets, one closet for outdoor clothes, one linen closet, one storage closet for wood, one storage closet for card tables, etc. Mr. Blandings specified a liquor closet, with spring lock. It all added up to twenty-four closets, and Mrs. Blandings would brook no counterproposals. (The closets alone were to account for just a little under 2,000 cubic feet on Mr. Simms's conscientious plans.)

The Blandings' watched their house grow on the drawing board with warmth and pride. A study for Mr. Blandings became necessary the instant an opportunity for it opened up. Mrs. Blandings put in for a small cubicle, off the master bedroom, which she referred to as a "sulking room"—something that could serve her either as a dressing room or tiny study. And it would be awfully nice to have a little place with a sink and shelves for vases to do her flower arranging, she thought. Mr. Blandings got the notion that a built-in bar off the living room hall, scarcely larger than a closet and piped for cold water only, would add immeasurably to the house's whole feeling of hospitality—and who was Mr. Simms, who liked a snort himself now and again, to dispute him? One day Mr. Simms said, "It's beginning to look more like a $22,000 house than anything else," and for the first time the word "mansion" was used in conversation—facetiously, of course. The plans progressed; the house grew.

Mr. John Tesavis, well driller, appeared one summer day on the Blandings acres with his rig, under contract to drill a deep ("artesian," in the usage of the community) well at $4 per foot for the first three hundred feet, and $6 a foot thereafter, if necessary. Mr. Blandings was momentarily dismayed by the empiricism of selecting a well site ("I sinks she might as good go here as anywhere," Mr. Tesavis had said, indicating a wide area that seemed no different from any other half acre on Bald Mountain), but once the work was in progress he would sit on the bank for hours in fascination as the rig lifted the five hundred-pound steel drill-bit up three feet, let it down with a shattering slam, and instantly repeated its cycle. By the time Mr. Tesavis was down thirty feet the Blandings could tell when the rig was working even when they were three miles away: a faint concussion would shake the ground under their feet every time the drill took its pulverizing bite. Mr. Tesavis was drilling through elemental rock.

"There ought to be some better way," Mr. Blandings moaned one night after Mr. Tesavis had announced that he was down 201 feet and his "string" was stuck. Mrs. Blandings voiced regret that her husband had refused the services of a neighborhood dowser who had offered to pick an infallible well site by means of his forked applewood stick, on payment of $25. Mr. Blandings had summarily rejected this suggestion and was now wondering if it might not have been worth $25 merely to have Mrs. Blandings on the defensive instead of, as was again the miserable case, vice versa. But his spirits rebounded next day on the news that Mr. Tesavis had been able to free his string and had also encountered liquids: somewhere in the bowels of geology the drill had struck a fissure through which one-half gallon of water per minute was now flowing into the Blandings' bore. This was far from the twenty gallons a minute that Mr. Blandings had always thought of as a desirable supply, but at least it kept down the cloud of pulverized rock in which Mr. Tesavis, unshakable as the Duke of Wellington at his nerve-racking task, had hitherto been working.

It was apparent at last that the plans would soon be finished. Mr. Blandings, having missed several sessions between his wife and Mr. Simms, had fallen seriously behind the procession and had the uneasy feeling that his house was now beyond his control. He would discover his wife and his architect discussing in familiar terms the breezeway, of which he had never heard. Matters of cabinets, shelving, random-width floor boards, gutters, dry wells, olive-knuckle butts, flues, muntins, mullions, tiles, shakes, ranges, pitches, and reveals came at him in unexpected ways and from unanticipated angles.

There was a bathroom on the second floor right above the front entrance to the house, and although Mr. Blandings was willing to accept this as part of the same cosmic plan that had put the rock under Mr. Tesavis, Mrs. Blandings fought it like a tigress, and more than once embarrassed Mr. Blandings by the vividness with which she embodied her objections. Eventually, Mr. Simms got the bathroom established in the rear, but if Mrs. Blandings had won a battle, history might still assess that here she had lost the war: the house length grew by four feet.

"I sometimes wonder if you people know what you're heading into," Mr. Simms said one night as he packed up to go home, but he and the Blandings' were in a relaxed mood, with highballs in their hands. It was a bad evening for warnings, anyway: a littler earlier, Mr. Tesavis had run crash into eight gallons of water at 297 feet and had telephoned the joyful news.

"When we build, let us think that we build for ever," John Ruskin once wrote. Mr. Blandings held a similar view. The curse of America was jerry-building, he was eloquent in saying, and the Blandings house bore out the philosophies of quality and permanence. The floors were to be oak, the waterlines red brass; the plumbing fixtures did not bear the tradename Sphinx for nothing; the incombustible shingles were the same as those developed to meet Mr. Rockefeller's wishes for the restoration of Williamsburg; the hardware was to be supplied by the nearest thing to Benvenuto Cellini in Connecticut.

When Mr. Simms, after going into a monastic seclusion for three weeks, emerged again, it was with a set of drawings and specifications that floored the Blandings' flat: the simple plans and elevations that they had seen grow on the drafting board were superseded now by section drawings, framing plans, wiring diagrams, and detail sheets; everything had become so dense with dimensions as to be undecipherable except to experts. There was also a set of specifications the thickness of a Chicago telephone directory. It was time to ask for bids.

Mr. Blandings now felt it appropriate to consult Mr. Anson Dolliver, the president of the local First National Bank, about borrowing some money. Mr. Blandings had had the foresight, a year earlier, to open a checking account in Mr. Dolliver's bank and to keep his balance at a level he was sure a country bank would consider opulent. Mr. Dolliver had been cordiality itself. "If we can ever help you out, up there on the hill," he had said, "just let us know." Now that at last Mr. Blandings was ready to apply for some mortgage money at Mr. Dolliver's bank, he envisioned cordiality in the extreme, the proffer of a fine cigar, the suggestion of a leisurely lunch at the tavern on the green, and an open line of credit at a nominal rate.

What he encountered was nothing like that at all. As Mr. Blandings stated his readiness to contract a loan, Mr. Dolliver bit off the end of a cigar for himself and spat daintily in Mr. Blandings' direction but proffered nothing. "Why, great grief," he said, as if he had been asked to do somebody's laundry, "we're loaned full up to our legal limit right now. Love to help you out, but ..." He left the sentence unfinished. Then he added, listlessly, "My brother's the president of the savings bank across the hall. He might be able to do something for you, although of course I couldn't know for sure...."

Mr. Blandings had three separate conversations with the savings bank brother, at the end of which the second-string Dolliver admitted that there might be circumstances under which he would make Mr. Blandings a $10,000 mortgage loan at 6 per cent. Feeling like Lord Keynes at the end of a tough mission, Mr. Blandings said that he had hoped for more money at less rate, and Mr. Dolliver responded with a concise lecture on the risks of rural real estate that Mr. Blandings wished he had been able to think up by himself a year ago. So Mr. Blandings contented himself by wondering aloud how soon he might have Mr. Dolliver's accommodation, since his bids were almost due and he hoped to begin breaking ground very soon.

Mr. Dolliver snapped forward in his chair. "You want this money for *construction?*" he asked, in a tone that made Mr. Blandings feel that he had sought a criminal abortion from an archbishop. Mr. Blandings said he did. He tried to make his voice firm, but in spite of his strongest efforts a tremulous harmonic crept into it.

"You've had me at a misapprehension," said Mr. Dolliver. "This bank never makes construction loans. If that's your situation and you have some government bonds, I think my brother in the commercial bank across the hall could work out something very satisfactory for you."

Mr. Blandings at this point discontinued negotiations with both Dolliver brothers and closed out his checking account. It had not been pleasant to deal with the Dollivers and their banks, but Mr. Blandings was at least able to congratulate himself that here was one episode in his building experience that had not cost him any money. He merely did not have his loan.

Mr. Simms arrived on a Saturday morning, looking a little constricted
about the mouth, but brisk. "We've got all our bids," he said. "I've
summarized them on the top sheet."

Mr. Blandings opened the manila folder, and leaped upward as from
a bayonet thrust through the chair bottom.

"Jesus H. Mahogany Christ!" cried Mr. Blandings, and let the folder
slip from his grasp. Mrs. Blandings, who had had her second child
without anesthesia on the grounds that she did not wish to miss the
experience, picked up the sheets as they slithered on the floor. She
bent a level gaze on them and read:

ESTIMATES	BLANDINGS JOB	BALD MOUNTAIN
Antonio Doloroso, Builders		*$32,117.00*
Caries & Plumline		*34,265.00*
Julius Akimbo & Co................................		*37,500.00*
Zack, Tophet & Payne		*28,920.50*
John Retch & Sons		*30,852.00*

"There are a couple of things to be noted from this," said Mr. Simms,
speaking in an even, level, slightly rapid voice. "In the first place, Julius
Akimbo obviously doesn't want the job or he wouldn't have put in any
round-figure bid that size. As for that bid from Zack, Tophet & Payne
I wouldn't touch it with a ten-foot pole. They have a reputation for
bidding low and then loading on the extras. That sort of gives us three
to choose between. They're all good builders; John Retch is as good
as any, and with that low figure I don't think you'll go wrong on him.
Even so, we'll have to cut some costs."

This, Mr. Blandings thought in a blurred way, was putting it mildly.
The cost-cutting job began then and there. What Mr. Blandings now
discovered was that you could cut the cost of a $31,000 house some-
what, but there is no way on earth of cutting a $31,000 house to $21,000,
to say nothing of anything lower. There were some things that were
irremediable; it was no longer possible to shrink the house even by
the process of restoring the fatal bathroom to its flaunting position
over the front door. Too much else had altered in the meanwhile, and
you could no more reverse the growth process of the house than you
could shrink an adolescent back into last year's clothes by denying him
food.

But there were, of course, some things to be done. The house could not be abandoned. Although Mr. Simms had never spoken of money and seemed wholly content to go on helping the Blandings' build their house forever, Mr. Blandings was aware that the standard architect's fee, according to the procedures of the American Institute of Architects, to which Mr. Simms belonged, was 10 per cent of the cost of the house—and God knows that if anyone had ever earned $3,100, it was Mr. Simms. With that obligation outstanding there was simply no turning back: the house must be built. As the deflation progressed, bronze casement windows changed to steel of the lightest cross section made. Red brass piping became galvanized iron. A whole flagged terrace disappeared. The roofing specifications came down in the world. The house would now be insulated only to the eaves—and to hell with having a cool attic in summer. The plumbing fixtures became notably less Pompeian.

Even so, it was slow, dispiriting work. It depressed Mr. Blandings deeply to observe that the elimination of the big flagged terrace, on which he had already, in anticipation, had a few delicious drinks, saved him, on Mr. Retch's figures, only $172.50. "If I was *adding* the terrace it wouldn't cost me a cent less than $700," said Mr. Blandings savagely. But he said it to himself, for he no longer had anyone to talk to. He was being cheated, he was being bilked, he was being made a fool of, but he could not find the villain because everyone was a villain—his wife, Mr. Simms, the local bank, John Retch and his burly, ugly, insolent sons, Mr. Funkhauser, Mr. Appolonio, Ephemus Halleck, and the real estate man—all, all had made him the butt and victim of a huge conspiracy, clever and cruel.

"There!" he heard Mrs. Blandings saying to Mr. Simms a fortnight later. "We've got Mr. Retch's figures down to $26,991.17. That's more like it."

"What's more like *what?*" snarled Mr. Blandings.

"I think we've pared it down as far as it will go," said Mr. Simms tactfully. "It's more money than you started out to spend, but you're getting a fine house. Retch is an honest builder, and that's about what your house will cost you *if* you don't start getting into extras with him."

With one voice Mr. and Mrs. Blandings assured Mr. Simms that there would be *no* extras. Far, far off in outer space, the Gods of Residential Construction offered a chirruping laugh.

Mr. Blandings' ego, scarred by forces too vast to identify, was powerfully restored a week later on his visit to the big, impressive savings bank in the industrial city of Seagate. Thither Mr. Blandings and his friend and attorney Bill Cole had gone to seek the mortgage that had come to naught with the local banks. In no more than an hour's conversation the bank agreed to advance Mr. Blandings $18,000 at 5 per cent, the loan to be amortized over twenty years, anticipation of repayments permitted. (That left plenty for Mr. Blandings to raise by other means, but he knew where he could hock the stock he held in his own company.) And, *of course,* it would be a construction loan; Mr. Blandings could have a wad of cash as soon as the bank's title attorneys completed their search on the old Halleck property.

This last puzzled Mr. Blandings but did not disturb him. "I thought we'd done that," he said to Bill Cole as they left the bank together. "What did I pay old Judge Quondam $125 for when I bought the property from Halleck originally?"

Bill Cole explained that that had been a title search, all right. "It would have satisfied the local bank if you'd been able to do business with them," he said. "But Seagate-Proletarian has five million dollars out in mortgages in a hundred communities besides yours, and they have to have their own guarantees and satisfactions, naturally. It won't amount to much. Their title attorneys are Barratry, Lynch & Replevin; they'll soak you $200 but it'll be worth it to have their stamp of approval. Mostly they'll just send a man up to check old Judge Quondam and his county records."

"Old Judge Quondam died last spring," said Mr. Blandings. "The whole town closed down the afternoon of his funeral."

"Oh," said Bill, and then, after a pause, "Well, he didn't take his records with him, I guess."

On a crisp autumn morning the steam shovel arrived. Mr. and Mrs. Blandings, Mr. Simms, and John Retch himself were present for the ground breaking, and Mrs. Blandings was delighted with the rugged honesty and great good humor of Mr. Retch—"A rough diamond with a heart of gold," she said afterward. Mrs. Blandings was also happy that Mr. Blandings seemed himself again, as indeed he was. Any man who can raise $18,000 in an hour's conversation with one of the biggest savings banks in the East has certainly no call to be so jumpy about finances as Mr. Blandings could now see, looking back on it all, he had permitted himself to become. The $10,000-odd he would have to borrow on his company stock was just about the net of his burden—that was one way of looking at it. Everything else had been cash he would have spent on something else if it hadn't been for the house: something silly, probably, and certainly not with all the solid permanence of a home for his wife and children, forever. As for the mortgage, that was the bank's worry, not his; they were going to get 5 per cent for their worrying, and if they were satisfied, so was he. Interest would be $900 the first year, but it would go down as he amortized his loan, and that was pretty piffling when you considered it as the rent on a twelve-room house. . . .

"I wonder why the steam shovel isn't working," said Mrs. Blandings. It had been over an hour now since they had last heard its snortings come drifting down the hill.

"He's been at it five hours," said Mr. Blandings, speaking of the villainous-looking man who had turned out to be the excavating subcontractor. "Let's see what things look like."

Hand in hand, the Blandings', like happy children, climbed the hill— *their* hill, as Mrs. Blandings put it. On the summit Mr. Attilio Campobasso's steam shovel rested unevenly on its treads. From the south portion of the staked-out ground it had dug a hole, gratifyingly sharp, that went down six feet at the edges. Toward the north end the excavation was ragged and uneven, and while the shovel operator sat in his cab and smoked, three men with hand shovels were at work with the earth. The noise that came forth from their instruments was the same sort of noise you heard in the morning when a light fall of snow was being scraped from the city pavement. As they worked, Mr. and Mrs. Blandings could see growing the outlines of what appeared to be a mammoth, ossified whale.

"Looka that," said Mr. Campobasso, in disgusted elation.

"Boulder?" asked Mr. Blandings.

"Boulder!" said Mr. Campobasso, uttering an unmusical laugh. "Atsa no boulder. Atsa *ledge*. We go home now, come back next week, start blasting, keep on blasting plenty, yes *sir*. One thing you never got to worry your house settle any, sitting on granite, no *sir*."

When he got back to his fireside, Mr. Blandings looked up Mr. Retch's estimates on excavation. The job was to be done for $500 flat, except for the proviso, "If rock is encountered, removal by blasting at $0.24

per cubic foot." It had not seemed much, but the nature of cubic equations had once before eluded Mr. Blandings. This time he put pencil to paper to discover that an excavation sixty feet long, twenty-eight feet wide, and six feet deep contains 10,080 cubic feet.

Mr. Blandings was just beginning to wonder what sizable fraction of this figure should be multiplied by $0.24 when the phone rang. With a leaden hand, Mr. Blandings placed the receiver at an ear that did not wish to hear. Bill Cole's voice greeted him with what Mr. Blandings instantly knew to be false cheer.

"I don't want you to fly off the handle, Jim," Bill's voice said, "but there's a little hitch."

"What kind of a hitch?" Mr. Blandings heard himself ask.

"I've just been talking to Barratry, Lynch's man, Joe Pugh, who's doing your legal job for the bank," said Bill Cole, becoming almost aggressively hearty.

"And so what?" said Mr. Blandings.

"There's a flaw in the title," said Mr. Blandings' attorney.

Excerpts from Mrs. Blandings' diary:

October 7

Jim's cold not any better. He has spent a miserable three days in bed, with more hot toddies than I think warranted. Mr. Campobasso's blasting foreman wanted to know if we had liability insurance: a sharp piece of rock apparently fell on one of old Mr. Lange's chickens half a mile down the road, and he was very nasty about it. Blasting probably to go on another two weeks, at least. Mr. C.'s foreman says the way the ledge is tilted (right?) almost straight up makes it impossible to get rock out even with picks and shovels even after the blast has gone off. Nervous headache.

October 10

I don't understand trouble over the title, and I don't think Bill Cole does either. The title lawyers say they have nothing to show them that Mr. Halleck was entitled to act as the administrator of *his father's estate,* from which it seems we bought, not from Mr. Halleck himself. Mr. Dolliver at First National Bank was *gleeful* when he bumped into me this morning, said anybody but a dumb city bank would know that of course Ephemus was his father's administrator, and had always "been so accepted" since the old man died in 1922. It would all never have happened if we'd done business with him, he said. Blatherskite! The law firm wants Mr. Halleck to post a $10,000 bond to guarantee his "performance as administrator," before we get our loan, but he won't. He doesn't speak to us anymore when we meet him, I don't know why.

October 22

Mr. Retch asked for some money today, and I guess he's entitled to it. He got Campobasso to compromise his blasting bill at a flat $1,900! A nasty man, if I ever saw one. Jim put up most of his Amalgamated stock to borrow $15,000 to tide us over until the bank loan comes through. We have to get something called a "waiver of lien" from every one of Mr. Retch's subcontractors before the bank gives us a penny, and there must be at least twenty of them! The subcontractors have to promise the bank they won't sue us if we don't pay their bills. Silly! Why shouldn't they?

November 4

It *would* freeze in November so hard the concrete man can't pour any forms for the cellar walls! No work on the house for the last eight days at all, but a man came around and wanted to sell us a tennis court this afternoon. There were also three tree salesmen on the premises. I didn't know trees *had* salesmen.

November 9

The men started pouring concrete for the cellar walls today, but when Mr. Simms saw what they were doing he stopped them and tried to get Mr. Retch on the phone. They were putting hardly any cement in with the sand and gravel at all—a fine situation! Suppose Mr. Simms hadn't just happened to come around. Mr. Retch was in Maryland on another job. A load of shingles came today but they're not the right kind. We won't need any shingles until spring, anyway at this rate, if then.

November 15

What are we going to do with all the rock that Campobasso man excavated for the cellar? Nobody will take any responsibility for it; even Mr. Simms just shrugs his shoulders and changes the subject. But there it is, a mountain of it, right in front of where the front door is supposed to be. I *insist* it be carted away. Mr. Retch says there is nothing about it in the contract, and I must say I couldn't find anything myself.

November 20
The woodwork is going up! I guess that's the wrong word for it, but there are a lot of square poles sticking up in the air from the concrete, and I never heard so much sawing and hammering. There must have been ten men working all around everything today.

November 25
I'm just sick about the whole house! The framing (right word!) is finished for the wing and it is all *miles too high!* I thought we were getting a sweet modest house that hugged the hills close in its arms, and here instead is something that looks like a skyscraper! It just goes up and up. Mr. Simms was very short when I telephoned him about it and ended up by suggesting that I "take a pill or something." I just know that *somebody* is making a *terrible* mistake. Jim very sullen.

November 27
Glory be! Bill Cole says the bank and its lawyers are ready for "the closing." This means now we get our money at last. All Jim has to do is give the law firm $500 "in escrow" in case anything should go wrong with those wretched "waivers of lien" from those filthy subcontractors. Jim turned purple at the idea of giving Barratry, Lynch another $500, but he wrote out a check just the same. Five toilets arrived today and they're lying all around the field. It looked *unspeakably* vulgar!

November 28
I must admit I was wrong about the wing framing being too high. Now that all the framing is up, it all looks very nice. Mr. Retch was a changed man today, after he got a check. He swears he will get the house "closed in" before the snow flies, and that everything is going to go "like clockwork" from now on.

November 29
The men nailed a little tree to the top of the roof this noon. Then they knocked off and came down to our cottage and stood around until one of them hinted that when the evergreen went up on the ridgepole, it was up to the owner to stand a round of drinks for all the workmen.

Jim didn't seem to think much of this idea at first, but it's remarkable how well he fell in with it after the first twenty minutes. To bed very late.

The winter was slowly closing in on Bald Mountain. The house as it stood now reminded Mr. Blandings of a flayed elephant: the brick veneer ended in different courses at different places; above it, the diagonal sheathing of yellow pine, crusty with resin and punctured with knotholes, rose to the eaves. The roof was a wavy expanse of tar paper, dotted with shiny metal disks. The house's appearance was the nakedness of muscle, stripped of skin and fat.

Mr. Blandings did not like the looks of the sheathing lumber; he felt that he could either speak of it and make a fool of himself or stay silent and be bilked. He chose the latter of course, not as the least painful but merely as the least conspicuous. He was dismayed by the ragged lopsidedness of the holes where some day windows were supposed to be. But the worst thing, the thing so bad that neither Mr. nor Mrs. Blandings dared speak of such a matter as blame, was the microscopic size of the rooms—of the spaces, that is, where studding indicated some sort of partition in the future. There were five times as many spaces as the Blandings' could in any way account for, but even the largest, in the Blandings' eyes, was a cubicle. "Is this the *living* room?" Mrs. Blandings had wailed from amidst a rectangular grove of two-by-fours. Mr. Blandings merely sat down on a nail keg and stared through a hole in the wall. He no longer had enough energy to appear dejected. "I guess so," he said. "Mr. Simms says a room always looks like this before the partitions go up and the furniture goes in."

"Where would we have space for any furniture?" sobbed Mrs. Blandings.

"Where would we have money for any furniture?" asked Mr. Blandings.

All work on the house had now come to a stop. The window casements had not come.

The truck had left the factory and would be on the site tomorrow. No, the truck had not left, but that was immaterial: the windows had been shipped by freight, and the car must have been lost by some negligent waybill clerk. No, the windows would be shipped by truck *when* they were ready, which would not be for another three weeks.

No, the windows must be there and mislaid by the contractor. No, an order for the windows had never been received, but "we would give your valued customer promptest attention should we be so favored."

Mr. Blandings actually felt a sense of triumph when, after a while, roughly half of the windows arrived and the truckmen dumped them in a disorderly pile in the roadway. Several days later two window installers arrived, very drunk, looked at the windows, and roamed away again, never to return. Mr. Blandings ventured to inquire of Mr. Retch why some work could not go forward, even in the absence of the remaining windows or any crew to install them. This inquiry struck Mr. Retch as in the most flagrant bad taste. Mr. Retch was himself in a pet. The window company, as the price of signing its waiver of lien, had stuck Mr. Retch for cash on the barrelhead and was now letting him whistle. In coarse tones he explained to Mr. Blandings that (*a*) the mason subcontractor was stalled since he could not complete his brick courses around the missing frames, all of which were for the first floor; (*b*) the heating subcontractor could make no further progress until the house was closed in; (*c*) the tiler hired for the bathrooms could affix no tile; (*d*) not even the subfloors could be laid when the house was still open to rain and snow; (*e*) it was manifest that plastering could never be started now until spring, if at all, and (*f*) the electrical subcontractor's workmen refused to run any more BX cable around wet joists and columns. He ended by confidently predicting that the whole house would shortly burn down from one of the half-dozen temporary oilstoves the workmen insisted on using to keep their hands warm enough to hold a hammer, and whose fault would the whole blinking business be then?

Suddenly, enough windows arrived to build a biscuit factory.

Out of an infinite variety of rectangular steel shapes Mr. Retch selected those frames that seemed to accord roughly with the dimensions on Mr. Simms's plans, and sought to get the window company to send back a crew of window installers, preferably sober enough to put the windows into the sheathing holes right side up. The window company called Mr. Blandings to say that his contractor had been grossly abusive over the telephone, that in twenty years' experience they had never been treated with such inhumanity by such a tin-pot contractor, and that Mr. Blandings would be held responsible for the fact that the contractor had given the window company a bad check for $1,407.56. When Mr. Blandings relayed this intelligence to Mr. Retch, Mr. Retch produced a canceled check to the order of the window company and told Mr. Blandings that in thirty years' experience in the construction trades this was the first time an owner had ever accused him of fraud, and if he'd like to take his glasses off they could settle it outside, and if Mr. Retch lost he would build the rest of Mr. Blandings' house at his own expense. Mrs. Blandings' diary for the year ended with a notation, dated December 27, that she was taking the children to Sarasota for the winter, and did not mention the house at all. Of Mr. Blandings she merely recorded that he was "better."

Letter from Mr. J. H. Blandings to Mr. John Retch:

February 5

Dear Retch:

It is some time since my wife or I have visited the house, and I can only hope that the work is progressing as fast as the receipt of money requisitions from you seems to indicate. We will hope to see things again as soon as the weather moderates.

Meanwhile, I am considerably disturbed by the number of "extras" that are accumulating on your bills. So far as my wife and I are aware, we have authorized only two changes from the original plans: the depth of the reveal at the front door was altered by Mr. Simms with our approval, and we also authorized relocation and redesign of the concrete cellar steps after Mrs. Blandings fell down them. Except for these items, which seem to total $577.60, God knows why, I am at a loss to understand the multitude of other matters being billed to me, or in most cases what the items specified refer to at all. I herewith quote and comment on the following from your latest requisition:

"Redesign of doors No. 102, 107, 108, 112 . . . . *$120.00"*

(Mr. Simms tells me that there was no redesign on any doors on the job whatsoever.)

"New installation of well casing . . . . *$96.50"*

(If, according to your own explanation, the well casing installed by Mr. John Tesavis on his contract with me was cracked by the blasting done by your excavating subcontractor, I fail to see why I should bear replacement cost.)

"Substitution of 220-volt main switch panel in cellar . . . . . *$139.89"*

(What is the meaning of this? It is the eighth major extra so far on the electrical subcontract. Why was a 220-volt switch panel "substituted" for something else?)

"Furring down ceiling for kitchen cabinets .... *$102.00"*

(Insofar as I understand this charge, I consider it outrageous. You must have known the dimensions of the kitchen cabinets from the beginning; if you did not, then either you or Mr. Simms appear guilty of negligence. But you bill *me* just the same.)

"Mortising five butts .... *$1.68"*

(This refers to something I do not understand and the charge is small—but apparently whenever a carpenter picks up an extra chisel it costs me extra money.)

"Furnishing and installing one Zuz-Zuz Water Soft-N-R .. *$365.50"*

(I will not have any such piece of equipment in my house. Who authorized it? I will not pay this charge, nor any subsequent extra for "Removal of Zuz-Zuz Water Soft-N-R.")

"Time and overtime relocating oil burner .... *$215.00"*

(The oil burner was never relocated; it is supposed to be where it is marked on the plans. If your heating contractor thought it would be a good idea to relocate it in the living room, I have no doubt I will have to endure it there, but the cost of this change should be borne by whomever it gave pleasure to make it.)

All this totals to $1,040.57—a not inconsiderable expenditure. I shall expect to hear from you directly.

From Mr. John Retch to Mr. J. H. Blandings:

". . . only time in our experience when an owner has taken any such position. We have passed up many extra items without bill, because we have wanted you to be satisfied all along the line. Pardon our suggestion that you and Mrs. Blandings ought to get together, but furring of kitchen ceiling was discussed with her and she said cabinets must fit exactly 'at all costs.' We could have left in the smaller electrical switch panel specified by the architect against advice of electrician and leave resulting fire hazard up to you, but preferred to take the honest course and bill you in the open. The Zuz-Zuz people make a fine water softener, and we were looking out for your interests in not letting the unusually corrosive water from your well ruin your fine boilers and water lines. We discussed this with Mr. Simms when we could not get ahold of you and he said he would explain, which it appears he has not. As to the oil burner . . ."

From Mr. J. H. Blandings to Mr. John Retch:

"...and I enclose a check for $1,040.57 but will positively not be responsible for any further..."

When Mr. and Mrs. Blandings resumed their visits to Bald Mountain it was in the flowering spring. They saw the house, and a cry escaped them. It was a cry of joy. There it stood in its gleaming whiteness, more lovely than the fairest drawings that ever Mr. Simms had drawn. The house seemed to wait them as a girl would wait with downcast eyes for her lover's first shy kiss.

The entrance to the citadel was not accomplished with ease; the house appeared, on closer examination, to be more like a full-rigged ship floating placidly on a sea of mud where the new grading had been liquefied by the warm rains. But once across this ten-foot moat, the Blandings' removed their ruined shoes and stood with reverence upon their gleaming oaken floors...

Of course, there were little misfortunes here and there. The fireplace molding was nothing like what Mrs. Blandings had had in her mind's eye all along, from somewhere. The elaborate and "very advanced" fluorescent lighting in the dining room was later discovered to turn a healthy roast of beef into a purple mass of putrescence on the dining table, and the hum of the ballasts hidden in the lighting cove was so distracting to conversation that the whole installation was eventually removed and replaced by the more conventional type of lamp invented by Thomas Alva Edison in 1879. "We have never recommended fluorescent equipment for rooms of low noise-level," the Nadir Electric Supply Co. wrote tartly in answer to Mr. Blandings' protest. For the thousandth time Mr. Blandings moaned his refrain: "Why didn't anybody tell me?"

One major boner by the otherwise flawless Mr. Simms was also upsetting: in changing the location of the electric hot-water heater on the plans one hot summer night he had relocated the waterlines but forgotten to specify electrical connections to the new position, and neither owner, architect, builder, plumber, electrical subcontractor, nor any other mortal soul, had discovered the oversight until the day the Blandings' moved in and turned on their first tap. Most of the cellar wiring had to be ripped out to permit the new stretch of heavy power cable to run from the main busses to the heater, and Mr. Simms had insisted on paying the $275 for this item himself. There was, too, the window hardware, which would not work, and one bathroom floor to which the linoleum would not adhere even under Gestapo-like methods of attack. All the doors stuck except those that would not latch at all.

But the Blandings' had built a good house—a very fine house indeed. Its process of morphology might, for a moment, be noted. The ovum had been the farmhouse on which $10,000 was to be spent for "restoration." The larva was the $15,000 house that Mr. Simms began to design. The pupal stage was reached when Mr. Retch began to build something for a contract price of $26,991.17. The eventually emerged home, in full adult form, bore (as in all organic processes) little resemblance to its embryo, either to the aesthete's or to the cost accountant's eye. Only Mr. Blandings *really* knows how much he spent on Bald Mountain, compared with the $20,000 concept for land and building with which he began, but no one would go wrong if he took something like $51,000 as a basic figure.

The Christmas House Number of *House & Home (Combined with The Home Lovely)* lay before Mr. Savington Funkhauser, A.I.A., who was wondering why, at the end of a hard day at the drafting board, he had opened it at all. "Our problem was to create a modern home in a community dominated by fine old colonial farmhouses that had stood the test of revolutionary days and before," he read, "and to achieve a youthful spirit without doing violence to the tradition of those stout forebears of ours whose indomitable strivings have been the heritage of..."

"Spittle," said Mr. Funkhauser in a toneless voice, aloud. He looked for a title at the top of the page to tell him what he was reading. In thin swash lettering he saw *"Home Lovely's* December House-of-the-Month is Tribute to Taste and Ingenuity with Materials Old and New." There seemed here no conveyance of information whatsoever, and Mr. Funkhauser would have tossed the magazine aside but could not rouse himself enough.

"It was a challenge to our ingenuity," he read on in a sort of mild hypnosis, "but my husband and I tackled the difficulties with a will, and out of a combination of budgeted planning, a determination to keep our primary objectives ever before us, and the closest and most friendly three-way cooperation between architect, owner, and builder, we were able to achieve our aims with a minimum of misunderstandings and additional items of expense that occasionally mar the joys of building that *sine qua non* of all normal couples' ambitions, the Home of One's Own."

"Whose bilge *is* this?" Mr. Funkhauser asked of the fireplace. On the instant, a picture caption answered him: "Mrs. J. Holocoup Blandings, whose delightful mountain dwelling is this month's *Home Lovely* choice as ..."

Mr. Funkhauser's right arm moved suddenly, and the Christmas House Number described a graceful arc, disappearing into the chromium-bound cylinder of Nutasote that served Mr. Funkhauser as a waste receiver. A moment later the young architect fished it out again, and turned back to the assistant editor's interview with "the chic and attractive Mrs. Blandings, mistress of 'Surrogate Acres.' " For some five wordless minutes he studied the dim halftones and spidery line cuts arranged ingeniously askew on the chalky paper. Suddenly he came on something familiar, and a flush darkened his face. He muttered for a moment and then, taking pen and paper, he commenced a letter:

"Dear Mr. Blandings," he wrote. "In the December issue of *House & Home* I notice, in the midst of the display of your new residence and in an interview that purports to be with your wife, a reference that says, 'Once the impracticalities of an earlier designer had been discarded as wholly unsuitable ...' I would scarcely have credited this to be a reference to myself and some work I did for you from which I later withdrew, were it not that on the following page an illustration labeled 'Discarded Study' is a manifest caricature of a rendering I submitted to you on June 3, 1938. Taken in conjunction, the sentence and drawing offer to my professional standing an affront and damage that I cannot afford to let pass unnoticed. I am instructing my attorneys, Messrs. Barratry, Lynch & Replevin, to communicate with you regarding possible steps toward redress which ..."

Miles away, on Bald Mountain, in the midst of Surrogate Acres, beneath an uninsulated composition roof that creaked slightly under the growing snow load of an early winter storm, Mr. Blandings stirred uneasily in his sleep. He was dreaming that his house was on fire.

PSYCHO

(1960)

THE REAL BAD FRIEND
ROBERT BLOCH

Made for the minimal sum of $800,000 and shot by a television crew, Alfred Hitchcock's *Psycho* is, without a doubt, the quintessential suspense-shocker of modern cinema, and a touchstone for almost everything in the genre that has since followed. Thirty years later, the famous shower scene is still firmly embedded in the cultural imagination. Throughout his long and influential career as a director, Hitchcock revelled in manipulating audiences by playing on their expectations, emotions, and private fears. In speaking of the film, Hitchcock once said, "It wasn't a message that stirred the audience, nor was it a great performance.... They were aroused by pure film." Indeed, as a purely visceral experience, *Psycho* is without equal. Hitchcock, with typically ironic humor, often referred to his terror classic as a "fun picture."

ROBERT BLOCH's prolific literary career has produced novels, short stories, film scripts, and television scripts for *Alfred Hitchcock Presents, Star Trek, Night Gallery,* and numerous other programs. Born in Chicago in 1917, Bloch sold his first story to *Weird Tales* at the age of seventeen and has been writing assiduously ever since.Certainly Hitchcock's most famous work, *Psycho,* was loosely based on the real-life story of Ed Gein, the Wisconsin murderer whose grisly activities included dressing up in "suits" made from the skins of his female victims. But according to Bloch, the original basis for the thriller came from the following story.

PSYCHO

Released: 1960
Production: Alfred Hitchcock for Paramount
Direction: Alfred Hitchcock
Screenplay: Joseph Stefano
Cinematography: John L. Russell
Editing: George Tomasini
Art direction: Joseph Hurley and Robert Clatworthy; set decoration, George Milo
Music: Bernard Herrmann
Title design: Saul Bass
Running time: 109 minutes

PRINCIPAL CHARACTERS:

Norman Bates	Anthony Perkins
Marion Crane	Janet Leigh
Lila Crane	Vera Miles
Sam Loomis	John Gavin
Milton Arbogast	Martin Balsam
George Lowery	Vaughn Taylor

It was really all Roderick's idea in the first place.

George Foster Pendleton would never have thought of it. He couldn't have; he was much too dull and respectable. George Foster Pendleton, vacuum cleaner salesman, aged forty-three, just wasn't the type. He had been married to the same wife for fourteen years, lived in the same white house for an equal length of time, wore glasses when he wrote up orders, and was completely complacent about his receding hairline and advancing waistline.

Consequently, when his wife's uncle died and left her an estate of some eighty-five thousand dollars after taxes, George didn't make any real plans.

Oh, he was delighted, of course—any ten-thousand-a-year salesman would be—but that's as far as it went. He and Ella decided to put in another bathroom on the first floor and buy a new Buick, keeping the old car for her to drive. The rest of the money could go into something safe, like savings and loan, and the interest would take care of a few little luxuries now and then. After all, they had no children or close relatives to look after. George was out in the territory a few days every month, and often called on local sales prospects at night, so they'd never developed much of a social life. There was no reason to expand their style of living, and the money wasn't quite enough to make him think of retiring.

So they figured things out, and after the first flurry of excitement and congratulations from the gang down at George's office, people gradually forgot about the inheritance. After all, they weren't really living any differently than before. George Foster Pendleton was a quiet man, not given to talking about his private affairs. In fact, he didn't have any private affairs to talk about.

Then Roderick came up with his idea.

"Why not drive Ella crazy?"

George couldn't believe his ears. "You're the one who's crazy," George told him. "Why, I never heard of anything so ridiculous in all my life!"

Roderick just smiled at him and shook his head in that slow, funny way of his, as if he felt sorry for George. Of course, he *did* feel sorry for George, and maybe that's why George thought of him as his best friend. Nobody seemed to have any use for Roderick, and Roderick didn't give a damn about anyone else, apparently. But he liked George, and it was obvious he had been doing a lot of thinking about the future.

"You're a fine one to talk about being ridiculous," Roderick said. That quiet, almost inaudible way he had of speaking always carried a lot of conviction. George was handicapped as a salesman by his high, shrill voice, but Roderick seldom spoke above a whisper. He had the actor's trick of deliberately underplaying his lines. And what he said usually made sense.

Now George sat in his five-dollar room at the Hotel LeMoyne and listened to his friend. Roderick had come to the office today just before George left on his monthly road trip, and decided to go along. As he'd fallen into the habit of doing this every once in a while, George thought nothing of it. But this time, apparently, he had a purpose in mind.

"If anyone is being ridiculous," Roderick said, "it's you. You've been selling those lousy cleaners since nineteen forty-six. Do you like your job? Are you ever going to get any higher in the company? Do you want to keep on in this crummy rut for another twenty years?"

George opened his mouth to answer, but it was Roderick who spoke. "Don't tell me," he said. "I know the answers. And while we're on the subject, here's something else to think about. Do you really love Ella?"

George had been staring at the cracked mirror over the bureau. Now he turned on the bed and gazed at the wall. He didn't want to look at himself, or Roderick, either.

"Why, she's been a good wife to me. More than a wife—like a mother, almost."

"Sure. You've told me all about that. That's the real reason you married her, wasn't it? Because she reminded you of your mother, and your mother had just died, and you were afraid of girls in the first place but you had to have someone to take care of you."

Damn that Roderick! George realized he never should have told him so much in the first place. He probably wouldn't, except that Roderick had been his best—maybe his only—friend. He'd come along back in '44, in the service, when George had been ready to go to pieces completely.

Even today, after all those years, George hated to remember the way he'd met Roderick. He didn't like to think about the service, or going haywire there on the island and trying to strangle the sergeant, and ending up in the stockade. Even so, it might have been much worse, particularly after they stuck him in solitary, if he hadn't met Roderick. Funny part of it was, Roderick had become his intimate friend and heard everything about him long before George ever set eyes on him. Roderick had been down in solitary, too, and for the first month he was just a voice that George could talk to in the dark. It wasn't what you'd call the best way in the world to develop a close friendship, but at the time it kept George from cracking up. He had someone to confide in at last, and pretty soon he was spilling his guts, his heart, his soul; telling things he hadn't even known about himself until the words came.

Oh, Roderick knew, all right. He knew the things George had carefully concealed from everyone—the kids back in school, the guys in the army, the gang at the office, the card-playing friends and neighbors, even Ella. Most especially, Ella. There were lots of things George wouldn't dream of telling Ella, any more than he would have told his mother, years ago.

Roderick was right about that. Ella did remind George of his mother. And when his mother died he'd married Ella because she was big and took care of him, and the way it worked out it was she who made most of the decisions. As a child he'd been taught to be a good little boy. Now he was a good little salesman, a good little potbellied householder, a fetcher-home of Kleenex, a mower of lawns, a wiper of dishes, a wrapper of garbage. Twelve years of it since the war. And if it hadn't been for Roderick, he never could have stood it.

Could he stand another twelve years of it? Or twenty, or thirty, or even more?

"You don't have to put up with it, you know," Roderick murmured, reading his thoughts. "You don't have to be mommy's boy any longer. This is your big chance, George. If you got rid of the house, you'd have over ninety thousand in cash. Suppose you settled down on one of those little islands in the Caribbean. There's dozens of them, according to the travel guide I saw on your desk in the office today."

"But Ella wouldn't like that," George protested. "She hates hot climates. That's why we've never traveled south on vacations. Besides, what on earth could she do down there?"

"She wouldn't be going," Roderick answered, patiently. "She'd stay here. That's the whole point of it, George. You could live like a king there for a few hundred a month. Have a big house, all the servants you want. Plenty to drink. And the *girls,* George! You've heard about the girls. Every color under the sun. Why, you can even buy them down there, the way those old Southern planters used by buy slaves. Quadroons and octoroons and mulattoes—probably can't even speak a word of English. But you wouldn't have to worry about that. All you'd want is obedience, and you could have a whip to take care of that. They'd have to do anything you wanted, because you'd be their master. You could even kill them if you liked. The way you'd like to kill Ella."

"But I don't want to kill Ella," George said, very quickly, and his voice was quite loud and shrill.

Roderick's answering laugh was soft. "Don't kid me," he said. "I know you. You'd like to kill her, the same way you'd have liked to kill that sergeant back on the island, but you can't because you're chicken. And besides, it isn't practical. Murder is no solution to this problem, George, but my way is. Drive Ella crazy."

"Preposterous."

"What's preposterous about it? You want to get rid of her, don't you? Get rid of your job, get rid of taking orders from a wife and a boss and every stinking customer with ninety bucks for a cleaner who thinks he can make you jump And here's your chance. The chance of a lifetime, George, sitting right in your lap."

"But I can't drive Ella insane."

"Why not? Take a look around you, man. It's being done every day. Ask the lawyers about the sons and daughters and in-laws of people who have money, and how they get the old folks put away in the asylum. Getting power of attorney from grandpa and grandma—things like that. Don't you think a lot of them help the deal along a little? You can drive anyone crazy, George, if you plan."

"Ella isn't the type," George insisted. "Besides, anything I did—don't you think she'd know about it and see through it? Even if I tried, it wouldn't work."

"Who said anything about you trying?" Roderick drawled. He seemed very sure of himself, now. "That's my department, George. Let me do it."

"You? But—"

"I wouldn't fool you. It's not merely a beautiful gesture of friendship. I want those West Indies, too. We can go there together. You'd like that, wouldn't you, George? The two of us down there, I mean, where we wouldn't have to be afraid of what we did, what people would say or think? I could help you, George. I could help you get hold of some of those girls. Do you remember that book you read once, about the Roman Emperor, Tiberius—the one who had the villa on the island, and the orgies? You told me about some of those orgies, George. We could do it, you and I."

George felt the sweat oozing down the insides of his wrists. He sat up. "I don't even want to think of such things," he said. "Besides, what if you got caught?"

"I won't get caught," Roderick assured him, calmly. "Don't forget, Ella doesn't even know me. I've steered clear of your friends all these years. I'm a free agent, George, and that's our ace in the hole. You've always treated me like a poor relation, never introducing me or even mentioning my name. Oh, I'm not complaining. I understand. But now that little situation is going to come in handy. Let me think things out, work up a plan."

George bit his upper lip. "Ella's too sensible," he said. "You'd never get her upset."

Roderick laughed without making a sound. "Nobody is really 'sensible,' George. It's just a false front, that's all. Like the one you've built up." He was suddenly quite serious again. "Think about it. How many people would believe you were capable of even talking to me the way you have just now, let alone of carrying out any such ideas? Would your boss believe it? Or Ella, even? Of course not! To the world, you're just another middle-aged salesman, a Willy Loman type, only worse. A spineless, gutless, chicken-hearted, yellow-bellied coward. A weak-kneed sissy, a little panty-waist, a mommy's boy, a—"

"*Shut up!*" George almost screamed the words, and then he was on his feet with his sweat-soaked hands balled into fists, ready to smash at the voice and the face, ready to kill . . . .

And then he was back on the bed, breathing hoarsely, and Roderick was laughing at him without making a sound.

"You see? I knew the words to use, all right. In one minute I turned you into a potential murderer, didn't I? You, the respectable suburban type who's never gotten out of line since they shoved you into the stockade.

"Well, there are words for everyone, George. Words and phrases and ideas that can churn rage, trigger emotion, fill a person with incoherent, hysterical fear. Ella is no different. She's a woman; there's a lot of things she must be afraid of. We'll find those things, George. We'll press the right buttons until the bells ring. The bells in the belfry, George. The bats in the belfry—"

George made a noise in his throat. "Get out of here," he said.

"All right. But you think over what I've said. This is your big opportunity—*our* big opportunity. I'm not going to stand by and see you toss it away."

Then he was gone.

Alone in his room, George turned out the light and got ready for bed. He wondered if there was a threat hidden in Roderick's last words, and that startled him. All his life George had been afraid of other people because they were violent, aggressive, cruel. At times he could sense the same tendencies in himself, but he always suppressed them. His mother had made him behave like a little gentleman. And except for that one terrible interlude in the service, he had always been a little gentleman. He'd kept out of trouble, kept away from people that could harm him.

And Roderick had helped. He'd gotten out of the army at the same time George had, settled down in the same city. Of course, he didn't really settle down, inasmuch as he had no wife or family and never kept a regular job. Still, he seemed to get by all right. In spite of his hand-to-mouth existence, he dressed as well as George did. And he was taller and leaner and darker and looked a good ten years younger. It often occurred to George that Roderick lived off women—he seemed to be that type, always hinting of sexual conquests. But he never volunteered any information about himself. "What you don't know won't hurt you," he'd say.

And George was satisfied with the arrangement, because as a result he could talk about himself. Roderick was the sounding board, the confessional booth, the one person who could really understand.

He'd drop in at the office from time to time when George was free, and sometimes he'd ride along with him for a day when George went out of town, or in the evenings when he called on prospects. After a few perfunctory overtures, George stopped trying to get Roderick to meet his wife. And he'd never mentioned Roderick to her—mainly because of the circumstances of their having been in the stockade together, and George had never dared to tell Ella about *that*. So Ella didn't know about Roderick, and somehow this made everything quite exciting. Once, when Ella had gone down to Memphis for her mother's funeral, Roderick consented to move in with George at the house for two days. They got violently and disastrously drunk together, but on the third morning Roderick left.

It was all very clandestine, almost like having a mistress. Only without the messy part. The messy part was no good, though it might be different if you were on one of those islands and nobody could see you or stop you and you owned those girls body and soul; then you could have a whip, a long black whip with little pointed silver spikes at the end, and the spikes would tear the soft flesh and you would make the girls dance and little red ribbons would twine around the naked bodies and then—

But that was Roderick's doing, putting such thoughts into his head! And suddenly George knew he was afraid of Roderick. Roderick, always so soft-voiced and calm and understanding; always ready to listen and offer advice and ask nothing in return. George had never realized until now that Roderick was as cruel as all the rest.

Now he had to face the fact. And he wondered how he could have escaped the truth all these years. Roderick had been in the stockade for a crime of violence, too. But the difference was that Roderick wasn't repentant. Repentance wasn't in him—only defiance and hatred, and the terrible strength that comes of being untouched and untouchable. It seemed as though nothing could move him or hurt him. He bowed to no conventions. He went where he pleased, did what he pleased. And apparently there was a streak of perversity in him; obviously he hated Ella and wanted George to get rid of her. If George had listened to him tonight . . . .

The little vacuum-cleaner salesman fell asleep in his sagging bed, his mind firmly made up. He was finished with Roderick. He wouldn't see him any more, wouldn't listen to any of his wild schemes. He wanted no part of such plans. From now on he'd go his way alone. He and Ella would be safe and happy together . . . .

During the next few days George often thought of what he'd say to Roderick when he turned up, but Roderick left him alone. Maybe he'd figured out the situation for himself and realized he'd gone too far.

Anyway, George completed his trip, returned home, kissed Ella, helped supervise the installation of the second bathroom, and finished up his paperwork at the office.

Being on the road had left him feeling pretty tired, but there came a time when he just had to catch up with his prospect list here in town, so he finally spent an evening making calls.

Since he was just plain fagged out, he violated one of his rules and stopped for a quick drink before he began his rounds. After the first call he had another, as a reward for making a sale, and from then on things went easier. George knew he had no head for alcohol, but just this once a few drinks helped. He got through his customer list in a sort of pleasant fog, and when he was done he had several more fast shots in a tavern near the house. By the time he put the car in the garage, he was feeling no pain.

He wondered vaguely if Ella would be waiting up to bawl him out. She didn't like him to drink. Well, perhaps she'd be asleep by now. He hoped so, as he went up the walk and started to unlock the door.

Before he could turn the key the door opened and Ella was in his arms. "Thank goodness you're here!" she cried. She *was* crying, George realized, and then he noticed that all the lights in the house were on.

"Hey, what's the matter? What's all this about?"

She began to gurgle. "The face, in the window—"

Alcohol plays funny tricks, and for a moment George wanted to laugh. Something about the melodramatic phrase, and the way Ella's jowls quivered when she uttered it, was almost painfully amusing. But Ella wasn't joking. She was frightened. She quivered against him like a big blob of Jello.

"I had this awful headache—you know the kind I get—and I was just sitting in the front room watching TV with the lights off. I guess I must have been dozing a little, when all of a sudden I got this feeling, like somebody was watching me. So I looked up, and there in the window was this awful face. It was like one of those terrible rubber masks the kids wear for Halloween—all green and grinning. And I could see hands clawing at the window, trying to open it and get in!"

"Take it easy, now," George soothed, holding her. "Then what happened?"

Gradually he got it out of her. She had screamed and turned on the big overhead light, and the face had disappeared. So she'd turned on all the lights and gone around locking the doors and windows. After that she'd just waited.

"Maybe we ought to call the police," she said. "I thought I'd tell you about it first."

George nodded. "Sensible idea. Probably was just what you thought— some kid playing a trick." He was quite sobered now, and thoughtful. "Which window did you see this through, the big one? Here, let me get a flashlight from the garage. I'm going to look for footprints."

He got the flashlight, and when Ella refused to accompany him, walked across the lawn himself. The flower bed beneath the window was damp from a recent rain, but there were no footprints.

When George told Ella about it, she seemed puzzled.

"I can't understand it," she said.

"Neither can I," George answered. "If it was a kid, he'd probably have run off when you spotted him, instead of waiting to smooth out his tracks. On the other hand, if it was a prowler, he'd cover up his traces. But a prowler wouldn't have let you see him in the first place." He paused. "You're sure about what you saw?"

Ella frowned. "Well . . . it was only for a second, you know, and the room was so dark. But there was this big green face, like a mask, and it had those long teeth . . . ."

Her voice trailed away.

"Nobody tried the doors or windows? You didn't hear any sounds?"

"No. There was just this face." She blinked. "I told you about my headache, and how I was dozing off, watching that late movie. It was all sort of like a nightmare."

"I see." George nodded. "Did you ever stop to think that maybe it was a nightmare?"

Ella didn't answer.

"How's the head? Still aching? Better take a couple of aspirins and go up to bed. You just had a bad dream, dear. Come on, let's go to bed and forget about it, shall we?"

So they went to bed.

Maybe Ella forgot about it and maybe she didn't, but George wasn't forgetting. He knew. Roderick must be starting to carry out his plan. And this would only be the beginning. . . .

It was only the beginning, and after that things moved fast. The next afternoon, George was sitting in the office all alone when Ella called him from the house. She sounded very excited.

"George, did you tell the plumbers to come back?"

"Why no, dear, of course not."

"Well, Mr. Thornton is here, and he said they got a call to come over and rip everything out again. I don't understand it, and I've been trying to explain that it's some kind of mistake and—"

Ella sounded very upset now, and George tried to calm her down. "Better put him on, dear. I'll talk to him."

So Ella put Mr. Thornton on and George told him not to bother, there was a mixup somewhere. And when Mr. Thornton got mad and said there was no mixup, he'd taken the call himself, George just cut him off and got Ella back on the wire.

"It's all taken care of now," he assured her. "Don't worry about a thing. I'll be home early."

"Maybe you'd better get something to eat downtown," Ella said. "I've got such an awful headache, and I want to lie down for a while."

"You go ahead," George said. "I'll manage."

So George managed, but if Ella lay down, she didn't get very much rest.

George found that out when he got home. She was quivering, her voice and body trembling.

"Somebody's trying to play a trick on us," she told him. "The doorbell's been ringing all afternoon. First it was Gimbel's delivery truck. With *refrigerators.*"

"I didn't order a refrigerator," George said.

"I know you didn't, and neither did I." Ella was trying to hold back the tears. "But somebody did. And not just one. They had four of them."

"Four?"

"That's not the worst of it. Some man from Kelly's called and asked when I was going to move. They'd gotten an order for a van."

"Let me get this straight." George paced the floor. "How did they get the order?"

"Over the phone," Ella said. "Just the way Mr. Thornton did. That's why I thought at first you might have called." She was sniffling now, and George made her sit down.

"So you said," George told her. "But I asked Mr. Thornton about that. He happened to take that particular call himself. And he was quite positive the caller was a woman."

"A woman?"

"Yes." George sat down next to Ella and took her hand. "He claimed he recognized your voice."

"But George, that's impossible! Why, I never even used the phone once today. I was lying down with my headache and—"

George shook his head. "I believe you, dear. But who else could it be? What other woman would know that Thornton was the plumber who put in our bathroom? Did you mention his name to anyone?"

"No, of course not. At least, I don't remember." Ella was pale. "Oh,

I'm so upset I can't think straight." She put her hands up to her forehead.
"My head feels like it's splitting wide open. I can't stand it. . . ." She
stared at George. "Where are you going?"

"I'm calling Dr. Vinson."

"But I'm not sick. I don't need a doctor."

"He'll give you a sedative, something for that head of yours. Now
just calm down and relax."

So Dr. Vinson came over, and he did give Ella a sedative. Ella didn't
mention anything about the calls, so he only went through a routine
examination.

But afterwards, when she was asleep upstairs, George took Dr. Vinson aside and told him the story—including the part about the face in
the window.

"What do you think, doc?" he asked. "I've heard about such things happening when women start going through change of life. Maybe—"

Dr. Vinson nodded. "Better have her call my office for an appointment later in the week," he said. "We'll see that she gets a complete
checkup. Meanwhile, don't let yourself get upset. It could be somebody's idea of a practical joke, you know."

George nodded, but he wasn't reassured.

The part that really bothered him was the business about Ella's voice
being recognized over the phone.

Next morning he left early, and Ella was still asleep. Down at the
office he called Gimbel's and then Kelly's. After much confusion he
was able to locate the clerks who had taken the orders. Both insisted
they had talked to a woman.

So George called Dr. Vinson and told him so.

No sooner had he hung up than Ella was on the phone. She could
scarcely speak.

A man had come from the Humane Society with a Great Dane. A
west side furrier, somebody Ella had never heard of, drove up with
samples of mink coats—mink coats in July! A travel agency had kept
calling, insisting that she had asked for information about a flight around
the world. Her head was killing her; she didn't know what to do; she
wanted George to phone the police and—

She broke off in the middle of her hysterical account, and George
quickly asked what was happening. A moment later he realized he
could have spared himself the question. The sound of what was hap-

pening was clearly audible over the wire: he recognized the hideous wailing.

"Fire engines!" Ella gasped. "Somebody called the fire department!"

"I'll be right home," George said, hanging up quickly.

And he went right home. The trucks were gone by the time he arrived, but a lieutenant was still there, and a detective from the police department. Ella was trying to explain the situation to them, and it was a lucky thing George was on hand to straighten things out. He had Ella go upstairs, and then he told the men the story.

"Please," he said. "Don't press any charges. If there's any expense, anything like a fine, I'll be glad to pay it. My wife is under doctor's care— she's going to have a complete examination later in the week. This is all very embarrassing, but I'm sure we can straighten things out. . . ."

The men were quite sympathetic. They promised to let him know what the costs would be, and the detective gave George his card and told him to keep in touch with him in case there was anything he could do.

Then George got on the phone and squared things with the Humane Society, the furrier, and the travel agency. After that he went up to Ella's bedroom, where he found her lying on the bed with all the shades pulled down. He offered to fix her something to eat but she said she wasn't hungry.

"Something's happening," she told him. "Somebody's trying to harm us. I'm frightened."

"Nonsense." George forced a smile. "Besides, we've got protection now." And then, to cheer her up, he told her that the detective had promised to put a watch on the house and tap the telephone.

"If there's anybody pulling any funny business, we'll catch him," George reassured her. "All you have to do is rest. By the way, Dr. Vinson said it would be a good idea if you stopped in for a checkup towards the end of the week. Why not call him for an appointment?"

Ella sat up. "You told him?"

"I had to, dear. After all, he's your doctor. He's in a position to help if—"

"If *what?*"

"Nothing."

"George. Look at me." He didn't, but she went on. "Do you think I made those calls? Do you?"

"I never said so. It's just that Thornton claims he recognized your voice. Why would he want to lie about a thing like that?"

"I don't know. But he's lying. He *must* be! I never called him, George. I swear it! And I didn't call anyone this morning. Why, I was in bed until almost noon. That sedative made me so dopey I couldn't think straight."

George was silent.

"Well, aren't you going to say something?"

"I believe you, dear. Now, try and get some rest."

"But I can't rest now. I'm not tired. I want to talk to you."

"Sorry, I've got to get back to the office and clean up my desk. Don't forget, I'm leaving town again tomorrow."

"But you can't go now. You can't leave me alone like this!"

"Only for three days. You know, Pittsville and Bakerton. I'll be back by Saturday." George tried to sound cheerful. "Anyway, the police will keep an eye on the house, so you needn't worry about prowlers."

"George, I—"

"We'll talk about it again tonight. Right now, I've got a job to attend to, remember?"

So George left her weeping softly on the bed and went back to his office. But he didn't pay much attention to his job.

Roderick was waiting for him when he came in.

The other salesmen were out that afternoon, and there was no one else near the hot stuffy little back-room cubicle George used for an office. He and Roderick were all alone, and Roderick spoke very softly. George was glad of that, at least, because he wouldn't have wanted anyone to hear the things Roderick told him. Nor, for that matter, would he have cared to have been overheard himself.

The moment he saw Roderick he almost shouted, "So it was you, after all!"

Roderick shrugged. "Who else?"

"But I told you I didn't want any part of it, and I meant it!"

"Nonsense, George. You don't know what you mean, or what you really want." Roderick smiled and leaned forward. "You talked to this Dr. Vinson and to the detective. Did you mention my name?"

"No, I didn't, but—"

"You see? That proves it. You must have realized who was responsible, but you kept silent. You *wanted* the scheme to work. And it is working, isn't it? I have everything all planned."

In spite of himself George had to ask the question. "How did you manage to imitate her voice?"

"Simple. I've called her on the phone several times—wrong number, you know, or pretending to be a telephone solicitor. I heard enough to be able to fake. She's got one of those whiney voices, George. Like this. *I think I'll lie down for a while. My head is killing me.*"

It was uncanny to hear Ella's voice issuing from those sardonically curled lips. George's heart began to pound.

"You—you said you had plans," he murmured.

Roderick nodded. "That's right. You're going out of town for a few days, I believe?"

"Yes. Tomorrow."

"Good. Everything will be arranged."

"What do you intend to do?"

"Maybe you'd better not ask that question, George. Maybe you ought to keep out of this completely. Just leave everything to me." Roderick cocked his head to one side. "Remember, what you don't know won't hurt you."

George sat down, then stood up again hastily. "Roderick, I want you to stop this! Lay off, do you hear me?"

Roderick smiled.

"Do you hear me?" George repeated. He was trembling now.

"I heard you," Roderick said. "But you're upset now, George. You aren't thinking straight. Stop worrying about Ella. She won't really come to any harm. They'll take quite good care of her where she's going. And you and I will take good care of ourselves, where we're going. That's what you want to concentrate on, George. The Caribbean. The Caribbean, with ninety thousand dollars in our pockets. A little boat, maybe, and those long, moonlit tropical nights. Think about the girls, George—those nice, slim young girls. They aren't fat and blubbery, always whining and complaining about headaches and telling you not to touch them. They like to be touched, George. They like to be touched, and held, and caressed, and—"

"Stop it! It's no use. I've changed my mind."

"Too late, George. You can't stop now." Roderick was very casual, but very firm. "Besides, you don't really want to stop. It's only that you're afraid. Well, don't be. I promise you won't be involved in this at all. Just give me three days. Three days, while you're gone—that's all I need."

"I won't go!" George shouted. "I won't leave her! I'll go to the police!"

"And just what will you tell them?" Roderick paused to let the question sink in. "Oh, that would be a fine idea, wouldn't it, going to the police? Not on your life, George. You're going out of town like a good little boy. Because this is a job for a bad little boy—like me."

He was laughing at George now, and George knew it. Any further protest on his part would be useless. Still, he might have tried to do something about it if the boss hadn't come in through the side entrance at that very moment. Roderick stood up, crossed the room, slipped out the door and was gone. And George, staring after him, realized that his last chance had gone with him.

Things seemed a little bit better that evening. Ella had had no further disturbances during the rest of the day, and as a result she was considerably calmer. By the time they had finished a makeshift supper and got ready for bed, both of them felt a trifle more reconciled to the coming separation.

Ella said she had phoned Dr. Vinson and made an appointment for Friday afternoon, two days hence. George, for his part, promised to call her faithfully every evening he was away.

"And if you need me, I'll drive right back," he told her. "I won't be much more than a hundred miles away any time during the trip. Come on now, I'll finish packing and we can get some sleep."

So they left it at that. And the next morning George was up and on the road long before Ella awakened.

He had a fairly easy day of it in Pittsville and finished his calls long before he had anticipated. Perhaps that's why he started to worry; he had nothing else to occupy his mind.

What was it Roderick had said? *What you don't know won't hurt you?*

Well, that wasn't true. Not knowing was the worst part of it. Not knowing and suspecting. Roderick had told him he had everything planned. George believed that all right. And Roderick had told him he wouldn't actually harm Ella. This part George wasn't certain about; he didn't know whether he could believe it or not. Roderick couldn't be trusted. He'd proved it by the way he'd gone ahead with the scheme despite George's protests. There was no telling what he might be capable of doing. After all, what did George know about the man? He might already be guilty of far greater crimes than the one he proposed.

George thought of Roderick with a knife, a gun, or even his bare hands. . . . And then he thought of those same bare hands ripping away a dress, fastening themselves like hungry mouths on naked flesh. And he saw his face, like the face of one of those fiends in that old copy of *Paradise Lost* with the Doré etchings, the one his mother had owned.

The thought made his hands tremble, made his voice quaver. But he forced himself to be calm as he dialed the long-distance operator from his hotel room, put through the call to the house.

And then he heard Ella's voice, and everything was all right. Everything was fine.

Yes, she could hear him. And no, nothing had happened. Nothing at all. Apparently, whoever had been playing those tricks had decided to stop. She'd been cleaning house all day. And how did he feel?

"Fine, just fine," George said. And meant it. His relief was tremendously exhilarating. He hung up, suddenly jubilant. Ella was undisturbed, and that meant Roderick had been scared off after all.

George went down to the bar for a few drinks. It was still early, and he felt like celebrating. He struck up a conversation with a leather goods salesman from Des Moines, and they hit a few of the local spots. Eventually his companion picked up a girl and wandered off. George continued on alone for quite a time, blacking out pleasantly every now and then, but always remaining under control; he liked the good feeling that came with knowing he was under control and would always behave like a little gentleman. He had the right to celebrate because he had won a victory.

Roderick had told the truth in a way; for a while George had been tempted to let the scheme go through. But he had changed his mind in time, and Roderick must have known he meant it. Now Ella was safe, and he was safe, and they'd be happy together. Ninety thousand dollars and an island in the West Indies—what a pipe dream! George Foster Pendleton wasn't that kind of a person. And now it was time to find the hotel, find his room, find the keyhole, find the bed, find the whirling darkness and the deep peace that waited within it.

The next morning George had a hangover, and he was feeling pretty rocky as he drove to Bakerton. He made a few calls around noon, but just couldn't seem to hit the ball. So in the afternoon he decided to call it quits, because he still had Friday to finish up there.

He went back to his room intending to take a late afternoon nap, but he slept right straight through. He didn't wake up to eat supper or call Ella or anything.

When he woke up the next morning, he was surprised to find that Ella had apparently called him several times; he had slept right through the rings. But he felt good, and he was out making the rounds by nine.

He called Ella immediately after supper. Her voice was relaxed and reassuring.

"Did you go to the doctor today?" he asked.

She had seen Dr. Vinson, she told him, and everything was fine. He had checked her over thoroughly—cardiograph, blood tests, even head X-rays. There was nothing wrong. He'd given her a few pills for her headaches, that was all.

"Any other disturbances?" George asked.

"No. It's been very quiet here." Ella sounded quite calm. "When are you coming in tomorrow?"

"Around noon, I hope. Right after lunch."

"Right after lunch," Ella repeated. "I'll see you."

"Good night," George said, and hung up.

He felt very happy, and yet there was something bothering him. He didn't quite know what it was, but there was an uneasy feeling, a feeling of having forgotten an important message. Like when he was a boy and his mother sent him to the store for groceries, and he couldn't remember one of the items on the list.

George sat there, holding the phone in his hand, and then he jumped when he heard the tapping on the door.

He got up and opened it and Roderick came into the room. Roderick was smiling gaily.

"Always stay at the best hotel in town, don't you?" he said. "Knew I'd find you here."

"But what—"

"Just thought I ought to take a run over," Roderick said. "You're coming back tomorrow, and I figured you'd better be prepared."

"Prepared for what?"

Roderick stood in front of the mirror and cocked his head. "I've been working hard," he told George. "But it's paid off. Like I told all I needed was three days."

George opened his mouth, but Roderick wasn't to be interrupted.

"While you've been snoozing away here, I've been up and doing," he chuckled. "No rest for the wicked, you know. Let me give you a quick rundown. Wednesday, the day you left, I made a few calls in the evening. The first one was to the savings and loan people—they're open Wednesday nights until nine, you know. I did the Ella impersonation and told them I wanted my money out as soon as I could get it. Talked to old Higgins himself. When he asked why, I told him I was planning on getting a divorce and going to Cuba."

Roderick nodded to himself and continued. "Then I went around to the house and did the mask routine again. Ella was in the kitchen, drinking a glass of milk before she got ready for bed. When she saw me I thought she was going to jump right out of her skin. She ran for the telephone, and I guess she called the police. I didn't wait to find out.

"Yesterday I figured it might be best to keep away from the house, so I went through the telephone gag again. I talked to Higgins once more and told him I needed the money at once, because you were deathly ill and had to have an operation on your brain. That was a neat touch, wasn't it?

"Then I talked to the bank, and after that I phoned a few stores and had them promise to make deliveries this morning. Just a few odds and ends—a piano, and two trombones from the Music Mart, and seventy-five dozen roses from the florist. Oh yes, as a final touch, I called Phelps Brothers and told them I wanted to stop in and look at a casket because I anticipated a death in the family."

Roderick giggled over that one, almost like a naughty little boy. But his eyes were serious as he continued.

"Finally, I called that old goat, Dr. Vinson, and told him I wanted to cancel my appointment. He couldn't quite figure out why until I told him I was leaving for Europe on a midnight flight. He wanted to know if you were going and I said no, it was a big surprise because I was going to have a baby over there and you weren't the father.

"After that, I went out to the house—but I was very careful, you understand, in case any cops should happen to be around. Lucky for me I'd anticipated them, because not only was there a prowl car parked

when I sneaked back through the alley and looked
ow, I could see this detective talking to Ella in the
f there. But it wasn't necessary to do any more. I
looked like the wrath of God. I don't imagine she'd
had any sleep two nights. And by today, word must have gotten
around. Old Higgins in savings and loan will do his share of talking.
So will Doc Vinson, and some of the others. And your wife will keep
insisting to the police that she saw this face. Now all you have to do
is go back and wrap everything up in one neat package."

"What do you mean?" George asked.

"I imagine they'll all be calling you. Your only job is to give the
right answers. Tell them that Ella *has* talked about taking a lot of crazy
trips. Tell them she wants to hide her money in the house. Tell Doc
Vinson she's afraid he wants to poison her, or attack her, or something.
You ever hear about paranoiac delusions? That's when people get the
idea that everybody's persecuting them. Build up a yarn like that. You
know what to tell Ella; she's so confused now that she'll go for anything
you say. Mix her up a little more. Ask her about things she's told you,
like trading in the Buick for a Cadillac. She'll deny she ever said anything
like that, and then you drop the subject and bring up something else.
A day or two—with a few more looks through the window at the
mask—and you'll have *her* convinced she's screwy. That's the most
important thing. Then you go to Vinson with a sob story, have her
examined while she's scared and woozy, and you've got it made."
Roderick laughed. "If you could have seen her face. . . ."

George shook his head in bewilderment. Why was Roderick lying
to him? He'd talked to Ella Wednesday night and tonight, and she'd
been quite normal. Nothing had happened, nothing at all. And yet here
was Roderick, coming a hundred miles and boasting about all kinds
of crazy stuff—

Crazy stuff.

Sudenly George knew.

Crazy stuff. A crazy scheme to drive someone crazy. It added up.

Roderick was the crazy one.

That was the answer, the real answer. He was more than cruel,
more than childish, more than antisocial. The man was psychotic, crim-
inally insane. And it was all a fantasy; he'd started to carry out his
delusions, then halted. The rest of it took place only in his disordered
imagination.

George didn't want to look at him, didn't want to hear his voice. He wanted to tell him to go away, wanted to tell him he had just talked to Ella and she was okay, nothing had happened.

But he knew that he mustn't. He couldn't. Roderick would never accept such an answer. He was crazy, and he was dangerous. There had to be some other way of handling him.

All at once, George found the obvious solution.

"I'm all through here," he said. "Thought I might drive back tonight. Want to ride along?"

Roderick nodded. "Why not?" Again the childish giggle. "I get it. You can't wait, isn't that it? Can't wait to see the look on her foolish fat face. Well, go ahead. One good thing, you won't have to look at it very much longer. They're going to put her on ice. And we'll have the sunshine. The sunshine, and the moonlight, and all the rest of it. The tropics are great stuff, George. You're going to be happy there. I know you don't like insects, but even they can come in handy. Take ants, for instance. Suppose one of these girls disobeys us, George. Well, we can tie her to a tree, see? Spread-eagle, sort of. Strip her naked and rub honey all over her. Then the ants come and . . ."

Roderick talked like that all during the drive back home. Sometimes he whispered and sometimes he giggled, and George got a splitting headache worse than anything Ella could ever have had. But still Roderick kept on talking. He was going to have Ella locked up. He was going to take George to the islands. Sometimes it even sounded as if he meant *the* island, the one where they'd been in the stockade. And he was going to do things to the girls the way the guards used to do things to the prisoners. It was crazy talk, crazy.

The only thing that kept George going was the knowledge that it *was* crazy talk, and if anyone else heard it they'd realize the truth right away. All he had to do was get Roderick into town, stall him on some pretext or other, and call in the police. Of course Roderick would try to implicate George in the scheme, but how could he? Looking back, George couldn't remember any slip-up on his part; *he* hadn't actually said or done anything out of line. No, it was all Roderick. And that was his salvation.

Still, the cold sweat was trickling down his forehead by the time he pulled up in front of the house. It must have been close to midnight, but the front-room lights were still burning. That meant Ella was up. Good.

"Wait here," George told Roderick. "I'm just going in to tell her I'm home. Then I'll put the car away."

Roderick seemed to sense that something was phony. "I shouldn't hang around," he said. "What if the cops have a stakeout?"

"Let me check on that," George said. "I've got an idea. If the cops aren't here you could give her one more taste of the rubber mask. Then I can deny seeing it. Get the pitch?"

"Yes." Roderick smiled. "Now you're cooperating, George. Now you're with it. Go ahead."

So George got out of the car and walked up to the front door and opened it.

Ella was waiting for him. She *did* look tired, and she jumped when she saw him, but she was all right. Thank God for that, she was all right! And now he could tell her.

"Don't say a word," George whispered, closing the door. "I've got a lunatic out in the car there."

"Would you mind repeating that?"

George looked around, and sure enough he recognized him. It was the detective he'd talked to after the fire alarm was turned in.

"What are you doing here this time of night?" George asked.

"Just checking up," said the detective. "Now what's all this you were saying about a lunatic?"

So George told him. George told him and he told Ella, and they both listened very quietly and calmly. George had to talk fast, because he didn't want Roderick to get suspicious, and he stumbled over some of his words. Then he asked the detective to sneak out to the car with him before Roderick could get away, and the detective said he would. George warned him that Roderick was dangerous and asked him if he had a gun. The detective had a gun, all right, and George felt better.

They walked right out to the car together and George yanked open the door.

But Roderick wasn't there.

George couldn't figure it out, and then he realized that Roderick might have been just crazy enough to pull his rubber mask trick without waiting, and he told the detective about that and made him look around under the front windows. The detective wasn't very bright; he didn't seem to understand about the mask part, so George showed him what he meant—how you could stand under the window on this board from the car and look in without leaving any footprints. The detective wanted to know what the mask looked like, but George couldn't quite describe it, and then they were back at the car and the detective opened the glove compartment and pulled something out and asked George if this was the mask he meant.

Of course it was, and George explained that Roderick must have left it there. Then they were back inside the house and Ella was crying, and George didn't want her to cry so he said there was nothing to be frightened about because Roderick was gone. And she didn't have to be afraid if somebody played tricks on her like imitating her voice because anyone could do that.

The detective asked him if he could, and of course he could do it perfectly. He was almost as good as Roderick, only he had such a splitting headache. . . .

Maybe that's why the doctor came, not Dr. Vinson but a police doctor, and he made George tell everything all over again. Until George got mad and asked why were they talking to him, the man they should be looking for was Roderick.

It was crazy, that's what it was. They were even crazier than Roderick, the way they carried on. There were more police now, and the detective was trying to tell him that he was the one who had made the calls and worn the mask. He, George! It was utterly ridiculous, and George explained how he had met Roderick on the island in solitary and how he looked like the fiend in the Doré book and everything, and how he was a bad boy.

But the detective said that George's boss had heard him talking to himself in the office the other afternoon and called Ella to tell her, and that she had talked to the police. Then when George went on his trip they'd checked up on him and found he drove back to town the night he got drunk and also the night he said he was sleeping in his hotel room, and that he was the one who had done it all.

Of course they didn't tell him this all at once—there was this trip to the station, and all those doctors who talked to him, and the lawyers and the judge. After a while, George stopped paying attention to them and to that nonsense about schizophrenia and split personalities. His head was splitting and all he wanted to do was get them to find Roderick. Roderick was the one to blame. Roderick was the crazy one. They had to understand that.

But they didn't understand that, and it was George whom they locked up. George Foster Pendleton, not George Roderick the naughty boy.

Still, George was smarter than they were, in the end. Because he found Roderick again. Even though he was locked up, he found Roderick. Or rather, Roderick found him, and came to visit.

He comes quite often, these days, moving in that quiet way of his and sneaking in when nobody's around to see him. And he talks to George in that soft, almost inaudible voice of his when George sits in front of the mirror. George isn't mad at him anymore. He realizes now that Roderick is his best friend, and wants to help him.

Roderick still dreams about getting his hands on all that money and going away with George to the Caribbean. And he has a plan. This time there won't be any slip-ups. He'll get George out of here, even if he has to kill a guard to do it. And he'll kill Ella, too, before he goes.

And then they'll travel on down to the islands, just the two of them. And there'll be girls, and whips gleaming in the moonlight. . . .

Oh, George trusts Roderick now. He's his only friend. And he often wonders just where he'd be without him.

REAR WINDOW

(1954)

REAR WINDOW
CORNELL WOOLRICH

CORNELL WOOLRICH (1903–1968) has been called "the Poe of the twentieth century" and "a master of pure suspense." He began writing in New York City in the early 1920s and over the next thirty years produced a string of short stories and novels, including *Phantom Lady* and *The Bride Wore Black,* many of which later appeared as films. Despite considerable financial and critical success, Woolrich led a lonely and unhappy life. On his motivation for writing, he once said that "it is a form of subconscious self-expression and as long as it supports me, I don't bother trying to find out what causes it."

Certainly the most famous of Cornell Woolrich's adaptations is Alfred Hitchcock's *Rear Window.* The film's protagonist, L. B. Jeffries (James Stewart) is a photographer laid up with a broken leg who busies himself by watching the activities of his neighbors through his apartment window and, in doing so, discovers a murder. The film deals with the attractions and dangers of voyeurism, and once again Hitchcock effectively manipulates his audience by making them part of the entire voyeuristic enterprise. "Of all the films I have made," said Hitchcock, "this to me is the most cinematic."

REAR WINDOW

Released: 1954
Production: Alfred Hitchcock for Paramount
Direction: Alfred Hitchcock
Screenplay: John Michael Hayes
Cinematography: Robert Burks
Editing: George Tomasini
Running Time: 112 minutes

PRINCIPAL CHARACTERS:

Jeff (L.B. Jeffries)	James Stewart
Lisa Fremont	Grace Kelly
Thomas J. Doyle	Wendell Corey
Stella	Thelma Ritter
Lars Thorwald	Raymond Burr

I didn't know their names. I'd never heard their voices. I didn't even know them by sight, strictly speaking, for their faces were too small to fill in with identifiable features at that distance. Yet I could have constructed a timetable of their comings and goings, their daily habits and activities. They were the rear-window dwellers around me.

Sure, I suppose it *was* a little bit like prying, could even have been mistaken for the fevered concentration of a Peeping Tom. That wasn't my fault, that wasn't the idea. The idea was, my movements were strictly limited just around this time. I could get from the window to the bed, and from the bed to the window, and that was all. The bay window was about the best feature my rear bedroom had in the warm weather. It was unscreened, so I had to sit with the light out or I would have had every insect in the vicinity in on me. I couldn't sleep, because I was used to getting plenty of exercise. I'd never acquired the habit of reading books to ward off boredom, so I hadn't that to turn to. Well, what should I do, sit there with my eyes tightly shuttered?

Just to pick a few at random: straight over, and the windows square, there was a young jitter-couple, kids in their teens, only just married. It would have killed them to stay home one night. They were always in such a hurry to go, wherever it was they went, they never remembered to turn out the lights. I don't think it missed once in all the time I was watching. But they never forgot altogether, either. I was to learn to call this delayed action, as you will see. He'd always come skittering madly back in about five minutes, probably from all the way down in the street, and rush around killing the switches. Then fall over something in the dark on his way out. They gave me an inward chuckle, those two.

The next house down, the windows already narrowed a little with perspective. There was a certain light in that one that always went out each night, too. Something about it, it used to make me a little sad. There was a woman living there with her child, a young widow I suppose. I'd see her put the child to bed, and then bend over and kiss her in a wistful sort of way. She'd shade the light off her and sit there painting her eyes and mouth. Then she'd go out. She'd never come back till the night was nearly spent. Once I was still up, and I looked and she was sitting there motionless with her head buried in her arms. Something about it, it used to make me a little sad.

The third one down no longer offered any insight, the windows were just slits like in a medieval battlement, due to foreshortening. That brings us around to the one on the end. In that one, frontal vision came back full-depth again, since it stood at right angles to the rest, my own included, sealing up the inner hollow all these houses backed on. I could see into it, from the rounded projection of my bay window, as freely as into a doll house with its rear wall sliced away. And scaled down to about the same size.

It was a flat building. Unlike all the rest it had been constructed originally as such, not just cut up into furnished rooms. It topped them by two stories and had rear fire escapes to show for this distinction. But it was old, evidently hadn't shown a profit. It was in the process of being modernized. Instead of clearing the entire building while the work was going on, they were doing it a flat at a time, in order to lose as little rental income as possible. Of the six rearward flats it offered to view, the topmost one had already been completed, but not yet rented. They were working on the fifth-floor one now, disturbing the peace of everyone all up and down the "inside" of the block with their hammering and sawing.

I felt sorry for the couple in the flat below. I used to wonder how they stood it with that bedlam going on above their heads. To make it worse the wife was in chronic poor health, too; I could tell that even at a distance by the listless way she moved about over there, and remained in her bathrobe without dressing. Sometimes I'd see her sitting by the window, holding her head. I used to wonder why he didn't have a doctor in to look her over, but maybe they couldn't afford it. He seemed to be out of work. Often their bedroom light was on late at night behind the drawn shade, as though she were unwell and he was sitting up with her. And one night in particular he must have had to sit up with her all night, it remained on until nearly daybreak. Not that I sat watching all that time. But the light was still burning at three in the morning, when I finally transferred from chair to bed to see if I could get a little sleep myself. And when I failed to, and hop-scotched back again around dawn, it was still peering wanly out behind the tan shade.

Moments later, with the first brightening of day, it suddenly dimmed around the edges of the shade, and then shortly afterward, not that one, but a shade in one of the other rooms—for all of them alike had been down—went up, and I saw him standing there looking out.

He was holding a cigarette in his hand. I couldn't see it, but I could tell it was that by the quick, nervous little jerks with which he kept putting his hand to his mouth, and the haze I saw rising around his head. Worried about her, I guess. I didn't blame him for that. Any husband would have been. She must have only just dropped off to sleep, after night-long suffering. And then in another hour or so, at the most, that sawing of wood and clattering of buckets was going to start in over them again. Well, it wasn't any of my business, I said to myself, but he really ought to get her out of there. If I had an ill wife on my hands. . . .

He was leaning slightly out, maybe an inch past the window frame, carefully scanning the back faces of all the houses abutting on the hollow square that lay before him. You can tell, even at a distance, when a person is looking fixedly. There's something about the way the head is held. And yet his scrutiny wasn't held fixedly to any one point, it was a slow, sweeping one, moving along the houses on the opposite side from me first. When it got to the end of them, I knew it would cross over to my side and come back along there. Before it did, I withdrew several yards inside my room, to let it go safely by. I didn't want him to think I was sitting there prying into his affairs. There was still enough blue night-shade in my room to keep my slight withdrawal from catching his eye.

When I returned to my original position a moment or two later, he was gone. He had raised two more of the shades. The bedroom one was still down. I wondered vaguely why he had given that peculiar, comprehensive, semicircular stare at all the rear windows around him. There wasn't anyone at any of them, at such an hour. It wasn't important, of course. It was just a little oddity, it failed to blend in with his being worried or disturbed about his wife. When you're worried or disturbed, that's an internal preoccupation, you stare vacantly at nothing at all. When you stare around you in a great sweeping arc at windows, that betrays external preoccupation, outward interest. One doesn't quite jibe with the other. To call such a discrepancy trifling is to add to its importance. Only someone like me, stewing in a vacuum of total idleness, would have noticed it at all.

The flat remained lifeless after that, as far as could be judged by its windows. He must have either gone out or gone to bed himself. Three of the shades remained at normal height, the one masking the bedroom remained down. Sam, my day houseman, came in not long after with my eggs and morning paper, and I had that to kill time with for awhile. I stopped thinking about other people's windows and staring at them.

The sun slanted down on one side of the hollow oblong all morning long, then it shifted over to the other side for the afternoon. Then it started to slip off both alike, and it was evening again—another day gone.

The lights started to come on around the quadrangle. Here and there a wall played back, like a sounding board, a snatch of radio program that was coming in too loud. If you listened carefully you could hear an occasional clink of dishes mixed in, faint, far off. The chain of little habits that were their lives unreeled themselves. They were all bound in them tighter than the tightest straitjacket any jailer ever devised, though they all thought themselves free. The jitterbugs made their nightly dash for the great open spaces, forgot their lights, he came careening back, thumbed them out, and their place was dark until the early morning hours. The woman put her child to bed, leaned mournfully over its cot, then sat down with heavy despair to redden her mouth.

In the fourth floor flat at right angles to the long, interior "street" the three shades had remained up, and the fourth shade had remained at full length, all day long. I hadn't been conscious of that because I hadn't particularly been looking at it, or thinking it, until now. My eyes may have rested on those windows at times, during the day, but my thoughts had been elsewhere. It was only when a light suddenly went up in the end room behind one of the raised shades, which was their kitchen, that I realized that the shades had been untouched like that all day. That also brought something else to my mind that hadn't been in it until now: I hadn't seen the woman all day. I hadn't seen any sign of life within those windows until now.

He'd come in from outside. The entrance was at the opposite side of their kitchen, away from the window. He'd left his hat on, so I knew he'd just come in from the outside.

He didn't remove his hat. As though there was no one there to remove it for any more. Instead, he pushed it farther to the back of his head by pronging a hand to the roots of his hair. That gesture didn't denote removal of perspiration, I knew. To do that a person makes a sidewise sweep—this was up over his forehead. It indicated some sort of harassment or uncertainty. Besides, if he'd been suffering from excess warmth, the first thing he would have done would be to take off his hat altogether.

She didn't come out to greet him. The first link, of the so-strong chain of habit, of custom, that binds us all, had snapped wide open.

She must be so ill she had remained in bed, in the room behind the lowered shade, all day. I watched. He remained where he was, two rooms away from there. Expectancy became surprise, surprise incomprehension. Funny, I thought, that he doesn't go in to her. Or at least go as far as the doorway, look in to see how she is.

Maybe she was asleep, and he didn't want to disturb her. Then immediately: but how can he know for sure that she's asleep, without at least looking in at her? He just came in himself.

He came forward and stood there by the window, as he had at dawn. Sam had carried out my tray quite some time before, and my lights were out. I held my ground, I knew he couldn't see me within the darkness of the bay window. He stood there motionless for several minutes. And now his attitude was the proper one for inner preoccupation. He stood there looking downward at nothing, lost in thought.

He's worried about her, I said to myself, as any man would be. It's

the most natural thing in the world. Funny, though, he should leave
her in the dark like that, without going near her. If he's worried, then
why didn't he at least look in on her on returning? Here was another
of those trivial discrepancies, between inward motivation and outward
indication. And just as I was thinking that, the original one, that I had
noted at daybreak, repeated itself. His head went up with renewed
alertness, and I could see it start to give that slow circular sweep of
interrogation around the panorama of rearward windows again. True,
the light was behind him this time, but there was enough of it falling
on him to show me the microscopic but continuous shift of direction
his head made in the process. I remained carefully immobile until the
distant glance had passed me safely by. Motion attracts.

Why is he so interested in other people's windows, I wondered
detachedly. And of course an effective brake to dwelling on that thought
too lingeringly clamped down almost at once: look who's talking. What
about you yourself?

An important difference escaped me. I wasn't worried about anything. He, presumably, was.

Down came the shades again. The lights stayed on behind their
beige opaqueness. But behind the one that had remained down all
along, the room remained dark.

Time went by. Hard to say how much—a quarter of an hour, twenty
minutes. A cricket chirped in one of the back yards. Sam came in to
see if I wanted anything before he went home for the night. I told him
no, I didn't—it was all right, run along. He stood there for a minute,
head down. Then I saw him shake it slightly, as if at something he
didn't like. "What's the matter?" I asked.

"You know what that means? My old mammy told it to me, and she
never told me a lie in her life. I never once seen it to miss, either."

"What, the cricket?"

"Any time you hear one of them things, that's a sign of death—
someplace close around."

I swept the back of my hand at him. "Well, it isn't in here, so don't
let it worry you."

He went out, muttering stubbornly: "It's somewhere close by, though.
Somewhere not very far off. Got to be."

The door closed after him, and I stayed there alone in the dark.

It was a stifling night, much closer than the one before. I could hardly get a breath of air even by the open window at which I sat. I wondered how he—that unknown over there—could stand it behind those drawn shades.

Then suddenly, just as idle speculation about this whole matter was about to alight on some fixed point in my mind, crystallize into something like suspicion, up came the shades again, and off it flitted, as formless as ever and without having had a chance to come to rest on anything.

He was in the middle windows, the living room. He'd taken off his coat and shirt, was bare-armed in his undershirt. He hadn't been able to stand it himself, I guess—the sultriness.

I couldn't make out what he was doing at first. He seemed to be busy in a perpendicular, up-and-down way rather than lengthwise. He remained in one place, but he kept dipping down out of sight and then straightening up into view again, at irregular intervals. It was almost like some sort of calisthenic exercise, except that the dips and rises weren't evenly timed enough for that. Sometimes he'd stay down a long time, sometimes he'd bob right up again, sometimes he'd go down two or three times in rapid succession. There was some sort of a widespread black V railing him off from the window. Whatever it was, there was just a sliver of it showing above the upward inclination to which the window sill deflected my line of vision. All it did was strike off the bottom of his undershirt, to the extent of a sixteenth of an inch maybe. But I hadn't seen it there at other times, and I couldn't tell what it was.

Suddenly he left it for the first time since the shades had gone up, came out around it to the outside, stooped down into another part of the room, and straightened again with an armful of what looked like varicolored pennants at the distance at which I was. He went back behind the V and allowed them to fall across the top of it for a moment, and stay that way. He made one of his dips down out of sight and stayed that way a good while.

The "pennants" slung across the V kept changing color right in front of my eyes. I have very good sight. One moment they were white, the next red, the next blue.

Then I got it. They were a woman's dresses, and he was pulling them down to him one by one, taking the topmost one each time. Suddenly they were all gone, the V was black and bare again, and his torso had reappeared. I knew what it was now, and what he was doing.

The dresses had told me. He confirmed it for me. He spread his arms to the ends of the V, I could see him heave and hitch, as if exerting pressure, and suddenly the V had folded up, become a cubed wedge. Then he made rolling motions with his whole upper body, and the wedge disappeared off to one side.

He'd been packing a trunk, packing his wife's things into a large upright trunk.

He reappeared at the kitchen window presently, stood still for a moment. I saw him draw his arm across his forehead, not once but several times, and then whip the end of it off into space. Sure, it was hot work for such a night. Then he reached up along the wall and took something down. Since it was the kitchen he was in, my imagination had to supply a cabinet and a bottle.

I could see the two or three quick passes his hand made to his mouth after that. I said to myself tolerantly: that's what nine men out of ten would do after packing a trunk—take a good stiff drink. And if the tenth didn't, it would only be because he didn't have any liquor at hand.

Then he came closer to the window again, and standing edgewise to the side of it, so that only a thin paring of his head and shoulder showed, peered watchfully out into the dark quadrilateral, along the line of windows, most of them unlighted by now, once more. He always started on the left-hand side, the side opposite mine, and made his circuit of inspection from there on around.

That was the second time in one evening I'd seen him do that. And once at daybreak, made three times altogether. I smiled mentally. You'd almost think he felt guilty about something. It was probably nothing, just an odd little habit, a quirk, that he didn't know he had himself. I had them myself, everyone does.

He withdrew into the room again, and it blacked out. His figure passed into the one that was still lighted next to it, the living room. That blacked next. It didn't surprise me that the third room, the bedroom with the drawn shade, didn't light up on his entering there. He wouldn't want to disturb her, of course—particularly if she was going away tomorrow for her health, as his packing of her trunk showed. She needed all the rest she could get, before making the trip. Simple enough for him to slip into bed in the dark.

It did surprise me, though, when a match-flare winked some time later, to have it still come from the darkened living room. He must be lying down in there, trying to sleep on a sofa or something for the night. He hadn't gone near the bedroom at all, was staying out of it altogether. That puzzled me, frankly. That was carrying solicitude almost too far.

Ten minutes or so later, there was another match-wink, still from that same living room window. He couldn't sleep.

The night brooded down on both of us alike, the curiosity-monger in the bay window, the chain-smoker in the fourth floor flat, without giving any answer. The only sound was that interminable cricket.

I was back at the window again with the first sun of morning. Not because of him. My mattress was like a bed of hot coals. Sam found me there when he came in to get things ready for me. "You're going to be a wreck, Mr. Jeff," was all he said.

First, for awhile, there was no sign of life over there. Then suddenly I saw his head bob up from somewhere down out of sight in the living room, so I knew I'd been right; he'd spent the night on a sofa or easy chair in there. Now, of course, he'd look in at her, to see how she was, find out if she felt any better. That was only common ordinary humanity. He hadn't been near her, so far as I could make out, since two nights before.

He didn't. He dressed, and he went in the opposite direction, into the kitchen, and wolfed something in there, standing up and using both hands. Then he suddenly turned and moved off side, in the direction in which I knew the flat entrance to be, as if he had just heard some summons, like the doorbell.

Sure enough, in a moment he came back, and there were two men with him in leather aprons. Expressmen. I saw him standing by while they laboriously maneuvered that cubed black wedge out between them, in the direction they'd just come from. He did more than just stand by. He practically hovered over them, kept shifting from side to side, he was so anxious to see that it was done right.

Then he came back alone, and I saw him swipe his arm across his head, as though it was he, not they, who was all heated up from the effort.

So he was forwarding her trunk, to wherever it was she was going. That was all.

He reached up along the wall again and took something down. He was taking another drink. Two. Three. I said to myself, a little at a loss: yes, but he hasn't just packed a trunk this time. That trunk has been

standing packed and ready since last night. Where does the hard work
come in? The sweat and the need for a bracer?

Now, at last, after all those hours, he finally did go in to her. I saw
his form pass through the living room and go beyond, into the bed
room. Up went the shade, that had been down all this time. Then he
turned his head and looked around behind him. In a certain way, a
way that was unmistakable, even from where I was. Not in one certain
direction, as one looks at a person. But from side to side, and up and
down, and all around, as one looks at—*an empty room*.

He stepped back, bent a little, gave a fling of his arms, and an
unoccupied mattress and bedding upended over the foot of a bed,
stayed that way, emptily curved. A second one followed a moment later.
She wasn't in there.

They use the expression "delayed action." I found out then what it
meant. For two days a sort of formless uneasiness, a disembodied
suspicion, I don't know what to call it, had been flitting and volplaning
around in my mind, like an insect looking for a landing place. More
than once, just as it had been ready to settle, some slight thing, some
slight reassuring thing, such as the raising of the shades after they had
been down unnaturally long, had been enough to keep it winging
aimlessly, prevent it from staying still long enough for me to recognize
it. The point of contact had been there all along, waiting to receive it.
Now, for some reason, within a split second after he tossed over the
empty mattresses, it landed—*zoom!* And the point of contact expanded—or exploded, whatever you care to call it—into a certainty
of murder.

In other words, the rational part of my mind was far behind the
instinctive, subconscious part. Delayed action. Now the one had caught
up to the other. The thought-message that sparked from the synchronization was: he's done something to her!

I looked down and my hand was bunching the goods over my
kneecap, it was knotted so tight. I forced it to open. I said to myself,
steadyingly: now wait a minute, be careful, go slow. You've seen nothing. You know nothing. You only have the negative proof that you don't
see her any more.

Sam was standing there looking over at me from the pantry way.
He said accusingly: "You ain't touched a thing. And your face looks
like a sheet."

It felt like one. It had that needling feeling, when the blood has left it involuntarily. It was more to get him out of the way and give myself some elbow room for undisturbed thinking, than anything else, that I said: "Sam, what's the street address of that building down there? Don't stick your head too far out and gape at it."

"Somep'n or other Benedict Avenue." He scratched his neck helpfully.

"I know that. Chase around the corner a minute and get me the exact number on it, will you?"

"Why you want to know that for?" he asked as he turned to go.

"None of your business," I said with the good-natured firmness that was all that was necessary to take care of that once and for all. I·called after him just as he was closing the door: "And while you're about it, step into the entrance and see if you can tell from the mailboxes who has the fourth floor rear. Don't get me the wrong one now. And try not to let anyone catch you at it."

He went out mumbling something that sounded like, "When a man ain't got nothing to do but just sit all day, he sure can think up the blamest things—" The door closed and I settled down to some good constructive thinking.

I said to myself: what are you really building up this monstrous supposition on? Let's see what you've got. Only that there were several little things wrong with the mechanism, the chain-belt, of their recurrent daily habits over there. 1. The lights were on all night the first night. 2. He came in later than usual the second night. 3. He left his hat on. 4. She didn't come out to greet him—she hasn't appeared since the evening before the lights were on all night. 5. He took a drink after he finished packing her trunk. But he took three stiff drinks the next morning, immediately after her trunk went out. 6. He was inwardly disturbed and worried, yet superimposed upon this was an unnatural external concern about the surrounding rear windows that was off-key. 7. He slept in the living room, didn't go near the bedroom, during the night before the departure of the trunk.

Very well. If she had been ill that first night, and he had sent her away for her health, that automatically canceled out points 1, 2, 3, 4. It left points 5 and 6 totally unimportant and unincriminating. But when it came up against 7, it hit a stumbling block.

If she went away immediately after being ill that first night, why didn't he want to sleep in their bedroom *last night?* Sentiment? Hardly. Two perfectly good beds in one room, only a sofa or uncomfortable easy chair in the other. Why should he stay out of there if she was already gone? Just because he missed her, was lonely? A grown man doesn't act that way. All right, then she was still in there.

Sam came back parenthetically at this point and said: "That house is Number 525 Benedict Avenue. The fourth floor rear, it got the name of Mr. and Mrs. Lars Thorwald up."

"Sh-h," I silenced, and motioned him backhand out of my ken.

"First he want it, then he don't," he grumbled philosophically, and retired to his duties.

I went ahead digging at it. But if she was still in there, in that bedroom last night, then she couldn't have gone away to the country, because I never saw her leave today. She could have left without my seeing her in the early hours of yesterday morning. I'd missed a few hours, been asleep. But this morning I had been up before he was himself, I only saw his head rear up from that sofa after I'd been at the window for some time.

To go at all she would have had to go yesterday morning. Then why had he left the bedroom shade down, left the mattresses undisturbed, until today? Above all, why had he stayed out of that room last night? That was evidence that she hadn't gone, was still in there. Then today, immediately after the trunk had been dispatched, he went in, pulled up the shade, tossed over the mattresses, and showed that she hadn't been in there. The thing was like a crazy spiral.

No, it wasn't either. *Immediately after the trunk had been dispatched—*

The trunk.

That did it.

I looked around to make sure the door was safely closed between Sam and me. My hand hovered uncertainly over the telephone dial a minute. Boyne, he'd be the one to tell about it. He was on Homicide. He had been, anyway, when I'd last seen him. I didn't want to get a flock of strange dicks and cops into my hair. I didn't want to be involved any more than I had to. Or at all, if possible.

They switched my call to the right place after a couple of wrong tries, and I got him finally.

"Look, Boyne? This is Hal Jeffries—"

"Well, where've you been the last sixty-two years?" he started to enthuse.

"We can take that up later. What I want you to do now is take down a name and address. Ready? Lars Thorwald. Five twenty-five Benedict Avenue. Fourth floor rear. Got it?"

"Fourth floor rear. Got it. What's it for?"

"Investigation. I've got a firm belief you'll uncover a murder there if you start digging at it. Don't call on me for anything more than that—just a conviction. There's been a man and wife living there until now. Now there's just the man. Her trunk went out early this morning. If you can find someone who saw *her* leave herself—"

Marshaled aloud like that and conveyed to somebody else, a lieutenant of detectives above all, it did sound flimsy, even to me. He said hesitantly, "Well, but—" Then he accepted it as was. Because I was the source. I even left my window out of it completely. I could do that with him and get away with it because he'd known me years, he didn't question my reliability. I didn't want my room all cluttered up with dicks and cops taking turns nosing out of the window in this hot weather. Let them tackle it from the front.

"Well, we'll see what we see," he said. "I'll keep you posted."

I hung up and sat back to watch and wait events. I had a grandstand seat. Or rather a grandstand seat in reverse. I could only see from behind the scenes, but not from the front. I couldn't watch Boyne go to work. I could only see the results, when and if there were any.

Nothing happened for the next few hours. The police work that I knew must be going on was as invisible as police work should be. The figure in the fourth floor windows over there remained in sight, alone and undisturbed. He didn't go out. He was restless, roamed from room to room without staying in one place very long, but he stayed in. Once I saw him eating again—sitting down this time—and once he shaved, and once he even tried to read the paper, but he didn't stay with it long.

Little unseen wheels were in motion around him. Small and harmless as yet, preliminaries. If he knew, I wondered to myself, would he remain there quiescent like that, or would he try to bolt out and flee? That mightn't depend so much upon his guilt as upon his sense of immunity, his feeling that he could outwit them. Of his guilt I myself was already convinced, or I wouldn't have taken the step I had.

At three my phone rang. Boyne calling back. "Jeffries? Well, I don't know. Can't you give me a little more than just a bald statement like that?"

"Why?" I fenced. "Why do I have to?"

"I've had a man over there making inquiries. I've just had his report. The building superintendent and several of the neighbors all agree she left for the country, to try and regain her health, early yesterday morning."

"Wait a minute. Did any of them *see* her leave, according to your man?"

"No."

"Then all you've gotten is a secondhand version of an unsupported statement by him. Not an eyewitness account."

"He was met returning from the depot, after he'd bought her ticket and seen her off on the train."

"That's still an unsupported statement, once removed."

"I've sent a man down there to the station to try and check with the ticket agent if possible. After all, he should have been fairly conspicuous at that early hour. And we're keeping him under observation, of course, in the meantime, watching all his movements. The first chance we get we're going to jump in and search the place."

I had a feeling that they wouldn't find anything, even if they did.

"Don't expect anything more from me. I've dropped it in your lap. I've given you all I have to give. A name, an address, and an opinion."

"Yes, and I've always valued your opinion highly before now, Jeff—"

"But now you don't, that it?"

"Not at all. The thing is, we haven't turned up anything that seems to bear out your impression so far."

"You haven't gotten very far along, so far."

He went back to his previous cliché. "Well, we'll see what we see. Let you know later."

An hour or so went by, and sunset came on. I saw him start to get ready to go out, over there. He put on his hat, put his hand in his pocket and stood still looking at it for a minute. Counting change, I guess. It gave me a peculiar sense of suppressed excitement, knowing they were going to come in the minute he left. I thought grimly, as I saw him take a last look around: if you've got anything to hide, brother, now's the time to hide it.

He left. A breath-holding interval of misleading emptiness descended on the flat. A three-alarm fire couldn't have pulled my eyes off those windows. Suddenly the door by which he had just left parted slightly and two men insinuated themselves, one behind the other. There they were now. They closed it behind them, separated at once, and got busy. One took the bedroom, one the kitchen, and they started to work their way toward one another again from those extremes of the flat. They were thorough. I could see them going over everything from top to bottom. They took the living room together. One cased one side, the other man the other.

They'd already finished before the warning caught them. I could tell that by the way they straightened up and stood facing one another frustratedly for a minute. Then both their heads turned sharply, as at a tip-off by doorbell that he was coming back. They got out fast.

I wasn't unduly disheartened, I'd expected that. My own feeling all along had been that they wouldn't find anything incriminating around. The trunk had gone.

He came in with a mountainous brown paper bag sitting in the curve of one arm. I watched him closely to see if he'd discover that someone had been there in his absence. Apparently he didn't. They'd been adroit about it.

He stayed in the rest of the night. Sat tight, safe and sound. He did some desultory drinking. I could see him sitting there by the window and his hand would hoist every once in awhile, but not to excess. Apparently everything was under control, the tension had eased, now that—the trunk was out.

Watching him across the night, I speculated: why doesn't he get out? If I'm right about him, and I am, why does he stick around—after it? That brought its own answer: because he doesn't know anyone's on to him yet. He doesn't think there's any hurry. To go too soon, right after she has, would be more dangerous than to stay awhile.

The night wore on. I sat there waiting for Boyne's call. It came later than I thought it would. I picked the phone up in the dark. He was getting ready to go to bed, over there, now. He'd risen from where he'd been sitting drinking in the kitchen, and put the light out. He went into the living room, lit that. He started to pull his shirttail up out of his belt. Boyne's voice was in my ear as my eyes were on him, over there. Three-cornered arrangement.

"Hello, Jeff? Listen, absolutely nothing. We searched the place while he was out—"

I nearly said, "I know you did, I saw it," but checked myself in time.

"—and didn't turn up a thing. But—" He stopped as though this was going to be important. I waited impatiently for him to go ahead.

"Downstairs in his letter box we found a post card waiting for him. We fished it up out of the slot with bent pins—"

"And?"

"And it was from his wife, written only yesterday from some farm upcountry. Here's the message we copied: "Arrived OK. Already feeling a little better. Love, Anna.' "

I said, faintly but stubbornly: "You say, written only yesterday. Have you proof of that? What was the postmark date on it?"

He made a disgusted sound down in his tonsils. At me, not it. "The postmark was blurred. A corner of it got wet, and the ink smudged."

"All of it blurred?"

"The year date," he admitted. "The hour and the month came out OK. August. And seven thirty P.M., it was mailed at."

This time I made the disgusted sound, in my larynx. "August, seven thirty P.M.—1937 or 1939 or 1942. You have no proof how it got into that mailbox, whether it came from a letter carrier's pouch or from the back of some bureau drawer!"

"Give up, Jeff," he said. "There's such a thing as going too far."

I don't know what I would have said. That is, if I hadn't happened to have my eyes on the Thorwald flat living room windows just then. Probably very little. The post card *had* shaken me, whether I admitted it or not. But I was looking over there. The light had gone out as soon as he'd taken his shirt off. But the bedroom didn't light up. A match flare winked from the living room, low down, as from an easy chair or sofa. With two unused beds in the bedroom, he was *still staying out of there*.

"Boyne," I said in a glassy voice. "I don't care what post cards from the other world you've turned up, I say that man has done away with his wife. Trace that trunk he shipped out. Open it up when you've located it—and I think you'll find her!"

And I hung up without waiting to hear what he was going to do about it. He didn't ring back, so I suspected he was going to give my suggestion a spin after all, in spite of his loudly proclaimed skepticism.

I stayed there by the window all night, keeping a sort of deathwatch. There were two more match flares after the first, at about half-hour intervals. Nothing more after that. So possibly he was asleep over there. Possibly not. I had to sleep some time myself, and I finally succumbed in the flaming light of the early sun. Anything that he was going to do,

he would have done under cover of darkness and not waited for broad
daylight. There wouldn't be anything much to watch, for a while now.
And what was there that he needed to do any more, anyway? Nothing,
just sit tight and let a little disarming time slip by.

It seemed like five minutes later that Sam came over and touched
me, but it was already high noon. I said irritably: "Didn't you lamp that
note I pinned up, for you to let me sleep?"

He said: "Yeah, but it's your old friend Inspector Boyne. I figured
you'd sure want to—"

It was a personal visit this time. Boyne came into the room behind
him without waiting, and without much cordiality.

I said to get rid of Sam: "Go inside and smack a couple of eggs
together."

Boyne began in a galvanized-iron voice: "Jeff, what do you mean by
doing anything like this to me? I've made a fool out of myself, thanks
to you. Sending my men out right and left on wild goose chases. Thank
God, I didn't put my foot in it any worse than I did, and have this guy
picked up and brought in for questioning."

"Oh, then you don't think that's necessary?" I suggested, drily.

The look he gave me took care of that. "I'm not alone in the department, you know. There are men over me I'm accountable to for
my actions. That looks great, don't it, sending one of my fellows one-
half-a-day's train ride up into the sticks to some Godforsaken whis-
tlestop or other at departmental expense—"

"Then you located the trunk?"

"We traced it through the express agency," he said flintily.

"And you opened it?"

"We did better than that. We got in touch with the various farmhouses in the immediate locality, and Mrs. Thorwald came down to
the junction in a produce truck from one of them and opened it for
him herself, with her own keys!"

Very few men have ever gotten a look from an old friend such as
I got from him. At the door he said, stiff as a rifle barrel: "Just let's
forget all about it, shall we? That's about the kindest thing either one
of us can do for the other. You're not yourself, and I'm out a little of
my own pocket money, time, and temper. Let's let it go at that. If you
want to telephone me in the future I'll be glad to give you my home
number."

The door went *whopp!* behind him.

For about ten minutes after he stormed out my numbed mind was in a sort of straitjacket. Then it started to wriggle its way free. The hell with the police. I can't prove it to them, maybe, but I can prove it to myself, one way or the other, once and for all. Either I'm wrong or I'm right. He's got his armor on against them. But his back is naked and unprotected against me.

I called Sam in. "Whatever became of that spyglass we used to have, when we were bumming around on that cabin cruiser that season?"

He found it some place downstairs and came in with it, blowing on it and rubbing it along his sleeve. I let it lie idle in my lap first. I took a piece of paper and a pencil and wrote six words on it: *What have you done with her?*

I sealed it in an envelope and left the envelope blank. I said to Sam: "Now here's what I want you to do, and I want you to be slick about it. You take this, go in that building 525, climb the stairs to the fourth floor rear, and ease it under the door. You're fast, at least you used to be. Let's see if you're fast enough to keep from being caught at it. Then when you get safely down again, give the outside doorbell a little poke, to attract attention.

His mouth started to open.

"And don't ask me any questions, you understand? I'm not fooling."

He went, and I got the spyglass ready.

I got him in the right focus after a minute or two. A face leaped up, and I was really seeing him for the first time. Dark-haired, but unmistakable Scandinavian ancestry. Looked like a sinewy customer, although he didn't run to much bulk.

About five minutes went by. His head turned sharply, profilewards. That was the bell-poke, right there. The note must be in already.

He gave me the back of his head as he went back toward the flat door. The lens could follow him all the way to the rear, where my unaided eyes hadn't been able to before.

He opened the door first, missed seeing it, looked out on a level. He closed it. Then he dipped, straightened up. He had it. I could see him turning it this way and that.

He shifted in, away from the door, nearer the window. He thought danger lay near the door, safety away from it. He didn't know it was the other way around, the deeper into his own rooms he retreated the greater the danger.

He'd torn it open, he was reading it. God, how I watched his expression. My eyes clung to it like leeches. There was a sudden widening, a pulling—the whole skin of his face seemed to stretch back behind the ears, narrowing his eyes to Mongoloids. Shock. Panic. His hand pushed out and found the wall, and he braced himself with it. Then he went back toward the door again slowly. I could see him creeping up on it, stalking it as though it were something alive. He opened it so slenderly you couldn't see it at all, peered fearfully through the crack. Then he closed it, and he came back, zigzag, off balance from sheer reflex dismay. He toppled into a chair and snatched up a drink. Out of the bottle neck itself this time. And even while he was holding it to his lips, his head was turned looking over his shoulder at the door that had suddenly thrown his secret in his face.

I put the glass down.

Guilty! Guilty as all hell, and the police be damned!

My hand started toward the phone, came back again. What was the use? They wouldn't listen now any more than they had before. "You should have seen his face, etc." And I could hear Boyne's answer: "Anyone gets a jolt from an anonymous letter, true or false. You would yourself." They had a real live Mrs. Thorwald to show me—or thought they had. I'd have to show them the dead one, to prove that they both weren't one and the same. I, from my window, had to show them a body.

Well, he'd have to show me first.

It took hours before I got it. I kept pegging away at it, pegging away at it, while the afternoon wore away. Meanwhile he was pacing back and forth there like a caged panther. Two minds with but one thought, turned inside-out in my case. How to keep it hidden, how to see that it wasn't kept hidden.

I was afraid he might try to light out, but if he intended doing that he was going to wait until after dark, apparently, so I had a little time yet. Possibly he didn't want to himself, unless he was driven to it—still felt that it was more dangerous than to stay.

The customary sights and sounds around me went on unnoticed, while the main stream of my thoughts pounded like a torrent against that one obstacle stubbornly damming them up: how to get him to give the location away to me, so that I could give it away in turn to the police.

I was dimly conscious, I remember, of the landlord or somebody bringing a prospective tenant to look at the sixth floor apartment, the one that had already been finished. This was two over Thorwald's; they were still at work on the in-between one. At one point an odd little bit of synchronization, completely accidental of course, cropped up. Landlord and tenant both happened to be near the living room windows on the sixth at the same moment that Thorwald was near those on the fourth. Both parties moved onward simultaneously into the kitchen from there, and, passing the blind spot of the wall, appeared next at the kitchen windows. It was uncanny, they were almost like precision-strollers or puppets manipulated on one and the same string. It probably wouldn't have happened again just like that in another fifty years. Immediately afterwards they digressed, never to repeat themselves like that again.

The thing was, something about it had disturbed me. There had been some slight flaw or hitch to mar its smoothness. I tried for a moment or two to figure out what it had been, and couldn't. The landlord and tenant had gone now, and only Thorwald was in sight. My unaided memory wasn't enough to recapture it for me. My eyesight might have if it had been repeated, but it wasn't.

It sank into my subconscious, to ferment there like yeast, while I went back to the main problem at hand.

I got it finally. It was well after dark, but I finally hit on a way. It mightn't work, it was cumbersome and roundabout, but it was the only way I could think of. An alarmed turn of the head, a quick precautionary step in one certain direction, was all I needed. And to get this brief, flickering, transitory give-away, I needed two phone calls and an absence of about half an hour on his part between them.

I leafed a directory by matchlight until I'd found what I wanted: *Thorwald, Lars. 525 Bndct.... SWansea 5-2114.*

I blew out the match, picked up the phone in the dark. It was like television. I could see to the other end of my call, only not along the wire but by a direct channel of vision from window to window.

He said "Hullo?" gruffly.

I thought: how strange this is. I've been accusing him of murder for three days straight, and only now I'm hearing his voice for the first time.

I didn't try to disguise my own voice. After all, he'd never see me and I'd never see him. I said: "You got my note?"

He said guardedly: "Who is this?"

"Just somebody who happens to know."

He said craftily: "Know what?"

"Know what you know. You and I, we're the only ones."

He controlled himself well. I didn't hear a sound. But he didn't know he was open another way too. I had the glass balanced there at proper height on two large books on the sill. Through the window I saw him pull open the collar of his shirt as though its stricture was intolerable. Then he backed his hand over his eyes like you do when there's a light blinding you.

His voice came back firmly. "I don't know what you're talking about."

"Business, that's what I'm talking about. It should be worth something to me, shouldn't it? To keep it from going any further." I wanted to keep him from catching on that it was the windows. I still needed them, I needed them now more than ever. "You weren't very careful about your door the other night. Or maybe the draft swung it open a little."

That hit him where he lived. Even the stomach-heave reached me over the wire. "You didn't see anything. There wasn't anything to see."

"That's up to you. Why should I go to the police?" I coughed a little. "If it would pay me not to."

"Oh," he said. And there was relief of a sort in it. "D'you want to— see me? Is that it?"

"That would be the best way, wouldn't it? How much can you bring with you for now?"

"I've only got about seventy dollars around here."

"All right, then we can arrange the rest for later. Do you know where Lakeside Park is? I'm near there now. Suppose we make it there." That was about thirty minutes away. Fifteen there and fifteen back. "There's a little pavilion as you go in."

"How many of you are there?" he asked cautiously.

"Just me. It pays to keep things to yourself. That way you don't have to divvy up."

He seemed to like that too. "I'll take a run out," he said, "just to see what it's all about."

I watched him more closely than ever, after he'd hung up. He flitted straight through to the end room, the bedroom, that he didn't go near any more. He disappeared into a clothes closet in there, stayed a minute, came out again. He must have taken something out of a hidden cranny or niche in there that even the dicks had missed. I could tell by the piston-like motion of his hand, just before it disappeared inside his coat, what it was. A gun.

It's a good thing, I thought, I'm not out there in Lakeside Park waiting for my seventy dollars.

The place blacked and he was on his way.

I called Sam in. "I want you to do something for me that's a little risky. In fact, damn risky. You might break a leg, or you might get shot, or you might even get pinched. We've been together ten years, and I wouldn't ask you anything like that if I could do it myself. But I can't, and it's got to be done." Then I told him. "Go out the back way, cross the back yard fences, and see if you can get into that fourth floor flat up the fire escape. He's left one of the windows down a little from the top."

"What do you want me to look for?"

"Nothing." The police had been there already, so what was the good of that? "There are three rooms over there. I want you to disturb everything just a little bit, in all three, to show someone's been in there. Turn up the edge of each rug a little, shift every chair and table around a little, leave the closet doors standing out. Don't pass up a thing. Here, keep your eyes on this." I took off my own wrist watch, strapped it on him. "You've got twenty-five minutes, starting from now. If you stay within those twenty-five minutes, nothing will happen to you. When you see they're up, don't wait any longer, get out and get out fast."

"Climb back down?"

"No." He wouldn't remember, in his excitement, if he'd left the windows up or not. And I didn't want him to connect danger with the back of his place, but with the front. I wanted to keep my own window out of it. "Latch the window down tight, let yourself out the door, and beat it out of the building the front way, for your life!"

"I'm just an easy mark for you," he said ruefully, but he went.

He came out through our own basement door below me, and scrambled over the fences. If anyone had challenged him from one of the surrounding windows, I was going to backstop for him, explain I'd sent him down to look for something. But no one did. He made it pretty good for anyone his age. He isn't so young any more. Even the fire escape backing the flat, which was drawn up short, he managed to contact by standing up on something. He got in, lit the light, looked over at me. I motioned him to go ahead, not weaken.

I watched him at it. There wasn't any way I could protect him, now that he was in there. Even Thorwald would be within his rights in shooting him down—this was break and entry. I had to stay in back behind the scenes, like I had been all along. I couldn't get out in front of him as a lookout and shield him. Even the dicks had had a lookout pistol.

He must have been tense, doing it. I was twice as tense, watching him do it. The twenty-five minutes took fifty to go by. Finally he came over to the window, latched it fast. The lights went, and he was out. He'd made it. I blew out a bellyful of breath that was twenty-five minutes old.

I heard him keying the street door, and when he came up I said warningly: "Leave the light out in here. Go and build yourself a great big two story whisky punch; you're as close to white as you'll ever be."

Thorwald came back twenty-nine minutes after he'd left for Lakeside Park. A pretty slim margin to hang a man's life on. So now for the finale of the long-winded business, and here was hoping. I got my second phone call in before he had time to notice anything amiss. It was tricky timing but I'd been sitting there with the receiver ready in my hand, dialing the number over and over, then killing it each time. He came in on the 2 of 5-2114, and I saved that much time. The ring started before his hand came away from the light switch.

This was the one that was going to tell the story.

"You were supposed to bring money, not a gun; that's why I didn't show up." I saw the jolt that threw into him. The window still had to stay out of it. "I saw you tap the inside of your coat, where you had it, as you came out on the street." Maybe he hadn't, but he wouldn't remember by now whether he had or not. You usually do when you're packing a gun and aren't an habitual carrier.

"Too bad you had your trip out and back for nothing. I didn't waste my time while you were gone, though. I know more now than I knew before." This was the important part. I had the glass up and I was practically fluoroscoping him. "I've found out where—it is. You know what I mean. I know now where you've got—it. I was there while you were out."

Not a word. Just quick breathing.

"Don't you believe me? Look around. Put the receiver down and take a look for yourself. I found it."

He put it down, moved as far as the living room entrance, and touched off the lights. He just looked around him once, in a sweeping, all-embracing stare, that didn't come to a head on any one fixed point, didn't center at all.

He was smilng grimly when he came back to the phone. All he said, softly and with malignant satisfaction, was: "You're a liar."

Then I saw him lay the receiver down and take his hand off it. I hung up at my end.

The test had failed. And yet it hadn't. He hadn't given the location away as I'd hoped he would. And yet that "You're a liar" was a tacit admission that it was there to be found, somewhere around him, somewhere on those premises. In such a good place that he didn't have to worry about it, didn't even have to look to make sure.

So there was a kind of sterile victory in my defeat. But it wasn't worth a damn to me.

He was standing there with his back to me, and I couldn't see what he was doing. I knew the phone was somewhere in front of him, but I thought he was just standing there pensive behind it. His head was slightly lowered, that was all. I'd hung up at my end. I didn't even see his elbow move. And if his index finger did, I couldn't see it.

He stood like that a moment or two, then finally he moved aside. The lights went out over there; I lost him. He was careful not even to strike matches, like he sometimes did in the dark.

My mind no longer distracted by having him to look at, I turned to trying to recapture something else—that troublesome little hitch in synchronization that had occurred this afternoon, when the renting agent and he both moved simultaneously from one window to the next. The closest I could get was this: it was like when you're looking at someone through a pane of imperfect glass, and a flaw in the glass distorts the symmetry of the reflected image for a second, until it has gone on past that point. Yet that wouldn't do, that was not it. The windows had been open and there had been no glass between. And I hadn't been using the lens at the time.

My phone rang. Boyne, I supposed. It wouldn't be anyone else at this hour. Maybe, after reflecting on the way he'd jumped all over me—I said "Hello" unguardedly, in my own normal voice.

There wasn't any answer.

I said: "Hello? Hello? Hello?" I kept giving away samples of my voice. There wasn't a sound from first to last.

I hung up finally. It was still dark over there, I noticed.

Sam looked in to check out. He was a bit thick-tongued from his restorative drink. He said something about "Awri' if I go now?" I half heard him. I was trying to figure out another way of trapping *him* over there into giving away the right spot. I motioned my consent absently.

He went a little unsteadily down the stairs to the ground floor and after a delaying moment or two I heard the street door close after him. Poor Sam, he wasn't much used to liquor.

I was left alone in the house, one chair the limit of my freedom of movement.

Suddenly a light went on over there again, just momentarily, to go right out again afterwards. He must have needed it for something, to locate something that he had already been looking for and found he wasn't able to put his hands on readily without it. He found it, whatever it was, almost immediately, and moved back at once to put the lights out again. As he turned to do so, I saw him give a glance out the window. He didn't come to the window to do it, he just shot it out in passing.

Something about it struck me as different from any of the others I'd seen him give in all the time I'd been watching him. If you can qualify such an elusive thing as a glance, I would have termed it a glance with a purpose. It was certainly anything but vacant or random, it had a bright spark of fixity in it. It wasn't one of those precautionary sweeps I'd seen him give, either. It hadn't started over on the other side and worked its way around to my side, the right. It had hit dead-center at my bay window, for just a split second while it lasted, and then was gone again. And the lights were gone, and he was gone.

Sometimes your senses take things in without your mind translating them into their proper meaning. My eyes saw that look. My mind refused to smelter it properly. "It was meaningless," I thought. "An unintentional bull's-eye, that just happened to hit square over here, as he went toward the lights on his way out."

Delayed action. A wordless ring of the phone. To test a voice? A period of bated darkness following that, in which two could have played at the same game—stalking one another's window-squares, unseen. A last-moment flicker of the lights, that was bad strategy but unavoidable. A parting glance, radioactive with malignant intention. All these things sank in without fusing. My eyes did their job, it was my mind that didn't—or at least took its time about it.

Seconds went by in packages of sixty. It was very still around the familiar quadrangle formed by the back of the houses. Sort of a breathless stillness. And then a sound came into it, starting up from nowhere, nothing. The unmistakable, spaced clicking a cricket makes in the silence of the night. I thought of Sam's superstition about them, that he claimed had never failed to fulfill itself yet. If that was the case, it looked bad for somebody in one of these slumbering houses around here—

Sam had been gone only about ten minutes. And now he was back again, he must have forgotten something. That drink was responsible. Maybe his hat, or maybe even the key to his own quarters uptown. He knew I couldn't come down and let him in, and he was trying to be quiet about it, thinking perhaps I'd dozed off. All I could hear was this faint jiggling down at the lock of the front door. It was one of those old-fashioned stoop houses, with an outer pair of storm doors that were allowed to swing free all night, and then a small vestibule, and then the inner door, worked by a simple iron key. The liquor had made his hand a little unreliable, although he'd had this difficulty once or twice before, even without it. A match would have helped him find the keyhole quicker, but then, Sam doesn't smoke. I knew he wasn't likely to have one on him.

The sound had stopped now. He must have given up, gone away again, decided to let whatever it was go until tomorrow. He hadn't gotten in, because I knew his noisy way of letting doors coast shut by themselves too well, and there hadn't been any sound of that sort, that loose slap he always made.

Then suddenly it exploded. Why at this particular moment, I don't know. That was some mystery of the inner workings of my own mind. It flashed like waiting gunpowder which a spark has finally reached along a slow train. Drove all thoughts of Sam, and the front door, and this and that completely out of my head. It had been waiting there since midafternoon today, and only now—more of that delayed action. Damn that delayed action.

The renting agent and Thorwald had both started even from the living room window. An intervening gap of blind wall, and both had reappeared at the kitchen window, still one above the other. But some sort of a hitch or flaw or jump had taken place, right there, that bothered me. The eye is a reliable surveyor. There wasn't anything the matter with their timing, it was with their parallel-ness, or whatever the word is. The hitch had been vertical, not horizontal. There had been an upward "jump."

Now I had it, now I knew. And it couldn't wait. It was too good. They wanted a body? Now I had one for them.

Sore or not, Boyne would *have* to listen to me now. I didn't waste any time, I dialed his precinct house then and there in the dark, working the slots in my lap by memory alone. They didn't make much noise going around, just a light click. Not even as distinct as that cricket out there—

"He went home long ago," the desk sergeant said.

This couldn't wait. "All right, give me his home phone number."

He took a minute, came back again. "Trafalgar," he said. Then nothing more.

"Well? Trafalgar what?" Not a sound.

"Hello? Hello?" I tapped it. "Operator, I've been cut off. Give me that party again." I couldn't get her either.

I hadn't been cut off. My wire had been cut. That had been too sudden, right in the middle of—and to be cut like that it would have to be done somewhere right here inside the house with me. Outside it went underground.

Delayed action. This time final, fatal, altogether too late. A voiceless ring of the phone. A direction-finder of a look from over there. "Sam" seemingly trying to get back in a while ago.

Surely, death was somewhere inside the house here with me. And I couldn't move, I couldn't get up out of this chair. Even if I had gotten through to Boyne just now, that would have been too late. There wasn't time enough now for one of those camera-finishes in this. I could have shouted out the window to that gallery of sleeping rear window neighbors around me, I supposed. It would have brought them to the windows. It couldn't have brought them over here in time. By the time they had even figured which particular house it was coming from, it would stop again, be over with. I didn't open my mouth. Not because I was brave, but because it was so obviously useless.

He'd be up in a minute. He must be on the stairs now, although I couldn't hear him. Not even a creak. A creak would have been a relief, would have placed him. This was like being shut up in the dark with the silence of a gliding, coiling cobra somewhere around you.

There wasn't a weapon in the place with me. There were books there on the wall, in the dark, within reach. Me, who never read. The former owner's books. There was a bust of Rousseau or Montesquieu, I'd never been able to decide which, one of those gents with flowing manes, topping them. It was a monstrosity, bisque clay, but it too dated from before my occupancy.

I arched my middle upward from the chair seat and clawed desperately up at it. Twice my fingertips slipped off it, then at the third raking I got it to teeter, and the fourth brought it down into my lap, pushing me down into the chair. There was a steamer rug under me. I didn't need it around me in this weather, I'd been using it to soften the seat of the chair. I tugged it out from under and mantled it around me like an Indian brave's blanket. Then I squirmed far down in the chair, let my head and one shoulder dangle out over the arm, on the side next to the wall. I hoisted the bust to my other, upward shoulder, balanced it there precariously for a second head, blanket tucked around its ears. From the back, in the dark, it would look—I hoped—

I proceeded to breathe adenoidally, like someone in heavy upright sleep. It wasn't hard. My own breath was coming nearly that labored anyway, from tension.

He was good with knobs and hinges and things. I never heard the door open, and this one, unlike the one downstairs, was right behind me. A little eddy of air puffed through the dark at me. I could feel it because my scalp, the real one, was all wet at the roots of the hair right then.

If it was going to be a knife or head-blow, the dodge might give me a second chance, that was the most I could hope for, I knew. My arms and shoulders are hefty. I'd bring him down on me in a bear hug after the first slash or drive, and break his neck or collarbone against me. If it was going to be a gun, he'd get me anyway in the end. A difference of a few seconds. He had a gun, I knew, that he was going to use on me in the open, over at Lakeside Park. I was hoping that here, indoors, in order to make his own escape more practicable—

Time was up.

The flash of the shot lit up the room for a second, it was so dark. Or at least the corners of it, like flickering, weak lightning. The bust bounced on my shoulder and disintegrated into chunks.

I thought he was jumping up and down on the floor for a minute

with frustrated rage. Then when I saw him dart by me and lean over
the window sill to look for a way out, the sound transferred itself
rearwards and downwards, became a pummeling with hoof and hip
at the street door. The camera-finish after all. But he still could have
killed me five times.

I flung my body down into the narrow crevice between chair arm
and wall, but my legs were still up, and so was my head and that one
shoulder.

He whirled, fired at me so close that it was like looking a sunrise
in the face. I didn't feel it, so—it hadn't hit.

"You—" I heard him grunt to himself. I think it was the last thing
he said. The rest of his life was all action, not verbal.

He flung over the sill on one arm and dropped into the yard. Two
story drop. He made it because he missed the cement, landed on the
sod strip in the middle. I jacked myself up over the chair arm and
flung myself bodily forward at the window, nearly hitting it chin first.

He went all right. When life depends on it, you go. He took the first
fence, rolled over that bellywards. He went over the second like a cat,
hands and feet pointed together in a spring. Then he was back in the
rear yard of his own building. He got up on something, just about like
Sam had— The rest was all footwork, with quick little corkscrew twists
at each landing stage. Sam had latched his windows down when he
was over there, but he'd reopened one of them for ventilation on his
return. His whole life depended now on that casual, unthinking little
act—

Second, third. He was up to his own windows. He'd made it. Something went wrong. He veered out away from them in another pretzel-
twist, flashed up toward the fifth, the one above. Something sparked
in the darkness of one of his own windows where he'd been just now,
and a shot thudded heavily out around the quadrangle-enclosure like
a big bass drum.

He passed the fifth, the sixth, got up to the roof. He'd made it a
second time. Gee, he loved life! The guys in his own windows couldn't
get him, he was over them in a straight line and there was too much
fire escape interlacing in the way.

I was too busy watching him to watch what was going on around
me. Suddenly Boyne was next to me, sighting. I heard him mutter: "I
almost hate to do this, he's got to fall so far."

He was balanced on the roof parapet up there, with a star right over his head. An unlucky star. He stayed a minute too long, trying to kill before he was killed. Or maybe he was killed, and knew it.

A shot cracked, high up against the sky, the window pane flew apart all over the two of us, and one of the books snapped right behind me.

Boyne didn't say anything more about hating to do it. My face was pressing outward against his arm. The recoil of his elbow jarred my teeth. I blew a clearing through the smoke to watch him go.

It was pretty horrible. He took a minute to show anything, standing up there on the parapet. Then he let his gun go, as if to say: "I won't need this any more." Then he went after it. He missed the fire escape entirely, came all the way down on the outside. He landed so far out he hit one of the projecting planks, down there out of sight. It bounced his body up, like a springboard. Then it landed again—for good. And that was all.

I said to Boyne: "I got it. I got it finally. The fifth floor flat, the one over his, that they're still working on. The cement kitchen floor, raised above the level of the other rooms. They wanted to comply with the fire laws and also obtain a dropped living room effect, as cheaply as possible. Dig it up—"

He went right over then and there, down through the basement and over the fences, to save time. The electricity wasn't turned on yet in that one, they had to use their torches. It didn't take them long at that, once they'd got started. In about half an hour he came to the window and wigwagged over for my benefit. It meant yes.

He didn't come over until nearly eight in the morning; after they'd tidied up and taken them away. Both away, the hot dead and the cold dead. He said: "Jeff, I take it all back. That damn fool that I sent up there about the trunk—well, it wasn't his fault, in a way. I'm to blame. He didn't have orders to check on the woman's description, only on the contents of the trunk. He came back and touched on it in a general way. I go home and I'm in bed already, and suddenly pop! into my brain—one of the tenants I questioned two whole days ago had given us a few details and they didn't tally with his on several important points. Talk about being slow to catch on!"

"I've had that all the way through this damn thing," I admitted ruefully. "I call it delayed action. It nearly killed me."

"I'm a police officer and you're not."

"That how you happened to shine at the right time?"

"Sure. We came over to pick him up for questioning. I left them planted there when we saw he wasn't in, and came on over here by myself to square it up with you while we were waiting. How did you happen to hit on that cement floor?"

I told him about the freak synchronization. "The renting agent showed up taller at the kitchen window in proportion to Thorwald, than he had been a moment before when both were at the living room windows together. It was no secret that they were putting in cement floors, topped by a cork composition, and raising them considerably. But it took on new meaning. Since the top floor one has been finished for some time, it had to be the fifth. Here's the way I have it lined up, just in theory. She's been in ill health for years, and he's been out of work, and he got sick of that and of her both. Met this other—"

"She'll be here later today, they're bringing her down under arrest."

"He probably insured her for all he could get, and then started to poison her slowly, trying not to leave any trace. I imagine—and remember, this is pure conjecture—she caught him at it that night the light was on all night. Caught on in some way, or caught him in the act. He lost his head, and did the very thing he had wanted all along to avoid doing. Killed her by violence—strangulation or a blow. The rest had to be hastily improvised. He got a better break than he deserved at that. He thought of the apartment upstairs, went up and looked around. They'd just finished laying the floor, the cement hadn't hardened yet, and the materials were still around. He gouged a trough out of it just wide enough to take her body, put her in it, mixed fresh cement and recemented over her, possibly raising the general level of the flooring an inch or two so that she'd be safely covered. A permanent, odorless coffin. Next day the workmen came back, laid down the cork surfacing on top of it without noticing anything, I suppose he'd used one of their own trowels to smooth it. Then he sent his accessory upstate fast, near where his wife had been several summers before, but to a different farmhouse where she wouldn't be recognized, along with the trunk keys. Sent the trunk up after her, and dropped himself an already used post card into his mailbox, with the year date blurred. In a week or two she would have probably committed 'suicide' up there as Mrs. Anna Thorwald. Despondency due to ill health. Written him a farewell note and left her clothes beside some body of deep water. It was risky, but they might have succeeded in collecting the insurance at that."

By nine Boyne and the rest had gone. I was still sitting there in the chair, too keyed up to sleep. Sam came in and said: "Here's Doc Preston."

He showed up rubbing his hands, in that way he has. "Guess we can take that cast off your leg now. You must be tired of sitting there all day doing nothing."

STAGECOACH

(1939)

STAGE TO LORDSBURG
ERNEST HAYCOX

If there is a single cinematic genre that can be considered uniquely American, it is most surely the Western. A groundbreaking classic of the genre, *Stagecoach* is an historical landmark for a number of reasons. It firmly established the careers of John Wayne as the archetypal cowboy actor and of director John Ford as the premier practitioner of the form. Most importantly, however, it raised the Western from its previous 'B'-grade status, replete with good guy vs. bad guy stock formulations, to the level of serious, mature film. Instead of using stereotypes like singing cowboys and one-dimensional action heroes, *Stagecoach* contained a wide variety of real characters that evinced depth and qualities well beyond their proscribed types. The film relates the stories of eight characters brought together on a stagecoach journey through the American Southwest which, during the 1870s, was terrorized by marauding Apaches. The individual subplots intertwine and finally merge in a climactic Indian attack. Because of its panoramic landscapes and diversified performances, *Stagecoach* has been called "a 'Grand Hotel' on wheels." Later memorable John Ford Westerns include *Fort Apache* (1948), *She Wore a Yellow Ribbon* (1949), and *The Man Who Shot Liberty Valance* (1962).

Although John Ford once cited Guy de Maupassant's story, "Boule-de-Suif," as the inspiration for *Stagecoach,* it was really the following story by ERNEST HAYCOX (1899–1950) that scriptwriter Dudley Nichols drew on as the basis for his script. Born in Portland, Oregon, Haycox wrote over twenty novels and hundreds of short stories. Perhaps because of his unswerving devotion to Western fiction, Haycox has never received widespread literary attention and this, in the words of one critic, ranks him "among the most seriously underrated of contemporary novelists." Haycox once wrote, "To me, some little faded town sitting out on the Nebraska sand hills . . . nourishing the memory of a more robust career, is more valid than any great city."

STAGECOACH

Released: 1939
Production: John Ford and Walter Wanger for United Artists
Direction: John Ford
Screenplay: Dudley Nichols
Cinematography: Bert Glennon
Editing: Dorothy Spencer and Walter Reynolds
Art direction: Alexander Toluboff
Costume design: Walter Plunkett
Music: Richard Hageman, Franke Harling, John Leipold, Leo Shuken
    (Academy Award)
Running time: 96 minutes

PRINCIPAL CHARACTERS:

Ringo Kid	John Wayne
Dallas	Claire Trevor
Doc Boone	Thomas Mitchell (Academy Award)
Buck	Andy Devine
Curly Wilcox	George Bancroft
Mr. Peacock	Donald Meek
Lucy Mallory	Louise Platt
Hatfield	John Carradine
Mr. Gatewood	Berton Churchill
Lieutenant Blanchard	Tim Holt
Luke Plummer	Tom Tyler
Ike Plummer	Joe Rickson

This was one of those years in the Territory when Apache smoke signals spiraled up from the stony mountain summits and many a ranch cabin lay as a square of blackened ashes on the ground and the departure of a stage from Tonto was the beginning of an adventure that had no certain happy ending. . . .

The stage and its six horses waited in front of Weilner's store on the north side of Tonto's square. Happy Stuart was on the box, the ribbons between his fingers and one foot teetering on the brake. John Strang rode shotgun guard and an escort of ten cavalrymen waited behind the coach, half asleep in their saddles.

At four-thirty in the morning this high air was quite cold, though the sun had begun to flush the sky eastward. A small crowd stood in the square, presenting their final messages to the passengers now entering the coach. There was a girl going down to marry an infantry officer, a whisky drummer from St. Louis, an Englishman all length and bony corners and bearing with him an enormous sporting rifle, a gambler, a solid-shouldered cattleman on his way to New Mexico and a blond man upon whom both Happy Stuart and the shotgun guard placed a narrow-eyed interest.

This seemed all until the blond man drew back from the coach door; and then a girl known commonly throughout the Territory as Henriette came quietly from the crowd. She was small and quiet, with a touch of paleness in her cheeks and her quite dark eyes lifted at the blond man's unexpected courtesy, showing surprise. There was this moment of delay and then the girl caught up her dress and stepped into the coach.

Men in the crowd were smiling but the blond one turned, his motion like the swift cut of a knife, and his attention covered that group until the smiling quit. He was tall, hollow-flanked, and definitely stamped by the guns slung low on his hips. But it wasn't the guns alone; something in his face, so watchful and so smooth, also showed his trade. Afterwards he got into the coach and slammed the door.

Happy Stuart kicked off the brakes and yelled, "Hi!" Tonto's people were calling out their last farewells and the six horses broke into a trot and the stage lunged on its fore and aft springs and rolled from town with dust dripping off its wheels like water, the cavalrymen trotting briskly behind. So they tipped down the long grade, bound on a journey no stage had attempted during the last forty-five days. Out below in the desert's distance stood the relay stations they hoped to reach and pass. Between lay a country swept empty by the quick raids of Geronimo's men.

The Englishman, the gambler, and the blond man sat jammed together in the forward seat, riding backward to the course of the stage. The drummer and the cattleman occupied the uncomfortable middle bench; the two women shared the rear seat. The cattleman faced Henriette, his knees almost touching her. He had one arm hooked over the door's window sill to steady himself. A huge gold nugget slid gently back and forth along the watch chain slung across his wide chest and a chunk of black hair lay below his hat. His eyes considered Henriette, reading something in the girl that caused him to show her a deliberate smile. Henriette dropped her glance to the gloved tips of her fingers, cheeks unstirred.

They were all strangers packed closely together, with nothing in common save a destination. Yet the cattleman's smile and the boldness of his glance were something as audible as speech, noted by everyone except the Englishman, who sat bolt upright with his stony indifference. The army girl, tall and calmly pretty, threw a quick side glance at Henriette and afterwards looked away with a touch of color. The gambler saw this interchange of glances and showed the cattleman an irritated attention. The whisky drummer's eyes narrowed a little and some inward cynicism made a faint change on his lips. He removed his hat to show a bald head already beginning to sweat; his cigar smoke turned the coach cloudy and ashes kept dropping on his vest.

The blond man had observed Henriette's glance drop from the cattleman; he tipped his hat well over his face and watched her—not boldly but as though he were puzzled. Once her glance lifted and touched him. But he had been on guard against that and was quick to look away.

The army girl coughed gently behind her hand, whereupon the gambler tapped the whisky drummer on the shoulder. "Get rid of that." The drummer appeared startled. He grumbled, "Beg pardon," and tossed the smoke through the window.

All this while the coach went rushing down the ceaseless turns of the mountain road, rocking on its fore and aft springs, its heavy wheels slamming through the road ruts and whining on the curves. Occasionally the strident yell of Happy Stuart washed back. "Hi, Nellie! By

God—!" The whisky drummer braced himself against the door and closed his eyes.

Three hours from Tonto the road, making a last round sweep, let them down upon the flat desert. Here the stage stopped and the men got out to stretch. The gambler spoke to the army girl, gently: "Perhaps you would find my seat more comfortable." The army girl said "Thank you," and changed over. The cavalry sergeant rode up to the stage, speaking to Happy Stuart.

"We'll be goin' back now—and good luck to ye."

The men piled in, the gambler taking the place beside Henriette. The blond man drew his long legs together to give the army girl more room, and watched Henriette's face with a soft, quiet care. A hard sun beat fully on the coach and dust began to whip up like fire smoke. Without escort they rolled across a flat earth broken only by cacti standing against a dazzling light. In the far distance, behind a blue heat haze, lay the faint suggestion of mountains.

The cattleman reached up and tugged at the ends of his mustache and smiled at Henriette. The army girl spoke to the blond man. "How far is it to the noon station?" The blond man said courteously: "Twenty miles." The gambler watched the army girl with the strictness of his face relaxing, as though the run of her voice reminded him of things long forgotten.

The miles fell behind and the smell of alkali dust got thicker. Henriette rested against the corner of the coach, her eyes dropped to the tips of her gloves. She made an enigmatic, disinterested shape there; she seemed past stirring, beyond laughter. She was young, yet she had a knowledge that put the cattleman and the gambler and the drummer and the army girl in their exact places; and she knew why the gambler had offered the army girl his seat. The army girl was in one world and she was in another, as everyone in the coach understood. It had no effect on her for this was a distinction she had learned long ago. Only the blond man broke through her indifference. His name was Malpais Bill and she could see the wildness in the corners of his eyes and in the long crease of his lips; it was a stamp that would never come off. Yet something flowed out of him toward her that was different than the predatory curiosity of other men; someting unobtrusively gallant, unexpectedly gentle.

Upon the box Happy Stuart pointed to the hazy outline two miles away. "Injuns ain't burned that anyhow." The sun was directly overhead,

turning the light of the world a cruel brass-yellow. The crooked crack
of a dry wash opened across the two deep ruts that made this road.
Johnny Strang shifted the gun in his lap. "What's Malpais Bill ridin' with
us for?"

"I guess I wouldn't ask him," returned Happy Stuart and studied
the wash with a troubled eye. The road fell into it roughly and he got
a tighter grip on his reins and yelled: "Hang on! Hi, Nellie! God damn
you, hi!" The six horses plunged down the rough side of the wash and
for a moment the coach stood alone, high and lonely on the break,
and then went reeling over the rim. It struck the gravel with a roar,
the front wheels bouncing and the back wheels skewing around. The
horses faltered but Happy Stuart cursed at his leaders and got them
into a run again. The horses lunged up the far side of the wash two
and two, their muscles bunching and the soft dirt flying in yellow
clouds. The front wheels stuck solidly and something cracked like a
pistol shot; the stage rose out of the wash, teetered crosswise and then
fell ponderously on its side, splintering the coach panels.

Johnny Strang jumped clear. Happy Stuart hung to the handrail with
one hand and hauled on the reins with the other; and stood up while
the passengers crawled through the upper door. All the men, except
the whisky drummer, put their shoulders to the coach and heaved it
upright again. The whisky drummer stood strangely in the bright sunlight shaking his head dumbly while the others climbed back in. Happy
Stuart said, "All right, brother, git aboard."

The drummer climbed in slowly and the stage ran on. There was a
low, gray 'dobe relay station squatted on the desert dead ahead with
a scatter of corrals about it and a flag hanging limp on a crooked pole.
Men came out of the 'dobe's dark interior and stood in the shade of
the porch gallery. Happy Stuart rolled up and stopped. He said to a
lanky man: "Hi, Mack. Where's the Goddamned Injuns?"

The passengers were filing into the 'dobe's dining room. The lanky
one drawled: "You'll see 'em before tomorrow night." Hostlers came
up to change horses.

The little dining room was cool after the coach, cool and still. A fat
Mexican woman ran in and out with the food platters. Happy Stuart
said: "Ten minutes," and brushed the alkali dust from his mouth and
fell to eating.

The long-jawed Mack said: "Catlin's ranch burned last night. Was a
troop of cavalry around here yesterday. Came and went. You'll git to

the Gap tonight all right but I do' know about the mountains beyond.
A little trouble?"

"A little," said Happy, briefly, and rose. This was the end of rest.
The passengers followed, with the whisky drummer straggling at the
rear, reaching deeply for wind. The coach rolled away again, Mack's
voice pursuing them. "Hit it a lick, Happy, if you see any dust rollin'
out of the east."

Heat had condensed in the coach and the little wind fanned up by
the run of the horses was stifling to the lungs; the desert floor projected
its white glitter endlessly away until lost in the smoky haze. The cattleman's knees bumped Henriette gently and he kept watching her, a
celluloid toothpick drooped between his lips. Happy Stuart's voice ran
back, profane and urgent, keeping the speed of the coach constant
through the ruts. The whisky drummer's eyes were round and strained
and his mouth was open and all the color had gone out of his face.
The gambler observed this without expression and without care; and
once the cattleman, feeling the sag of the whisky drummer's shoulder,
shoved him away. The Englishman sat bolt upright, staring emotion-
lessly at the passing desert. The army girl spoke to Malpais Bill: "What
is the next stop?"

"Gap Creek."

"Will we meet soldiers there?"

He said: "I expect we'll have an escort over the hills into Lordsburg."

And at four o'clock of this furnace-hot afternoon the whisky drummer made a feeble gesture with one hand and fell forward into the
gambler's lap.

The cattleman shrugged his shoulders and put a head through the
window, calling up to Happy Stuart: "Wait a minute." When the stage
stopped everybody climbed out and the blond man helped the gambler
lay the whisky drummer in the sweltering patch of shade created by
the coach. Neither Happy Stuart nor the shotgun guard bothered to
get down. The whisky drummer's lips moved a little but nobody said
anything and nobody knew what to do—until Henriette stepped forward.

She dropped to the ground, lifting the whisky drummer's shoulders
and head against her breasts. He opened his eyes and there was something in them that they could all see, like relief and ease, like grate-
fulness. She murmured: "You are all right," and her smile was soft and

pleasant, turning her lips maternal. There was this wisdom in her, this knowledge of the fears that men concealed behind their manners, the deep hungers that rode them so savagely, and the loneliness that drove them to women of her kind. She repeated, "You are all right," and watched this whisky drummer's eyes lose the wildness of what he knew.

The army girl's face showed shock. The gambler and the cattleman looked down at the whisky drummer quite impersonally. The blond man watched Henriette through lids half closed, but the flare of a powerful interest broke the severe lines of his cheeks. He held a cigarette between his fingers; he had forgotten it.

Happy Stuart said: "We can't stay here."

The gambler bent down to catch the whisky drummer under the arms. Henriette rose and said, "Bring him to me," and got into the coach. The blond man and the gambler lifted the drummer through the door so that he was lying along the back seat, cushioned on Henriette's lap. They all got in and the coach rolled on. The drummer groaned a little, whispering: "Thanks—thanks," and the blond man, searching Henriette's face for every shred of expression, drew a gusty breath.

They went on like this, the big wheels pounding the ruts of the road while a lowering sun blazed through the coach windows. The mountain bulwarks began to march nearer, more definite in the blue fog. The cattleman's eyes were small and brilliant and touched Henriette personally, but the gambler bent toward Henriette to say: "If you are tired—"

"No," she said. "No. He's dead."

The army girl stifled a small cry. The gambler bent nearer the whisky drummer, and then they were all looking at Henriette; even the Englishman stared at her for a moment, faint curiosity in his eyes. She was remotely smiling, her lips broad and soft. She held the drummer's head with both her hands and continued to hold him like that until, at the swift fall of dusk, they rolled across the last of the desert floor and drew up before Gap Station.

The cattleman kicked open the door and stepped out, grunting as his stiff legs touched the ground. The gambler pulled the drummer up so that Henriette could leave. They all came out, their bones tired from the shaking. Happy Stuart climbed from the box, his face a gray mask of alkali and his eyes bloodshot. He said: "Who's dead?" and looked into the coach. People sauntered from the station yard, walking with the indolence of twilight. Happy Stuart said, "Well, he won't worry about tomorrow," and turned away.

A short man with a tremendous stomach shuffled through the dusk. He said: "Wasn't sure you'd try to git through yet, Happy."

"Where's the soldiers for tomorrow?"

"Other side of the mountains. Everybody's chased out. What ain't forted up here was sent into Lordsburg. You men will bunk in the barn. I'll make out for the ladies somehow." He looked at the army girl and he appraised Henriette instantly. His eyes slid on to Malpais Bill standing in the background and recognition stirred him then and made his voice careful. "Hello, Bill. What brings you this way?"

Malpais Bill's cigarette glowed in the gathering dusk and Henriette caught the brief image of his face, serene and watchful. Malpais Bill's tone was easy, it was soft. "Just the trip."

They were moving on toward the frame house whose corners seemed to extend indefinitely into a series of attached sheds. Lights glimmered in the windows and men moved around the place, idly talking. The unhitched horses went away at a trot. The tall girl walked into the station's big room, to face a soldier in a disheveled uniform.

He said: "Miss Robertson? Lieutenant Hauser was to have met you here. He is at Lordsburg. He was wounded in a brush with the Apaches last night."

The tall army girl stood very still. She said: "Badly?"

"Well," said the soldier, "yes."

The fat man came in, drawing deeply for wind. "Too bad—too bad. Ladies, I'll show you the rooms, such as I got."

Henriette's dove-colored dress blended with the background shadows. She was watching the tall army girl's face whiten. But there was a strength in the army girl, a fortitude that made her think of the soldier. For she said quietly, "You must have had a bad trip."

"Nothing—nothing at all," said the soldier and left the room. The gambler was here, his thin face turning to the army girl with a strained expression, as though he were remembering painful things. Malpais Bill had halted in the doorway, studying the softness and the humility of Henriette's cheeks. Afterwards both women followed the fat host of Gap Station along a narrow hall to their quarters.

Malpais Bill wheeled out and stood indolently against the wall of this desert station, his glance quick and watchful in the way it touched all the men loitering along the yard, his ears weighing all the night-softened voices. Heat died from the earth and a definite chill rolled down the mountain hulking so high behind the house. The soldier was in his saddle, murmuring drowsily to Happy Stuart.

"Well, Lordsburg is a long ways off and the damn' mountains are squirmin' with Apaches. You won't have any cavalry escort tomorrow. The troops are all in the field."

Malpais Bill listened to the hoofbeats of the soldier's horse fade out, remembering the loneliness of a man in those dark mountain passes, and went back to the saloon at the end of the station. This was a low-ceilinged shed with a dirt floor and whitewashed walls that once had been part of a stable. Three men stood under a lantern in the middle of this little place, the light of the lantern palely shining in the rounds of their eyes as they watched him. At the far end of the bar the cattleman and the gambler drank in taciturn silence. Malpais Bill took his whisky when the bottle came, and noted the barkeep's obscure glance. Gap's host put in his head and wheezed, "Second table," and the other men in here began to move out. The barkeep's words rubbed together, one tone above a whisper. "Better not ride into Lordsburg. Plummer and Shanley are there."

Malpais Bill's lips were stretched to the long edge of laughter and there was a shine like wildness in his eyes. He said, "Thanks, friend," and went into the dining room.

When he came back to the yard night lay wild and deep across the desert and the moonlight was a frozen silver that touched but could not dissolve the world's incredible blackness. The girl Henriette walked along the Tonto road, swaying gently in the vague shadows. He went that way, the click of his heels on the hard earth bringing her around.

Her face was clear and strange and incurious in the night, as though she waited for something to come, and knew what it would be. But he said: "You're too far from the house. Apaches like to crawl down next to a settlement and wait for strays."

She was indifferent, unafraid. Her voice was cool and he could hear the faint loneliness in it, the fatalism that made her words so even. "There's a wind coming up, so soft and good."

He took off his hat, long legs braced, and his eyes were both attentive and puzzled. His blond hair glowed in the fugitive light.

She said in a deep breath: "Why do you do that?"

His lips were restless and the sing and rush of strong feeling was like a current of quick wind around him. "You have folks in Lordsburg?"

She spoke in a direct, patient way as though explaining something he should have known without asking. "I run a house in Lordsburg."

"No," he said, "it wasn't what I asked."

"My folks are dead—I think. There was a massacre in the Superstition Mountains when I was young."

He stood with his head bowed, his mind reaching back to fill in that gap of her life. There was a hardness and a rawness to this land and little sympathy for the weak. She had survived and had paid for her survival, and looked at him now in a silent way that offered no explanations or apologies for whatever had been; she was still a pretty girl with the dead patience of all the past years in her eyes, in the expressiveness of her lips.

He said: "Over in the Tonto Basin is a pretty land. I've got a piece of ranch there—with a house half built."

"If that's your country why are you here?"

His lips laughed and the rashness in him glowed hot again and he seemed to grow taller in the moonlight. "A debt to collect."

"That's why you're going to Lordsburg? You will never get through collecting those kind of debts. Everybody in the Territory knows you. Once you were just a rancher. Then you tried to wipe out a grudge and then there was a bigger one to wipe out—and the debt kept growing and more men are waiting to kill you. Someday a man will. You'd better run away from the debts."

His bright smile kept constant, and presently she lifted her shoulders with resignation. "No," she murmured, "you won't run." He could see the sweetness of her lips and the way her eyes were sad for him; he could see in them the patience he had never learned.

He said, "We'd better go back," and turned her with his arm. They went across the yard in silence, hearing the undertone of men's drawling talk roll out of the shadows, seeing the glow of men's pipes in the dark corners. Malpais Bill stopped and watched her go through the station door; she turned to look at him once more, her eyes all dark and her lips softly sober, and then passed down the narrow corridor to her own quarters. Beyond her window, in the yard, a man was murmuring to another man: "Plummer and Shanley are in Lordsburg. Malpais Bill knows it." Through the thin partition of the adjoining room she heard the army girl crying with a suppressed, uncontrollable regularity. Henriette stared at the dark wall, her shoulders and head bowed;

and afterwards returned to the hall and knocked on the army girl's door and went in.

Six fresh horses fiddled in front of the coach and the fat host of Gap Station came across the yard swinging a lantern against the dead, bitter black. All the passengers filed sleep-dulled and miserable from the house. Johnny Strang slammed the express box in the boot and Happy Stuart gruffly said: "All right, folks."

The passengers climbed in. The cattleman came up and Malpais Bill drawled: "Take the corner spot, mister," and got in, closing the door. The Gap host grumbled: "If they don't jump you on the long grade you'll be all right. You're safe when you get to Al Schrieber's ranch." Happy's bronze voice shocked the black stillness and the coach lurched forward, its leather springs squealing.

They rode for an hour in this complete darkness, chilled and un comfortable and half asleep, feeling the coach drag on a heavy-climbing grade. Gray dawn cracked through, followed by a sunless light rushing all across the flat desert now far below. The road looped from one barren shoulder to another and at sunup they had reached the first bench and were slamming full speed along a boulder-strewn flat. The cattleman sat in the forward corner, the left corner of his mouth swollen and crushed, and when Henriette saw that her glance slid to Malpais Bill's knuckles. The army girl had her eyes closed, her shoulders pressing against the Englishman, who remained bolt upright with the sporting gun between his knees. Beside Henriette the gambler seemed to sleep, and on the middle bench Malpais Bill watched the land go by with a thin vigilance.

At ten they were rising again, with juniper and scrub pine showing on the slopes and the desert below them filling with the powdered haze of another hot day. By noon they reached the summit of the range and swung to follow its narrow rock-ribbed meadows. The gambler, long motionless, shifted his feet and caught the army girl's eyes.

"Schrieber's is directly ahead. We are past the worst of it."

The blond man looked around at the gambler, making no comment; and it was then that Henriette caught the smell of smoke in the windless air. Happy Stuart was cursing once more and the brake blocks began to cry. Looking through the angled vista of the window panel Henriette saw a clay and rock chimney standing up like a gaunt skeleton against the day's light. The house that had been there was a black patch on the ground, smoke still rising from pieces that had not been completely burnt.

The stage stopped and all the men were instantly out. An iron stove squatted on the earth, with one section of pipe stuck upright to it. Fire licked lazily along the collapsed fragments of what had been a trunk. Beyond the location of the house, at the foot of a corral, lay two nude figures grotesquely bald, with deliberate knife slashes marking their bodies. Happy Stuart went over there and had his look; and came back.

"Schriebers. Well—"

Malpais Bill said: "This morning about daylight." He looked at the gambler, at the cattleman, at the Englishman who showed no emotion. "Get back in the coach." He climbed to the coach's top, flattening himself full length there. Happy Stuart and Strang took their places again. The horses broke into a run.

The gambler said to the army girl: "You're pretty safe between those two fellows," and hauled a .44 from a back pocket and laid it over his lap. He considered Henriette more carefully than before, his taciturnity breaking. He said: "How old are you?"

Her shoulders rose and fell, which was the only answer. But the gambler said gently, "Young enough to be my daughter. It is a rotten world. When I call to you, lie down on the floor."

The Englishman had pulled the rifle from between his knees and laid it across the sill of the window on the side. The cattleman swept back the skirt of his coat to clear the holster of his gun.

The little flinty summit meadows grew narrower, with shoulders of gray rock closing in upon the road. The coach wheels slammed against the stony ruts and bounced high and fell again with a jar the springs could not soften. Happy Stuart's howl ran steadily above this rattle and rush. Fine dust turned all things gray.

Henriette sat with her eyes pinned to the gloved tips of her fingers, remembering the tall shape of Malpais Bill cut against the moonlight of Gap Station. He had smiled at her as a man might smile at any desirable woman, with the sweep and swing of laughter in his voice; and his eyes had been gentle. The gambler spoke very quietly and she didn't hear him until his fingers gripped her arm. He said again, not raising his voice: "Get down."

Henriette dropped to her knees, hearing gunfire blast through the rush and run of the coach. Happy Stuart ceased to yell and the army girl's eyes were round and dark. The walls of the canyon had tapered off. Looking upward through the window on the gambler's side, Henriette saw the weaving figure of an Apache warrior reel nakedly on a calico pony and rush by with a rifle raised and pointed in his bony elbows. The gambler took a cool aim; the stockman fired and aimed again. The Englishman's sporting rifle blasted heavy echoes through the coach, hurting her ears, and the smell of powder got rank and bitter. The blond man's boots scraped the coach top and round small holes began to dimple the paneling as the Apache bullets struck. An Indian came boldly abreast the coach and made a target that couldn't be missed. The cattleman dropped him with one shot. The wheels screamed as they slowed around the sharp ruts and the whole heavy superstructure of the coach bounced high into the air. Then they were rushing downgrade.

The gambler said quietly, "You had better take this," handing Henriette his gun. He leaned against the door with his small hands gripping the sill. Pallor loosened his cheeks. He said to the army girl: "Be sure and keep between those gentlemen," and looked at her with a way that was desperate and forlorn and dropped his head to the window's sill.

Henriette saw the bluff rise up and close in like a yellow wall. They were rolling down the mountain without brake. Gunfire fell off and the crying of the Indians faded back. Coming up from her knees then she saw the desert's flat surface far below, with the angular pattern of Lordsburg vaguely on the far borders of the heat fog. There was no more firing and Happy Stuart's voice lifted again and the brakes were screaming on the wheels, and going off, and screaming again. The Englishman stared out of the window sullenly; the army girl seemed in a deep desperate dream; the cattleman's face was shining with a strange sweat. Henriette reached over to pull the gambler up, but he had an unnatural weight to him and slid into the far corner. She saw that he was dead.

At five o'clock that long afternoon the stage threaded Lordsburg's narrow streets of 'dobe and frame houses, came upon the center square and stopped before a crowd of people gathered in the smoky heat. The passengers crawled out stiffly. A Mexican boy ran up to see the dead gambler and began to yell his news in shrill Mexican. Malpais Bill climbed off the top, but Happy Stuart sat back on his seat and stared taciturnly at the crowd. Henriette noticed then that the shotgun messenger was gone.

A gray man in a sleazy white suit called up to Happy. "Well, you got through."

Happy Stuart said: "Yeah. We got through."

An officer stepped through the crowd, smiling at the army girl. He took her arm and said, "Miss Robertson, I believe. Lieutenant Hauser is quite all right. I will get your luggage—"

The army girl was crying then, definitely. They were all standing around, bone-weary and shaken. Malpais Bill remained by the wheel of the coach, his cheeks hard against the sunlight and his eyes riveted on a pair of men standing under the board awning of an adjoining store. Henriette observed the manner of their waiting and knew why they were here. The blond man's eyes, she noticed, were very blue and flame burned brilliantly in them. The army girl turned to Henriette, tears in her eyes. She murmured: "If there is anything I can ever do for you—"

But Henriette stepped back, shaking her head. This was Lordsburg and everybody knew her place except the army girl. Henriette said formally, "Good-bye," noting how still and expectant the two men under the awning remained. She swung toward the blond man and said, "Would you carry my valise?"

Malpais Bill looked at her, laughter remote in his eyes, and reached into the luggage pile and got her battered valise. He was still smiling as he went beside her, through the crowd and past the two waiting men. But when they turned into an anonymous and dusty little side street of the town, where the houses all sat shoulder to shoulder without grace or dignity, he had turned sober. He said: "I am obliged to you. But I'll have to go back there."

They were in front of a house no different from its neighbors; they had stopped at its door. She could see his eyes travel this street and comprehend its meaning and the kind of traffic it bore. But he was saying in that gentle, melody-making tone:

"I have watched you for two days." He stopped, searching his mind to find the thing he wanted to say. It came out swiftly. "God made you a woman. The Tonto is a pretty country."

Her answer was quite barren of feeling. "No. I am known all through the Territory. But I can remember that you asked me."

He said: "No other reason?" She didn't answer but something in her eyes pulled his face together. He took off his hat and it seemed to her he was looking through this hot day to that far-off country and

seeing it fresh and desirable. He murmured: "A man can escape nothing. I have got to do this. But I will be back."

He went along the narrow street, made a quick turn at the end of
it, and disappeared. Heat rolled like a heavy wave over Lordsburg's
housetops and the smell of dust was very sharp. She lifted her valise,
and dropped it and stood like that, mute and grave before the door
of her dismal house. She was remembering how tall he had been
against the moonlight at Gap Station.

There were four swift shots beating furiously along the sultry quiet,
and a shout, and afterwards a longer and longer silence. She put one
hand against the door to steady herself, and knew that those shots
marked the end of a man, and the end of a hope. He would never
come back; he would never stand over her in the moonlight with the
long gentle smile on his lips and with the swing of life in his casual
tone. She was thinking of all that humbly and with the patience life
had beaten into her. . . .

She was thinking of all that when she heard the strike of boots on
the street's packed earth; and turned to see him, high and square in
the muddy sunlight, coming toward her with his smile.

2001:
A SPACE ODYSSEY

(1968)

THE SENTINEL
ARTHUR C. CLARKE

Arguably the most important science-fiction film ever made, *2001: A Space Odyssey* was initially viewed by critics as ponderous, pretentious, and vague. However, any critical confusion surrounding Stanley Kubrick's message on man's evolution from beast to machine to cosmic fetus was quickly dispelled by the film's widespread popular and commercial success—*Variety* magazine ranked it among the fifty highest-grossing movies of all time. Relying almost solely on powerful visual imagery (there are a mere forty minutes of dialogue) and innovative special effects provided by Douglas Trumbull (who later lent his expertise to *Close Encounters of the Third Kind* (1977), *2001* has firmly established itself both in the history of cinema and in the modern cultural imagination.

Stanley Kubrick's interest in literature as a source of material can also be seen in such films as *Paths of Glory* (1958), *Lolita* (1962), *A Clockwork Orange* (1969), *Barry Lyndon* (1975) and *The Shining* (1980).

Co-scripted by Kubrick and sci-fi writer ARTHUR C. CLARKE, *2001* is one of the very few instances in which a short story adapted into film spawned, in essence, a "novelization" that later became a major work of modern fiction. Born in England in 1917, Clarke has for many years lived in relative seclusion on the island of Sri Lanka where he continues his writing as well as research in the field of satellite communications.

2001: A SPACE ODYSSEY

Released: 1968
Production: Stanley Kubrick for MGM
Direction: Stanley Kubrick
Screenplay: Stanley Kubrick and Arthur C. Clarke
Cinematography: Geoffrey Unsworth
Editing: Ray Lovejoy
Special effects: Stanley Kubrick and special effects team (Academy Award)
Music: Richard Strauss, Johann Strauss, Aram Ilich Khatchaturian, and György Ligeti
Running time: 141 minutes

PRINCIPAL CHARACTERS:

David Bowman	Keir Dullea
Frank Poole	Gary Lockwood
Dr. Heywood Floyd	William Sylvester
Moonwatcher	Daniel Richter
HAL 9000	Douglas Rain

The next time you see the full moon high in the south, look carefully at its righthand edge and let your eye travel upward along the curve of the disk. Round about two o'clock you will notice a small, dark oval: anyone with normal eyesight can find it quite easily. It is the great walled plain, one of the finest on the Moon, known as the Mare Crisium— the Sea of Crises. Three hundred miles in diameter, and almost completely surrounded by a ring of magnificent mountains, it had never been explored until we entered it in the late summer of 1996.

Our expedition was a large one. We had two heavy freighters which had flown our supplies and equipment from the main lunar base in the Mare Serenitatis, five hundred miles away. There were also three small rockets which were intended for short-range transport over regions which our surface vehicles couldn't cross. Luckily, most of the Mare Crisium is very flat. There are none of the great crevasses so common and so dangerous elsewhere, and very few craters or mountains of any size. As far as we could tell, our powerful caterpillar tractors would have no difficulty in taking us wherever we wished to go.

I was geologist—or selenologist, if you want to be pedantic—in charge of the group exploring the southern region of Mare. We had crossed a hundred miles of it in a week, skirting the foothills of the mountains along the shore of what was once the ancient sea, some thousand million years before. When life was beginning on Earth, it was already dying here. The waters were retreating down the flanks of those stupendous cliffs, retreating into the empty heart of the Moon. Over the land which we were crossing, the tideless ocean had once been half a mile deep, and now the only trace of moisture was the hoarfrost one could sometimes find in caves which the searing sunlight never penetrated.

We had begun our journey early in the slow lunar dawn, and still had almost a week of Earth-time before nightfall. Half a dozen times a day we would leave our vehicle and go outside in the space suits to hunt for interesting minerals, or to place markers for the guidance of future travelers. It was an uneventful routine. There is nothing hazardous or even particularly exciting about lunar exploration. We could live comfortably for a month in our pressurized tractors, and if we ran into trouble, we could always radio for help and sit tight until one of the spaceships came to our rescue.

I said just now that there was nothing exciting about lunar exploration, but of course that isn't true. One could never grow tired of those incredible mountains, so much more rugged than the gentle hills of Earth. We never knew, as we rounded the capes and promontories of that vanished sea, what new splendors would be revealed to us. The whole southern curve of the Mare Crisium is a vast delta where a score of rivers once found their way into the ocean, fed perhaps by the torrential rains that must have lashed the mountains in the brief volcanic age when the Moon was young. Each of these ancient valleys was an invitation, challenging us to climb into the unknown uplands beyond. But we had a hundred miles still to cover, and could only look longingly at the heights which others must scale.

We kept Earth-time aboard the tractor, and precisely at 22:00 hours the final radio message would be sent out to Base and we would close down for the day. Outside, the rocks would still be burning beneath the almost vertical sun, but to us it would be night until we awoke again eight hours later. Then one of us would prepare breakfast, there would be a great buzzing of electric razors, and someone would switch on the shortwave radio from Earth. Indeed, when the smell of frying sausages began to fill the cabin, it was sometimes hard to believe that we were not back on our own world—everything was so normal and homely, apart from the feeling of decreased weight and the unnatural slowness with which objects fell.

It was my turn to prepare breakfast in the corner of the main cabin that served as a galley. I can remember that moment quite vividly after all these years, for the radio had just played one of my favorite melodies, the old Welsh air "David of the White Rock." Our driver was already outside in his space suit, inspecting our caterpillar treads. My assistant, Louis Garnett, was up forward in the control position, making some belated entries in yesterday's log.

As I stood by the frying pan, waiting, like any terrestrial housewife, for the sausages to brown, I let my gaze wander idly over the mountain walls which covered the whole of the southern horizon, marching out of sight to east and west below the curve of the Moon. They seemed only a mile or two from the tractor, but I knew that the nearest was twenty miles away. On the Moon, of course, there is no loss of detail with distance—none of that almost imperceptible haziness which softens and sometimes transfigures all far-off things on Earth.

Those mountains were ten thousand feet high, and they climbed steeply out of the plain as if ages ago some subterranean eruption had smashed them skyward through the molten crust. The base of even the nearest was hidden from sight by the steeply curving surface of the plain, for the Moon is a very little world, and from where I was standing the horizon was only two miles away.

I lifted my eyes toward the peaks which no man had ever climbed, the peaks which, before the coming of terrestrial life, had watched the retreating oceans sink sullenly into their graves, taking with them the hope and the morning promise of a world. The sunlight was beating against those ramparts with a glare that hurt the eyes, yet only a little way above them the stars were shining steadily in a sky blacker than a winter midnight on Earth.

I was turning away when my eye caught a metallic glitter high on the ridge of a great promontory thrusting out into the sea thirty miles to the west. It was a dimensionless point of light, as if a star had been clawed from the sky by one of those cruel peaks, and I imagined that some smooth rock surface was catching the sunlight and heliographing it straight into my eyes. Such things were not uncommon. When the Moon is in her second quarter, observers on Earth can sometimes see the great ranges in the Oceanus Procellarum burning with a blue-white iridescence as the sunlight flashes from their slopes and leaps again from world to world. But I was curious to know what kind of rock could be shining so brightly up there, and I climbed into the observation turret and swung our four-inch telescope round to the west.

I could see just enough to tantalize me. Clear and sharp in the field of vision, the mountain peaks seemed only half a mile away, but whatever was catching the sunlight was still too small to be resolved. Yet it seemed to have an elusive symmetry, and the summit upon which it rested was curiously flat. I stared for a long time at that glittering enigma, straining my eyes into space, until presently a smell of burning from the galley told me that our breakfast sausages had made their quarter-million-mile journey in vain.

All that morning we argued our way across the Mare Crisium while the western mountains reared higher in the sky. Even when we were out prospecting in the space suits, the discussion would continue over the radio. It was absolutely certain, my companions argued, that there had never been any form of intelligent life on the Moon. The only living things that had ever existed there were a few primitive plants and their slightly less degenerate ancestors. I knew that as well as anyone, but there are times when a scientist must not be afraid to make a fool of himself.

"Listen," I said at last, "I'm going up there, if only for my own peace of mind. That mountain's less than twelve thousand feet high—that's only two thousand under Earth gravity—and I can make the trip in twenty hours at the outside. I've always wanted to go up into those hills, anyway, and this gives me an excellent excuse."

"If you don't break your neck," said Garnett, "you'll be the laughingstock of the expedition when we get back to Base. That mountain will probably be called Wilson's Folly from now on."

"I won't break my neck," I said firmly. "Who was the first man to climb Pico and Helicon?"

"But weren't you rather younger in those days?" asked Louis gently.

"That," I said with great dignity, "is as good a reason as any for going."

We went to bed early that night, after driving the tractor to within half a mile of the promontory. Garnett was coming with me in the morning; he was a good climber, and had often been with me on such exploits before. Our driver was only too glad to be left in charge of the machine.

At first sight, those cliffs seemed completely unscalable, but to anyone with a good head for heights, climbing is easy on a world where all weights are only a sixth of their normal value. The real danger in lunar mountaineering lies in overconfidence; a six-hundred-foot drop on the Moon can kill you just as thoroughly as a hundred-foot fall on Earth.

We made our first halt on a wide ledge about four thousand feet above the plain. Climbing had not been very difficult, but my limbs were stiff with the unaccustomed effort, and I was glad of the rest. We could still see the tractor as a tiny metal insect far down at the foot of the cliff, and we reported our progress to the driver before starting on the next ascent.

Inside our suits it was comfortably cool, for the refrigeration units were fighting the fierce sun and carrying away the body heat of our exertions. We seldom spoke to each other, except to pass climbing instructions and to discuss our best plan of ascent. I do not know what Garnett was thinking, probably that this was the craziest goose chase he had ever embarked upon. I more than half agreed with him, but the joy of climbing, the knowledge that no man had ever gone this way before, and the exhilaration of the steadily widening landscape gave me all the reward I needed.

I don't think I was particularly excited when I saw in front of us the wall of rock I had first inspected through the telescope from thirty miles away. It would level off about fifty feet above our heads, and there on the plateau would be the thing that had lured me over these barren wastes. It would be, almost certainly, nothing more than a boulder splintered ages ago by a falling meteor, and with its cleavage planes still fresh and bright in this incorruptible, unchanging silence.

There were no handholds on the rock face, and we had to use a grapnel. My tired arms seemed to gain new strength as I swung the three-pronged metal anchor round my head and sent it sailing up toward the stars. The first time it broke loose and came falling slowly back when we pulled the rope. On the third attempt, the prongs gripped firmly and our combined weights could not shift it.

Garnett looked at me anxiously. I could tell that he wanted to go first, but I smiled back at him through the glass of my helmet and shook my head. Slowly, taking my time, I began the final ascent.

Even with my space suit, I weighed only forty pounds here, so I pulled myself up hand over hand without bothering to use my feet. At the rim I paused and waved to my companion, then I scrambled over the edge and stood upright, staring ahead of me.

You must understand that until this very moment I had been almost completely convinced that there could be nothing strange or unusual for me to find here. Almost, but not quite; it was that haunting doubt that had driven me forward. Well, it was a doubt no longer, but the haunting had scarcely begun.

I was standing on a plateau perhaps a hundred feet across. It had once been smooth—too smooth to be natural—but falling meteors had pitted and scored its surface through immeasurable eons. It had been leveled to support a glittering, roughly pyramidal structure, twice as high as a man, that was set in the rock like a gigantic, many faceted jewel.

Probably no emotion at all filled my mind in those first few seconds. Then I felt a great lifting of my heart, and a strange, inexpressible joy. For I loved the Moon, and now I knew that the creeping moss of Aristarchus and Eratosthenes was not the only life she had brought forth in her youth. The old, discredited dream of the first explorers was true. There had, after all, been a lunar civilization—and I was the first to find it. That I had come perhaps a hundred millions years too late did not distress me; it was enough to have come at all.

My mind was beginning to function normally, to analyze and to ask questions. Was this a building, a shrine—or something for which my language had no name? If a building, then why was it erected in so uniquely inaccessible a spot? I wondered if it might be a temple, and I could picture the adepts of some strange priesthood calling on their gods to preserve them as the life of the Moon ebbed with the dying oceans, and calling on their gods in vain.

I took a dozen steps forward to examine the thing more closely, but some sense of caution kept me from going too near. I knew a little of archaeology, and tried to guess the cultural level of the civilization that must have smoothed this mountain and raised the glittering mirror surfaces that still dazzled my eyes.

The Egyptians could have done it, I thought, if their workmen had possessed whatever strange materials these far more ancient architects had used. Because of the thing's smallness, it did not occur to me that I might be looking at the handiwork of a race more advanced than my own. The idea that the Moon had possessed intelligence at all was still almost too tremendous to grasp, and my pride would not let me take the final, humiliating plunge.

And then I noticed something that set the scalp crawling at the back of my neck—something so trivial and so innocent that many would never have noticed it at all. I have said that the plateau was scarred by meteors; it was also coated inches deep with the cosmic dust that is always filtering down upon the surface of any world where there are no winds to disturb it. Yet the dust and the meteor scratches ended quite abruptly in a wide circle enclosing the little pyramid, as though an invisible wall was protecting it from the ravages of time and the slow but ceaseless bombardment from space.

There was someone shouting in my earphones, and I realized that Garnett had been calling me for some time. I walked unsteadily to the edge of the cliff and signaled him to join me, not trusting myself to speak. Then I went back toward that circle in the dust. I picked up a fragment of splintered rock and tossed it gently toward the shining enigma. If the pebble had vanished at that invisible barrier, I should not have been surprised, but it seemed to hit a smooth, hemispheric surface and slide gently to the ground.

I knew then that I was looking at nothing that could be matched in the antiquity of my own race. This was not a building, but a machine, protecting itself with forces that had challenged Eternity. Those forces, whatever they might be, were still operating, and perhaps I had already come too close. I thought of all the radiations man had trapped and tamed in the past century. For all I knew, I might be as irrevocably doomed as if I had stepped into the deadly, silent aura of an unshielded atomic pile.

I remember turning then toward Garnett, who had joined me and was now standing motionless at my side. He seemed quite oblivious to me, so I did not disturb him but walked to the edge of the cliff in

an effort to marshal my thoughts. There below me lay the Mare Crisium—Sea of Crises, indeed—strange and weird to most men, but
reassuringly familiar to me. I lifted my eyes toward the crescent Earth,
lying in her cradle of stars, and I wondered what her clouds had covered
when these unknown builders had finished their work. Was it the
steaming jungle of the Carboniferous, the bleak shoreline over which
the first amphibians must crawl to conquer the land—or, earlier still,
the long loneliness before the coming of life?

Do not ask me why I did not guess the truth sooner—the truth that
seems so obvious now. In the first excitement of my discovery, I had
assumed without question that this crystalline apparition had been built
by some race belonging to the Moon's remote past, but suddenly, and
with overwhelming force, the belief came to me that it was as alien to
the Moon as I myself.

In twenty years we had found no trace of life but a few degenerate
plants. No lunar civilization, whatever its doom, could have left but a
single token of its existence.

I looked at the shining pyramid again, and the more I looked, the
more remote it seemed from anything that had to do with the Moon.
And suddenly I felt myself shaking with a foolish, hysterical laughter,
brought on by excitement and overexertion: for I had imagined that
the little pyramid was speaking to me and was saying, "Sorry, I'm a
stranger here myself."

It has taken us twenty years to crack that invisible shield and to reach
the machine inside those crystal walls. What we could not understand,
we broke at last with the savage might of atomic power and now I have
seen the fragments of the lovely, glittering thing I found up there on
the mountain.

They are meaningless. The mechanisms—if indeed they are mechanisms—of the pyramid belong to a technology that lies far beyond
our horizon, perhaps to the technology of paraphysical forces.

The mystery haunts us all the more now that the other planets have
been reached and we know that only Earth has ever been the home
of intelligent life in our Universe. Nor could any lost civilization of our
own world have built that machine, for the thickness of the meteoric
dust on the plateau has enabled us to measure its age. It was set there
upon its mountain before life had emerged from the seas of Earth.

When our world was half its present age, *something* from the stars swept through the Solar System, left this token of its passage, and went again upon its way. Until we destroyed it, that machine was still fulfilling the purpose of its builders; and as to that purpose, here is my guess.

Nearly a hundred thousand million stars are turning in the circle of the Milky Way, and long ago other races on the worlds of other suns must have scaled and passed the heights that we have reached. Think of such civilizations, far back in time against the fading afterglow of Creation, masters of a universe so young that life as yet had come only to a handful of worlds. Theirs would have been a loneliness we cannot imagine, the loneliness of gods looking out across infinity and finding none to share their thoughts.

They must have searched the star clusters as we have searched the planets. Everywhere there would be worlds, but they would be empty or peopled with crawling, mindless things. Such was our own Earth, the smoke of the great volcanoes still staining the skies, when that first ship of the peoples of the dawn came sliding in from the abyss beyond Pluto. It passed the frozen outer worlds, knowing that life could play no part in their destinies. It came to rest among the inner planets, warming themselves around the fire of the Sun and waiting for their stories to begin.

Those wanderers must have looked on Earth, circling safely in the narrow zone between fire and ice, and must have guessed that it was the favorite of the Sun's children. Here, in the distant future, would be intelligence; but there were countless stars before them still, and they might never come this way again.

So they left a sentinel, one of millions they scattered throughout the Universe, watching over all words with the promise of life. It was a beacon that down the ages patiently signaled the fact that no one had discovered it.

Perhaps you understand now why that crystal pyramid was set upon the Moon instead of on the Earth. Its builders were not concerned with races still struggling up from savagery. They would be interested in our civilization only if we proved our fitness to survive—by crossing space and so escaping from the Earth, our cradle. That is the challenge that all intelligent races must meet, sooner or later. It is a double challenge, for it depends in turn upon the conquest of atomic energy and the last choice between life and death.

Once we had passed that crisis, it was only a matter of time before we found the pyramid and forced it open. Now its signals have ceased, and those whose duty it is will be turning their minds upon Earth. Perhaps they wish to help our infant civilization. But they must be very, very old, and the old are often insanely jealous of the young.

I can never look now at the Milky Way without wondering from which of those banked clouds of stars the emissaries are coming. If you will pardon so commonplace a simile, we have set off the fire alarm and have nothing to do but to wait.

I do not think we will have to wait for long.

SELECTED SHORT LIST
OF OTHER STORIES
MADE INTO FILMS

1. **THE ABSENT-MINDED PROFESSOR (1960)**
   from "A Letter to the President" by Samuel W. Taylor
2. **BABETTE'S FEAST (1988)**
   from "Babette's Feast" by Isak Dinesen
3. **THE BEAST FROM 20,000 FATHOMS (1953)**
   from "The Foghorn" by Ray Bradbury
4. **THE BIRDS (1963)**
   from "The Birds" by Daphne du Maurier
5. **A BOY AND HIS DOG (1975)**
   from "A Boy and his Dog" by Harlan Ellison
6. **CHARLY (1968)**
   from "Flowers for Algernon" by Daniel Keyes
7. **THE DEVIL AND DANIEL WEBSTER (1941)**
   from "The Devil and Daniel Webster" by Stephen Vincent Benet
8. **THE BEACHCOMBER (1938)**
   from "Vessel of Wrath" by W. Somerset Maugham
9. **BROKEN BLOSSOMS (1919)**
   from "The Chink and the Child" by Thomas Burke
10. **CHAMPION (1949)**
    from "Champion" by Ring Lardner
11. **A CHRISTMAS MEMORY (1969)**
    from "A Christmas Memory" by Truman Capote
12. **CRACK UP (1946)**
    from "Madman's Holiday" by Fredric Brown
13. **THE DEAD (1987)**
    from "The Dead" by James Joyce

14. THE FALLEN IDOL (1948)
    from "The Basement Room" by Graham Greene
15. FATHER BROWN, DETECTIVE (1934)
    from "The Blue Cross" by G. K. Chesterton
16. FORT APACHE (1948)
    from "Massacre" by James Warner Bellah
17. GUN CRAZY (1950)
    from "Gun Crazy" by MacKinlay Kantor
18. THE HUSTLER (1961)
    from "The Hustler" by Walter Tevis
19. THE IMMORTAL STORY (1968)
    from "The Immortal Story" by Isak Dinesen
20. THE INNOCENTS (1961)
    from "The Turn of the Screw" by Henry James
21. THE KILLERS (1946)
    from "The Killers" by Ernest Hemingway
22. LADY FOR A DAY (1933) & POCKETFUL OF MIRACLES (1961)
    from "Madame La Gimp" by Damon Runyon
23. THE LAST TIME I SAW PARIS (1954)
    from "Babylon Revisited" by F. Scott Fitzgerald
24. THE LEMON DROP KID (1951)
    from "The Lemon Drop Kid" by Damon Runyon
25. THE LONG HOT SUMMER (1958)
    from "Barn Burning" and "Spotted Horse" by William Faulkner
26. A MAN CALLED HORSE (1970)
    from "A Man Called Horse" by Dorothy Johnson
27. THE MAN WHO COULD WORK MIRACLES (1936)
    from "The Man Who Could Work Miracles" by H. G. Wells
28. THE MOST DANGEROUS GAME (1936)
    from "The Most Dangerous Game" by Richard Connell
29. NIGHT OF THE DEMON (1957)
    from "Casting the Runes" by M. R. James
30. NOTHING SACRED (1937)
    from "A Letter to the Editor" by James H. Street
31. THE PASSION OF ANNA (1971)
    from "The Passion of Anna" by Ingmar Bergman
32. THE SECRET LIFE OF WALTER MITTY (1947)
    from "The Secret Life of Walter Mitty" by James Thurber

33. **SEVEN BRIDES FOR SEVEN BROTHERS (1954)**
    from "The Sobbin' Women" by Stephen Vincent Benet
34. **THE SHOUT (1978)**
    from "The Shout" by Robert Graves
35. **THE SPIDER'S STRATAGEM (1970)**
    from "Theme of the Traitor and the Hero" by Jorge Luis Borges
36. **SUNRISE (1927)**
    from "The Excursion to Tilsit" by Hermann Sudermann
37. **THE SWIMMER (1968)**
    from "The Swimmer" by John Cheever
38. **THE THING (1951)**
    from "Who Goes There?" by John W. Campbell, Jr.
39. **TOMORROW (1972)**
    from "Tomorrow" by William Faulkner
40. **WITNESS FOR THE PROSECUTION (1957)**
    from "Witness for the Prosecution" by Agatha Christie
41. **THE YOUNG ONE (1960)**
    from "Travelling Man" by Peter Matthiessen

INDEX